Swapping Stories

Swapping Stories

FOLKTALES FROM LOUISIANA

*   *   *

Carl Lindahl, Maida Owens, and C. Renée Harvison

EDITORS

UNIVERSITY PRESS OF MISSISSIPPI · JACKSON
in association with
LOUISIANA DIVISION OF THE ARTS · BATON ROUGE

This publication is supported by a grant from the National Endowment
for the Arts, the Louisiana Division of the Arts, Office of Cultural
Development, Department of Culture, Recreation and Tourism.

The paper in this book meets the guidelines for permanence and
durability of the Committee on Production Guidelines for Book
Longevity of the Council on Library Resources.

Library of Congress Cataloging-in-Publication Data

Swapping stories : folktales from Louisiana / Carl Lindahl, Maida
Owens, and C. Renée Harvison, editors.
     p. cm.
   Includes bibliographical references and index.
   ISBN 0-87805-930-X (cloth : alk. paper).—ISBN 0-87805-931-8
(pbk. : alk. paper)
     1. Tales—Louisiana.   2. Oral tradition—Louisiana.   3. Louisiana—
Social life and customs.   I. Lindahl, Carl, 1947– . II. Owens,
Maida.   III. Harvison, C. Renée.
   GR110.L5S93   1997
   398.2'09763—dc20   96-41265
                                                                    CIP

British Library Cataloging-in-Publication data available

Contents

Acknowledgments

Various collections and studies of Louisiana folktales have appeared since Alcée Fortier's pioneering works were published a century ago. But all share the same limitation: restriction to a particular genre or to a single locale or ethnic group. It is time to build upon and to move beyond the work of such notable collectors as Fortier, Calvin Claudel, and Corinne Saucier to create a more inclusive picture of Louisiana storytelling.

This project could not have been accomplished without the assistance of many folklorists from Louisiana and elsewhere. They are to be commended for realizing that good stories are valuable. Thanks to all the folklorists and community members who either shared their personal collections or assisted with fieldwork of some kind: Dr. Barry Jean Ancelet, University of Southwestern Louisiana in Lafayette, for his work with Cajun and Creole storytellers (in particular for this project Creole raconteur Wilson "Ben Guiné" Mitchell) and for his assistance in transcribing or translating French stories; Dr. Samuel G. Armistead, for contributing and annotating Isleño texts; Dr. Harry Becnel, whose collecting efforts with Italians in Livingston Parish are archived with the Center for Regional Studies at Southeastern Louisiana University; Debra Anderson Forney, for her work in contributing and interpreting the tales of her father, Alfred Anderson; Dr. H. F. "Pete" Gregory, Northwestern State University for his expertise concerning Native American storytellers, particularly Bel Abbey; Dr. Donald W. Hatley, Louisiana Folklife Center at Northwestern State University in Natchitoches, and Dr. Nicholas R. Spitzer for their work with African-American Clifford Blake, Sr.; Annette Huval, folklorist, for her work with Cajun and Creole storytellers, especially Enola Matthews; Dr. Geoffery Kimball, a linguist at Tulane University, for his work with Koasati tribal leader Bel Abbey; Pat Mire, filmmaker and community scholar, for his work with Bel Abbey; Dr. Susan Roach, Louisiana Tech University in Ruston, for her work with Harold Talbert, David Allen, and Lonnie Gray; and Fran Slaton, folklorist, for her work with the Vietnamese community. Other folklorists who provided guidance and encouragement are Dr. Eric Montenyohl, University of Southwestern Louisiana; Ben Sandmel, researcher and writer; and Dr. Carolyn Ware, 1989–91 Louisiana Folklife Festival programming coordinator.

Partly responsible for the breadth of storytelling represented herein is the extensive narrative collection that resulted from Louisiana Open House 1990. We thank Charlie Fisher, Bruce Morgan, and Myra Peak of the Office of Tourism for their vision; and Judith Barrow, Debi Bennett, Ellen Blue, Monty Brown, Cordelia Cale, Susan Eddington, Randall LaBry, Dayna Lee, Pat Mire, and Norris Rousse for their hard work and commitment to the project goals. We also applaud the local coordinators who invited storytellers to participate, those who moderated narrative stage sessions, and others who worked with the program. Together, they provided communities throughout Louisiana the opportunity to present local folk storytellers and to share their culture with visitors and friends alike.

We would like to thank the National Endowment for the Arts Folk Arts Program for the support that made the Louisiana Storytelling Project possible. This project was also funded in part by the Louisiana State Arts Council and the Louisiana Division of the Arts, Office of Cultural Development, Department of Culture, Recreation, and Tourism. Support services were provided by the Division of the Arts staff. Dr. Frank de Caro, Mary Anne Sternberg, Dr. Carl Brasseaux, Dr. H. F. "Pete" Gregory, Dr. Donald W. Hatley, and Dr. Susan Roach provided comments while the manuscript was being developed. Dr. Denise Wenner and Dr. Lee Winnifred of the University of Houston performed meticulous and artful editorial work.

The article on the peoples of Louisiana by Maida Owens draws on the work of many people. Susan Roach, Barry Ancelet, Michael Smith, H. F. "Pete" Gregory, Donald W. Hatley, Carl Brasseaux, Pam Breaux, Joyce Jackson, and James Borders assisted by reading drafts, and many more provided information through their research.

Finally, due credit should go to the book's true composers, the numerous storytellers from whom hundreds of narratives were collected. These people opened their hearts and jogged their memories and told their stories to our willing ears. For their generosity, we are truly grateful. Regrettably, four of the featured storytellers—Bel Abbey, Alfred Anderson, Lonnie Gray, and Wilson "Ben Guiné" Mitchell—passed away before publication. In addition, Alex Bartus, Clifford Blake, Sr., Eck Bozeman, John T. Campbell, Clarence Broussard, Mary Gray, J. Maxwell Kelley, James B. Rider, and John Verret have died since their stories were recorded. At least their artistry was documented before their deaths.

With so many involved in this project, it was not possible to create a system for sharing the profit from book sales. Consequently, proceeds will be used to support folklife research through the Louisiana Folklife Program. However, the genuine reward of this team effort—the stories—are here for all to enjoy. We hope that reading them will bring almost as much pleasure as hearing the tellers themselves personally swapping stories.

The Louisiana Storytelling Project

Maida Owens

To promote understanding of Louisiana's traditional cultures, the Louisiana Folklife Program within the state's Division of the Arts strives to assist cultural specialists in public presentation of their findings by means of various formats appropriate to their subjects. These include publications, concerts, recordings, festivals, videotapes, and exhibits. The Louisiana Storytelling Project is one such project. The Folklife Program also tries to focus attention upon neglected cultures and folklife genres. A special concern is to assist communities with identifying their cultural resources and determining the most culturally appropriate means to support or use these resources. The ultimate goal is self-determination, which will be accomplished by providing each group the appropriate and specific tools necessary for the presentation and support of its own cultural resources. The Division of the Arts grants program is one resource available to communities to assist them in this process of self-empowerment.

The collecting efforts of many are presented in *Swapping Stories,* the culmination of a much larger project by the Louisiana Folklife Program. This multiyear focus on storytelling began with a collaboration with the Office of Tourism on its Open House 1990 Storytelling Program. As Folklife Program director, I worked with Bruce Morgan and Myra Peak, of the Louisiana Office of Tourism, to design and implement a public presentation program that for the first time made storytelling a major focus at Louisiana fairs and festivals. The 1990 Open House Storytelling Program provided two thirty-by-thirty-foot pavilions, which were featured at seventy-one festivals. Local coordinators selected 1,051 storytellers to participate in 504 storytelling sessions in the pavilions. Regional coordinators for the Open House 1990 Storytelling Program—Judith Barrow, Debi Bennett, Ellen Blue, Monty Brown, Cordelia Cale, Susan Eddington, Randall LaBry, Dayna Lee, Pat Mire, and Norris Rousse—worked with community members and served as liaisons to identify the best storytellers in their regions. Most storytelling sessions were recorded and the audiotapes deposited with the Louisiana Folklife Program (Owens 1992). The dynamics of the storytelling sessions is further discussed in Carl Lindahl's essay on Louisiana's folktale traditions, below.

The Storytelling Pavilion, a 30 foot by 30 foot structure, was featured at 71 festivals during Open House 1990. Local communities selected 1,051 storytellers to participate in 504 storytelling sessions, of which 441 were recorded and deposited in an archive. Here, the Pavilion is on the steps of the State Capitol where politicians shared stories about their experiences. Photo: Courtesy of Louisiana Office of Tourism.

I then initiated this folklife publication project, and C. Renée Harvison joined the team to document individual storytellers more thoroughly. The original intent was to create a small publication featuring approximately ten storytellers from various Louisiana cultures. As the regional coordinators began providing contacts with many outstanding narrators, it became apparent that the publication project had the potential to be much more substantial. The call went out to folklorists and researchers throughout the state who had worked with storytelling, and many responded by contributing unpublished data or providing leads for others to document. So many good stories were gathered that publication plans were greatly expanded. Harvison spent hundreds of hours listening to and transcribing stories to be considered for this volume. Carl Lindahl then joined the team as a folk narrative specialist to introduce, annotate, and further edit the tales. The project has taken much longer than originally planned, but we hope it was worth it.

After the book was well under way, it became apparent that the subject deserved an additional presentation format: a video program. I then collaborated with Pat Mire, an independent filmmaker who had also served as one of the regional coordinators for the Open House 1990 Storytelling Program. Together we designed a video documentation project, also entitled *Swapping Stories,* featuring some of the finest storytellers identified in the project.

Louisiana's Traditional Cultures: An Overview

Maida Owens

A basic principle in the study of folklore and anthropology is that in order to understand a cultural feature, one must understand the context in which it exists. Therefore, to understand a basket, dance, song, ritual, or story, one must know about the maker, dancer, singer, practitioner, or teller. One must understand the culture or setting in which it is made or performed. Only then can one know its significance and function within the cultural region for the people. One must take a holistic look at the integrated system to understand each part.

Therefore, when one examines the storytelling traditions of an entire state, it is important to understand the cultures within the state and how they relate to each other. This is particularly true of Louisiana, because of the state's complex cultural milieu. Hence, here follows a brief overview of Louisiana's traditional cultures, provided to assist the reader in placing the stories in context. Although no article can do justice to the folk cultures of the state, it is important to provide a sketch of the peoples and their regions as a background for the stories that follow. Regrettably, not all groups mentioned in this article have stories in this volume—either because their storytelling traditions have not been documented or because in the scope of this project, tellers were not identified.

It is trite to say that Louisiana is culturally diverse. The truth is that few people realize the degree of complexity and variation in the cultures of the state. Many are aware that New Orleans and French-speaking South Louisiana are juxtaposed against the African-American/British-American culture of North Louisiana, but few are familiar with subtle differences within these regional groups and the cultural complexities resulting from the presence of Native Americans and the waves of immigrations by Irish, Germans, Italians, Czechs, Hungarians, Croatians, Filipinos, Latins (Isleño, Mexican, Cuban, Guatemalan), and East Asians (Chinese, Vietnamese, Laotian, Thai). Each group has added to the cultural environment of Louisiana and in varying ways influenced the storytelling traditions found here.

Geographers and historians have documented many of the settlement patterns and the waves of immigration into most parts of Louisiana. Louisiana State University geographer Fred Kniffen laid the foundation for understanding Louisiana's settlement patterns during the 1930s (Kniffen 1936). More recently, Malcolm Comeaux (1972) investigated the Atchafalaya Basin settlement patterns and folk occupations, University of Southwestern Louisiana historian Carl Brasseaux focused on French Louisiana settlement patterns (Brasseaux 1987 and 1992), and historian Gwendolyn Midlo Hall documented the earliest influx of Africans into Louisiana via slavery from the Senegambian region of West Africa (Hall 1992).

Building on this base of cultural geography and history, Louisiana folklore research has led to several publications that provide a foundation, stimulating further study. The Louisiana Folklife Program's *Louisiana Folklife: A Guide to the State* (1985), edited by the program's first director, Nicholas R. Spitzer, is the most comprehensive state publication of its type. Frank de Caro's *Folklife in Louisiana Photography* (1990) provides a comprehensive overview of the photographic record. Other publications have focused tightly on a specific group, region, or genre: for example, *Gifts from the Hills: The Folk Traditions of North Central Louisiana* (Roach-Lankford 1984), *Folklife in the Florida Parishes* ([Gardner et al.] 1989), *Doing It Right and Passing it On: North Louisiana Crafts* (Gregory 1981), *Cajun and Creole Folktales* (Ancelet 1994), and *The Spanish Tradition in Louisiana* (Armistead 1992).

Since the advent of the Louisiana Folklife Program in 1978, many researchers have worked with the program to present their research in various formats to the general public. These researchers have explored numerous topics, but most generally focus on certain aspects of particular ethnic communities or folklore genres, including North Louisiana quilters (Roach 1986), north-central Louisiana British- and African-American folk cultures (Roach-Lankford 1984), Cajun musicians and culture (Ancelet 1984 and 1989a; Ancelet et al. 1991; Savoy 1984), Creole language (Ricard 1977, Snyder 1990), South Louisiana wooden boatbuilding (Knipmeyer 1976, Comeaux 1985, Brassieur 1989), Mardi Gras Indians (Smith 1984 and 1994), Hungarian dance and costume (Romero 1989), African-American gospel (Jackson 1989), Cajun Mardi Gras (Ancelet 1989b, Lindahl 1996a, Lindahl 1996b, Mire 1993, Ware 1995), Czechs (Walker 1989), Louisiana crafts (Bergeron 1988, de Caro and Jordan 1980, Roach-Lankford 1984), commercial fisherfolk (Knipmeyer 1956, Comeaux 1985, Gregory 1966), and Native American cultures (Gregory 1992, Kniffen, Gregory, and Stokes 1987), languages (Kimball 1989, Dreschel 1979), and crafts (Medford, Gregory, and Sepulvado 1990).

The Louisiana Crafts Program and Folklife Program also produced publications featuring individuals involved with the Craft, Apprenticeship, and other programs: for example, *Fait à la Main: A Sourcebook of Louisiana Crafts* (Bergeron 1988) and *Keeping It Alive: Cultural Conservation Through Apprenticeship* (Dunbar and Owens 1993). This essay draws on these publications and the research conducted by cultural specialists (folklorists, cultural anthropologists, cultural geographers, ethnomusicologists) and the non-academically-trained community scholars. Readers seeking more detailed information should refer to these publications and for a historical overview of folklife research to de Caro's article in *Louisiana Folklife: A Guide to the State* (1985, 12–34).

Many of the folk crafts mentioned in this article are displayed in *The Creole State: An Exhibition of Louisiana Folklife* located in the Louisiana State Capitol. First curated by Nicholas R. Spitzer in 1985 and renovated by myself in 1994, this permanent exhibit by the Louisiana Folklife Program presents folk crafts from Louisiana's traditional cultures in seven sections: folk toys; folk instruments; occupational crafts; domestic crafts; decorative folk arts; ritual, festival, and religion; and cultural conservation.

Scholars divide the state into three major cultural regions, New Orleans, South Louisiana, and North Louisiana, each of which contains groups whose cultures remain distinct from that of the larger region.

New Orleans

When Louisiana is mentioned, many people think only of New Orleans and neglect other regions of the state. Many misunderstandings exist about the distinct and complex culture that evolved in this metropolitan center. New Orleans, like Louisiana as a whole, has been governed by the French, Spanish, and Americans, with each making distinctive contributions. In addition, other ethnic groups, in particular Native Americans (especially Choctaw), Africans (both French-speaking African Creoles and English-speaking African Americans), Italians (primarily Sicilian), Germans, and Irish, have also made significant contributions to the cultural landscape of the city. Today, New Orleans is a multicultural metropolis with significant communities of Jews, Latins (from throughout the Caribbean and Central and South America), Greeks, Haitians, Filipinos, and Asians, including a large concentration of Vietnamese (Cooke and Blanton 1981).

Contrary to some tourism promotions, New Orleans is not a Cajun town, even though many Cajuns moved to New Orleans after World War II and grew to dominate certain parts of the city, such as Westwego and Marrero on the West Bank. The first and largest migrations of the French to New Orleans were not Acadian. French nobles and army officers blended with the Spanish to create a Creole community. "Creole," as used in New Orleans, refers either to the descendants of the French and Spanish settlers or to people of French, Spanish, and African descent who were known as *gens de couleur libres* or free-people-of-color (Snyder 1990, Tregle 1992). These two groups were culturally intertwined, yet maintained separate identities.

Most Africans in Louisiana arrived as slaves from Francophone West Africa, but later some arrived as free-people-of-color from the Caribbean. Two-thirds of the Africans arriving before 1730 were from the Senegambia region of West Africa. Senegambia was home to many culturally related groups with similar languages, but most Africans brought to Louisiana during this time were either Wolof or Bambara (Hall 1992). After the Haitian Revolution of 1791–1804, another influx of Africans, including many free-people-of-color, arrived by way of the Caribbean. Most of these Africans from the Caribbean were originally from Dahomey (now the Republic of Benin) and Nigeria (Hunt 1988).

The fact that a significant number of Africans from closely related cultures came to Louisiana was a factor in their ability to retain many cultural traits and contribute to the Creole culture that was developing in New Orleans and South Louisiana. For example, the Haitians brought the shotgun house and the voodoo religion to Louisiana. The word "voodoo" is derived from the African word *voudun,* which means "deity" in Yoruba or "insight" in Fon (Bodin 1990). Free-people-of-color dominated many building trades in New Orleans, were often highly educated, and as chefs played an important role in the development of Creole cuisine for which the city is known (Reinecke 1985). Okra, an important ingredient of gumbo, and the word "gumbo" itself (derived from Bantu *nkombo*) are African.

After the Louisiana Purchase in 1803, British Americans, referred to as *Les Américains,* arrived and settled upriver or uptown from the central Creole district, with Canal Street being the dividing line. Irish fleeing the potato famine of the 1840s settled in the area that became known as the Irish Channel between the Mississippi River and the Uptown Garden District. The 1850s saw an influx of Germans. After the Civil War, even more English-speaking African Americans arrived to join the population of freed slaves. The distinction between African Creoles and African Americans began to blur after 1918 (Reinecke 1985, 58–59), but still today Louisianans at times refer to people not descended from the French or Creole culture as Americans. Jazz played a role in this cultural fusion because ethnic groups that did not otherwise mingle were drawn together through jazz. African Americans, African Creoles, Italians, Germans, and Irish were all instrumental in the development of this new art form. In New Orleans, musical traditions range from brass jazz bands to African Creole and African-American Mardi Gras Indians chanting call-responses that have been called the most African of all musics found in North America. African-American Delta blues and Latin salsa are some of the most frequently heard musics today in local clubs, along with the distinctive New Orleans rhythm and blues made famous by the likes of Fats Domino, Professor Longhair, and the Neville Brothers (Smith 1990).

Parading is another cultural expression cherished by New Orleanians. Mardi Gras, or Shrove Tuesday, celebrated the day before Lent begins, is a community-wide celebration that embraces all segments of society. The elite *krewes* (festive societies) sponsor elaborate parades and balls, neighborhood groups celebrate with organized walking clubs or less elaborate truck parades, and working-class blacks celebrate dressed as Mardi Gras "Indians." Garbed in elaborate feather and bead costumes and identifying themselves as tribes to emulate and honor Native Americans, Mardi Gras Indian tribes such as the Wild Magnolias, the Golden Star Hunters, and the Yellow Pocahontas, compete for recognition of their costumes, songs, and dances while parading on Mardi Gras day.

Parades also occur at other times of the year. The Irish, who also contributed to the distinctive "Yat" dialect (the name of which is derived from the contraction of 'Where you at?') spoken by many New Orleanians, celebrate St. Patrick's Day (March 17) with what is essentially a Mardi Gras parade with green floats filled with revelers who throw to the crowd the ingredients for potato stew. Jazz parades still accompany some funerals, and the Mardi Gras Indians return to the streets for Super Sunday (the Sunday closest to St. Joseph's Day, March 19). It is still common among African Americans for the male-oriented, secular Social Aid and Pleasure Clubs to enter the streets throughout the fall, and the female-dominated organizational counterparts to have second-line parades as part of their spring celebrations. The marching and parading traditions inspire and incorporate specific craft traditions, such as ribbon baskets and sashes for the Benevolent Societies' marching clubs, and costume- and maskmaking for Mardi Gras.

South Louisiana

Nicholas R. Spitzer has described rural South Louisiana as a cultural gumbo in which each of the different ingredients is identifiable, yet all have blended, affecting each other (Spitzer 1977). A complex blend of French, Spanish, German, African, Irish, and Native American influences created a unique regional culture. Yet, when one looks closer, one becomes aware of local variations: in spite of its deep French roots, South Louisiana is not a monolithic, homogeneous Francophonic culture.

French traditional culture in Louisiana is largely contained in a great triangular area with its apex below Alexandria and its base stretching from New Orleans to Lake Charles. Small enclaves dominated by one or more of Louisiana's French-influenced traditions exist, however, even in North Louisiana, near Natchitoches and Hebert in Caldwell Parish, and along Bayou Pierre (the Rambin community) and in Big Island in Rapides Parish.

The dominant regional culture of South Louisiana results from successive waves of French (Canadian traders, Acadians from Nova Scotia and New Brunswick, French royalists, Bonapartists, apolitical French civilians, French soldiers, French from the West Indies), Spaniards (from Spain, the Adaeseños from Texas-Mexico, and the Isleños from the Canary Islands), Germans (arriving as early as the Spanish period and continuing into the nineteenth century), Irish, Africans, and a variety of Caribbean transplants. Many of these groups blended with the Louisiana Native American groups (some aboriginal tribes and others who resettled in the area during the eighteenth and nineteenth centuries). Some Native Americans retain their own unique cultures, virtually unmodified by European contact in a number of ways.

Many people think of South Louisiana as "Cajun," the term being a local version of "Acadian." Today's Cajun culture resulted from the blending of several groups, primarily the Acadians, the descendants of French Acadians who were expelled from Nova Scotia by the British in 1755 and who began arriving in Louisiana in 1765. Two primary cultural regions exist within South Louisiana. While still basically French, the area east of the Atchafalaya Swamp and along the Mississippi River and Bayou Lafourche between Baton Rouge and New Orleans received a significant influx of wealthy Lowland South planters of English descent. Those plantation owners influenced the area in many ways, particularly by teaching their slaves English rather than French. Also, being closer to New Orleans and on major transportation routes, the Germans, Spanish, French, English, and later the "Kaintucks"

(Americans from up the Mississippi River) were more cosmopolitan than people in the swamps and on the prairies to the west. A large number of Germans arrived during the Spanish period, settled upriver from New Orleans along the German Coast, and provided most of the vegetable crops needed by New Orleans. These Germans are not as easily identified today, because they gradually assimilated into the dominant French culture, and many of their names were translated into French or English (Reinecke 1985).

Living in relative isolation on the Louisiana bayous and the southwest Louisiana prairie and being the dominant cultural group, the French-speaking Acadians, French nationals, French royalists, and French army officers absorbed Germans, Spanish, British Americans, and Native Americans who settled among them or married into their families. During the late nineteenth century, large numbers of Midwesterners settled the Cajun prairie to take part in the newly developing rice industry and the railroad. Within a relatively short time period, many were absorbed into Cajun culture. Today, many French-speaking people who identify themselves as Cajuns may have surnames such as Frey (German), Smith (English), McGee (Irish), and Manuel or Rodrigue (Spanish) in addition to Acadian surnames like Bergeron, Broussard, LeBlanc, or Mire, and the French colonial army surnames of Fontenot or Fusilier (Brasseaux 1992).

The French-speaking black Creoles of the southwest Louisiana prairie lived alongside the Cajuns and were often free-people-of-color and landowners. While remaining racially distinct from their Cajun neighbors, they share many cultural traits, including the food, Mardi Gras, Catholicism, musical repertoire, and often the French or Creole language. But one of their most significant contributions is zydeco, a distinctly black Creole music known for its blending of French songs and African/Caribbean rhythms. To be of African descent in South Louisiana certainly does not presume a French-speaking heritage. English-speaking blacks, many of whom descended from freed slaves, also made cultural contributions (Fontenot 1994a and 1994b). For example, the zydeco repertoire shows heavy influence from Deep South rhythm and blues.

Many people are aware that the Cajun and Creole cultures have contributed Cajun dance music, with two-steps, waltzes, and haunting ballads; and Creole zydeco music, with its African influence. But more recently—in the early 1950s—this unique cultural mix also created "swamp pop", a regional variation of rhythm and blues music common throughout South Louisiana and into East Texas. Swamp pop combines rhythm and blues with Cajun and black Creole music and country and western. A strong horn section and honky-tonk piano characterizes this blend (Bernard 1996). The region also has a vital jazz community (Sonnier 1990). Cajuns and Creoles are as well known to outsiders for their special foods as for the distinctive music, and a delectable array of food dishes (crawfish étouffée, gumbo, bisque, sauce piquante, jambalaya) can be found in the region (Gutierrez 1992). Many restaurants and dance halls provide Cajun and Creole music for both tourists and locals. Saturdays often mean jam sessions, radio shows, or dances for Cajun music lovers. Outsiders seldom know about Cajun and Creole crafts, such as cowhide chair bottoms, wooden boats (skiffs, luggers, pirogues), Acadian brown cotton weaving, accordion building, fiddlemaking, and Job's Tears rosaries (Latimer and Vermillion 1988) or lesser known food delicacies such as *langue boureé* (stuffed beef tongue) or *chaudin* (sausage-stuffed pork stomach).

Some communities in South Louisiana have always been predominantly English-speaking. Fishing and gathering settlements in the Atchafalaya Basin were different from those on the bayous and prairies to the east and west. Many of these predominately white communities relocated to the levees surrounding the basin when the U.S. Corps of Engineers transformed the basin for flood control. Many individuals also moved to the Morgan City area, which was already primarily English-speaking. Other English-speaking people in Morgan City came from the Carolinas' coastal fishing communities and became shrimpers or menhaden ("poggie") fishermen.

South Louisiana also has pockets of ethnic groups that have resisted total absorption by French/Cajun culture. In St. Bernard Parish, the Isleños, who are descended from Canary Islanders who settled the area in the 1760s, continue to retain their archaic Spanish dialect and perpetuate the singing of *décimas* (narrative songs). In Acadia Parish, Germans of Robert's Cove, who settled the area during the nineteenth century, begin the Christmas season with a procession on December 5, the eve of the religious feast of St. Nicholas. St. Nick, Lil' Black Peter, Santa Claus, and the church choir visit German homes in the community. Croatians from the Dalmatian Coast settled in Plaquemines Parish, introduced the oystering industry, and continue to control it. These groups remain culturally distinct after more than one hundred years of Louisiana residency.

Throughout South Louisiana and New Orleans, Catholicism, the dominant religion since colonial times, is shared by many cultural groups. As a result, cultural or folk Catholicism, incorporating the specific religious traditions of each group, has contributed practices that persist today. For example, on November 7, New Orleanian Nicaraguans build home altars for

Purissima, the Feast of the Blessed Mother; and in Cajun prairie communities Mardi Gras, Fat Tuesday, is observed with *le courrir de Mardi Gras* (Mardi Gras run) by community members proceeding from house to house on horseback or by truck to gather ingredients for a communal gumbo, one last good meal and lively party before the solemn observance of Lent begins on Ash Wednesday.

North Louisiana

The rest of Louisiana is populated primarily by English-speaking British Americans and African Americans. This includes the Florida Parishes north of Lake Pontchartrain (in the "toe of the boot" as locals say) and parishes north of the French triangle (see map 1). The term "British American" as used in this volume refers to various English-speaking peoples from the British Isles who arrived at various times in Louisiana history. The term is intended to replace Anglo American, Anglo-Scotch-Irish, and Anglo-Celtic. Within what is commonly called "North Louisiana" there are two primary subcultures: the Upland South hill culture and the Lowland South plantation culture along the river bottoms. Both are primarily Protestant, but there are significant differences. The Upland South region was primarily populated by Scotch-Irish who migrated from Georgia, Alabama, South Carolina, Mississippi, and Tennessee (Roach-Lankford 1985). The majority of these immigrants were Baptist or Methodist small farmers with a strong Protestant work ethic. Few had slaves in large numbers. The Lowland South region in Louisiana was populated by the descendants of Englishmen and Scots from other Southern states and New England. This group established plantations, especially cotton, along the bottoms of the Mississippi, Red, and Ouachita Rivers. More often, these settlers were Methodists, Presbyterians, or Episcopalians. Their plantations depended on a large slave population, a fact reflected in the high concentration of rural blacks who inhabit the region today (Cash 1941, Frantom 1993, Roach-Lankford 1985).

Culturally, North Louisiana is akin to a patchwork quilt, as described by H. F. Gregory (1981). Each piece has remained intact, coexisting with the others. But just as South Louisiana is not a uniform French/African culture, North Louisiana is not a uniform British/African culture. Variations and subtleties exist through the region. Distinctive traits differentiate the communities of the northeast, northwest, and central regions.

In the Mississippi River delta in northeast Louisiana, the land is low and has few large towns. On the high bluffs of the Mississippi side of the river,

Louisiana Folk Regions

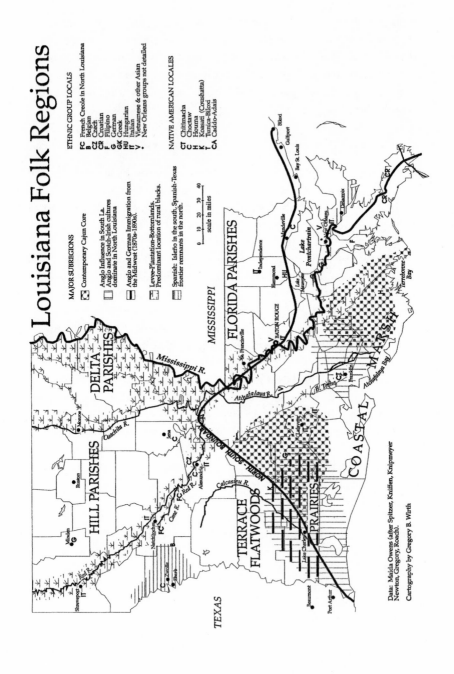

MAJOR SUBREGIONS

▨ Contemporary Cajun Core

☐ Anglo Influence in South La.
  Anglo and Scotch-Irish cultures
  dominate in North Louisiana

▤ Anglo and German Immigration from
  the Midwest (1870s–1890s).

▥ Levee-Plantation-Bottomlands.
  Predominant location of rural blacks.

▦ Spanish: Isleño in the south, Spanish-Texas
  frontier remnants in the north.

ETHNIC GROUP LOCALS

FC   French Creole in North Louisiana
B   Belgian
CZ   Czech
CR   Croatian
F   Filipino
G   German
GK   Greek
HU   Hungarian
IT   Italian
V   Vietnamese & other Asian
•   New Orleans groups not detailed

NATIVE AMERICAN LOCALES

CT   Chitimacha
C   Choctaw
H   Houma
K   Koasati (Coushatta)
T   Tunica-Biloxi
CA   Caddo-Adais

0   10   20   30   40
scale in miles

Data: Maida Owens (after Spitzer, Kniffen, Knipmeyer
Newton, Gregory, Roach).

Cartography by Gregory B. Wirth

Louisiana Parishes

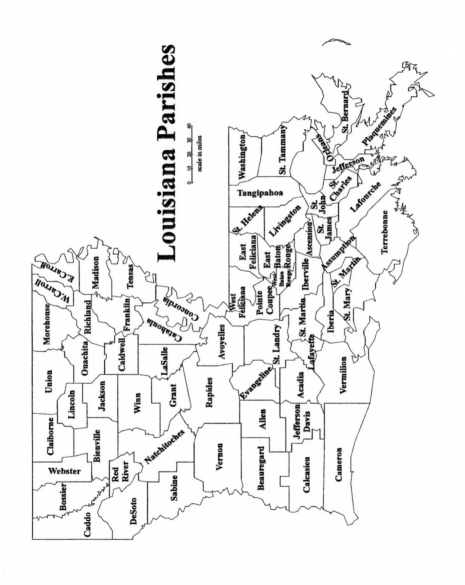

scale in miles
0 10 20 30 40

larger towns, including Vicksburg and Natchez, were founded. They also served the lowland Louisiana side. The Mississippi River left natural levees, creating backswamp areas dividing the region into what was called "front lands" and "back lands." The front lands were the flat, higher, siltier levees near the active Mississippi River where the plantation economy flourished. As the artificial levees expanded, these lands were extensively cleared and planted. The back lands remained swamps until drained in the 1970s.

This area, the Louisiana delta from the Red River to the Arkansas border, was home to a folk culture based on open-range hogs managed by Catahoula curs, a dog breed developed in the area. While this method of raising hogs was not unique to this area, it predominated this region more than others. From the late 1800s until the mid-1900s, settlers raised free-ranging hogs for pork and lard to be sold in New Orleans (LeBon 1970). Today, Catahoula curs are still valued. A few people still raise free-ranging hogs, and pork remains a staple of the diet.

Between the lowlands of the Mississippi River and the Boeuf River/ Ouachita River basins is Maçon Ridge, high land settled by Upland South farmers. Along the Mississippi River and to the south on Catahoula Lake and other lakes, British-American fishing communities are found. Here, commercial fishermen and their families maintain the occupational traditions of boatbuilding, trapmaking, and netmaking.

The twin cities of Monroe and West Monroe on the Ouachita River illustrate the juxtaposition of North Louisiana's two dominant cultures: Lowland and Upland South. Monroe on the east bank with rich delta soil was settled first by Lowland South planters who were more likely to have larger tracts of land and to allow alcohol and dancing in social settings. A second wave, bringing small farmers of Upland South heritage, settled on the west bank with higher land and piney woods. This area, known as West Monroe, is less likely to have alcohol at community and social events.

Shreveport, Natchitoches, and Alexandria are Lowland South cities along the Red River. Each was tied economically to the large plantations in this rich river delta. Shreveport, the largest city in North Louisiana, is home to a culturally diverse mix of British Americans (especially Scotch-Irish), African Americans, Italians, Lebanese, Germans, Greeks, Chinese, and Jews. At one time, Shreveport had a significant downtown community of Italian grocers, Chinese restaurants, Jewish merchants, and a German bakery. While few downtown merchants remain, Shreveport is still home to their descendants. Nearby, German socialists started a colony at Minden that broke up in 1871.

Founded in 1713, Natchitoches, the earliest settlement in the Louisiana Purchase, was settled by the French, creating a unique cultural pocket in North Louisiana. Current evidence of the Creole French influence is seen in the foodways (Natchitoches meat pies and Cane River cakes) and the architecture, more reminiscent of New Orleans's than that of its surrounding communities. On nearby Cane River, a rural community of Creoles of color exists, descended from a freed slave woman who established what is now known as Melrose Plantation. This French-African-Creole community was isolated until World War II, after which many members moved away to Houston, Chicago, and southern California for economic reasons. Yet, the community remains tight-knit, with most returning annually just after the cotton harvest for the St. Augustine Catholic Church fair (Mills 1977; Breaux 1995).

To the west along the Texas-Louisiana border, one finds the remains of "No-Man's Land," otherwise known as the Neutral Strip, which was formerly a refuge for outlaws and others not wanting to be bothered with the trappings of "civilized" society. This area has not been extensively documented but is home to a diverse group, including colonial Spanish to the west of Natchitoches in Sabine Parish. The colonial town of Los Adais near Robeline was once a capital of Texas. In Los Adais, colonial Spanish influence is evident in the Catholicism and the food traditions of tamales and chilies. Elders speak a unique, archaic Spanish filled with Nahuatl Indian and French loanwords (Armistead and Gregory 1986). These Spanish and Indian groups work at cattle raising and lumbering. Further south around Beauregard Parish, a group emerged in the mid-nineteenth century when a Native American community absorbed British-American settlers and other populations. These people became known as Redbones, from the West Indian term *red ibo*, which refers to any racial mixture (Kniffen, Gregory and Stokes 1987).

Most of the Florida Parishes are Protestant and rural, and dominated by Upland South culture. Here small farms and towns thrive among the piney woods that were at one time part of the colonial Spanish territory of Florida. Exceptions are St. Francisville in West Feliciana, which is part of the Lowland South plantation culture, and the capital Baton Rouge, a British-American town in spite of its French name, that is home to a multicultural community of Italians, Cajuns, African Americans, Lebanese, Asians (particularly Vietnamese), and others.

As in French Louisiana, pockets of ethnic groups remain intact among the Upland and Lowland South cultures. Hungarians in Tangipahoa Parish continue their dance, music, food, and costume traditions, and the Hungarian language is taught in the elementary school in an effort to save it (Romero 1987). Czechs in Rapides Parish east of Alexandria have revitalized their dance, song, food, and costume traditions.

North Louisiana craft traditions include many that reflect the skills used on farms and plantations relying upon available resources. Some crafts, such as whipmaking, knifemaking, saddlery, trapmaking, split-oak basketmaking, and quilting are still vital and practiced by many. Others—including whittling toys, blacksmithing, tatting, carving walking sticks, soapmaking, and fashioning gourd birdhouses—are relatively rare and maintained by only a few individuals.

Food traditions include a vast array of relishes and chow chow (to enhance field peas and cornbread); jellies, jams, and preserves; vegetable crops (corn, sweet potatoes, greens, beans, peas); hogs; and cattle. Many still relish wild game (venison, squirrel, raccoon, rabbit, and quail) and fish (both farm-raised catfish and gamefish such as crappie and bream). All of these may be fried. Sunday dinners at noon, fish fries, and barbecues are common occasions.

Ritual traditions reflect the Protestant heritage. All-day singings and dinners on the grounds still take place after church services in many rural communities, frequently on the fifth Sunday in a month. Both black and white rural churches have gatherings such as Homecoming, bringing together extended families. Memorial Day, which commemorates all the deceased and not only military veterans, also provides an opportunity for extended families to visit graveyards, decorate graves with silk flowers, and tell stories. North Louisiana graveyards are relatively unadorned compared with those in South Louisiana. Some rural church congregations still conduct baptisms in the same river or lake used for generations. Many church families, especially among the African Americans, continue to make the special baptismal robes and headgear.

The music of North Louisiana reflects its cultural roots. Gospel music is probably the strongest traditional form of music among both blacks and whites. Quartets and choirs are heard in churches, on the radio, and at festivals throughout the region. Shape-note singing, a musical notation system using seven shapes to represent the musical scale, is still practiced in North Louisiana, and singing conventions are held annually. Quartet singing remains strong, and a strong emphasis on harmony is seen in family performing groups. Most churches have large choirs, and many still learn to sing by ear rather than by musical notation. Church services featuring gospel performances are broadcast on radio and television.

Other music traditions shared by British Americans include old-time country and bluegrass. Weekly country music shows such as the Dixie Jamboree in Ruston and the former Louisiana Hayride radio show in Shreveport reflect this heritage. Country music is also performed at benefits to raise funds to help families cover the costs of such emergencies as catastrophic illnesses and rebuilding fire-damaged houses. Benefits often include auctions of donated goods. Bluegrass festivals, which usually forbid alcohol, have been popular since the introduction of bluegrass in the 1940s. The region is also the home of a relatively new form of music that grew out of Ferriday in Concordia Parish—rockabilly. This regional, early form of rock and roll, blending country music with Mississippi Delta blues, was made famous by Ferriday's Jerry Lee Lewis and others (Tucker 1989, 1029).

African Americans made their mark with traditional Delta blues and more recently rhythm and blues, both of which have become popular with many of the state's cultural groups. Country blues, derived from the field hollers and slave songs of the past, more often feature a single musician who accompanies himself and uses much improvisation. City blues is usually more structured and is more often accompanied by a band. Both forms abound in North Louisiana. Juke joints dot the rural and small-town landscape, and urban centers such as Baton Rouge and Shreveport feature blues clubs (Beyers 1980).

Cowboy culture is one trait shared by both North and South Louisiana. Cowboys in Louisiana may be British American, African American, Cajun, or Creole. Rodeos, trail rides, and the making of braided whips, horsehair ropes, and leather saddles flourish from Monroe to Cameron Parish, from Shreveport to Hammond. Since Louisiana's landscape does not include the vast rangelands of the American West, adaptations were needed in both North and South Louisiana. The marsh cowboys have made extra long reins to allow cowboys to stay out of the way of horses lunging through the mud. They learned how to put spurs on rubber boots and herd cattle by boat. Creole ponies successfully survived the heat and mosquitoes and could cope with the marsh with their small hooves. Cattle are wintered in the marshes but moved to higher ground during the summer to avoid mosquitoes in the marsh. Cattle drives continue, but eighteen-wheel trucks have taken the place of the horseback cowboy. North Louisiana, with its piney woods and thickets, also required special adaptations of cowboy lifestyle. Largely untended woods cattle required hardy cowboys that could round them up in thickets and swamps using Catahoula curs (Spitzer 1991). The commonality of the ranch and rodeo culture persists throughout Louisiana. Performance genres found in cowboy culture include reciting cowboy poetry, auctioneering in French or English, and singing cowboy ballads in clubs and at festivals.

Other Cultural Groups

Some cultural groups are found throughout Louisiana. Italians, one of the largest such groups, began arriving en masse from Sicily at the turn of the twentieth century. Most settled first in rural agricultural communities, later moved into cities to start small businesses, and soon dominated the food distribution systems. But some rural Italian communities remain. One is in and around the town of Independence in the Florida Parishes, where strawberry farming persists and families make strawberry wine. Another rural, conservative Italian community is located around Powhattan in North Louisiana.

One tradition closely tied to Italian-American ethnic identity is the St. Joseph altar, which has seen a resurgence of popularity since the 1970s from Shreveport to New Orleans. Catholics often promise God that they will build an altar if a favor is granted or in hopes of having a favor granted. The altar contains religious icons and food for the community, including special breads in the form of Catholic symbols, casseroles, cookies, and cakes, while guests are given dried fava beans for luck. While an altar can be promised at any time to any saint, most commonly an Italian family will build an altar in their home for St. Joseph, the patron saint of Sicily. The altar is usually built on or near St. Joseph's Day, March 19. Family, friends, and the community are invited to attend the blessing of the altar and the Feeding of the Saints, and to eat the food on the altar (Orso 1990; Owens 1989, 134; Warren 1982). More recently, Italian-American associations, such as the Grandsons of Italy, build a community altar that is publicized for the general public. It functions as an ethnic identity marker for the organization (Gardner 1983).

Many people are surprised to discover that Louisiana has a significant Native American population—the largest within the eastern United States. Although they do not fit the stereotyped image of what most people think of as Indians, the Louisiana tribes and bands have played a significant role in shaping the distinctive culture of the state, both north and south. Many of the original inhabitants of Louisiana shared their culture with the newly arrived Europeans and Africans, teaching them how to take advantage of the natural bounty of the land. So filé (powdered sassafras for gumbo), place names (Atchafalaya, Kisatchie), and hunting and fishing practices, such as handfishing, sometimes attributed to European-American pioneers should be credited to the Native Americans (Mire 1990). The Attakapas, Chitimacha, Houma, Tunica-Biloxi, and Caddo are the only surviving tribes that were in Louisiana at European contact, although they were not necessarily settled in their present locations. The others, including the Choctaw and Koasati, were relocated to the state during the Spanish period. Four of the tribes—the Tunica-Biloxi, Chitimacha, Koasati, and most recently the Jena Band of Choctaw—have been federally recognized and have reservations, although these are relatively small when compared with the reservations of the American West. State recognition has been extended to the Houma, Clifton-Choctaw, Choctaw-Apache of Ebarb, Caddo-Adais, and East Baton Rouge Choctaw. Quite aside from these "recognized" groups, numerous other Native Americans live in the state. The tribes are presently gaining more recognition, and one of their cultural survival strategies—isolation—may not have as important a role in their cultural conservation efforts as it had in the past. But the trade-off is that more tribal members are making greater economic progress.

The Chitimacha, a small tribe of about three hundred members located at Charenton, in St. Mary Parish, is world-renowned for its river cane basketry. A handful of individuals continue to make the double and single weave baskets in traditional patterns. This is one of the most conservative of the state's traditions, and it is passed on exclusively within the culture.

The Houma, the largest tribe, numbering about ten thousand, live in the marshes and along the bayous of Terrebonne and Lafourche Parishes. Until recently, they have maintained a lifestyle close to the land, with emphasis on fishing and trapping. Weaving palmetto (a native palm); curing Spanish moss to make dolls, bags, and mattresses; and carving duck decoys and model pirogues are some of the current craft traditions maintained (United Houma Nation n.d.).

The Koasati (also known as Coushatta), located outside of Elton in Allen Parish, are perhaps the most conservative of the tribes. They have maintained their native language, and most families speak only Koasati in their homes. This tribe is known for its pine straw baskets. They also make traditional river cane baskets for their own use as well as for sale (Coushatta Tribe of Louisiana 1992).

Several Choctaw bands are located in Louisiana. Those in Jena (La-Salle Parish) and in Clifton (Rapides Parish) maintain close-knit communities. The folk art of the Clifton Choctaw has been documented (Gregory and Hatley 1992). Other Native American tribes include the Apache-Choctaw (Sabine Parish), the Caddo-Adais (Natchitoches Parish), and the Tunica-Biloxi (Avoyelles Parish). Each community has its own crafts traditions. The Tunica-Biloxi maintain their annual sacred corn feast and continue to live on lands they have held for over two centuries. Their storytelling traditions and some of their songs survive. The Choctaw-Apache and Caddo-Adais still live in the vicinity of the eighteenth-century Spanish outpost of Los Adais. Because their ancestors converted to Catholicism and learned Spanish, these groups are in some ways more like Southwestern mission Indians than Southeastern tribes. Tamales and salsas are included in their food traditions; they often carve, plait whips, and do leatherwork.

Many other ethnic groups live in Louisiana, but their traditional culture, including storytelling, has not yet been documented by either folklife researchers or community scholars for presentation to others. Some are particularly strong in urban areas or university communities, while others are dispersed in rural communities. Some ethnic groups are closely identified with certain occupations. For example, many independent, small-town motels are owned and operated by East Indians. Other groups specialized in merchant trades. Lebanese peddlers followed the railroads and rivers and settled in many small towns as merchants and grocers (Saloom and Turner 1994). Chinese merchants can also be found in both large cities and such small towns as Lake Providence and Ferriday. Louisiana is also home to Africans, Greeks, Pakistanis, Iranians, Japanese, Koreans, and Vietnamese. Fortunately, the Louisiana Library Association has initiated efforts to facilitate research by publishing surveys of archival collections focused on some ethnic groups (Riquelmy 1994).

Conclusion

Multiculturalism, a buzzword of the 1990s coined to acknowledge and honor cultural diversity, has already produced a backlash. Many now claim that diversity promotes fragmentation and that assimilation or the blending of different traditional cultures is more in the national interest of the United States as a whole; according to some, the old melting-pot theory should be revived and a uniform mass culture promoted. In reality, the United States has never had and never will have such a seamless culture.

Furthermore, to attempt to create a melting pot would deny the importance of traditional culture in the lives of individuals. People's sense of community and validation must be protected and honored. This need not threaten our national unity. The challenge for the future is to make diversity work—to help all of us better understand not only our own cultures but also those of others.

Efforts by public cultural programs can produce tools, such as this volume and its companion video production on Louisiana storytelling, that can assist in this process of creating mutual respect among diverse cultures. By assembling stories from the many cultural groups that comprise Louisiana, by examining the individual parts, we can better understand the whole. Through public programs such as the Louisiana Folklife Program within the Division of the Arts, traditional Louisiana cultures have a means to be documented and validated with public presentations of their traditional art forms. The partnering of communities and trained researchers will help ensure that all of the traditional cultures within Louisiana will be better understood and appreciated. In the future, the Louisiana Folklife Program hopes to assist the communities covered in this volume to document more thoroughly their folk traditions and to empower those communities that have not yet made such efforts to document their unique folk cultures.

Louisiana Folklife Bibliography

Readers are invited to use the following bibliography on Louisiana folklife to learn more about the cultural groups discussed in this brief sketch. A bibliography of Louisiana storytellers, their stories, and related stories and storytelling traditions from elsewhere in the United States and throughout the world is found following the Notes on the Tales.

Bibliography

Ancelet, Barry Jean. 1984. *Musiciens cadiens et creoles: The Makers of Cajun Music.* Austin: University of Texas Press.

———. 1989a. *Cajun Music: Its Origins and Development.* Lafayette: University of Southwestern Louisiana, Center for Louisiana Studies.

———. 1989b. *Capitaine, Capitaine: Voyage Ton Flag.* Lafayette: University of Southwestern Louisiana, Center for Louisiana Studies.

———. 1994. *Cajun and Creole Folktales: The French Oral Tradition of South Louisiana.* Jackson: University Press of Mississippi.

Ancelet, Barry Jean, Jay Edwards, and Glen Pitre. 1991. *Cajun Country.* Jackson: University Press of Mississippi.

Armistead, Samuel G. 1992. *The Spanish Tradition in Louisiana.* Newark, Del.: Juan de la Cuesta.

Armistead, Samuel G., and H. F. Gregory. 1986. "French Loan Words in the Spanish Dialect of Sabine and Natchitoches Parishes." *Louisiana Folklife* 10:21–30.

Bergeron, Maida. 1988. *Fait à la Main: A Sourcebook of Louisiana Crafts.* Baton Rouge: Office of Cultural Development.

Bernard, Shane K. 1996. *Swamp Pop: Cajun and Creole Rhythm and Blues.* Jackson: University Press of Mississippi.

Beyer, Jimmy. 1980. *Baton Rouge Blues: A Guide to Baton Rouge Bluesmen and Their Music.* Baton Rouge: Arts and Humanities Council of Greater Baton Rouge.

Bodin, Ron. 1990. *Voodoo, Past and Present.* Louisiana Life Series, No. 5. Lafayette: University of Southwestern Louisiana, Center for Louisiana Studies.

Brasseaux, Carl A. 1987. *The Founding of New Acadia: The Beginning of Acadian Life in Louisiana, 1765–1803.* Baton Rouge: Louisiana State University Press.

———. 1992. *Acadian to Cajun: The Transformation of a People, 1803–1877.* Jackson: University Press of Mississippi.

Brassieur, Ray. 1989. "Louisiana Boatbuilding: An Unfathomed Fortune." In *1989 Louisiana Folklife Festival.* Ed. Carolyn Ware and Maida Owens. Baton Rouge: Office of Cultural Development.

Breaux, Pamela. 1995. "The Folklore of Cane River and the Creoles of Color Who Live There." M.A. thesis, University of Southwestern Louisiana.

Cash, W. J. 1941. *The Mind of the South.* New York: Vintage Books.

Comeaux, Malcolm. 1972. *Atchafalaya Swamp Life: Settlement and Folk Occupations.* Vol. 2 of *Geoscience and Man.* Baton Rouge: Louisiana State University School of Geoscience.

———. 1985. "Folk Boats of Louisiana." In Spitzer 1985, 161–78.

Cooke, John, and Mackie J-V Blanton. 1981. *Perspectives on Ethnicity in New Orleans.* New Orleans: University of New Orleans, Committee on Ethnicity in New Orleans.

Coushatta Tribe of Louisiana. 1992. *Red Shoes' People: A History of the Sovereign Nation of the Coushatta Tribe of Louisiana.* Elton: Coushatta Tribe of Louisiana.

de Caro, F. A. 1985. "A History of Folklife Research in Louisiana." In Spitzer 1985, 12-34.

———. 1990. *Folklife in Louisiana Photography.* Baton Rouge: Louisiana State University Press.

de Caro, F. A., and R. A. Jordan. 1980. *Louisiana Traditional Crafts.* Baton Rouge: Louisiana State University Union Gallery.

Dreschel, Emanuel. 1979. "Mobilian Jargon: Linguistic, Sociocultural, and Historical Aspects of an American Indian Lingua Franca." Ph.D. diss., University of Wisconsin, Madison.

Dunbar, Sheri, and Maida Owens. 1993. *Keeping It Alive: Cultural Conservation Through Apprenticeship.* Baton Rouge: Office of Cultural Development.

Fontenot, Wonda, ed. 1994a. *1994 Malaki Festival: A Community Reunion to Celebrate Rural African American Traditions.* Opelousas, La.: Wannamuse Institute for Arts, Culture, and Ethnic Studies.

———. 1994b. *Secret Doctors: Ethnomedicine of African Americans.* Westport, Conn.: Bergin and Garvey, Greenwood Publishing Group.

Frantom, Marcy. 1993. *Louisiana Folklife.* Special Issue: African-American Folklife in Louisiana, vol. 17. Natchitoches: Northwestern State University, Louisiana Folklife Center.

Gardner, Joel, ed. 1983. *A Better Life: Italian-Americans in South Louisiana.* New Orleans: American-Italian Federation of the Southeast.

[Gardner, Joel, et al.] 1989. *Folklife in the Florida Parishes.* Baton Rouge: Office of Cultural Development.

Gregory, Hiram F., Jr. 1966. "The Black River Commercial Fisheries: A Study in Cultural Geography." *Louisiana Studies* 5:3–36.

Gregory, H. F. 1981. *Doing It Right and Passing It On: North Louisiana Crafts.* Alexandria, La.: Alexandria Museum of Art.

———. 1992. "Stories of the Old People." In *1992 Louisiana Folklife Festival.* Ed. Maida Owens and Peter Schwarz. Baton Rouge: Office of Cultural Development.

Gregory, H. F., and Donald W. Hatley, eds. 1992. *Splittin' on the Grain: North Louisiana Crafts.* Alexandria, La.: Alexandria Museum of Art.

Gutierrez, C. Page. 1992. *Cajun Foodways.* Jackson: University Press of Mississippi.

Hall, Gwendolyn Midlo. 1992. *Africans of Colonial Louisiana: The Development of Afro-Creole Culture in the Eighteenth Century.* Baton Rouge: Louisiana State University Press.

Hunt, Alfred H. 1988. *Haiti's Influence on Antebellum America: Slumbering Volcano in the Caribbean.* Baton Rouge: Louisiana State University Press.

Jackson, Joyce. 1989. "Music of the Black Churches." In [Gardner et al.] 1989. Pp. 97–103.

Kimball, Geoffery. 1989. *Koasati Grammar.* Lincoln: University of Nebraska Press.

Kniffen, Fred. 1936. " Louisiana House Types." *Annals of the Association of American Geographers* 26:179–93.

Kniffen, Fred, H. F. Gregory, and George A. Stokes. 1987. *The Historic Indian Tribes of Louisiana: From 1542 to the Present.* Baton Rouge: Louisiana State University Press.

Knipmeyer, William. 1956. "Settlement Succession in Eastern French Louisiana." Ph.D. diss., Louisiana State University.

———. 1976. "Folk Boats of Eastern French Louisiana." In *American Folklife.* Ed. Don Yoder. Austin: University of Texas Press.

Latimer, Beverly D., and Phoebe D. Vermillion. 1988. *Craft Talk: Visits with Five Traditional Louisiana Craftspeople.* Lafayette: Lafayette Natural History Museum.

LeBon, Joseph Walter, Jr. 1970. "The Catahoula Hog Dog: A Cultural Trait of the Upland South." M.A. thesis, Louisiana State University.

Lindahl, Carl. 1996a. "Bakhtin's Carnival Laughter and the Cajun Country Mardi Gras." *Folklore* 107:49–62.

————. 1996b. "The Presence of the Past in Cajun Mardi Gras." *Journal of Folklore Research* 33:101–29.

Medford, Claude, Jr., H. F. Gregory, and Don Sepulvado. 1990. *The Old Ways Live: The Claude Medford, Jr. Collection.* Natchitoches: Northwestern State University, Williamson Museum.

Mills, Gary B. 1977. *The Forgotten People: Cane River's Creoles of Color.* Baton Rouge: Louisiana State University Press.

Mire, Pat. 1990. *Anything I Catch: The Handfishing Story.* Eunice, La.: Attakapas Productions. Video.

————. 1993. *Dance for a Chicken: The Cajun Mardi Gras.* Eunice, La.: Attakapas Productions. Video.

Orso, Ethelyn. 1990. *The St. Joseph Altar Traditions of South Louisiana.* Louisiana Life Series, no. 4. Lafayette: University of Southwestern Louisiana, Center for Louisiana Studies.

Owens, Maida. 1989. "St. Joseph Altar." In [Gardner et al.] 1989, 134–36.

Reinecke, George F. 1985. "The National and Cultural Groups of New Orleans." In Spitzer 1985, 55–64.

Ricard, Ulysses. 1977. *Lagniappe: A Louisiana French Reader.* Private printing.

Riquelmy, Christina, ed. 1994. *Documenting Selected Louisiana Ethnic Groups: A Theme Issue of LLA Bulletin* 57:1. Baton Rouge: Louisiana Library Association. (Includes Italians, Lebanese, Vietnamese, and prehistoric, historic, and present-day Louisiana Indians: Chitimacha, Coushatta, Tunica-Biloxi, Caddo, Choctaw Apache, Clifton Choctaw, Jena Band of Choctaw, and the United Houma Nation.)

Roach, Susan. 1986. "The Traditional Quiltmaking of North Louisiana Women: Form, Function, and Meaning." Ph.D. diss., University of Texas at Austin.

Roach-Lankford, Susan. 1984. *Gifts from the Hills.* Ruston: Louisiana Tech Art Gallery.

————. 1985. "The Regional Folklife of North Louisiana." In Spitzer 1985, 87–102.

Romero, Ginger. 1987. *Hungarian Folklife: "The Sweet Taste of Yesterday" in the Florida Parishes of Southeast Louisiana.* Folklife in the Florida Parishes Series, vol. 3. Hammond: Southwestern Louisiana University, Center for Regional Studies.

Romero, Virginia. 1989. "Hungarian Folklife in the Florida Parishes of Louisiana." In [Gardner et al.] 1989, 68–76.

Saloom, Yvonne Nassar, and I. Bruce Turner. 1994. "Roots of the Cedar: The

Lebanese Heritage in Louisiana." *Louisiana Library Association Bulletin* 57, no. 1 (Summer): 31–42.

Savoy, Ann. 1984. *Cajun Music: A Reflection of a People.* Eunice, La.: Bluebird Press.

Smith, Michael. 1984. *Spirit World.* Gretna, La.: Pelican Publishing.

————. 1990. *Make a Joyful Noise: A Celebration of New Orleans Music.* Dallas: Taylor Publishing.

————. 1994. *Mardi Gras Indians.* Gretna, La.: Pelican Press.

Snyder, Karen. 1990. "The Creole Controversy." *Cultural Vistas* 1, no. 1 (Spring).

Sonnier, Austin, Jr. 1990. *Second Linin': Jazzmen of Southwest Louisiana, 1900–1950.* Louisiana Life Series, no. 3. Lafayette: University of Southwestern Louisiana, Center for Louisiana Studies.

Spitzer, Nicholas R. 1977. "Cajuns and Creoles: The French Gulf Coast." In *The Long Journey Home: Folklife in the South.* Ed. Allen Tullos. Chapel Hill, N.C.: Southern Exposure.

————, ed. 1985. *Louisiana Folklife: A Guide to the State.* Baton Rouge: Office of Cultural Development.

————. 1991. "Lifelines of a Woods Cowboy." *Cultural Vistas* 2, no. 2 (Summer): 15, 28–31.

Tregle, Joseph G., Jr. 1992. "Creoles and Americans " In *Creole New Orleans: Race and Americanization.* Ed. Arnold R. Hirsch and Joseph Logsdon. Baton Rouge: Louisiana State University Press.

Tucker, Stephen. 1989. "Rock and Roll." In *Encyclopedia of Southern Culture.* Ed. Charles Reagan Wilson and William Ferris. Chapel Hill: University of North Carolina Press.

United Houma Nation. [n.d.] *The Houma People of Louisiana: A Story of Indian Survival.* Golden Meadow, La.: United Houma Nation.

Walker, Rose. 1989. "Textile Uses in the Homes of Central Louisiana Czechs." In *1989 Louisiana Folklife Festival.* Ed. Carolyn Ware and Maida Owens. Baton Rouge: Office of Cultural Development.

Ware, Carolyn E. 1995. " 'I Read the Rules Backward': Women, Symbolic Inversion, and the Cajun Mardi Gras Run." *Southern Folklore* 52 (2): 137–60.

Warren, Karen, 1982. *Feast of St. Joseph: Labor of Love by the Faithful.* Folklife in the Florida Parishes Series, vol. 1. Hammond: Southeastern Louisiana University, Center for Regional Studies.

In addition to the works above, readers may wish to consult the following reference works and periodicals which contain substantial information on Louisiana's traditional cultures.

Cultural Vistas. New Orleans: Louisiana Endowment for the Humanities.
Louisiana Folklife. Natchitoches: Louisiana Folklife Society.
Louisiana Folklife Festival [series of booklets]. Baton Rouge: Office of Cultural Development.
Louisiana Folklore Miscellany. New Orleans: Louisiana Folklore Society.
Southern Folklore. Lexington: University Press of Kentucky.
Wilson, Charles Reagan, and William Ferris, eds. 1989. *Encyclopedia of Southern Culture.* Chapel Hill: University of North Carolina Press.

Swapping Stories

Louisiana's Folktale Traditions: An Introduction

Carl Lindahl

This broad-based collection of Louisiana tales belongs to a current surge of interest in the ageless art of storytelling. Many recent fine and successful collections—including Barry J. Ancelet's *Cajun and Creole Folktales* (1994), John A. Burrison's *Storytellers: Folktales and Legends from the South* (1991), James P. Leary's *Midwestern Folk Humor* (1991), and W. K. McNeil's *Ghost Stories from the American South* (1985)—attest to a growing interest in state and regional samplers, books that showcase the narrative variety and cultural diversity of living American folktale traditions. In the last years of the twentieth century, readers and listeners are returning to the deceptively simple, limitlessly rich art of oral taletelling.

Not since the early 1940s has American storytelling enjoyed such popularity. The Depression Era work of the Federal Writers' Project sought to help fend off poverty and boost national morale by enlisting professional writers to capture the stories of the country's great amateur artists: storytellers whose jokes and legends, whose imagination and sense of history had created a folk art nurtured in hard work and hard times, a body of tales both extraordinarily rich in detail and essentially free, to be shared by all who cared to listen (Mangione 1972).

The Federal Writers did not merely collect folktales but substantially reworked them, mixing professional journalism with traditional artistry. The resulting blend was not entirely successful. In spite of the fact that the collectors of the 1930s and early 1940s amassed voluminous bodies of texts and traditions not fully digested or appreciated even today, most of the work published by the Federal Writers ultimately displayed far more journalism than folk artistry. As a case in point, *Gumbo Ya-Ya*—the survey of Louisiana lore compiled by Lyle Saxon, Edward Dreyer, and Robert Tallant, and released in 1945—was filled with valuable stories and impressive bits of oral history, but these tales were not rendered in the actual words of the storytellers, nor were they free of the biases of the collectors. For example,

Gumbo Ya-Ya's description of African-American lore in New Orleans limits itself to such negative outsiders' stereotypes as drunkenness and sexual excess. Instead of listening for the values and artistry of the African-American storytellers, the authors of *Gumbo Ya-Ya* simply heard and repeated the tales that reinforced their own prejudices.

The many failures of the Federal Writers' Project underline some of the daunting problems involved in attempting to translate even the greatest oral performances into readable stories. Storytelling may be the oldest, most popular, and most durable form of entertainment, but it is also, paradoxically, the most delicate and perishable. Louisiana's expert folk narrators rely on face-to-face communication and small audiences; they spice their tales with innumerable subtle references to their physical and social environments. They use gestures and vocal modulations to enrich their performances. They change their tales constantly, tailoring each telling to the interests and understanding of their listeners. When the tales are written down, and the speaker is no longer present to gauge the audience and reshape the tale for them, it is reasonable to ask how much of the storyteller's art can survive.

Collectors and editors face the enormous task of preserving the intimacy of oral storytelling on the cold, impersonal written page. The Federal Writers' Project met this challenge with a curious blend of reverence and condescension. True, the writers found the plots of the stories and some of the tellers' folk speech impressive enough to share with the outside world, but they did not trust the folk artists sufficiently to record the stories in the tellers' own words. Such famous collections as Richard Chase's *The Jack Tales* (1943) became American children's classics, but the stories were not faithful to the styles of the Appalachian taletellers (Perdue 1987).

More than fifty years after the Federal Writers' Project began, the question of how best to retell folktales remains unanswered. The current storytelling surge breaks into two great waves, the first represented by folklorists and the second by performers, with two distinct notions of how to retell a folktale. The first group turns toward the taletellers' community, seeking to understand the tales as organic parts of the group's daily life. Folklorists see storytellers as entertainers but also as guardians of the artistry and values of their local groups. Told in its natural setting—for example, during a fishing trip or at a family gathering—a folktale binds together the teller and the listeners; it is shaped to its surroundings by artists who invoke the immediate environment and imagination of listeners to create a tale that grows naturally from shared experience. Folklorists solve the problem of representation by sharing with their readers as much of the teller's background and context as possible.

The second wave, the performers, represented by such groups as NAPPS (National Association for the Preservation and Perpetuation of Storytelling), are usually less interested in the local dynamics of folk traditions than in acquiring material for performance. At such large gatherings as the National Storytelling Festival in Jonesboro, Tennessee, a Florida librarian may reshape a Scottish ballad he has learned from a book into a prose tale and attempt to entertain an audience of hundreds of strangers from around the world. Such performers seldom attempt to duplicate the style of the borrowed tales—or to share with the audience much knowledge of the original taletellers and their communities. Although often artful and entertaining, such performances rest on the premise that the tale itself is more important than the folk artist who told it, more important than that artist's folk community.

Folklorists are sometimes so intent on being faithful to the tellers that they leave the general public behind; but performers are often so intent on pleasing their audience that they distort their folk sources beyond recognition.

This book shares the goals of the contemporary folklorists, yet, like today's performers, strives to reach a wide audience. The great innovation of *Swapping Stories* lies in the circumstances of its collection. Most of the tales included here were recorded during a one-year period as part of a statewide public arts program. Like the old Federal Writers' Project, the Louisiana effort originated with a government-sponsored agency that sent fieldworkers into unfamiliar territory to locate master narrators and record their stories. As such, it ran the risk of missing a great deal of the living traditions and substituting in their place some very unrepresentative tales based on outsiders' partial views and stereotypes. Furthermore, the state project focused its attention on public programming, seeking to identify artists who would perform on festival stages.

Yet, from the beginning, the Louisiana Folklife Program Director Maida Owens and the fieldworkers strove to collect and represent these tales on the tellers' own terms. In order to coax storytellers to share intimate traditions with a broader public, the state folklorists developed innovative strategies. One of the most successful was a storytelling pavilion originally conceived by folklorist Barry Jean Ancelet of the University of Southwestern Louisiana and Bruce Morgan of the state's Office of Tourism. The taletellers would sit at the center of the pavilion, next to a collector familiar with

Fieldwork is an important step in the process of documenting a folk tradition such as storytelling. Here, folklorist Susan Roach and filmmaker Pat Mire interview storyteller Reverend Thadis Payne (left) and a restaurant visitor in Sarah's Kitchen during preliminary fieldwork in Ruston for the video program, Swapping Stories. *Photo: Maida Owens.*

their tales who would help elicit stories and fill in background for the audience. Chairs were arranged in concentric circles around the storytellers. Interested listeners could sit in the inner circles and share an intimate storytelling experience. Newcomers could listen at the fringes of the pavilion and—if interested—move closer to the center of the action. Others could come and go at will without disturbing the storytellers, who were insulated from the crowd by a tight circle of intent listeners (Owens 1992).

Even with these innovations, the tales told at public gatherings did not always reach the range or depth characteristic of tales told in more intimate circumstances. Therefore, to balance and enrich the collection, the editors supplied tales collected offstage, in more familiar and small-scale surroundings. C. Renée Harvison visited several master storytellers in their homes (Christian 1993). Barry Jean Ancelet, Samuel G. Armistead, Annette Huval, Nicholas R. Spitzer, and I also contributed tales and narrative songs collected earlier in private settings. Pat Mire and Maida Owens added tales recorded in a barber shop, at a backyard cookout, and in other contexts in which Louisiana's folktales are commonly told today.

Swapping Stories thus presents Louisiana folktales as they were told both in intimate home settings and on public stages. The editors aspire to present these tales in a way that is both faithful to the tellers' speech and friendly to the reader. We have tried to reproduce every word spoken by the taletellers and have added nothing to "touch up" their artful accounts. Unlike many contemporary folklorists, however, we do not reproduce pauses or certain "incidental" sounds—the "uhs," "ahs," and "ahems" that tellers sometimes unconsciously utter when searching for the right word. Even with this slight polish, however, a number of the tales will seem awkward to readers accustomed to traditional storybooks. Tales that grow out of conversation are often the joint creations of one major narrator and several assistants in the audience (see, for example, tale #68). When accomplished joke tellers are swapping stories (as in tale #80), they use all sorts of gestures and sounds that cannot be translated to the page, and they often speak in brief allusions rather than in complete sentences. Such storytelling styles, natural and flowing when witnessed firsthand, appear clumsy on the page, but—difficult to read as they may be—we have decided to include some such performances here, in hopes of giving the reader a better sense of the variety of ways in which stories emerge in daily life.

These Louisiana tales span a great range of folk narration, from historical accounts to belief tales, jokes, and fantasy creations. Some are told in the everyday language of conversation, some artfully embellished, some—such as the Isleño *décimas* and African-American toasts—spoken or sung in poetic form. This book contains two parts, the first presenting tales from six of Louisiana's most gifted narrators and the second arranged topically to present some of the most prominent themes and types of tales told throughout the state. Both sections begin with the most "realistic" tales, accounts of personal experiences, rich in themselves, but also useful for drawing the reader into the daily environment of the taletellers and setting the stage for their fictional tales. Each part then proceeds to tales more distant from the everyday world, tales focused on the distant past, supernatural occurrences, and, finally, mythic events and folk fiction.

Every folktale will bear the stamp of at least three styles: the style of the individual narrator, that of the narrator's community, and that of the type, or genre, of tale being told (Ball 1959). This book is arranged to take all three styles into account.

Individual Styles

Swapping Stories begins with a series of tales from some of Louisiana's most gifted narrators, people who stand out as oral artists in their various communities. Many tellers simply repeat what they have heard with little change, embellishment, or inventiveness. The narrators featured at the beginning of this book, however, are experts who have devoted much of their lives to storytelling; in the process, they have given their narratives a personal, artful stamp.

Few generalizations can be made about this diverse group of artists. But, beyond the fact that they are all great entertainers, it is also true that most of them are old; thus, their stories, drawing upon decades of life experience, tell us much about Louisiana's past. In Harold Talbert's tales of Depression-era Ruston and Wilson "Ben Guiné" Mitchell's accounts of sharecropping in the vicinity of Parks, the 1980s and 1990s are barely visible, but the 1930s, 1940s, and 1950s emerge in sharp focus. We are welcomed into a world that we can no longer see but that comes alive in their words.

This emphasis on times past is common in storytelling collections, the inevitable outgrowth of one important fact: storytelling is a lifelong profession. As a rule, taletellers don't retire. They simply tell more tales, and, as a rule, they simply grow better. If you were to ask to meet the best taleteller in any given Louisiana community, you would usually be led to an older man or woman whose art has been formed and refined by decades of performing for the entertainment of neighbors and friends. More often than not, this person would be respected in his or her community not only as a narrator but as a recognized expert in other skills. Lonnie Gray, a great tall tale teller, was also a master at basketmaking and wood carving; Harold Talbert, a specialist in small-town stories, also directed the local bank; Clifford Blake, possessing a repertoire of African-American tales from plantation days, was also a singer and composer, and the last person in his community to practice the skill of calling the cotton press; Jimmie Davis, a master jokester and tall tale teller, also served as governor of Louisiana. These people, like many others whose stories are found here, have become great storytellers not only because of their verbal skills but because they have been "elected" by their friends and neighbors to represent them in these stories.

Thus, even the most individualistic folktale teller will tell you more than one woman's—or one man's—experience. The taleteller presents a community narrative that encapsulates, to a great extent, the shared experiences, values, and sense of humor of his or her neighborhood or cultural background. For all their uniqueness, Alfred Anderson's magic tales draw upon the group experience of poor African Americans who worked as laborers and sharecroppers for wealthy whites. Learned from his father and neighbors, and told in turn to his children and grandchildren, these stories were shaped as much by the tastes and experience of his teachers and audience as by his own artistry. Alfred Anderson was such an accomplished storyteller that his children and grandchildren always deferred to him and did not try to imitate him. Nevertheless, his stories were their stories as well; he achieved his position of preeminence largely because he was sensitive to their tastes.

Cultural Styles

Each of the taletellers here represents the cultural style of at least one Louisiana community. Cultural style is conditioned by the shared values and experiences of each of the myriad groups that retell tales. A magic tale such as *The Two Brothers* may be well over a thousand years old and found in hundreds of different cultures, but each culture will appropriate the tale for its own uses and reshape it continually to correspond with its own constantly changing world view.

European versions of *The Two Brothers* are often extremely long and complicated, presenting a series of magical encounters in which a young man with magical animal helpers slays a dragon and wins a princess but is then enslaved by a witch's magic and finally rescued by his brother. American versions of *The Two Brothers* (AT 303)[1]—such as Alfred Anderson's "The Toodling Horn" (#57) and Barry Jean Ancelet's "*Gaillum, Singo, et Moliseau*" (#210)—tend to be much shorter than European versions, and to focus on one episode in which a boy walks into the woods, encounters a monstrous being that attempts to kill him, and finally saves himself by calling his dogs—that magically hear him from miles away and run to save him. Ancelet's and Anderson's tales were probably influenced by an African tale type, *Dogs Rescue Master from Tree Refuge* (AT 315A), similar in many ways to *The Two Brothers*. But, despite the fact that Ancelet's tale represents a French-American tradition and Anderson's an African-American tradition, the two tales, when considered together, represent a shared *American* tradition—derived from two streams of Old World story that merged into a new, unique tradition representative of the United States. American versions of this tale, as a rule, do not mention dragons, princesses, marriage, or a second brother—but focus instead on a boy alone in the woods. The differences between the two is largely a difference of cultural styles: American magic tales as a corpus tend to be shorter than their European and African counterparts, less concerned with such magical figures as dragons, and far less likely to end with marriages.

Cultural styles are not only national but regional, ethnic, and local as well. In addition to being distinctly American, many of the tales in *Swapping*

Stories are unmistakably Southern. Many of Harold Talbert's masterfully told reminiscences evoke small-town America, both North and South, but many more carry special Southern accents. Talbert speaks of Baptist revival meetings, cotton crops, the close proximity and playful relations of black and white children. The African-American narratives—in both English and French—project less positive aspects of Southern cultures. Clifford Blake's "Saul and Skeleton" (#208), Alfred Anderson's "The Old Coon" (#60), and Wilson "Ben Guiné" Mitchell's *"Vieux Nèg et Vieux Blanc"* (#35) recreate a world of masters and slaves in which whites are wealthy landowners and blacks abused workers.

Beyond their Southern coloring, some of the individual tales are pure Louisiana, deeply seasoned by local environment and lifestyle. Tall tales such as "The Alligator Peach Tree" (#134) and animal tales such as "The Girls and the Alligator" (#56) are special local variants of internationally distributed tales. Only in Louisiana do these stories feature the alligator, which—along with the crawfish—serves as a virtual totem animal for the southern reaches of the state. Julia Huval's tales impart the flavor of Louisiana's unique cuisine. In *"La Chaudiérée de couche-couche"* (#188), the wily rabbit devours a pot of couche-couche—a Cajun and Creole corn mush—instead of the tub of butter consumed by other tricksters when similar tales are told elsewhere. One reason for this unique change becomes obvious when the reader considers the context: when Julia Huval was growing up, her family had no butter to eat.

Political and historical tales also feature local phenomena and bind together Louisiana's people in a weave of shared experience often quite mysterious to outsiders. Tales of Huey Long and his dynasty of politicians form a narrative common ground; stories of other legendary figures, such as Jean Lafitte (#148, 163, 169) and Bonnie and Clyde (#138–42)—though generally more localized than the Long tales—engage imaginations throughout the state.

Swapping Stories reflects the combination of cultures that has made Louisiana unique. Enola Matthews's tales (#49–55) have much in common with those told by other Creoles in Louisiana and the Caribbean, but Mme. Matthews also passes on certain plots and traits of tales brought from Europe into her family tradition by her Irish grandfather. The English-language tales of Alfred Anderson (#56–62) show clear Creole influence, but they belong to a wider community of African Americans who share a common history as former slaves and sharecroppers. Thus, some of the historically underprivileged Louisiana groups—African-American, Cajun, and Creole—

shared far more than their poverty. They shared stories, and the richness of their overlapping repertoires testifies not only to their struggles but also to their wealth of imagination and artistry. Although some of the storytellers featured here suffered from effects of racial and cultural segregation, their stories affirm that, on at least one important level, these cultures were integrated: their stories leaped social barriers.

Generic Styles

Each folklore form or genre—the joke, belief legend, historical legend, magic tale, animal tale, or tall tale—bears a distinctive style, shaped by the purpose of the teller and the understandings of the audience. A teller of belief legends, for instance, often dwells on supernatural figures—such as ghosts and *loups garoux* (or werewolves)—that many believe to exist. Because legends tend to assert the reality of certain supernatural events, the tellers tend to use sincere, straightforward styles to persuade their listeners of hidden dangers lurking in the world. Tellers of magic tales will also introduce supernatural beings—like the talking bear in Alfred Anderson's "The Toodling Horn"(#57)—but these creatures are considered fictional by teller and listeners alike. In legends, the supernatural is often terrifically frightening; in magic tales, it is often entertaining and humorous; thus, even when they resemble each other in content, legends and magic tales possess different generic styles, because they treat the topic of the supernatural in entirely different ways.

Personal experience stories compose one of the richest and most varied bodies of Louisiana folklore. These autobiographical accounts of memorable events are retold dozens, even hundreds of times, recrafted at each telling, evolving into artistic statements to entertain family and friends, often at special ritualistic occasions such as Thanksgiving dinners and family reunions (Stahl 1977). When told by older people, such tales are sometimes strung together in a running account of the "good old days," as listeners are treated not simply to scenes from one man's or woman's past, but also to an entire, vanished world of community life. In telling their own stories, narrators also evoke a whole network of community events and values. Through innumerable retellings, most personal experience narratives become—intentionally or otherwise—at least slightly idealized or fictionalized to express more clearly a community's evolving notions of what is important about its past. Most "personal" experience narratives are thus also community stories, statements about the lifestyle of the teller's group.

The tales of two great personal experience narrators, featured in the first part of this book, reveal much about the diversity of the genre and how it reflects the unique values of each community. Both Harold Talbert, a British American from Ruston (#1-14), and Bel Abbey, a Native American of the Koasati culture (#37–48), possess rich repertoires of stories describing their boyhood experiences. Both dwell on transitional moments in the growing-up process and upon their individual—and sometimes lonely—paths toward adulthood. Beyond these facts, however, the two bodies of stories hold little in common, for they are set apart by the greatly different personalities, styles, and cultures of the two men.

Harold Talbert, a man of many words, speaks at loving length about his boyhood friends and foes. In his small-town world, such fixtures as popcorn, watermelons, freight trains, and movie theaters—unremarkable to today's children—assume enormous importance. As Harold recounts his long walks to and from the movie house, the listener begins to see, through a young boy's eyes, how a small town can present a very large and dangerous world. Harold describes how he used his wits to negotiate his way home from the movie theater in the dark. Like most folktale heroes, the young Harold encounters strange and threatening figures—men in red masks or disguised as gorillas—who invade his town.

Bel Abbey also must deal with strange and threatening forces, but his personal experience stories are set in a world of nature rather than of people. Although he knew many kinds of tales and shared them often with his fellow Koasati, Bel's growing-up stories are all set in the woods, and Bel is always alone (#39–41, 43). Like many folktale heroes, he loses his way in the woods and must confront and overcome his fears there.

The different cultural backgrounds of the two men are made vividly real in their stories. In order to grow up, Harold Talbert must come to terms with hostile strangers; Bel Abbey, on the other hand—brought up in relative isolation among the Koasati—must master the secrets of nature.

Elsewhere in this collection, tellers of personal experience stories dwell upon the basic themes of daily life: courtship, marriage, playing games. Yet all of the stories presented here—like nearly all personal experience narratives—involve common situations with uncommon twists. Such tales are popular because they give everyday experience the aura of a magical event. Master storytellers like Harold Talbert push reality to the verge of fantasy: a tale that begins in a sleepy town ends in frenzied flights from a wild "gorilla"; a baptism nearly becomes a drowning. Such stories walk the thin line between the personal experience story and the tall tale.

Tall tales, like personal experience stories, are presented as true accounts and usually told in the first person. Tellers tend to begin by describing common situations; the tales unfold in environments familiar to their listeners. Yet, as the narrator continues, he (for tall tales are most often told by males [Brown 1987, 12–14]) adds more and more unusual features to his story, until the believable and the utterly absurd tangle together, transforming fact into fantastic fiction. The typical tall tale teller performs in a monotone, as if he found nothing unusual about the incredible events he relates; neither his voice nor his facial expression betrays the fact that he is attempting to disguise a monstrous lie as an ordinary fact. Tellers often spice their stories with expressions—such as "this is the dying truth"; "if I'm lying, I'm dying"; "this is no damned lie"—aimed at persuading listeners to believe them (Biebuyck-Goetz 1977).

Also called "whoppers," "yarns," "windies," "trash," and "lies" in Louisiana and elsewhere, tall tales are told throughout the world but are particularly popular in the United States. According to one folklorist's study of published folktales, there are more than one hundred American tall tales for every one recorded in England (Baughman 1966, xiii). The tall tale certainly did not originate in the New World, but Americans have adopted it as their preferred, distinctive folktale form.

Many explanations have been offered for the American fascination with tall tales. Folklorists have pointed out that these stories tend to celebrate the limitless possibilities and magical aspects of nature. In Lonnie Gray's yarns, giant fish provide shingles for houses (#27); Harry Methvin tells of mosquitoes that sacrifice their lives to suck poison from the body of a snakebit man (#127). In such stories, nature becomes a magically friendly force that provides food, shelter, even life itself, and presents a world of "unlimited good" (Dundes 1971) in which all may prosper and no one has to suffer want. Newcomers to America often left behind crowded quarters and limited opportunities. Arriving in a region with seemingly inexhaustible land and possibilities, they may well have felt that they had entered a world where magic and reality came together, just as they do in the tall tale.

Furthermore, tall tales—wherever they are told throughout the world —are particularly popular among all-male occupational and recreational groups: sailors, soldiers, lumberjacks, and hunters. The huge and shifting American frontier was settled by just such populations. Like much of America, Louisiana attracted many all-male communities of trappers, hunters, and cowboys. Even in more settled, family-based communities, there were many predominately-male pastimes—such as gambling, horse racing, and fishing—that served as ideal environments for the exchange of such tales. Nineteenth-century newspapers are filled with written versions of the tall tales that circulated in North Louisiana (Anderson 1960).

Finally, tall tales tend to thrive in mobile, dynamic social settings, where they are used to test and initiate newcomers. In such situations, the tall tale teller strives to establish his turf by shocking the newcomer, testing his gullibility and his sense of humor. *We Always Lie to Strangers* reads the title of Vance Randolph's great collection of Ozark tall tales (1951). Randolph describes how groups of men gathered at a local store would begin exchanging tall tales with each other as soon as a stranger would come within earshot. The newcomer would hear the men describing impossible events in matter-of-fact voices, and the tellers would watch from the corners of their eyes to gauge the effect of their performance on the stranger. Nineteenth-century Louisiana—like Louisiana today—saw a constant stream of newcomers invading the turf of established residents, and these immigrants provided a steady supply of victims for the tall tale teller.

Tall tales are particularly popular in rural environments; the great majority of tall tale motifs center on farm life or wildlife. Farmers will explain about one summer day so hot that the sun popped whole acres of corn, turning it into popcorn. Hunters will describe mosquitoes so large that they carry off children. Thriving in the woods of northern Louisiana as well as in the southern bayous, tall tales populate all the rural regions of the state and are told endlessly among people who spend significant portions of their lives hunting, farming, or fishing.

In certain situations, one expert narrator—for example, a hunting guide—will dominate a tall tale session, regaling listeners with an endless string of impossible stories. Just as often, however, tall tale telling is a group-participation event, in which several men vie to tell the most outlandish story. On fishing trips, at favored bars, on benches—sometimes called "liar's benches"—in front of stores or on courthouse lawns, tall tales are often swapped by close-knit groups. Barry Jean Ancelet has described an especially vital group of older Cajun men who congregate at a bar in Mamou to perpetuate the adventures of a hero named Pascal (Ancelet 1980a). One man may start a Pascal story but another may finish it; all present add their own embellishments, sending Pascal on trips to the North Pole or to the moon.

In the male-dominated world of the tall tale, women are sometimes present as listeners. The women often express disbelief, thus goading the men toward greater efforts to tell outlandish stories (Cothran 1979; Dégh 1976). In the section of tales collected from Lonnie Gray by Renée Harvison,

Lonnie's wife, Mary, was also present, and she told two stories (#19, 22), but hers were legends—tales that she not only claimed to be true but also *believed* to be true. Mary's more emphatic voice contrasted with Lonnie's deadpan monotone. Her presence added to the tale telling session but served largely as a spur for Lonnie to expand upon his lies.

The public nature of tall taletelling makes it particularly well suited for the festival stage. One stage performance appearing in this collection underlines the fact that tall tales often suffer little when transported from the liar's bench to the public arena. In the summer of 1991 at Ruston, Harold Talbert, Bill Cox, and Lonnie Gray took the stage to swap stories about possum (#14). Their repartee is characteristic of the group nature of tall tale telling and produces mind-dizzying results as three expert narrators conspire to create a shared world of imagination.

Historical anecdotes and legends are heavily represented in this collection. From accounts of the pirate Jean Lafitte (#148, 163, 169) to recent sightings of Elvis (#150), these tales of local heroes and villains who have made their mark on Louisiana present a rich and highly varied folk history of the state.

A handful of historical figures are celebrated throughout the state: these are the politicians. What the Kennedys are to Massachusetts, what the Daleys are to Chicago—and then some—the Longs are to Louisiana. All regions of the state and nearly all ethnic groups have shared in creating and maintaining the extraordinarily rich body of lore centered on Huey Long, the charismatic governor assassinated at the height of his powers, in 1935, in the Louisiana Capitol that he had had built. Huey's brothers Earl and Julius also figure largely in the legends collected here, but Huey dominates, just as he has in state history.

The Long legends seem to present two different Hueys. In John Campbell's "He Knew How to Get Votes" (#91), Huey is the hero who "revitalized" the Railroad Commission and public life in Louisiana; but as seen by Hiram Wright (#81, 82), Huey is a nearly subhuman monster. John Campbell comes closest to describing the intensely two-sided nature of Huey Long: "Huey was the most outstanding individual I've ever known. . . . He could be a statesman among statesmen. He could get down with the lowest people in the world. Or he could be an s.o.b. among s.o.b.'s. . . . He was smarter than any of them" (#92).

Many of these tales about the Longs depict common people in the act of talking back to, or facing up to, the powerful. In Hiram Wright's account of "Earl's Grave" (#81), the craftsman who puts the finishing touches on the tomb also condemns Earl to hell. In "Hugh Goes Courting" (#89), Eck Bozeman tells how a recently widowed woman responds heroically to Huey's father's tasteless proposition. In stories, if not elsewhere, Louisianans control, humiliate, and govern their politicians.

Although no other figures dominate statewide legendry as the Longs do, a substantial number of stories has clustered around the names of Jean Lafitte and Bonnie and Clyde. Lafitte's name is kept alive largely in connection with the various treasures he is rumored to have concealed along the south coast of Louisiana; tales by British Americans Arthur Irwin (#162–63) and Wendell Lindsay of Calcasieu Parish (#148), and Cajun Velma Duet of Lafourche Parish (#169) testify to the breadth of Lafitte's notoriety as well as to the fact that his legends thrive in diverse regions and cultures in the state.

More typically, however, folk historical anecdotes and legends tend to take on a specifically local character. A case in point is the body of tales about the outlaws Bonnie and Clyde thriving in Bienville Parish, where the couple was shot to death (#138–42). In contrast to American popular culture, which has cast Bonnie and Clyde, Jesse James, and others as Robin-Hood-style outlaw heroes, local folk culture portrays the two robbers in extremely negative terms.

Most of the other heroes and villains depicted in this collection are local figures, people whose reputations may extend no farther than a day's walk from their place of birth but who are extremely important in neighborhood legendry. Ben Lilly, of Morehouse Parish, comes alive in the words of James B. Rider (#147). Such local strongmen are extremely popular in small-town legendry: Maine's Barney Beale (Dorson 1964, 40–54) and Florida's Acrefoot Johnson (Reaver 1987, 61) are just two examples from other regional traditions. Like Barney Beal, Ben Lilly isn't merely strong; he's good as well. He is so exemplary in his piety that he would rather lose his cattle than violate the Sabbath. Ben's size merely magnifies his goodness. Yet there is something almost supernatural about him as well. Like such famous heroes as the Roman Romulus, suckled by a wolf, and the Icelandic Bothvar, a bear's son, Ben is "more animal than human." Ben Lilly legends illustrate how even the most familiar local characters can take on superhuman proportions as their tales are retold by their neighbors and descendants.

In certain traditions, such as the African-American toast and the Isleño *décima*, legends are rendered in verse or song. Arthur Pfister's toast of "Shine and the Titanic" (#149) provides a masterful example of how African-

American legends can be transformed into poetry. Behind the current craze for rap music is a long-lived tradition of tightly rhymed, rhythmically chanted narratives known as toasts, which have formed a major part of black oral tradition in the South and urban North throughout this century. Discussed at length by Abrahams (1970, 97–172), the toast has served traditionally as an expression of protest, a compensation fantasy in which the black underdog proves superior to his white would-be oppressors. "Shine and the Titanic" is one of the best-known toasts. After the sinking of the Titanic, legends sprang up about boxer Jack Johnson, the first African-American Heavyweight Champion of the World: denied a berth on the Titanic, Johnson was left on shore and thus spared a watery death. Within a few years, rhymes similar to those in Arthur Pfister's toast began to celebrate Shine, a presumably fictional black hero who escaped the doomed ship and swam to shore. Although Shine is generally considered a fictional character by performers and audience alike, the toast celebrates an actual historic event; furthermore, Arthur Pfister updates the story for a 1990 audience with references to Rambo, Dolly Parton, Robin Givens, and Mike Tyson.

The toast is principally a memorized tradition, but innovative oral artists will always elaborate on the material they have received. Raised in a New Orleans neighborhood where he and his peers often spoke in rhyme, Pfister—like other great toast performers—has taken a largely memorized text and added his own special flourishes.

History and the supernatural often meet in legend, but never more often than in *buried treasure stories*. Though extremely common in the United States, treasure tales have been underrepresented in even the best recent regional collections (see, for example, Burrison 1989). This collection, however, contains a rich and varied sampling of such stories. Some of these narratives, such as "The Widow's Buried Gold" (#157), unfold in the everyday world, while others, such as "A Moaning Ghost and Buried Treasure" (#165), are filled with otherworldly occurrences. Even when ghosts fail to appear (as in the tale of "Buried Treasure Money Used to Build a Catholic Church" [#158]) the teller often suggests that there is something eerie or cursed about the treasure. The idea that one cannot get something for nothing is embedded in these tales' descriptions of elusive, buried riches—and in the curses that accompany the treasure when it is finally discovered.

Belief legends are largely stories of the supernatural, accounts of the eerie consequences experienced when ordinary people confront inexplicable forces beyond their understanding or control. Legends are also about boundaries—moral and social limits that, once crossed, open up worlds of punishing terror. Such legend villains as "The Red-Headed Witch of Bogalusa Creek" (#179) help set the geographical and social perimeters of the taleteller's community: lovers' lanes, isolated woods, and cemeteries are "off limits," particularly to young people, and especially after dark. Other legend villains, such as the *loup garou* (or werewolf) described by John Verret (#170), are transformed humans who have become monsters by crossing invisible but equally real moral boundaries: unlike the Hollywood werewolf—a man who becomes a monster simply when bitten by another werewolf—the folk *loup garou* is a man who is transformed by committing a sin such as missing mass on Sunday (Dorson 1975, 465; Ancelet et al. 1991, 215). As John Verret explains, "you do something wrong, . . . then . . . God turn His back on you. Then the devil take over."

Legends are about belief, but they are not always told by believers. Legend is best characterized as a "debate about belief" engaged by believers and nonbelievers alike, as they negotiate together the boundaries of the possible in their view of the world (Dégh 1972).

Because so many legends are told by believers to warn their friends and neighbors about the powers of the supernatural, content is often much more important than style in legend telling. "True believers" are usually much more intent upon sharing important beliefs than upon creating art; these narrators dwell upon the informational aspects of the stories and try to make their accounts persuasive by stressing their own convictions and the credibility of the people who have reported encounters with otherworldly events. A legend may be told at any moment by a believer who feels the need to warn or inform others about the dangers of the supernatural. Nevertheless, there are many situations in which the legend tellers cast doubt on the truth of their tales. Loulan Pitre, for example, sees a substantial difference between what younger Cajuns believe today and what the older Cajuns believed when his father was a boy. In his tales about a werewolf, mermaids, and a shadow that haunts an old man, Pitre calls attention to ways in which beliefs have changed: the older people "actually got each other to believe" in the existence of werewolves (#174); stories that were tragic in the old days seem funny now (#177).

In other cases, legend telling is recognized as an art form. Around the fire at summer camps, or during slumber parties, or on Halloween night, adolescents often congregate to exchange "scary stories" or "ghost stories." In such situations, the teller often uses art to enhance the effects of a chilling tale.

Furthermore, legends are not merely stories or debates; they are often rituals as well. Stories of ghosts that haunt forbidden settings give rise to ritual visits in which teenagers search for these monstrous figures. Across America, ghosts stalk lovers' lanes, and adolescents who travel with their dates to visit lonely places tell each other hair-raising accounts of the spirits of frustrated lovers or sex maniacs preying upon teens who are "too interested" in sex. Folklorist Alan Dundes (1971) once attempted to explain such strange stories simply as warnings. But if they are warnings, they are the most singularly ineffective warnings imaginable, because these stories are told again and again by people visiting the haunted sites, by couples intent on "making out," or by people like Mary Etta Scarborough Moody (teller of "The Red-Headed Witch" [#179]), who have to see for themselves if the ghosts are there. Obviously, these stories are more than warnings; they also serve as challenges to young people, testing if they are grown-up enough to make such nighttime visits. During the ritual visits, storytellers act out the plot of the legend, and when they return to the company of friends, they tell the story of their experiences; these accounts become a part of the legend process. Like so many lovers' lane legends told across the country, Mary Etta Scarborough Moody's story is in two parts: half is the story she heard as a child, and half is an account of her own trip to visit the Red-Headed Witch.

Like most serious folktale genres, legends generate parody forms. Sometimes called "humorous anti-legends" (Vlach 1971), such tales as "Who's Gon'na Sleep with Me?" (#184) begin as potentially frightening supernatural accounts. The taleteller builds suspense; listeners steel themselves for a horrifying ending. But in the end the teller deflates the terror by turning the scary story into a joke. Anti-legends suggest just how terrifying serious legends can be: in legend-swapping sessions, tellers often turn to the anti-legend to dispel the growing mood of horror created by a chain of frightening, presumably true stories.

Jokes are among the richest oral traditions in Louisiana, as in the country at large. This collection conveys only a hint of the range and popularity of this vital folk form. The editors have chosen to concentrate on the older and longer humorous narratives (labeled *Schwänke* by folklorists) which present vivid portraits of traditional life in Louisiana's past. Such tales typically present the stereotyped characters who act out common conflicts of neighborhood life.

Among the oldest joke cycles represented here is a series of African-American tales dedicated to John and Old Master. John is a clever old slave or servant who is continually finding ways of impressing his master. Often, as in Alfred Anderson's tales of "Skullbone" (#61) and "The Old Coon" (#60), John proves too clever for his own good. In "The Old Coon," John finally saves himself by mistake, but in "Skullbone" he is beheaded by his merciless master. Such stories affirm that even the funniest oral narratives may embed serious social messages. "Skullbone" and Clifford Blake's "Saul and Skeleton" (#208)—based on an African tale type (Bascom 1992, 17–39)—are often told among African Americans to warn listeners that they should watch what they say when speaking to whites, or else suffer painful consequences (Levine 1978; Lindahl 1982).

One joke cycle unique to French Americans concerns Jean Sot (or Foolish John), featured in Enola Matthews' tales, *Les trois couillons* (#52) and *Jean Sot, la vache, les chiens, et sa petite soeur* (#53). This numskull continually falls into trouble by confusing the meanings of words or failing to adapt to changing situations.

Jokes based on religious topics are popular among many of Louisiana's folk groups. As Barry Ancelet has shown, Cajun Catholics, though deeply religious, tend to single out clerics and such religious rituals as confession for playful treatment (1985). In Évélia Boudreaux's tale "Bless Me, Father" (#114), a priest is brought down to size when he utters a curse right after warning his parishioner of the evils of swearing; in "Curing Corpses" (#115), a young boy misinterprets the ritual use of incense as an attempt to "smoke" a dead body.

Louisiana Baptists and other Protestant groups focus many of their jokes on lengthy sermons that often put parishioners to sleep. Harry Methvin (#121) and Harold Talbert (#9, 10) tell similar tales about a sleeping man who wakes up at just the wrong time. Other Protestant jokes take aim at holier-than-thou attitudes; in "A Heaven Joke" (#30), Lonnie Gray makes light of certain congregations that take themselves too seriously, and in "The Reverend Gets the Possum" (#120), Sarah Albritton parodies the sanctimonious attitude of certain parsons.

Magic tales. For parents who read storybooks to children—or for people of all ages who have been enraptured by Disney's feature-length cartoons—the words "folktale" and "fairy tale" are synonymous. In reality, however, fairy tales—most often known as märchen, wonder tales, or magic tales by folklorists who study the oral forms of such stories—constitute a relatively small part of America's—and Louisiana's—oral traditions.

Oral magic tales, once told largely to entertain adults (Dégh 1989), are now told in America principally by parents and grandparents to children. These tales tend to center on growing-up experiences. Typically, a girl (like the clever heroine of Alfred Anderson's "The Smart Sisters and the Lazy Sister" [#59]) or boy (like the protagonist in Julia Huval's "*Quatorze*" [#189]) will leave home alone, enter the wilderness, and encounter such frightening figures as monsters, giants, and witches. Sometimes aided by magic, sometimes armed only with his or her wits or virtue, the child overcomes these formidable foes, growing up in the process. Folklorists have long noted that, while storybook tales based on European magic tales most often end with the marriage of the hero or heroine, American oral tales do not emphasize marriage nearly as often. The magic tales presented here offer a telling confirmation of this point, for not one of them ends with a wedding. Although earlier collections of Cajun Louisiana's märchen (Saucier 1962; Ancelet 1994) contain some tales that end in marriage, the state's oral repertoire tends to emphasize the American notion that growing up is a process that does not necessarily entail "tying the knot."

As magical as magic tales seem on the surface, they are also realistic in many ways. The heroines and heroes of Alfred Anderson's African-American stories (#56-62)—like the neighbors and family members to whom he told his tales—are hardworking and resourceful people who must do all in their power to succeed in a world of limited opportunities. Similarly, such Cajun heroes as Julia Huval's Quatorze use their wits to confront and conquer poverty. In their adventures, such characters may encounter fantasy villains, but they also face real problems, problems that are familiar to the taletellers and their listeners. No matter how fantastic they may be, magic tales offer real lessons in character, survival, and success—and these lessons are important and relevant enough to help explain why the stories continue to be told.

The British Americans who settled Appalachia, upstate New York, and the Ozarks brought with them and developed a considerable body of magic tales—many about a young boy named Jack who fights giants (Lindahl 1994)—but scarcely a trace of such tales can be found in Louisiana, even among surviving records of nineteenth-century storytelling. Yet magic tales did form an extensive part of the repertoire of African Americans and French Americans in the state. Cajuns, black French-speaking Creoles, and English-speaking African Americans exchanged many tales, building a shared repertoire.

A great range of folk narratives—including tall tales, jokes, and magic tales—feature animals, but folklorists assign the term *animal tales* particularly to fantasy stories populated principally—or entirely—by animals that play stereotyped roles representing certain human traits. In Louisiana, animal tales have most often been collected from African-American, Cajun, Creole, Native American, and Vietnamese-American storytellers.

Fables featuring animal characters were transmitted by European Americans to Creoles and African Americans. Wilson "Ben Guiné" Mitchell's colorful telling of "The Ant and the Grasshopper" (#32) can be traced back to the influence of Lafontaine, a seventeenth-century French poet. Clifford Blake's tale of the "Snake in a Wagon Rut" (#206) is as old as Aesop, but it may also have been derived from African tradition, where it has been quite popular.

More common than fables among Louisiana's African-American, Cajun, and Creole populations are animal trickster tales featuring the wily Brer Rabbit, who is known simply as *Lapin* in French-language tradition. West African peoples have a long and rich tradition of animal trickster tales, many of which feature the spider Anansi. When brought as slaves to the Caribbean, the Africans brought their trickster tales with them. Anansi the spider is a popular trickster hero in Caribbean tales to the present day (see, for example, Bennett 1979).

In the North American colonies, and on some of the neighboring islands (including the Bahamas), the tales that had been told of the spider Anansi were transferred to the trickster Brer Rabbit (or "Brabby," as he is known in the Bahamas [Crowley 1966]). Exactly how and why the spider became a rabbit is unclear, but some believe that Native American trickster tales featuring a sly rabbit were primarily responsible for the change. Whatever the reason, many of Louisiana's African-American storytellers—including Alfred Anderson and Clifford Blake—delight in telling Brer Rabbit tales similar to the Uncle Remus stories made famous by Georgia folklorist Joel Chandler Harris. In "Brer Bear Meets Man" (#62), Alfred Anderson treats us to a typical example. Brer Rabbit knows man, and he is fully aware of the dangers presented by him. But the dull-witted Bear has never met man. Refusing to heed Brer Rabbit's warning, Brer Bear walks up to the man and is shot in the behind.

Creole and Cajun narrators tell similar tales concerning the wily Lapin, but they replace Brer Bear and other dupes with *Bouki,* a character whose name means "Hyena" in the West African Wolof language (Gaudet 1992). Though they found no hyenas in the New World, African Americans retained the name "Bouki," and they continue to identify this character as a stupid and often ugly creature. "Bouki" is often a nickname given to an ugly or funny man in Cajun and Creole communities.

If Louisiana fables are principally derived from Europe, the trickster tales come primarily from Africa. Rich traditions of cultural exchange have ensured that both blacks and whites in Louisiana now participate in both traditions. Wilson "Ben Guiné" Mitchell's tale of "The Little Tar-Man" (#33) (known throughout the English-speaking world from Joel Chandler Harris's "Br'er Rabbit and the Tarbaby" and its Disney cartoon adaptation) is also known to white Cajuns such as Max Greig (#190); both versions appear in this book.

Brer Rabbit is a trickster with two sides. Sometimes he serves as a hero for the powerless, as a "little man" who uses his wits to get the better of powerful people who would otherwise take advantage of him. In this role, he is an essentially moral figure who overcomes social injustices. More often than not, however, Brer Rabbit, or *Lapin*, is amoral or immoral. His trickery serves only himself, and although tellers and audiences enjoy his antics, they derive a certain amount of pleasure from his occasional defeats. Occasionally Brer Rabbit proves too tricky for his own good—or for anyone else's. Wilson "Ben Guiné" Mitchell ends the Tarbaby story uncharacteristically, by having Lapin captured (in most versions—for example, Max Greig's, the rabbit escapes to the briar patch). Wilson "Ben Guiné" Mitchell is aware of the typical ending, but he feels that the trickster should lose once in a while: "it was high time to catch Lapin, you understand? It was past time."

Myths and aetiological tales are folk stories that hearken to the distant past and serve to explain the origins of current phenomena. These tales depict the ancient actions of gods and people that caused the world to take on its present form and properties. Myths have special religious significance. They may be believed literally (as fundamentalists read the Bible); or figuratively, as explanations about the origins of certain natural phenomena; or as metaphorically moral truths about the workings of the world. Bel Abbey's and Bertney Langley's Koasati myths (#37, 42, 45–46, 196–98) explain the workings of nature, the relationships between the natural and the human world, and the relationship between Native American and European peoples. Nicholas L. Stouff, Jr., a member of the Chitimacha culture, tells two stories that illustrate his tribe's close attachment to snakes. In "A Chitimacha Flood Story" (#191), snakes and people become close friends when riding out a massive flood together inside the same clay pot; for Nicholas Stouff, this incident explains why snakes are so special to the Chitimacha people. A second tale (#192) concerns the creation of Bayou Teche from the dying motions of a giant snake. In the world of the Chitimacha, traces of the snake are everywhere: in the bayou, in their past; it is not surprising that Chitimachas once tattooed the images of snakes on their bodies.

Aetiological tales answer the question, "Why?": Why does the mosquito suck blood? Why is the crow black? The answers are sometimes serious but often humorous or fanciful. African-American culture, for example, possesses a rich body of "why" stories (see Abrahams 1986, 39–79), almost none of which are literally believed but nearly all of which possess at least a kernel of serious content. African American Sarah Albritton tells a story about how the first woman and the first man obtained different social powers by bargaining with God (#193): the man gets greater strength, but God gives the woman a key which she can use to lock out the man if she needs to control him. This tale is both fanciful and serious. Although no one would mistake it for history, the story possesses a submerged seriousness which does indeed reflect certain aspects of gender roles in some contemporary African-American communities, where women, relatively powerless in many other respects, exercise great control over the household environment (Stack 1974). All of the Vietnamese tales in the present collection are aetiological tales. As Tang Thi Thanh Van, the skillful teller of the Vietnamese stories presented here, explains in "Why the Ocean is Salty" (#204), "[this is] another why [story]. We have a lot of that kind of story."

The Vietnamese myths retold in this collection are among the most recent additions to Louisiana's oral repertory. When American troops withdrew from Vietnam in the 1970s, floods of refugees entered the States, and they brought their tales with them to help maintain crucial cultural ties to their homeland. These tales were so important to the Vietnamese that they were broadcast over loudspeakers in American resettlement camps to help bolster the morale of the refugees. Tang Thi Thanh Van learned her tales from her grandmother and now retells them often to her students in bilingual education programs. For Vietnamese-American children who have never seen their country of origin, Tang Thi Thanh Van's tales provide a vital link to old and respected traditions. Whether or not her tales are regarded as literally true, they clearly possess extraordinary value for her and for many other Vietnamese Americans.

As earlier remarked, most of the tales in *Swapping Stories* bear significant relationships to other tales told internationally. In order to identify the broader traditions behind each tale, as well as the special features of many, I have provided comparative notes at the end of this collection. These notes, I hope, will help illustrate the extraordinary balance of the unique and the common that characterizes Louisiana folktales. Each tale is one person's special story, but all are part of a richly varied pattern that represents the state of Louisiana and ties it to the entire world through the universal love for a well-told tale.[2]

Notes

1. The abbreviation AT refers to the *Types of the Folktale* (Aarne and Thompson 1961), a classificatory catalogue of internationally distributed folktale plots. The "Notes on the Tales," near the end of the book, employ the *Types of the Folktale* as one tool for illustrating the similarities between the Louisiana narratives assembled here and other stories told elsewhere throughout the world.

2. In terms of variety of folk narratives presented, and in terms of the cultural range and the number of the narrators included, *Swapping Stories: Folktales from Louisiana* is the most diverse and comprehensive anthology of Louisiana folktales yet published; indeed we believe it to be the most diverse and comprehensive collection from any state. Nevertheless, certain important folktale genres and taletelling groups are underrepresented.

Two important kinds of legend receive little or no attention. Although we have included many tales that emphasize monstrous aspects of the supernatural—the workings of witches and werewolves, for example—there are only a few legends that dwell on positive aspects of belief (for example, #185, 186). Among the most commonly told tales in Louisiana today are accounts of miracles, comforting visits from the spirits of dead loved ones, and visions of saints or deities. The tellers of many such tales consider them to be too private or personal to share with large or unfamiliar audiences.

A second type of legend underrepresented here is a category of nonsupernatural stories often called contemporary legends, modern horror legends, or urban legends. Some of these tales—such as "The Hookman," often told among teenagers at summer camps or during slumber parties—are grisly accounts of madmen who stalk young lovers (these are similar in many ways to such supernatural horror stories as "The Silk Lady" [#178] and "The Red-Headed Witch" [#179]). Other contemporary legends are accounts of people caught in perversely unpleasant or painful situations: finding a mouse in a cola bottle; putting a wet poodle in a microwave to dry if off; entertaining a prostitute in a hotel room and awakening alone to find "Welcome to the world of AIDS" written on the bathroom mirror. Although told daily across the state, such tales often fail to find their ways to storytelling stages, partly because they are often told as news and believed to be true, and are therefore not regarded by the tellers to be folktales at all. Many such urban legends are available in the collections of Baker (1986) and Brunvand (1981, 1984, 1986, etc.).

Nearly missing from *Swapping Stories* are narrative poems and songs. We have included some Spanish-language *décimas* (#153–58) but have omitted the substantial traditions of ballads sung by Cajuns and British Americans, among other groups. Also missing are those personal experience narratives known as testimonials, used to convert or persuade members of certain congregations, social causes, or twelve-step programs.

As Maida Owens noted earlier in this volume, there are also many Louisiana culture groups missing from or underrepresented in *Swapping Stories*. Many of these groups are simply undocumented by folklorists at present; in other cases, we simply lacked the staffing or the resources to represent these groups adequately in this collection.

Swapping Stories also admittedly features an age bias. As mentioned earlier, the most celebrated narrators tend to be older people. Younger storytellers, as well as the tales they most often tell—contemporary legends, supernatural tales, and many types of up-to-date jokes about current events and situations—are all but absent from this anthology.

Finally, there is a substantial gender bias in *Swapping Stories*: at least three times as many male as female narrators appear here. The public, staged nature of the collecting process has something to do with this phenomenon, because in American culture men are more likely to narrate public stories than are women (see Baldwin 1985; Mitchell 1971). The tall tale, for example, is one genre very popular in public settings, and it is also seldom told by women (Cothran 1979). Thus, although Mary Gray was present while her husband Lonnie was telling tall tales, Mary contributed only two stories (compared with Lonnie's fifteen), and these were not tall tales.

Another reason for the imbalance is that women's storytelling often tends to be collaborative: every woman in a small group may lend a hand in a communal performance. Such small-scale group productions are often difficult for fieldworkers to collect and, once collected, are even more difficult to translate to the written page. For example, Sidna Coughlin's "Down the Wrong Hill" (#68) was shared with eleven close women friends who meet regularly, and it could be said that all present contributed to the narrative. When Sidna came to the climax of her story, she was overcome with laughter, and several members of her audience took over by saying "Oh, God!" When Sidna returned to her tale, she made "Oh, God!" the first words of one of the characters in the story. This type of group interaction, richly rewarding to experience in person, is almost impossible to represent in a written collection; hence we have included no further examples in *Swapping Stories*.

The Texts of the Tales

Most of the following tales were collected in 1990 and transcribed by C. Renée Harvison in 1991. As the book developed, however, seven other transcribers (four of whom also contributed translations of foreign-language performances) added fifty-three tales to the volume.[1]

As there is no universally accepted or entirely satisfactory method for representing an oral performance on the printed page, the transcribers varied greatly in their approaches. Carl Lindahl, Maida Owens, and Denise Wenner have worked to create a consistent transcription style that would make the tales both as readable and as faithful to the spoken originals as the printed word allows.

A normalized style required us to avoid "eye dialect"—attempts to make texts "look the way they sound." Many folktale collections present partial attempts at eye dialect—for example, by using "Ah" to represent the pronoun "I" as pronounced by some African-American and European-American Southerners; spelling "shore" to represent a certain pronunciation of "sure"; or writing "runnin'" or "'cause" to indicate that the speaker has not pronounced all the sounds in the standard forms of the words "running" and "because." All such systems, however, are ultimately subjective and distorting (Preston 1982; Ancelet 1994). Thus, we chose to use standard English, French, and Spanish spellings throughout.[2]

Although the editors have provided the titles for these tales, the texts themselves come directly from the storytellers. Our ideal has been to reproduce the spoken tales word for word, with four notable exceptions:

1. We have eliminated incidental sounds, such as "er" and "ah," made by storytellers when searching for the right word.

2. Ellipses— . . . —are used to represent words eliminated from the oral original. In certain cases, the tape-recorded voice of the storyteller was inaudible, or a member of the audience broke in with a comment that would make no sense to a reader who was not present at the original telling. In other cases, the speaker mentioned the name of an individual who has not given us permission to refer to him or her in this book. Only in such cases are words removed and ellipses substituted in their place.

3. Square brackets—[ ]—supply information that cannot be gleaned merely from listening to the teller's words. A phrase in brackets may describe

a gesture made by the speaker that is important to the sense of the story; describe significant audience reactions; translate foreign-language expressions (for example, *elle a cassé la paille* [she broke it off]); or correct an inconsistency (if, for example, the teller uses "she" in describing a male character, the word will be replaced by [he]).

4. We have used *italics* for three specific purposes: a) to represent stories, phrases, and words in foreign languages; b) to render onomatopoeic and nonlexical sounds made by the narrators: *Sshboom, psst, mama-li-to,* etc.; c) to signal words that the narrator spoke with obvious emphasis, in cases in which we felt that providing such stress would enhance the reader's sense of the story.

In a few cases, particularly when the narrator relied heavily on onomatopoeic sounds (for example, tales #56, 133) or when two or more people contributed to the storytelling (tales #68, 80, 121–23), we have had to use brackets, ellipses, and italics, and to transcribe a relatively large number of nonlexical sounds and audience remarks. As a rule, however, we have attempted to use these intrusive markers sparingly in hopes that the reader will experience the stories as directly as possible.

Notes

1. Barry Jean Ancelet transcribed and translated the tales of Wilson "Ben Guiné" Mitchell (#32–36) and oversaw the transcription and translation of all other tales told originally in Cajun or Creole French; Samuel G. Armistead transcribed and translated the Isleño *décimas* of Irvan Perez (#153–56) and the tales of Joseph "Chelito" Campo (#194–95); Annette Huval transcribed the Creole tales of Enola Matthews (#49–55) and Julia Huval (#188–89); Geoffrey Kimball transcribed and translated two of Bel Abbey's tales told in Bel's native Koasati (#45 and 47); Carl Lindahl transcribed the English-language tales of Alfred Anderson (#56–62), translated the Creole language tales of Enola Matthews (#49–55) and Julia Huval (#188–89), and transcribed and translated Barry Ancelet's *Gaillum, Singo et Moliseau* (#210); Arthur "Arturo" Pfister contributed his own written version of "Shine and the Titanic" (#149), which he treats both as an oral piece and as a literary text; and Denise Wenner transcribed twenty-two tales collected for the video production *Swapping Stories* by Pat Mire and Maida Owens from Sarah and Robert Albritton (#69, 70, 120, 193), Barry Ancelet (#122), Sidna Coughlin (#68), Bertney Langley (#196–98), Harry Lee Leger (#67), Dave Petitjean (#80, 131-33), Loulan and Glen Pitre (#174–77), and A. J. Smith (#79, 80, 121, 123, 130).

2. In three instances we have included "eye dialect" at the insistence of the storytellers. After reading our transcription of "The Politician Gets His" (#103)

Hubert L. "Anatoo" Clement, a professional storyteller who tells his jokes in an exaggerated Cajun accent, wrote out his own version of the story to convey his idea of the way his accent should look on paper. Arthur Pfister submitted his own written version of the toast "Shine and the Titanic" (#149). Mildred Osborne's tale, initially titled "Who's Going to Sleep with Me?" (#184), has been changed to "Who's Gon'na Sleep with Me?" because, according to Osborne, "My family would hardly recognize the story without 'Gon'na.' "

PART I

Individual Storytellers

Harold Talbert: Arcadian Anecdotes

ARCADIA, BIENVILLE PARISH

Introduced by C. Renée Harvison

Afolklorist friend in Ruston, Susan Roach, knew about Harold Talbert from listening to him at a storytelling session at the Piney Hills Kite and Art Festival in the spring of 1990. Along with Clarence Faulk from Ruston and a couple of friends from Arcadia, Rodney Cook and Julienne Cole, Harold discussed ornery critters from Bienville Parish. The subjects ranged from Bienville Parish's preservation of possum in the parish to two outlaws who found their demise there, Bonnie Parker and Clyde Barrow.

When I called Susan to find out if she knew of anybody who told good folktales in North Louisiana, she referred me to Harold. Other than the few stories she had already heard him tell, Susan didn't know what other types of or how many stories Harold knew. But as a trained folklorist with a keen eye and ear, Susan had a hunch that Harold would be a good source. Her hunch proved fruitful. Talbert, aged sixty-three, was delighted to share his numerous anecdotes about Arcadia.

I met Harold in town around ten o'clock in the morning on July 20, 1990, and we drove to his family's farmhouse just outside of Arcadia's limits. A bag of potato chips, a couple of Coca-Colas, and several hours later, he told me his stories and transported me back in time to the Arcadia of the 1930s, a place as bucolic as its name suggests. His repertoire included some oral history, such as his personal remembrance of the posse that finally killed Bonnie and Clyde in Bienville Parish in the 1930s. We briefly discussed that and a bit of other area history, such as the Free State of Sabine and the area known as the neutral strip.

But after settling comfortably in his chair, taking off his shoes, and warming up to me, he soon brought out his best stories—personal remembrances of growing up in Arcadia. As he was beginning his first story, names of real-life characters soon emerged. He was beginning to talk to me as though I were a native Arcadian, as though he and I were just sitting around swapping stories about mutual friends. But then he stopped his story and asked if I would change the names if these stories were going to be in print. When I suggested that he just not call names, he said, "I'm going

Harold Talbert at his family farm outside of Arcadia.
Photo: Susan Roach.

to have to call names on some things because you can't tell a story without names involved." With that, I agreed to change the names and keep his trust.

Harold is a well-read, thoughtful man. He was raised a Baptist, but after studying various religions and their doctrines, he now considers himself to be a nondenominational believer in God. He has traveled extensively, most recently to India. His open mind and contact with other cultures, however, have not resulted in a stiff, scholarly style of narration. Quite the contrary. Harold maintains a pleasant North Louisiana drawl and during the interview he frequently animated his stories by acting them out. More than once did Harold crank an invisible, early model telephone, as though he were calling up the operator at Arcadia's central office, or grab his neck as though he were being choked by the villain in the movie The Clutching Hand, or *sail a make-believe watermelon rind through the air, or jump up on his chair, prepared to run from the "gorilla" brought to Arcadia by a traveling animal act.*

Harold Talbert was born and raised in Arcadia, a town located in the hills of Bienville Parish in North Louisiana, where he has spent most of his life. Although the town has grown and changed over the years since Harold's Mayberry-like childhood, it still resembles its namesake: the Arcadia of North Louisiana remains as pastoral as the Arcadia of ancient Greece. Harold briefly attended Louisiana Tech University but transferred to Louisiana State University in Baton Rouge, where he graduated in 1950. He then worked for various companies away from Arcadia. He eventually made his way back home and opened a finance company, which he owned and operated for twenty years. He has had other business interests, such as oil and gas leasing, shallow well drilling, and serving as director of the bank in Arcadia for four years. Since 1989, he has been tending to his own property and traveling. "Just first one thing and another," as he says. This includes telling good stories, like the ones found here.

1. Wrestling Mania

Gus lived here in Arcadia and had a wrestling match here. One of the first real kind of wrestling matches. That was before it got to where you see them on TV, of course. It wasn't as popular then as it is now. But anyway, Gus had a wrestling place here in Arcadia. And he'd have these wrestlers come in.

One day, he had a fellow named Red Flash. Every Tuesday night we had a wrestling match. He wore a mask. You know how phony and what ham actors these wrestlers are. So he had this mask on. And he comes, and oh, they get in there. Course, he makes out like he's putting pepper in Gus's eyes. He'd hold his head away from the referee, put something in his eyes, and Gus would come out and couldn't see and all this.

So Joe Johnson's boys lived right down the road here by Oak Grove Church. Joe had some of the toughest boys in America. I mean, they were tough. . . . They thought that Red Flash [starts chuckling] put the pepper in Gus's eyes, and the referee wouldn't do anything about it, they just jumped up in the wrestling ring. They got Red Flash and like to have beat him to death. Took his mask off of him. [Laughs.] I mean, they were whipping him! Mr. Brown was the deputy sheriff. He had to get up there and beat Joe's boys off of Red Flash. They whipped Red Flash!

Renée Harvison: Did he ever come back?

Harold Talbert: He never did come back!

2. The Arcadia Dating Game

Then, we had a central office here. That was so nice. Much better than anything they have now. All this progress that you young folks think you have, you're really going backwards on most of it. We had a central office here. Miss Sarah ran it.

Renée Harvison: What's a central office?

Harold Talbert: The central office was where they had a big old panel, with stick-in cords that they connected you. You didn't have to know a number. We didn't have any numbers. You just called up. You'd call and say, "Sarah, I want to talk to Dr. Bridges."

And she'd say, "Well, Harold, Dr. Bridges isn't in this morning. Mrs. So and So is having a baby, and he's gone. Dr. Wiley is in town over at his office if you want to talk to him." Or, "Doc Bridges will be back this afternoon at such and such time."

Or you could say, "I want to talk to Mrs. Smith," and Sarah would hook you up. So we didn't have to remember numbers, and we didn't have to have a book. [This was] the most wonderful dating service in the world. We'd go somewhere and we'd see a girl. Like to the ball game in Homer. This is an instance that actually happened. We saw this girl up there. She was a cheerleader, and oh, she was so pretty. Had long, black hair. We didn't know who the girl was, but we played [the Homer team] in football.

So we decided the next morning. And as long as I live, I never called a girl from my house. My mother or daddy certainly wouldn't have objected, but it was an unwritten law. We didn't ever talk on the phone at home to a girl. We'd always go to the central office. Sarah—the operator—had a booth there. She had a little rail fence up right here [gestures]. Then all this equipment that she stuck things in, the connecting equipment, was here [gestures]. And the booth was over here [gestures].

And what was so nice about it, like, we didn't know this girl. So we go up to Sarah's the next morning. All the boys. We go up there. We spent Friday afternoons there. We had some chairs out on the porch. We'd wait out there while she was trying to get our call through to some girl in Ruston or Homer or somewhere. [Laughs.] And she'd take care of all this and call us to this phone in there. So we went in that day. We told Sarah, said, "Sarah, we were up to Homer to the game last night. And there was a girl there, a cheerleader or majorette or something."

We'd tell her what [the girl] looked like, describe her—what she had on and everything. And said, "We want to talk to her." So Ṣarah would get on the phone and call the central office in Homer. And, of course, she knew the lady up there. And she said, "Now, last night at that game, I got some boys down here who want to talk to this girl. They saw her up there last night. She's a cheerleader. Got long black hair."

Maybe the lady on the other end would say, "What was she wearing? What did she look like?" And such and such thing. Then she'd ask us and we'd get it all straightened out. And she'd say, "Oh yeah, I know. That's Dr. So-and-so's daughter." Or Mr. So-and-so. "Oh yeah, I know her."

She said, "Well, I got a boy here that wants to talk to her, and he's a nice boy." She'd tell her something about us. So she then would call the girl. The central office would get the girl on the line in Homer. [Laughs.] We'd get a date, see. It'd all be arranged. It was kind of like an introduction by people that knew you and knew them. It was a nice thing! [Laughs.] We'd come back. If we could get an accurate description of the girl, and what clothes she had on the night before, that's all we had to do for the central office in the other towns to know who she was. Then we'd call and Sarah would fix us up for the dates. Then she'd check back with us to see how everything went. It was nice.

Then later on we got a phone book. Got a number first. I believe before we got the phone book, it got to where you had to know the number. And got a book. And that wasn't too bad because it was printed in big, and it was just Arcadia's book. But then, now, the print keeps getting smaller and smaller and smaller. And now we've got Ruston, Grambling, Simsboro, Bernice. Everybody in the world in the phone book. You can't even find your town. You have to look for the town much less the number. If you're getting older, you got to get you some glasses or a magnifying glass. When you put your glasses down to dial your number, before you can get it all dialed you've forgotten it. Can't go back in and redial it again.

But here a few years ago, the phone service just got so horrible till—I don't remember what I was—but I called over at Ruston, and I said, "I tell you, this phone service is awful." And I said, "I don't mean this wrong, young lady. I'm sure you're a sweet lady and everything. But I want to gripe and I want to complain and I want to tell people what I think about it. And I don't want you to get offended because I know you just work for the phone company, but I am sick and tired of this damn telephone. I want to tell somebody about it!" So I says, "I want to talk to the supervisor."

She says, "Well, I'm going to give her to you." So she gets me the supervisor, and I start off and I'm just raising Cain and complaining. So finally, the lady says, "Who is this?"

I says, "This is Harold Talbert in Arcadia."

She says, "Harold, you know who you talking to?"

I says, "No I don't know who I'm talking to."

She says, "This is Sarah."

I says, "Oh my God, Sarah!" I says, "Oh my God!" [Laughs.] I says, "I didn't know what had happened to you. I didn't know you were over in Ruston now!"

She says, "Yeah."

We had a nice visit and reminisced about our old days at the central office. I was so much better now.

She says, "How are things at home? How are things in Arcadia?"

I says, "Sarah, to tell you the truth, they've been going downhill ever since we got rid of central office!" [Laughs.]

3. Popcorn as the Price for Protection

We had a picture show here, and oh we had some good times. First started off, we had a movie and a feed store. Uncle Tommy's feed store. He had a feed store downtown. Horse and mule feed store. And he had an old brick wall back there, and they hung up a sheet over it. And on Saturday afternoons, some Saturdays, we'd have a picture show down there. Charge us a nickel to get in, and they'd project the thing up on this old wall of the feed store. It was five cents at the time.

Then later on we got a picture show, the Joy Theater. It's still here, same place it was; it's always been there. Still there. So we had this picture show there. We used to have a show on Tuesday, Thursday, Friday, Saturday, and Sunday afternoon if the preacher allowed it. He closed it down four or five times just because we went to it. It didn't matter what was showing. Sunday, wasn't supposed to go; it didn't matter what the show was. If it was *Miss Minerva,* you wasn't supposed to go on Sunday. So he closed the show up every once and a while.

But we had it all these other nights. Had a big popcorn machine out on the street. Oh, you could smell the popcorn popping for several blocks. It smelled so wonderful. It was so good. But anyway, we'd go to this show, and on Tuesday night they had a continued piece. It was like a serial now. It would be something like *Dr. Fu Manchu* or *The Clutching Hand*—he came out at the end and he'd get them around the throat and bind them somewhere. You never saw him, but you always saw this hand reach out and grab them.

Now, I'm going to—I can't keep from calling names—I can't tell my stories otherwise—I also am going to have to tell it like it was. So if I use the term "colored people," I do it with no disrespect. They were friends of mine, playmates, and everything else. But I'm going to tell it just like it happened.

At the time, the show was segregated. We had a balcony upstairs where the colored people sat. That was the best night, Tuesday. The serial was always on. And we could hardly wait from one evening to the next to see what happened to Flash Gordon when he was thrown off the cliff. Or Charlie Chan was about to find a murderer, him and Number One Son. Oh, it was good. Everybody wanted to go to the picture show.

And I lived down here on a street on Highway 80 then, coming out of Arcadia. I lived in the last house. Everybody on that street, on both sides of the road from there to town, were kin to me, except the preacher and two other houses. All of them were my relatives. But nevertheless, it was a long way to run. I'd go up there to the show on Tuesday night. It'd just scare me so bad till once I'd start running I couldn't quit. It didn't have any street lights except right in town. About a block out of town the street lights ended. I'd walk to that street light, and once I got started running I had to run all the way home. It was a little too far for me to hold out, and I couldn't afford to stop. It was dark. I held the world's record. I never was timed officially. But I held the world's record, I know, between the street light and the house because I'd run it with my heart just beating. I was running for my life. I know I held the world's record if I'd been clocked.

But anyway, we had a particular scary show out there. I think it was *Dr. Fu Manchu* going on. And every Tuesday night I'd go to the show. People from all over the country would come. The negroes who were working in the fields, picking cotton and stuff, they'd get off and they'd come to the show. They'd get off a little early if they could. They'd come walking. So I'd walk to the show with them, with the colored people from down in the quarters there. And when we got to the show, and we started home that night, I'd come back with them if they were there. If they didn't come to the show that night, well, I was just into it; I just had to run.

So one night, they were getting the cotton in, and my escorts didn't show up. So I had a boy that I played with; he worked for us at the auction sales. A little colored boy. He was like this little old hybrid corn; he didn't grow very tall. He just grew about this high [gestures] and just spread out.

But he was built up like Charles Atlas on a small scale and just as muscular as could be. Course, I was skinny and didn't weigh hardly fifteen pounds wringing wet. But I was taller than him by a good bit. Anyway, I told him, I said, "I tell you what. I want you to walk me home after this show. This show has got me scared, and I want you to walk me home."

He says, "I tell you what I'll do, Harold." Says, "If you'll buy the popcorn, and we can eat it together, I'll walk you home."

I says, "All right." Rather than buying the popcorn when I went in the show, I bought the popcorn when I came out the show. He was going to walk me home. So we started eating the popcorn, and he was just gobbling the popcorn. I had to eat fast to get any of it. The popcorn, I could see, wasn't going to hold out until we got home. Well, sure enough, the popcorn played out just about time we got to the street light, about two blocks from town. He just stopped when the popcorn played out.

I said, "Wait a minute now." I said, "You were supposed to walk me home." Said, "This is the scary part from here on where it's dark."

He says, "No, I'm not going any further. You ate all the popcorn."

I said, "Oh, no. You ate all the popcorn." I said, "I had to eat fast to keep you from eating it all. That wasn't the deal. You're going to take me home."

He said, "No I'm not. I'm going back." So he turned around and went back. So the next week, I saw him next Tuesday night, and I was negotiating with him again. He said this time, "If I'm going to walk you home tonight, I want all the popcorn. Don't you eat any of it."

I said, "All right. I'm going to do it." So we came out of the show. He got the nickel bag of popcorn, and we started for the house. And the popcorn lasted till we got down there, going through the woods. Where the street light ended, we had a trail through the woods. You could get out in the road and walk, but if a car was coming you wasn't supposed to be out there. But we had a trail through the woods. So we had just gotten in the woods and were just about to cross this little old branch. I could see the popcorn was going to run out again. But I hadn't had one grain.

So I saw a limb laying down there that had fallen off of an old pine tree. It was just an old, rotten limb. But I figured he was going to try and turn back. And when he did, I decided I was just going to take that limb and whip him good if he didn't keep his bargain. So I picked up this limb. [Laughs.] I was walking along with it like I was walking with a walking stick. We got down there and the popcorn played out about the branch.

He said, "Well, I'm going back."

I said, "Oh, no, uh-uh. That wasn't the deal. You were going to take me all the way home."

He said, "No, the popcorn's through, I'm through." [Laughs.]

So I just hauled off and hit him in the head with this stick because I knew he could whip me, and I knew I had to hit him good! So I hit him right across the head with that stick just as hard as I could. The stick, of course, was rotten; it just crumbled. It didn't do anything. It just folded up and crumbled. That boy whipped me. He beat me to where he got me down *in* the branch and everywhere. [Laughs.] He liked to have beat me to death! So I went on home.

The next week, I told him, "I tell you what I'm going to do this time. We're going to change this thing up. I'm going to keep the nickel, and you're going to have to walk me all the way home. When I get in the house, I'll give you the nickel out the door. You can come back." He had to come back towards town to go home. "You can come back and get your popcorn when you pass the show."

So we had that deal. . . . I'd smell that popcorn every Tuesday night. I never got to have a sack of that popcorn because he took my nickel, and I didn't want to tell Daddy about it. And even today, I love popcorn and I love to smell it because I remember how I used to long for it at that show and never could eat it because I had to save my nickel.

4. You're Going to Shoot Me Where?

The colored maid that worked for us was named Esther. She had a boy the same age I was, O. D. And she'd bring O. D. to work with her. O. D. was my first playmate.

O. D. and I—he's still living—would play all day. She had a nephew that she was raising—and he was older than we were—named Adam. So Adam would come with her, too. Adam was in charge of O. D. and I. He was supposed to lead us, watch out for us and lead us on our horse and everything.

We had a Shetland pony, called Comet, and O. D. and I rode that pony. Halley's Comet came over about the time that I was born. And my daddy bought me a Shetland pony before I was born, and he named him Comet. Before I was born, my daddy bought me this pony in anticipation of me coming and being born. My horse was named Comet after Halley's Comet.

An interesting sidelight to that: before my first child was born—while my wife was pregnant with my first girl, the oldest child—my daddy bought another Shetland pony for her. A spotted Shetland pony. This was the time that the Russians had launched their Sputnik. So my daddy named the horse Sputnik. That was kind of prophetic. We had come here from a comet, something that was remote. Here we were, by the time my daughter got here, we were actually—we had surpassed the comets in a way. Here we were—civilization was in outer space just like this comet was. Who would ever have believed that would happen? But anyway, her horse was named Sputnik.

Anyway, this is a funny instance that happened. We had a doctor, Dr. Wright, who had an office here in town. You had to be in good health to go to Dr. Wright. If you were, as people say, if you were "poorly," and you went to him, you never survived it. He was so tough and rough. He didn't give any anesthetics. He was a good doctor, but these old country doctors—I'm telling you they were rough!

Dr. Wright had an office downtown. The state was going around—the state health department was going around inoculating people. I don't remember whether it was diphtheria, typhoid fever—I don't remember what it was. Anyway, they were inoculating the people according to the political precincts. You would go to the voting precinct. All the people in this voting precinct would come to this precinct, and he would come out there, the doctor would, and inoculate them according to a schedule.

But we lived in town. We were supposed to get our shot at the doctor's office. He had it beside the old drugstore.

So one afternoon, after dinner, Esther had cooked dinner that day. We ate dinner and went to town to get our shot. Of course, we came back. I was crying with my arm, and it was hurting where Dr. Wright had shot me and everything. Esther lived out in the quarters. When she got through working that day, she had to go through town to get home. She had to go through town, so she just stopped at Dr. Wright's office to get her shot, thinking since we'd got our shot, she'd get her shot.

The next morning, Esther shows up for work. She's in there scrambling eggs, and we'd come in for breakfast. Esther is all sulled up, kind of talking, mumbling to herself over there. Obvious she was crying or had been crying.

So Daddy said, "Esther, what's the matter with you this morning?" He said, "Have you and Jasper"—Jasper was her husband—"have you and Jasper had a fight? What in the world is the matter with you? You're kind of sulled up, your eyes are red, you've been crying." Said, "What's the matter?"

She says, "Well, I tell you the truth." Says, "I just don't think it's fair."

Daddy says, "Well, what are you talking about?"

She says, "Well, yesterday when you all went up to town and got your shot. Yesterday, when I got through working, I went by Dr. Wright's office to get *my* shot." And said, "He told me, said, 'No, you'll just have to wait. I'm going to shoot you colored people in your precinct. I'm going to shoot you in your precinct. You'll just have to wait.' Well, he shot you white folks in the arm!" Says, "Now he's going to shoot us in our precinct! I don't think it's right." [Laughs.]

That tickled Daddy to death. Esther didn't think it was right because he was going to shoot her in the precinct, and he'd shot us in the arm. I don't know where she thought her precinct was, but it does sound rather bad. Anyway, I guess she thought it was a bad place.

5. Paying the Price for a Free Train Ride

J. T. and I played down here, caught the train everywhere. The train would stop and come to Arcadia then to unload the feed off the train. It would also put cross-ties on the train. They had a lot of horse and mule feed, and they'd unload the feed for all the feed stores. Flour sacks and shorts for hogs. There'd be a bunch of cars over there. We'd play in the cars, in these old box cars. We'd go to the show up here, and we'd see all these train shows. We'd go down there and play on the train. The train would come, pull off the side track and hook into these empty cars, then get back on the main track. We'd ride a little way on the train.

There were so many people riding then on the train, there were more people riding the freight train than there was the passenger train. You'd just see a few people on the passenger train, because nobody could afford the fare. This was back during the Depression. But every hobo in the world was on the freight train. Had so many they had to have what they call *bulls* at the yard. People that worked in the big train yards, not Arcadia, but like Shreveport or Monroe, the bigger towns. They'd have a guy they called the bull. He would get the hobos and knock them off the train, keep them off the train, to where the train wouldn't be so many people riding it. Wasn't supposed to be that many on the train. There'd be hundreds of them on it. Looked like a Mexican bus—if you've ever seen a Mexican bus—in one of these third world countries. They were just riding all over it. That's the way the freight train was.

Anyway, we'd play on this freight train. We'd ride it from one side of town to the other. When they got down here, they had a water tank back there. This was during the time when they had steam engines. They didn't have diesel engines. So they'd take on water up here at Morgan and Lindsay's Store.

So one day, J. T., he was the marshall's boy, and I were playing up in the train. High up in one of these old box cars. When the train picked it up, we just thought we'd ride it down to the water tank and get out, which was what we'd usually do. This day, I don't know that the train didn't stop for water, and it was a short train. By the time he got to the water tank, he was flying. We were way up high. We wasn't down by the rails where we could jump off. We were up in the box car. It was just flying. We kept looking for a place to jump off, never could find one. He kept picking up speed so we thought, "Oh my God! We are into it now! We don't know where we're going!"

But we'd already been whipped once about riding the train. I rode it all the time. Daddy had already gotten after me about that train. I did hate to leave home and wound up on that train. Anyway, the train just keeps going. So J. T. is crying. Not that I wasn't just as afraid as he was, but I was still trying to look for a place to jump off. Never did find one.

Finally, we wound up over here at Gibsland, and the train, fortunately, stopped. Course, now, Gibsland was eight miles down the road. But that was a long way. Finally, the train pulled in over at Gibsland. We got off and went into the depot. Depot agent asked us, "Who are you all?"

So we told him, we said, "We're from Arcadia. Wish you'd telegraph Mr. Howard Moses." He was the depot agent in Arcadia, big old tall, white-headed fellow. Said, "Telegraph Mr. Howard Moses and tell him we're over here."

He said, "How did you boys get over here?" We told him what happened. Course, he acted like we'd violated some federal law. Just scaring us to make us feel bad. We thought maybe we were going to get sent to the penitentiary. I didn't know what was going to happen to us. [Laughs.]

Anyway, he telegraphed Mr. Howard and tells him he's holding us over there. Boy, I hated to see that car coming to pick us up because I knew it was going to be trouble. But anyway, Ms. Taylor came to get us in an old T-model car. You talk about mixed feelings. But I was glad to see her arrive because I wanted to go home. But I hated to see her, at the same time, because I knew we were going to face hell. I knew that woman, she was going to come over and beat me and J. T. [Laughs.]

She showed up, mad as a wet hen, and got out of that T-model car. I'm telling you the truth, she beat us every step we walked. We finally got in the T-model, and I thought, "One good thing about it, she'll have to take both hands to drive it. When we get in there, maybe she'll quit beating us. She won't have another hand to beat us with." We finally got in there and started home. We had that train ride every once and a while, even after that.

6. A Unique Way of Picking Cotton

It wasn't just a little piece from the railroad tracks to our house. So I told [my friend] Jim, I said, "Let's catch that freight train and ride it on home. We'll jump off when we get close to the house." By that time, it usually wasn't going too fast.

And Jim said, "You know, Mr. Andy's already whipped us once about that train." I said, "I know it, but we'll get on the other side of the train and catch it on the other side. He can't see us." [Laughs.]

So Jim thought that sounded like pretty good strategy, so we go on the other side of the train and get on the train. But this time we don't get up in the car. I've already learned from this other experience. We're hanging on the iron thing, on the side, Jim and I.

And we got down here, and that train again, by the time we got to where we was supposed to jump off, Miss Margaret Pittman had a field of cotton there. And she had planted cotton, and the cotton stalks was up about this high. If you've ever noticed cotton, they've got a sticker on the end of a cotton burr. It'll make your hands bleed if you don't know how to pick cotton and aren't used to it. It'll really hurt you.

But anyway, we got down there. When we got to that field, well, we were going to get off at the crossing. But by the time we got to the crossing, the train was going so fast that we couldn't find a place to jump off.

Well, Jim got to crying. And so, we got to that field. That was our last chance to jump off in soft ground. . . . A lot of times, the track was built up, and you just couldn't make it. You'd jump off, and you'd jump off right into the trees, and you'd kill yourself. But here was Miss Margaret's cotton field. So it was jump now or never. Ride it on to Ruston. And I sure wasn't going to Ruston after all the other trouble I'd been in.

Well, we got down there to Miss Margaret's field. I said, "This is it, Jim. We got to jump right now." [Laughs.] So we jumped off, and we must've rolled from here to that pecan tree out there [about 200 yards] before we stopped. Through that field. I was so scratched up, it looked like I'd been drug through a briar patch where that cotton had got me. I rolled two or three rows of cotton down. So did old Jim. But we kind of brushed our faces off, and got ourselves cleaned up to where it didn't look too bad, and walked on to the house, and ate dinner.

7. Gorilla Warfare

One time, we'd have these magicians. Like Willard the Magician. He'd come to town with a tent show, and he'd perform all these magic acts. They'd put these billboards up on the buildings. He'd have a goatee. He would be some man, maybe with a turban on his head, from some far-off, Asian country. He was going to mesmerize them and hypnotize them.

They'd have this tent show. We had the shows down at the pond pen. The pond pen is down where City Hall is now. The pond pen is where you impounded animals. Everybody in town had a cow. A milk cow, a Jersey cow, that you milked. Oftentimes, a horse or cow would get out. If they got out, well they had what they called a "pond pen," short for "pound pen," where they'd impound them. They caught them, put them in the pen, and you had to pay a dollar or two and come get them out. But that's where we'd have all the traveling tent shows.

Then, in the summer, they'd have a skating rink down there. A man came through with a portable skating rink. We had a big tent, and we'd skate all summer. That's all there was to do, other than what we made up.

On Saturday night, these acts would also use the picture show. They'd use the stage at the picture show. There was a big sign out in front of the picture shows. They'd give out circulars on Saturday. They'd print up circulars that they were having a tent show. Everybody would come to town on Saturday, and they'd put a circular in your wagon or on your car. Or they'd tack one to the telephone pole. You'd see what was going on at the picture show. Willard the Magician was coming. Clyde Beatty would come sometimes with his animal acts, like Ringling Brothers' Circus. Or Frank Buck, "Bring them back alive!" He had him one of these cardboard hats that came down in front like the English used to wear in India. They called them the "Frank Buck hat" then. He and Clyde Beatty had all the different, exotic animals.

This time, some man, with just a half-wild gorilla that he's gotten out of the jungles of Africa, was going to be there. Where old Tarzan was great. So we all knew about gorillas and the big chimpanzees because we saw Tarzan and Jane every Saturday. So this man is coming with his gorilla—*go*-rilla, as some used to say. This gorilla show is coming to town on Tuesday night. We were going to see this gorilla show prior to the picture show. [Of course, the gorilla was just a man dressed up in a suit. But we weren't knowledgeable enough to know that.]

Well, we all get up there, and they had a different booth where they sold tickets for the blacks, upstairs. The white ticket booth was here. [Gestures.] But you could go in the picture show, and as you went in the picture show, you could go in the colored booth here. That's where the manager sold the tickets. He went in the door there. Everybody was out to see the gorilla act. They had that gorilla out there, and he looked like he was just monstrous. He looked like King Kong. We all thought it was real. I didn't know anything like that could be made up. None of us did.

So this huge, looming thing looks like King Kong. This man [the gorilla's owner] has a pistol and a whip! [Gestures.] He pops it and he's got his gun on. That show is packed, from the front row all the way to the back. Standing room. They were all standing in the aisles. You couldn't get in or out to save your life. The colored section upstairs was full, too. They were all standing up. The man comes up on stage and the lights come on. Boy, we all watching. I'm about midway back, in the middle. I was sitting there watching. This man comes out, and he puts this gorilla through one or two little tricks. He makes the gorilla roll over. Of course, the gorilla is going, *Roooaarr!* Going on. He makes him roll over and turn, and do one or two little things. Seems like they had a little dispute over something, and the gorilla acts like he's going to attack the man. The man takes the whip and pops it! His whip doesn't work, so he takes out his gun and *Bam!*

Of course, it was all put up. When he shot, the lights went out. That was part of the act, the suspense. Well, when the lights went out, I mean the people in the back that were standing up had already checked out. They'd left when the gorilla got loose and jumped off the stage. That's when they left. And that's when the man shot. They left then. But the rest of us was in the dark, in the picture show, with the lights out! We didn't know what to do! You could've heard a pin drop. We didn't anybody want to make a noise because we didn't know where the gorilla was. I'd already gotten up. I was standing in my seat like this [squats in his chair], on the arms of the chair, poised for flight. I'd already gotten up. I was just waiting for the gorilla.

Well, one woman down in the front yells, "*Aaaaggghh!* He touched me!" Another one hollered something else. Then it all got quiet again, and I was poised for going. I was waiting to hear the next scream and know where he was. Then I was going to check out. I didn't want to run into him if he was running up my aisle. All of a sudden, the woman down there hollered, "*Aaaagghh!*" Well, when she did that, I just jumped and landed out in that aisle. I start back out running in that aisle, going a hundred miles an hour.

There's a big, fat girl here in town. She's still living, so I won't call her name. Let's call her Mildred, but that's not her name. So Mildred was a big old, tall, fat girl. She was older than I was and bigger, too. And Mildred and I, she seemed like she had the same idea I did. So she was out in the aisle when I landed out there. She was out there at the same time, running. [Jumps out of his chair and starts running.] We were just neck and neck, running. I wasn't going to give an inch, and she wasn't either. We both got to the door, and we couldn't both make it through the door. She wasn't going to give, and neither was I. So we both just hit the door and went through it. When we did, she went on out this way. I wasn't big as she was. I got knocked down into the black ticket booth. Right in the gorilla's path for coming out the show. I knew I couldn't come back out and face the gorilla. So I just had to go on out. So I just kicked it back. [Kicks.] The ticket salesman was with me. He wasn't going to come out, either! So we just went through the bottom. Crawled on out the bottom and came out on the street! Wasn't anything but ply-board. We went on out, and people ran out of that show. I'm telling you the truth, if it had been like it is now, there'd have been some lawsuits. Somebody could have died of a heart attack in there. They knocked the glass out of the doors. The doors were fancy with a half-moon. The half-moon was glass. Well, when the people got to these swinging doors, man, they knocked the glass out of them, knocked them off their hinges. Just tore the place up. That's to say nothing of the stampede up in the balcony. We ran. When we got out of that show, we ran clear down to the depot, about a block down the street. We were flying. Looked back up, and we had demolished that picture show. [Laughs.] I don't know what ever happened to the man and his gorilla! They were lucky if they didn't get mauled in the stampede. We didn't have any more gorilla shows come. It was too real. It was like Red Flash and the wrestling match. Things got out of hand!

8. A Thorough Baptizing

Everything in the world funny would happen at the church. When you wasn't supposed to laugh. For some reason, it made it more exciting and more suspenseful if you were on the front row. Now, children, I think, want to sit on the back row. But when I was a boy, we wanted to sit on the front row. I think it's because all the people's eyes were on us, and we knew we had to behave. It just made everything so funny.

So one Sunday, we had a revival. Brother Collins was preaching. He was a little fellow. Real nice man and a good preacher, but he was a little fellow. Bald-headed. He's dead now, but Brother Collins was the preacher at the Baptist church. We had a revival that Sunday. It was customary that whoever joined the church during the revival was baptized. We waited and baptized them all the following Sunday, after the revival was over. So they'd had a revival, and a bunch of people had joined the church.

The following Sunday comes, after the revival, and they're going to baptize them. The church was built up like a theater was. It was kind of slanted. The floor was built up like an amphitheater. Right down at the bottom, we had an area like an amphitheater. Above it, we had a platform. That's where the pulpit was, and the baptistry was right behind the curtains there. They had some steps that led down into it, and a metal tank. He filled it up with water, and he got down in there. You could see Brother Collins from about head up, he was so short. Didn't quite get his shoulder in. He baptized these people.

Back then, you didn't have any swimming pools or lifeguards. Children just learned to swim. But some just didn't know how to swim!

He was baptizing this Sunday. We was all sitting down there on the front row. Everything had gone pretty good that day. Nobody had to be sent out of the church. Everything was going all right, looked like. So he gets up to baptize. And he baptized them all, gets them out of the water, and they come on back up.

This one woman had hung back to the last. I guess because she was afraid of the water. She had hung back, and she was huge. A big old fat girl. *Way* bigger than Brother Collins. She came on up there, and she didn't like the idea too much anyway. She had on this dress. You brought an old dress you didn't care anything about, because it was going to ruin it when you got in. She steps down, and she gets up there, and she goes to walk down, steps down into this baptistry. He's holding his hand up for her. He gets her down here, and she's way up above him.

He had a [laughs] handkerchief. Everyone of them that would come, he'd say, "I baptize you in the name of the Father, the Son, and the Holy Ghost." He'd put this handkerchief over their nose [takes his handkerchief out of his pocket and places it over his nose], and then he would hold them down, push them down, then bring them back. Well, when he got this girl, he put this handkerchief over her nose. Great big woman! We were all wondering how he was going to hold her. And so, she wasn't too confident about it, either, so she grabbed him by the wrist. Kind of grabbed him around his shoulder. He put her under, and of course when her feet slipped out from under her and she went backward, she just reached up and she just jerked him on under!

Down he went! All we could see was feet and arms. And every once in a while, his foot would come up. Sometimes hers would come up. Sometimes his. And water sloshing around everywhere! They wallowed around in there, and it was just a question of who was going to survive the drowning. It looked like [laughs] both were underwater. Neither one of them could get their feet on. That tub was slick. That girl had that preacher, and he was under there. Sometimes his arm would come up, sometimes hers. Sometimes it would be a foot, sometimes a leg. We just screamed and hollered. I laughed so hard, I cried.

About this time, after all that thrashing and wallowing around, this girl finally comes climbing up the steps [acts it out] just like a drowned rat. Mad as a wet hen. She was sulled up. She come climbing up the thing, and he was left back in there. [Laughs.] So after a while, he came up, bald-headed you know. He came up, and oh, it tickled us so bad we just screamed.

9. Responding to the Sermon

Then one Sunday, we got in there. We was sitting down on the front row. They got to passing notes, the boys did. Singing. Some of them would sing too loud. The preacher got to preaching along. He gave us bad eyes two or three times. He stopped and told the deacon to take us out. He came down there, about six or seven of us, and got us out of there. Took us to the education building to wait until church was over and our parents could get us. So oh boy, did we have some rough times there that next week. Wasn't too long after this, one Sunday, I went to church with Mother. I saw David, a friend of mine. He's a red-headed boy. David was sitting there on the front row. And I told Mama, I said, "Mama, I see David down here. I want to go sit with him."

She says, "All right. I'm going to let you go. But I'm going to tell you one thing, young man. If that preacher looks at you all—just so much as looks at you all one time—just one time—when I get you home, I'm going to give you something to remember."

I said, "Oh no, I'm not going to get in any trouble, Mama. I'm going to mind my own business. I'm not going to do anything wrong."

She said, "All right. You go on down there. I'm just going to tell you now. I'm making you that promise."

I said, "Yes ma'am." I went on down there. I was on the end of the bench. The bench had an old armrest right here on the end of it. David was on the other side of me. It was only two of us. We were being real good. We hadn't done a thing wrong. I hadn't even whispered, and David hadn't either.

It was hot, no air-conditioning. Had those little old hand fans. The undertaking parlor always gave out the fans. You'd sit there in church, and you was fanning with the undertaker's fan. I always thought it was kind of interesting that we were sitting there, talking about eternal life, and had the undertaker's fan.

But anyhow, this Sunday, Brother Collins was preaching on David and Goliath. David had gotten sleepy. He laid down on the bench. He just gave it up and laid down on the bench. I myself was propped up over here on this armrest, and I was going to sleep, too.

So Brother Collins had a habit of hitting on the pulpit and raising his voice for emphasis. I think he did it to keep people awake. He was preaching along, and he says, "They were fighting—the children of Israel were fighting"—with the Philistines, as well as I remember. And Goliath was the giant. He was just whipping up on them something awful. And Brother Collins says [raises his voice], "And the children of Israel called for *David! David!*"

And when he did, David jumped right up, straight up out of his sleep, hollered, *"Yes, Sir!"* Stood right up. He was a little bitty, red-headed, freckle-faced boy. Not enough room in the face for another freckle. Said, *"Yes, Sir!"*

When he stopped and looked and realized where he was and saw that preacher, he turned back around and looked for his mama. He had the most pitiful look. It was obvious what had happened. Everybody just sat down. The preacher even sat in the chair behind the pulpit. He sat down and he just cried. He got his handkerchief out and cried, laughing. Tickled him so bad.

He got up and he starts again. Poor old David, he's sitting down next to me just like the condemned man. So I leaned over and told him, "Boy, you in for it when you get home." Said, "Look at your mama back there."

He said, "I see her. She's looking at me mean."

I said, "Man, she's going to beat you this afternoon till it's a shame."

So the preacher got back up to preach, and every time something would come up about David, he'd get tickled again. Finally, he just cut the sermon short, and we left. I could see David's mama. She was going up the hill there to her car. David was kind of lingering around. She had him by the wrist and [he gets up to demonstrate] she'd walk a little piece and just jerk him. Snatch him. She carried him on up the road.

I was waiting when the bus came to school, Monday. He got off the school bus, and I was waiting for him. I said, "Well, how did it go yesterday when you got home?"

He said, "I climbed up in the barn, and I got up in the pigeon loft. I didn't come out all day long." He said that she didn't whip him. He hadn't done anything wrong.

We had a time at that church!

10. He Prayed a Good Prayer

One Sunday, we had a big old tall man that didn't hear too good. People didn't get hearing aids back then like they do now. You just had to holler at them. Once and a while they had some old cow horn they'd hold up. But this old man was elderly, gray-headed. He had a short wife. She was real spry, but he was hard of hearing.

The preacher had a habit of calling on this man to pray. A lot of times, he'd give the benediction at the end of the sermon and dismiss us. This particular Sunday, the preacher had started his sermon. Hadn't gotten very far into it till the old man went to sleep. He was sitting there and just [makes a snoring noise] got to snoring real loud. [Snores again.] Every once and a while, he'd hit a knot. [Snores three short times.] Everybody could hear him!

Anyway, when the preacher would call on him to pray, he couldn't hear. His wife had a habit of elbowing him, and he would give the benediction. This particular Sunday, the preacher started his sermon. Gets a pretty good piece into it, and the old man goes to sleep and starts snoring. His wife, when he started snoring, she just reached over with an elbow and elbowed him. I guess he thought it was time. That the preacher had called on him to give the benediction. He just stood up, closed his eyes, and said, "Oh, Lord, we give thee thanks for this beautiful Sunday, for being together in thy house. Be with us through the following week, and bring us back next Sunday. Bless everybody here, go with us through the rest of the day." Right in the middle of the sermon! [Laughs.] He just goes through the whole thing. [Laughs.] He prays the nicest prayer you ever did hear!

She just grabbed him by the coat and jerks him. Finally, he gets through. Looks around and nobody leaves the church. Everybody just crying. Just laughing. The preacher standing there with his mouth open!

[Laughs.] Everybody didn't realize what happened. Everybody knew he was snoring, but all of them didn't see his wife gouge him and see the whole sequence of events. That tickled us to death. We cried over that.

11. She Got the Spirit

We had a revival meeting up there one time. It was so hot we had it in a tent, outside of the church. With the sides of the tent rolled up. It didn't start until dark, and that way it would be a little cooler. We had the sides of the tent rolled up, and that way the air could come on through.

There was a little old boy, a lot younger than I was, mischievous little fellow. He was always into something, and his mother was a real, kind of sanctimonious, pious, self-righteous kind of lady. She was a nice lady, but she was that way. Had the worst boy you ever saw.

So he came to the revival, but his mama wasn't sitting right there. He was sitting down there with us boys. We wasn't on the front row this time. We was back there on some benches. This boy, I'm going to call him Joe, that wasn't his name. He had some bubble gum. Preacher got to preaching. We had an out-of-town preacher, and oh, he was leading this revival. He was singeing us good. It was hellfire and brimstone that night. Old Joe got to pulling his gum out. He'd chew on this gum. He'd blow him a bubble, and then he'd take his gum and see how far he could pull it before it would break. One time, he held his bubble gum up, and he pulled it out like this. [Gestures.] The thing popped loose and landed in a lady's hair. She had long hair. It landed in her hair, and he reached in there to get it out.

It got his other gum stuck in it. He got that lady by the head, and he was just going to have his gum one way or the other. He got her by the head, and she was jerking around like this [jerks his head around], pulling back. The preacher got to watching [starts laughing], and I guess he thought she had the Saint Vitus' dance or something, her head going like this!

That boy's mama saw it. Finally, she saw what happened, and she ran down there to get him. He had that woman almost down to the ground by that time. She got him out of there, and he was just hollering for his gum, all the way up the hill. He wanted his gum.

12. An Extra Passenger on the Bus

We had a lady here. She just died the other day, Miss Evelyn. She ran the bus station for years, when we had a Tri-State bus station. And Miss Evelyn was a wonderful lady and a real character; she was, I believe, a hundred and two when she died last year. Or maybe it was this year. When things got slow and there wasn't anything to do, we'd go downtown and sit with Miss Evelyn in the bus station. She had some cold drinks in there, and she'd give us some cold drinks. And I'd go sit over there with Miss Evelyn.

Miss Evelyn was the first person that I ever knew that had a small car. She had an American Austin. Now, these little cars were the forerunners of the little-type foreign cars that you see now—the Volkswagen Bug and these little Hondas. But American Austin built this little car, and it was a little bitty thing. It was just a real curiosity to see one. And Miss Evelyn bought her a little American Austin.

So she'd ride us. If she had to go somewhere, she'd ride me in that little American Austin. I couldn't get in one now, but then I could get in the back seat and ride with Miss Evelyn.

So one day, Miss Evelyn had her little American Austin parked down at the bus station. She would come down, a little before the time for the bus to arrive, and she'd sell tickets. A lot of times she'd go back home when the bus left. When the bus went to leave, she'd leave, too, because there wouldn't be another one for several hours or maybe only once or twice a day.

So Miss Evelyn goes out that day. And when the bus is getting ready to go, and she's through selling tickets, she locks up and gets in her little Austin. About that time, the bus pulls out. But the bus is so big and so tall, and he's not used to looking down that low for some little, old car, so he doesn't see Miss Evelyn, and he just drives on out. The back bumper of the bus hooks the front bumper of Miss Evelyn's little American Austin! And we look up downtown, and here comes the bus with Miss Evelyn in her little Austin, just blowing her horn in the back of it, and he's driving through town! So they got him stopped and got Miss Evelyn unhooked from the Tri-State bus! And oh, she was a character.

13. The Case of the Missing Sister

Miss Evelyn went over to Shreveport one time. Her daughter was Marilyn. Marilyn was a professor at Northwestern [State University] down here at Natchitoches. Marilyn is a sweet lady and lives here now. She retired and came back.

But Marilyn came home one weekend. She had bought her a new car, Marilyn, a new Ford. So Miss Evelyn—her sister had been real bad sick over at Shreveport, Miss Kitty. And Miss Kitty was in the hospital over at Shreveport—and Miss Evelyn was supposed to go get her that Saturday and bring her home.

So Marilyn shows up and tells Miss Evelyn, says, "Mama, I don't want you driving that old car of yours over there. My car is a bigger car. It's got two seats and it's new." Says, "You take my car. Get a pillow and a blanket and you can put Aunt Kitty on the back seat. She can rest on the way home. You drive my car. It's in good shape. You just leave yours at home."

She said, "All right."

So Miss Evelyn leaves, and she goes over to Shreveport to the hospital and picks Miss Kitty up. They put the blanket down on the back seat, put the pillow down. They got it fixed up nice. She starts home. Right there at the end of the Texas Street Bridge, they used to have a feed store called Lane Wilson. They had chicken feed and goldfish feed, every kind of thing. It was a hardware and a feed store. She told her sister, they had the windows rolled down because it was hot. She told her sister, said, "Kitty, I'm going to park this car here, and I'm going to run in Lane Wilson's here and get me some birdseed. You just lay right here, and you wait for me. I'll be right back out."

And she parked kind of up the street from the store, where there was a parking spot. In the same block, not far. She just ran in Lane Wilson's to get the feed. Got in there and got to talking, got her bird feed and everything else, and came out. Miss Evelyn came out and looked down the street, and she couldn't see her car. Anywhere!

So she's standing there looking, and the man comes out the store and he says, "Is something the matter?"

She says, "Well, yes it is." Says, "I parked my car right up the street, right yonder, and it's not there now. I don't know. Somebody's stolen my car!" She says, "The bad part of it is, I had my sick sister in there from the hospital, on the back seat! She's gone, too! Got the car and her both!"

He said, "Well, my Lord! Let's call the police!" So they call the police. They turn on the sirens and everything. They run up, two cars of them. They jump out. Been a kidnapping and Miss Evelyn standing there on the street, telling them about taking her car and Miss Kitty. She forgot that she came over in Marilyn's car.

In the middle of all the police sirens and Miss Evelyn out on the street going through the ordeal, Miss Kitty raised up down there on the back seat. Looks out and says, "Evelyn! [Laughs.] What in the world is the matter!"

She says, "Oh, Lord! Yonder's my sister, yonder! Yonder she is, yonder!" So it all comes out then, that she's over there in Marilyn's car and she forgot. She was looking for her car and thought they'd captured Miss Kitty.

14. Talking Trash

Harold Talbert is joined by friends at the Piney Hills Kite and Art Festival, March 31, 1990. The topic of discussion is one of Bienville Parish's most endangered natural resources, the possum. So endangered is this oft-misunderstood creature that Arcadia resident Rodney Cook founded an organization dedicated to its preservation, Possum's [contraction for Possum Is] Unlimited, patterned after Ducks Unlimited. The lifetime membership fee to Possum's Unlimited is $2.89 and includes a subscription to Tracks: The Official Newsletter of Possum's Unlimited; *a road kill body bag, in case any unfortunate possum is spotted along the highway; an official t-shirt; and a suitable-for-framing Honorary Degree of Possumcology.*

Harold Talbert: I said, you know, the trouble with the duck hunting is, nobody kills ducks anymore. Everybody goes hunting and nobody comes back. They just keep sending in money to raise these ducks. And I said, "That's the trouble. The trouble is they're feeding them so good up there in Canada and all the way down til the ducks are so strong they're flying so high to when they get down to Louisiana, they hadn't got a gun to reach them anymore."

I said, "They got to stop. It's too much help." I said, "Used to, they just flew a little piece, landed, and ate again, flew to the next pond, landed, and ate again; a fellow could kill them." But I said, "Now they're just like these jet planes. Eating up here in Canada, feeding them all this corn, ducks are flying so high, they're going to have to shoot them with anti-aircraft guns!"

Rodney Cook: He mentioned, too, you could put your money in possums. You got a garbage barrel, you can go out there and get him.

Harold Talbert: That's right. The ducks will fly off and leave you, but the possums stay right here at home. You move out of the country and come to town—they come with you. All you got to bring is your garbage can.

Susan Roach: But you can eat duck.

Harold Talbert: Oh, you can eat these possums, too. It's a delicacy here. I have to tell you that. My grandmother used to cook them. They'd shave them and singe them like you do a roast pig. You don't skin a possum and then cook it in there. Get some sweet potatoes and it's good!

Susan Roach: Well, you boil it or what?

Harold Talbert: Well, I think they baked it. It was good.

Rodney Cook: Probably our biggest convert is the tax assessor. He ate possum every Thanksgiving, and we stopped that.

Julienne Cole: This is the preservation movement.

Rodney Cook: We're in the preservation business.

Julienne Cole: Susan, you misunderstood. Our whole purpose in being in Possum's Unlimited is to try to further these lovely creatures. They're sort of true-hearted. They'll stay home with you. Like Harold said, wherever your garbage can goes, you've got one.

Roseanne Lankford: Well, you're right in there with [Governor Buddy] Roemer and his plan, what is it? One product for each parish. Well, you probably have two, sweet potatoes and possums.

Harold Talbert: That's right. That's like the man told me. He said, we were riding down the road one day, and every time we'd pass a field I'd notice him tip his hat. We passed a nice field where there was some peas planted, he tipped his hat. I said, "What do you keep doing that for?"

He said, "Well, I tell you what. Whenever I see a patch of peas, I tip my hat." He said, "They kept me alive so long in the Depression to where I think I owe them some respect. Every time I pass by one of them, I tip my hat."

So I was the same way with the possums in North Louisiana. The good thing about them was, you go coon hunting you had to stay out all night, the dogs ran all over the country, you had to work the next day, you couldn't go back and get them. But if you went possum hunting and they treed it, he never got far up. You could always see him. He'd look right at you. A coon will look up and close his eyes. But a possum will stand there and look you right in the face. You didn't have to do a thing. You could even take a stick and knock him out.

So that's our mascot over there in Bienville Parish. It's hard times over there. We didn't ever come out of the Depression, we just go from one to the next. Some a little worse than other's. Good times in other places are just a mini-depression over there. So the possum and the peas, they have a big respect for them over there.

Rodney, I bought some possums at his auction. He has registered possums, stud possums. He gave me a big plaque and I have it at home hung up, and it was about the pedigree of this possum I bought. I believe his daddy was named Fast Fuzzy Rambler, and his mother was named Good Time Sally.

Rodney Cook: We advertised we were going to have a bull possum auction one year. We were just selling breeding rights, but the Wildlife Department took it kind of serious. They said, "If you all sell a possum, we're going to arrest you." We weren't actually selling them, but we didn't have any there. We took my brother's dog and we actually shaved his tail and left a little ball of fur.

Harold Talbert: They had a Catahoula and he was blue with white eyes. He looked good!

Rodney Cook: Yeah, that was Dudley. But the next year, we got an early start. I told the wildlife agent, we're going to sell possums this year. He said, "We're going to arrest you." I said, "That's what we want. Look at all the publicity we're going to get." Baton Rouge actually called me, a guy over in the Wildlife Department.

He said, "I'm going to send you a special permit to have some possums for two weeks in your possession. You're going to have to turn them loose."

But that's not what's funny. They paid three men to catch those possums, biologists from Ruston. I'd get to work every morning and these guys from Ruston would drive up with all these possums. Drop them off at the office!

Harold Talbert: We had that auction and the bidding was going pretty good. We sold those possums for about $60 a piece at first. Then the money kind of played out. So I told Rodney, I said, "You know, on a thoroughbred horse, they syndicate him. We're going to have to syndicate the rest of these bull possums here because we hadn't got anybody in this crowd whose got the money. We've already got all the money from the politicians, the sheriff, and the tax assessor, and the clerk of court. I said, "We're going to have to syndicate this possum." So I went around and got $5 bids. We got down low, we had to syndicate our possums. But we sold them, and Rodney gave some wonderful certificates. Told all about their mother and daddy and their background.

Rodney Cook: We'd always launch an expedition to search the swamps for the flying possum. And I had written that when we finally found that one, about throwing plastic persimmons down on the ground and attracting him. He came in to get it. Tube had the net and fell on the possum. That's why we had him mounted. We thought that was the last one.

I brought what's left of the flying possum in this box. We've had a lot of fun. You can imagine, for the last two weeks it's been in my house on top of the refrigerator. My wife doesn't really like that. People come in, they look up there and see that possum sitting up there.

Julienne Cole: Be sure and tell them what the name of it is, because this is real serious business here. Rodney is not fooling at all.

Rodney Cook: We got to name this possum, and it's Possa Delphi Airplanus; it's an original specimen.

Julienne Cole: Very Greek.

Rodney Cook: The original one was Snow White. It had wings and it stayed out in my shop. Mice did away with him; there's nothing but a little wire frame left and a lot of stuffing around him when I found him. But that's the flying possum.

Clarence Faulk: He looks like he came out of the dinosaur age.

Rodney Cook: He's from Bienville Parish. He lives right south of town. There's not too many of them. That's a long story. The [possum]—we were going to catch this one—[the guy who hunted him] threw a persimmon down, then he tried to catch him in a net, and he fell on him and mashed him. So we had to stuff it. But there's still a few around. We've never found another one. A few people not too reliable have seen them, you know. This one was originally spotted by a guy. There used to be a guy named Mr. Beck that slept on the hood of his car downtown across from City Hall. He saw this one night.

Clarence Faulk: Must've been a Saturday night. The Smithsonian Institution would want to get that.

Lonnie Gray: "They're All Lies"

BERNICE, UNION PARISH

Introduced by C. Renée Harvison

Fortunately, Susan Roach's roll of North Louisiana talkers did not end with Harold Talbert. Before giving me Harold's name, she told me about Lonnie Gray, whose work with folk crafts she had previously documented. Before Lonnie died in 1992, he wove white oak baskets and chair bottoms. But as he wove with his hands, he also wove oral narratives: some of the best and tallest tales heard in the piney hills of North Louisiana.

Lonnie Gray was born in Bernice in Union Parish in 1908. He farmed and then worked for the state Highway Department for thirty years, maintaining roads. When he retired, he needed something to do, so he learned how to make white oak baskets. Lonnie remembered that when he was a boy, his father made baskets for storing corn and cotton, as well as other gifts from the field. But he didn't pay the technique much mind. When Lonnie was seventy, he decided to make a basket, but it didn't sit square on the ground. So he went and visited a fellow in Bernice who had quit making baskets but still remembered how. Lonnie learned, and he said that "it got to where I couldn't keep enough baskets around."

He may not have had enough baskets to supply the demand, but he never seemed to run out of the stories he learned from back porch and kitchen talk while growing up. He told me that when he was a kid, the menfolk would sit around and try to out-tell each other. Lonnie listened, and soon he was swapping yarns with them as well. But as the years passed, most of his friends either died or moved away. Lonnie performed principally at festivals or for interested collectors like myself.

When I called him up and told him I wanted to hear his stories, he didn't even ask who I was. He simply said, "Come on by for a visit anytime, and I'll tell you some good ones." A first-time visitor to Lonnie's home should be equipped with a sense of direction, or of adventure, or both. After following a curvy road outside of Bernice on July 19, 1990, several sharp turns to the left and right, a battered wooden sign that read "Mt. Pisgah Church," and a dirt road that seemed to take me deeper into the depths of the Corney Creek woods, I found an unassuming Lonnie on his back patio carving some flowers out of maple branches. My brave trek into the woods was well worth the search, because I soon discovered that I had also found a five-star tall tale teller.

Mary and Lonnie Gary at their home in Bernice. Photo: Renée Harvison.

After some talk about his twenty-acre homestead, his homemade gourd bird-houses, his vegetable garden, his carving techniques, and the hot weather, Lonnie casually began to spin his yarns. As he talked, he carved from the maple branches. His wife, Mary, who has also passed away, got up to leave because she said she'd heard all of his stories many times over. But as Lonnie began to talk, she sat back down because he started off with an old cowboy story she'd never heard. "Don't think I've heard that one," she said. Neither had I, at least that day's version. Mary and I both learned that the same story is never told twice.

When I left that afternoon, I had collected from Lonnie both stories and a bouquet of beautiful hand-carved maple flowers.

15. The Bear-Riding Cowboy

I'll start off with an old cowboy story. There were two cowboys riding across the plains. Decided they'd stop and make some coffee. They had a bucket—that's what they made it in. A bucket. Pour water in that bucket, heat it, pour the coffee in there, and drink it.

Well, they stopped and got off their horses to make some coffee. They looked, and in the distance they saw dust coming at them. One of them said,

"I see somebody coming." He kept getting closer. About time they'd gotten the coffee hot, he rode up. He was riding—big, rough-looking fellow. He was riding a bear. And he had two rattlesnakes, one in each hand, whooping him, making him go.

He stopped, jumped off. They said, "Do you want some coffee?"

He grabbed up that bucket of hot coffee and drank some of it. He said, "Boys, I got to keep going. There's a tough fellow following me." Said, "I've got to get out of his way."

And got his rattlesnakes, got back up on that bear, whooped him, and made him go! [Laughs.]

Renée Harvison: Where did you hear that one?

Mary Gray: I never have heard that one!

Lonnie Gray: Oh, I don't know. [Laughs.] I've heard them all my life. I've heard my daddy tell them. You might not understand some of them.

16. A Smart Bear

I'll tell you another one about a bear. Fellow had a field of corn. It was getting ready to eat. He got to missing some of it. Something was getting some of it. So he got down there one morning to watch and see what was coming and getting his corn. He got down and sat down by a tree.

An old, big black bear come in there and got to pulling corn, putting it in his arms. You know, a bear can walk straight up. He got him an armful of it, and he watched him to see what he was going to do with it.

He followed him. Stayed to where he couldn't see him. He had caught one of them old pine-rooter hogs. You know what they are, don't you? An old hog. He'd caught one of them and put him in a hollow stump, and he was so poor, he was too poor to eat. He was feeding him, fattening him up. Getting him fat enough to eat. He was feeding him that corn.

17. A Man-Eating Varmint

I'll tell you about one. A fellow in Louisiana went up, his family went up, to the Ozarks on vacation. He got up there late in the evening, camped at the foot of a mountain. Next morning he got up early. He carried his motorcycle with him. Mountain went right straight up. It was an old cripple lived up in that mountain—never had been out of it. Been up there all his life. Had a little trail.

[The fellow] started up that trail on his motorcycle. This old fellow that lived up there—he was sitting on the porch, his wife sitting back in the house. He told his wife, said, "Ma, I hear some kind of animal coming up the mountain, some kind of varmint." Said, "Bring me my shotgun."

Never had seen a motorcycle. So this fellow rode up in front of the house on that motorcycle, and that fellow shot him. Cut down on him. He jumped off the motorcycle. The motorcycle went one way, the man went the other way!

Man's wife said, "Pa, did you kill him?"

Said, "Naw, but I made him turn that man loose!" [Laughs.]

Renée Harvison: Did your family tell a lot of these stories?

Lonnie Gray: Well, used to. A lot of people used to.

18. The Mean Mountaineer

There was another old man that lived up in the Ozarks. He was mean. Meanest old fellow around there. He got sick. They carried him down to the little river that came down through the mountains and baptized him. He was so mean that it killed the fish for a hundred yards down that river when they baptized him. He went back home, and a little while later he got sick and died. Well, they buried him, his neighbors. They put him in a casket and started out the yard. Had a yard gate. Went through that yard gate, bumped a corner of the casket, and the lid flew off. He jumped out and went back in the house and got back in the bed!

Went on a while and he died *again*. They went back and got him and put him in the casket. Started out the yard and out the gate. This old mountaineer's wife was sitting on the porch. She said, "Now you all watch that gate this time!" She wanted to get rid of him.

Mary Gray: She was wanting him to be put in the ground.

Lonnie Gray: She was wanting to get rid of him! I'll tell you about—

19. A Rattlesnake Tale (by Mary Gray)

Mary Gray: Well, I want to tell one first, then I'm going into the house. Way back yonder, people didn't have any fears. They just went to bed and left the doors and windows open. This woman woke up during the night; something was cold to her back. She told her husband, "Get up and get the scissors and cut my gown, the sleeves all the way from me. Then grab me out of this bed." And he did, and it was a rattlesnake.

Renée Harvison: It was a rattlesnake?

Mary Gray: At her back.

Renée Harvison: Is that true?

Mary Gray: Well, that's what my grandmother used to tell me.

Lonnie Gray: It's all jokes! [Laughs.]

Mary Gray: It could have been true. You see, he was hunting a warm place, and he found a warm place up against her back.

20. It Was So Cold

Lonnie Gray: You were saying something about the geese carrying the pond. Well, a farmer had a nice pond. And in the wintertime, it began to turn cold one evening, real cold. Just about dark, a big drove of geese come over and lit in that pond. It was about dark. Everything froze over that night. It had turned freezing cold.

Fellow decided he'd go down there and shoot a few of them out of there before they got off. Geese'd come through and stop. Well he got down there with his gun and began to shoot them. They couldn't get their feet out of there. They began to flop their wings. They all got to flopping their wings together and they carried that pond off! Carried it off.

Renée Harvison: Now, did you see that happen?

Lonnie Gray: [Laughs hard.]

Renée Harvison: I believe it!

Mary Gray: I don't!

Renée Harvison: You got anymore tall tales like that?

Mary Gray: Shoot! He's made of them!

21. How the Farmer Saved His Pigs

Lonnie Gray: A fellow, a farmer, had an old hog sow. She had eight pigs. She was running out in the field. One night, she come up about dark, and she didn't have her pigs with her. He couldn't figure what happened to his pigs. It had got dark.

So the next morning, he got out looking for them, and over by the back side of the place, there was an old well. Been there a long time, an old, dried-up well. Didn't have any water in it. They'd fell in that well. Them pigs. He couldn't figure how he was going to get them out of there. But he had a good milk cow, an old Holstein cow, give lots of milk. So he got her over there, got her straddled over that well, and milked that well full of milk and floated them pigs out.

Mary Gray: Oh shoot! That was some cow, wasn't it?

22. They Buried Her Too Soon (by Mary Gray)

Mary Gray: I know one more. There was a man's wife, and just he and his daughter, grown daughter, and the woman lived together. Well the woman died, and they buried her. That night after supper, they was sitting there, and some grave diggers—stealers, you know, people that rob graves—had gone and dug her up. And her finger was swollen, and they couldn't get the ring off—so they was going to cut it off.

When they did, she flinched. She told them, says, "Now I know who you all are. If you all just take me home, I'll never tell anybody."

So they carried her home. She went walking in. He said, "If your mama wasn't dead, I'd say that was her."

And she went walking in the door.

My grandmother told it. I always thought it was true.

23. Even After Death Did Them Part

Lonnie Gray: You've heard of hen-pecked husbands.

Mary Gray: He's one of them!

Lonnie Gray: What?

Renée Harvison: She said you're one of them!

Lonnie Gray: Oh! [Laughs.] Well, this hen-pecked husband, he died and went to heaven. Got up there and run up on Saint Peter. He told him where to go—the gate down there, wasn't anybody down there. Somebody come along and asked the man, "What you doing standing off down here at this gate all by yourself?"

He said, "Well, my wife told me to come here when I died. So that's where I'm at." [Laughs.] He was doing what she said to.

24. It Was So Hot

Lonnie Gray: I'll tell you one about hot weather. Several years ago it was real hot and dry. One day I walked out to take a look at my garden about one o'clock. Hot, about 95 degrees. It was pretty sandy in my garden. I noticed a lizard crawling through that sand. He had a forked stick in his mouth. I was wondering. I'd just watch him to see what he was going to do with that forked stick. That sand would get so hot to his feet that he'd stick that stick in the ground, crawl up in that fork, let his feet cool off, then he'd get down and go again.

25. Lonnie's First Trip to Town

I'll tell you about the first time I ever come to Bernice. I was about, you know, when we was growing up, kids didn't get to come to town until they were seven or eight years old. I was about seven years old, and my daddy let me come to town with him in a wagon. Well, you know, now you have to watch out for cars, not walk in front of a car. But then, they'd teach you not to walk behind a mule or he'd kick you. Mules was all over the town here—and wagons. They'd caution you about not walking behind them mules when you went to town. It wasn't any cars then.

So I come to town with my daddy one day—and the drugstore, the old drugstore, I saw people coming out of there with ice cream. Eating ice cream. I looked at them, and I couldn't figure it all out. I didn't know what that was they had it in. So the next time I come, I got my daddy to give me a nickel and buy me an ice cream. I went in the drugstore there, and he filled it up, I mean he stacked it up high on that cone. I didn't know what a [ice] cream cone was then.

I come on outside, and I ate that cream down; he'd piled it up high. I eat it down to that cream cone, and I looked at that thing, and I didn't think it'd be good to eat. So I held it a few minutes, and I drank it. Melted. I threw that thing down on the ground, but the next time I was here, I watched another fellow who went in there and got him a cream cone. He come out, and I watched him and he eat that cone! So I've been eating ice cream cones ever since. That's how ignorant we was back then. We didn't know anything.

26. The Big Fish of Corney Creek

Lonnie Gray: I spent a lot of time on Corney Creek. One time we was down there fishing, and we was in a boat. We was floating down the creek, you know, and we stopped and fished a little bit.

We noticed and looked, and there was a big fish come up to the top of the water on the side of the boat there. We sat there and looked at him just a little bit. He was a big one! And after a while, he batted his eyes and made such a wave that he sunk that boat.

Mary Gray: Now, I hadn't ever heard that one.

Renée Harvison: She said she'd heard all your stories!

Mary Gray: I did say that, didn't I?

27. Another Big Fish Story

Lonnie Gray: I heard another one about a big fish, a gar. You know what a gar is. They can get big. Well, a fellow caught one in a net, got him out and put him in the wagon, brought him home. The scales were big things. They scaled that gar, and they used the scales for shingles and covered a four-room house.

28. The Devil Made Her Say It

Renée Harvison: You ever tell any preacher jokes?

Lonnie Gray: No, not too many of them. Well, I know one preacher story. The black people were having like a revival, and this preacher announced one day that he was going to cut the devil's tail off right behind his head. So that night, one of the members, he dressed up like the devil, horns and all.

There was one old lady that come there in a wheelchair. They rolled her up in the church, in the wheelchair. The preacher got to preaching. He said, "I'm going to cut the devil's tail off right behind his head!" About the time he said that, the fellow come walking in, had the horns on, dressed like the devil. All the members went out of the church. Preacher went out the back door.

This old lady couldn't go. Couldn't get out. He come walking on up to her. She said, "Mr. Devil, I come to church here every Sunday, but I've been on your side the whole time!"

29. How to Get a Mule's Attention

I'll tell you one about a mule. You don't know anything about mules, how contrary they was. This old colored fellow, he sold a mule. Used to plow mules. The colored fellow that bought him said he wouldn't plow. And he went and told this fellow, he said, "That mule I bought from you," he said, "he won't plow."

[The old fellow] said, "I'll go over there with you. You've got to get his attention." He went over there; the mule was standing over there, wouldn't move. This colored fellow picked up a limb and knocked him down. Mule got up and went on plowing.

Fellow said, "You just got to get his attention!" Mules was contrary, they sure was.

30. A Heaven Joke

I'll tell you one about Church of Christ. A Baptist died, and he went up to heaven, come up on Saint Peter. He was carrying him around.

You know Church of Christ, most of them think ain't nobody going to heaven but them. Well, they passed by a big building. This fellow asked Saint Peter, said, "What kind of people in there?"

He said, "Be quiet." He said, "Them's Church of Christ. They don't think there's anybody else here but them."

31. A Home Run Inside the Hog

I'll tell you one about a baseball game we played. You know, every community used to have a ball team. We'd play ball every Saturday evening. One Saturday, when it was hot, in July, we was playing ball in a cow pasture. That's where we played, in the cow pasture. So we used dry cow chips for the first, second, and third bases and a stick of wood for the home plate.

Well, we was playing out there about three o'clock one evening. An old, tall boy come up in about the third inning. The fellow that owned this pasture, he had a hog pen out past center field. He had hogs in the pen, way out behind center field. This old boy come up about the third inning, and the pitcher throwed him one.

He hit that ball, and it went over the center fielder, went over the center fielder's head and hit the ground and bounced into that hog pen. The old sow run up and grabbed that ball up and chewed it up and swallowed it. The center fielder never come back, and the umpire went out to find out what happened.

That center fielder said, "That old sow chewed that ball up and swallowed it."

The umpire went back, and he ruled that it was a home run inside the hog!

Wilson "Ben Guiné" Mitchell: Creole Tales

PARKS, ST. MARTIN PARISH

Introduced by Barry Jean Ancelet

In January 1974, I began collecting folktales in collaboration with Barbara F. Ryder, who was involved in a monthlong individual study project as a student of Colby College. It soon became obvious to us that the discovery of traditional oral performance of Louisiana French folklore required a fair amount of intensive fieldwork. What we had naively expected to be a "cakewalk" proved to be a complex research project. Accordingly, we foraged around the countryside in the Lafayette area searching for the elusive storytellers and singers.

On a lead from Richard Guidry, a teacher in the St. Martin Parish bilingual program, we went to Parks, where there was supposedly an abundance of black Creole storytellers in a section of town on the east bank of Bayou Teche referred to locally as the "Promised Land." We faithfully sought out the persons on our list of potential informants, but to no avail. Disheartened, we paused on the road to regroup our forces. We asked a group of young black children for directions, and the quickest one persuaded us to take him along for the ride. Our last hope also proved to be a "dry hole." As we were leaving the house, however, our perceptive young guide exclaimed, "My grandfather knows some old stories." He took us to his house where we met Wilson Mitchell, better known in the community by his nickname, Ben Guiné, who proved to be a masterful storyteller and easily one of our most impressive finds of the month.

Despite our protests, Ben Guiné immediately abandoned a plate of steaming crawfish étouffée, took his place in the living room, and assumed the role of oral entertainer—a role obviously not unfamiliar to him. Our party of three had varying degrees of competence in his native Creole dialect, but we were all immediately swept away by his extraordinary style. For Ben Guiné, storytelling was not just a tradition of memory. Here was truly active performer, complete with gestures, exceptional oral ability, and an uncanny sense of timing.

Ben Guiné was truly an artist in oral performance. He was acutely aware of his craft. This, however, did not prevent him from enjoying his experience as much as anyone else. Most noticeable in his performance was his engaging laughter at the end of almost every story. In addition to indicating the end of an oral text to those in

At his home in Parks in St. Martin Parish, storyteller Wilson "Ben Guiné" Mitchell shares Creole animal tales with folklorist Barry Ancelet and Toute Mitchell. Photo: Caroline Ancelet.

the audience who sometimes are lost in the heavy Creole, Ben Guiné's laughter also expressed his genuine appreciation of the storytelling experience.

    True to the generally held notion of black Creole storytelling in French Louisiana—fostered since Alcée Fortier's groundbreaking, century-old collection (1895), dominated by Creole animal tales—one, one of the first stories Ben Guiné related was an animal tale involving Bouki and Lapin. This tale was Guiné's version of the well-known Ant and the Lazy Cricket (AT 249). His forceful style is apparent in *the beginning when he handily disposes of Richard Guidry's attempt to suggest the French word for grasshopper. It is also noteworthy that the Grasshopper's musicianship is adapted to the French Louisiana region: he plays the accordion. Ben Guiné's interpretation of the story is striking in its down-home simplicity.*

Still thinking in terms of animal tales, Ben Guiné began a second tale about Bouki and Lapin. Since he had already used the usual briar patch escape ending in an earlier tale of the session, Guiné surprised us by ending his story with Lapin hopelessly stuck to Bouki's tarbaby trap. When asked about this unusual turn of events, Guiné deftly explained that it was high time Lapin was caught.

After telling a few animal tales, Guiné turned to another oral genre. Often called "John and Old Master stories" in African-American tradition, this genre focuses on the relationship between the crafty black servant and the plantation owner or boss. In this tale, the boss ridicules the servant for believing that animals can talk. He then hears for himself that it is possible—twice—and reacts in a manner unbecoming of a plantation boss seeking to debunk superstition.

Later visits with Ben Guiné produced other stories, including "Vieux Nèg et Vieux Blanc té gain une course." *In this story about how the black man came to work in the fields and the white man in the books, Guiné takes on the racial issue from both sides at once. The wholesale cheating that goes on during the race and the greed that causes the winner to take the larger sack filled with tools give a rather misanthropic picture on the surface, but the reader should know that Guiné laughed heartily throughout the telling, demonstrating that there can be humor even in the most pitiful circumstances, even if it is a matter of laughing to keep from crying. In* "Métayer Joe," *the servant charged with safeguarding the corn reserves steals from his master. When he is later caught, no one pities him. This story deftly demonstrates the master's growing loss of confidence as he begins to unravel Joe's story with a series of questions. He eventually catches him in a trap and leaves him to suffer in his misery and shame before banishing him.*

What made Ben Guiné a great storyteller was not the nature of his repertoire but his mastery of verbal art. His performance is impossible to render solely through transcription. He made effective use of vocal inflection and pause, and his timing was flawless. Even in recording, much was lost, especially his many gestures and facial expressions. To appreciate Ben Guiné fully as a storyteller, a personal encounter was essential and usually welcomed by him. While being filmed for a video-documentary on storytelling in America, with many of his neighbors around admiring the proceedings, he intimated to me that he relished having someone pay attention to his stories after such a long time. As I had discovered the first night we met, Ben Guiné would even leave a plate of crawfish étouffée for the chance to tell a few stories. When Ben Guiné died, Louisiana lost one of its greatest narrators.

32. Froumi et Grasshopper (The Ant and the Grasshopper)

Ah, well, *et ça semble vrai, tout ça, vous comprends? Une froumi travaille tout l'été. Il t'apé ramasser des quoi et pi il emplit une maison. Il mandé Grasshopper, comme ça, li dit, "Comment ça se fait to viens pas aider moi? Mo pourras donne toi quelque chose."*

"O!" Grasshopper dit, "O non!" Li dit, "Moi, mo pas gain le temps pour embêter avec toi!" Li dit, "Mo joue l'accordéon pour mon living."

Froumi dit, "All right, go ahead, *mais," li dit, "mo va, quand li parti, sauterelle, commencer mettre du manger à côté." Li met.*

Et là, well, *quand ça rivé dans l'hiver, il y avait la glace. Tout quelque chose té glacé! Vous comprends ça? Tout quelque chose té glacé! Froumi, li té dans sa maison.*

Li cogné, "Tac, tac, tac."

Li dit, "Hé, hé, hé, who's there?"

Li dit, "C'est moi, Grasshopper, let me in!"

Li dit, "To pas connais comment mo dis toi dans l'été-là? Mo travaille avec vous autres." Et li dit, "T'étais apé jouer la musique." Li dit, "O, poor Grasshopper, go and play for your living!" *Li frémé sa petite porte, Kabô! Li té couché dans sa maison et Grasshopper té gelé. Yé trouvé li en haut les cannes maïs. C'est pas vrai, ça? Hein?*

Li travaille tout le temps l'été, mais quand ça fait froid, vous p'alé oir li. Vous peux passer en haut où li gain nique-là. Li dans sa maison, li. Mais

Ah well, and this seems true, you understand? An ant works all summer long. He was gathering things to fill his house. He asked Grasshopper, this way, he said, "Why don't you come help me? I could give you something."

"Oh!" Grasshopper said, "Oh no!" He said, "I don't have the time to bother with you!" He said, "I play the accordion for a living."

Ant said, "All right, go ahead, but," he said, "I'm going, when the grasshopper is gone, to start putting food away." He did.

And then, well, when winter arrived, there was ice. Everything was frozen! You understand? Everything was frozen! Ant was in his house.

He knocked, "Tac, tac, tac."

He said, "Hey, hey, hey, who's there?"

He said, "It's I, Grasshopper, let me in!"

He said, "Don't you remember what I told you during the summer? I would work with you." And he said, "You were playing music." He said, "Oh, poor Grasshopper, go and play for your living!" He closed his little door. *Kabo!* He was in bed in his house and Grasshopper was frozen. They found him on top of the corn stalks. Isn't that true? Eh?

The ant works all summer long, but when it's cold, you won't see him. You can pass right above his nest. He's in his house. But Grasshopper,

Grasshopper, li dans l'été, c'est là li n-homme. C'est là li n-homme. Ça apé jouer, mais quand ça fait frette-là, li gelé. Li voulait rentrer, mais Froumi dit li, "O non! Peux pas vini. O non!" Et ça semble vrai, hein? Il n'y a rien qu'est plus malin qu'une froumi, mais ça qu'est plus bête qu'un grasshopper?

during the summertime, that's when he's a man. That's when he's a man. He's playing, but when it's cold, he freezes. He wanted to come inside, but Ant told him, "Oh no! You can't come in. Oh no!" And it seems true, eh? There's nothing more clever than an ant, but what's more stupid than a grasshopper?"

33. Le petit bonhomme en Coal Tar (The Little Tar-Man)

Ouais, mais Bouki té gain un jardin. Li acheté un homme, et fait un petit n-homme en coal tar *dans le milieu du jardin.*

Ah, well, Bouki vient, li gardé comme ça-là. Lapin vient, li gardé comme ça-là. Li hélé li, li dit, "Qui c'est ça, cil-là?"

A rien répond pas.

"O!" li dit, "c'est bligé d'être quelque chose de malicieux que Bouki rangé moi." Li dit, "M'alé couri apé li, n-homme."

Quand il a arrivé là-là, il sacré gaillard-là un coup de poing. Kabô! Ça c'était les jambes en bas, vous comprends? Li dit, "Moi dis toi lâcher moi, moi té toi!"

C'est comme ça!

"Moi dis toi lâcher moi, moi gain l'autre oui! Moi dis toi lâcher moi, moi gain l'autre, oui!" Li piqué un autre coup encore! Li lâchait pas, li restait collé! Li restait collé! Li . . . Là, li voyé la tête, tout quelque chose restait collé comme ça-là.

Ah ouais, mais Bouki toujours

Yes, well, Bouki had a garden. He bought a mannikin and made a little man out of coal tar in the middle of the garden.

Ah, well, Bouki came, he looked like this. Lapin came, he looked like that. He called to him [the mannikin], he said, "Who's this?"

Nothing answered.

"Oh!" he said, "this must be some evil things that Bouki has prepared for me." He said, "I'll go to him, this man."

When he arrived there, he hit the guy with his fist. *Kabo!* That was his legs, you know? He said, "I'm telling you to let me go, if I were you!"

That's how it was!

"I'm telling you to let me go, I have another! I'm telling you to let me go, I have another." He stung him again! He didn't let go. He stayed stuck! He stayed stuck! He—then, he hit him with his head, everything stayed stuck like that.

Oh yes, but Bouki always came

resté en arrière. *Lapin sorti devant.*

Richard Guidry: *Mais cette fois-là-là, Bouki sorti en avant!*

Ben Guiné: *Ouais, mais, li sorti en avant, mais li tient bon li, vous comprends ça? Bien là, c'était temps pour trapé Lapin, vous comprends? C'était passé. C'était temps pour trapé li! C'est pas une affaire, non. Pas jouer avec Lapin, non!*

out behind. Lapin always came out ahead.

Richard Guidry: But that time, Bouki came out ahead!

Ben Guiné: Yes, well, he came out ahead, but he had him, you understand? Well, then, it was high time to catch Lapin, you understand? It was past time. It was time to catch him! That was really something. You can't play with Lapin!

34. O, Fiva! (Oh, Fiva!)

Il y avait un boss, *un gros boss d'une grosse habitation, grosse habitation. Et il té travaillé tous les mulets. Il té gain à peu près . . . cinquante et quelques* teams. *Il y avait tous des vieux boug,' des vieux nèg-là, qui labouraient tout la semaine. C'est manière comme l'esclavage, vous comprends?*

Ah well, *il té gain un vieux nèg qui té donné manger les mulets, tu comprends? Ah well, tous les dimanches, il té gain un vieux mulet, c'était toujours so kèn tour. C'était jamais les autres! Li té toujours apé travailler, vieux mulet a toujours travaillé. Les autres té tous assis apé* enjoy *eux-mêmes manger.*

Et Vieux Nèg a vu le même. Li couri là, li couri là, li tourné back. *Li dit, li couri au ras là, li hélé,* "O, Fiva!"

Fiva dit, li dit, "Ça to lé?" *Mais li dit,* "mo pas aller aujourd'hui!"

Vieux Nèg a couté ça. Té gain

There was a boss, a big boss on a big farm, big farm. And they worked all the mules. There were about . . . fifty or so teams. There were a lot of old guys, old black men, who worked all week long. This was like slavery time, you understand?

Ah well, there was one old black man who fed the mules, you understand? Ah well, every Sunday, there was one old mule, and it was always his turn. Never the others! He was always working, the old mule worked all the time. The others were all sitting around enjoying themselves and eating.

And the old black man saw the same one. He went there, and came back. He said, he went over there and yelled, "Oh Fiva!"

Fiva said, "What do you want?" And he said, "I'm not going today!"

The old black man listened to this.

un de ces grosses chiques tabac. Li coupé paquet de tabac en deux. En deux! Li va. Li retourné back. Li dit ça à so boss, li dit, "Maître," li dit, "ça to crois c'est? Mo couri pour hélé à Fiva. Fiva dit moi li pas aller couri beau matin. Li travaille pas. C'est jamais so kèn tour."

"O," Boss a dit, "Va donc, toi. To fou, toi!"

"Mais," li dit, "All right!"

Boss-là part. Li parti, Vieux Boss-là. Li parti ayoù tous les autres-là dînaient. Li hélé. Et li dit à so ti chien [sifflements]. Li pélé ti chien-là Gyp. Li dit, "O, Fiva!"

Li dit, "Si mo vas, to vas mourir à soir, toi!"

Tonnerre m'écrase! Boss a parti galoper comme ça-là, c'était un assassin. Et li va arrêter en bas un ti n'arbre, à force li té gain chaud. Li té apé venter à so chapeau. Ti chien té accroupi au ras li.

Li dit, "Hot dog, c'est première fois mo vois une bêtaille causer."

Ti chien a dit, comme ça-là, "Moi aussi!" Tonnere! Ça a parti, et ça a parti. Yé té parti chacun ses côtés.

He had one of those big chews of tobacco. He cut that pack of tobacco in two. In two! He went. He came back. He told this to his boss, he said, "Master," he said, "what do you think is going on? I went to yell for Fiva. Fiva told me he was not going this morning. He's not working. It's always his turn."

"Oh," Boss said. "Go on, you. You're crazy!"

"Well," he said, "all right."

Boss left. Old Boss left. He went where all the others were eating. He yelled. And he called his little dog. [Whistles.] His little dog was named Gyp. [Boss] said, "Oh, Fiva!"

[Fiva] said, "If I go today, you'll die tonight!"

May thunder crush me! Boss took off running as though there were an assassin. And he stopped under a little tree, he was so hot. He was fanning himself with his hat. The little dog was crouched next to him.

He said, "Hot dog, that's the first time I hear an animal speak."

The little dog said, "Me, too!" Thunder! They took off again. They took off each in his own direction.

35. Vieux Nèg et Vieux Blanc té gain une course (An Old Black Man and an Old White Man Had a Race)

Well, il y avait un nèg, un vieux nèg avec un vieux blanc. Yé té gain une course. Il té gain ça dans gazette. Il té affiché tout le monde. Il y avait vieux nèg-là

Well, there was a black man—an old black man—and an old white man. They had a race. They announced it in the papers. They advertised it to everyone. There was

et vieux blanc. Yé té gain une course.

Là, well, *vieux nèg et vieux blanc-là, yé parti. Yé sorti de dans le* chute. *T'étais apé tendé les nègs et les blancs, "Hé, Monsieur Tom Jones! Hé, Monsieur Foff!"*

Vieux Nèg est parti la course. Li dit, "Lord, Lord!" Vieux Nèg-là tourné en arrière. Vieux Nèg té juste devant Vieux Blanc-là. Vieux Blanc-là té tombé par terre. Vieux Nèg-là té passé on *li.*

Quand Vieux Nèg arrivé au bout des sept arpents, blanc a passé. Vieux Nèg a passé devant blanc-là. Li fout vieux blanc une jambette, vieux n-homme-là tombé par terre.

Quand vieux nèg arrivé là-bas, li té gain un de ces gros sacs. Li té gain un gros sac. Là, li té gain un vieux petite affaire comme ça. Li té pélé ses partners. *Li dit, "Venez aider moi." Les autres vieux macaques-là, yé té tous campés à côté. Yé vini là. Vieux Nèg-là té gagné. Yé té hélé, "Hééé! Li gagné! Li gagné!"*

Ça to crois il y avait en dedans-là? Des vieilles charrues, des vieilles pioches . . . Il y avait pas de vieilles affaires qu'il té pas gain!

Blanc-là vini. Li ramassé vieux petite affaire-là. Il té gain un livre avec un crayon—pour lire et écrire. Là, vieux blanc-là, li té là, mais vieux nèg-là té gain pour couri dans le clos. Li té misérable toute sa vie.

Hein? C'est pas vrai, ça?

the old black man and the old white man. They had a race.

Then, well, the old black man and the old white man took off. They took off out of the chute. You could hear the blacks and the whites, "Hey, Mister Tom Jones! Hey, Mister Foff!"

The old black man took off running. He said, "Lord, Lord!" The old black man turned around. The old black man was just in front of the old white man. The old white man had fallen down. The old black man had passed over him.

When the old black man had covered seven arpents, the white man passed him. The old black man got back in front. He tripped the old white man, and he fell down.

When the old black man arrived, there was one of those big sacks. There was a big sack. Then there was a little old thing like this. He called his friends. He said, "Come and help me." The other old fools were all around. They came. The old black man had won. They yelled, "Heeey! He won! He won!"

What do you think was in there? Some old plows, some old hoes . . . There weren't just any old tools that weren't in there!

The white man came. He picked up the little old sack. There was a book and a pencil—to read and write. Then, the old white man, he was there, but the old black man had to go into the fields. He was miserable all his life.

Eh? Is this not true?

36. Métayer Joe (Joe the Overseer)

Et là, well, *il y avait un vieux nèg, li té resté dans la cour d'un vieux blanc. Vieux blanc té gain confiance en vieux nèg-là. Yé té appelé vieux nèg Métayer. Vieux nèg té gain toutes les clefs à vieux blanc. Vieux blanc té pas tracassé. Yé té gain plusieurs nèg qu'apé travailler, to comprends? Quand yé té parlé pour vieux nèg, yé parlé pour quelque chose!*

Li dit à vieux blanc, "Ah! Li tel comme ma femme," parce que vieux nèg, ça, c'était un vieux nèg qui droite. Li pas dans des bêtises. Li té gain toutes les clefs de magasin.

Li dit à vieux nèg, "Joe! O, Joe!"

Joe pas répond.

Li dit, "Joe!"

Joe pas répond.

"O, Joe!" Li dit, "Ça semble comme mon maïs apé manquer ici, Joe."

Joe répond li, "Le maïs apé manquer dans le magasin?"

Li dit, "O, Joe."

Li dit, "Non. T'apé fait un mistake. N'a pas maïs qu'apé manquer icitte."

"Mais," li dit, "oui, magasin apé baisser."

Li dit, "Non."

Li dit, "Qui c'est ça qu'apé baisser li comme ça, Joe?"

Joe dit, "C'est les rats qu'apé baisser comme ça."

So then, well, there was an old black man. He lived in an old white man's yard. The old white man had lots of confidence in the old black man. They called the old black man Métayer. The old black man had all the old white man's keys. The old white man wasn't worried. There were several black men working, you understand? When they spoke of the old black man, they were speaking of someone important!

He said to the old white man, "Ah! He's just like my wife," because the old black man was straight. He wasn't involved in foolishness. He had all the keys to the store.

He said to the old black man, "Joe! Oh, Joe!"

Joe didn't answer.

He said, "Joe!"

Joe didn't answer.

"Oh, Joe!" He said, "It seems that some of my corn is missing here, Joe."

Joe answered him, "Some corn is missing in the store?"

He said, "Yes, Joe."

He said, "No. You're making a mistake. There's no corn missing here."

"But," he said, "yes, the store is going down."

He said, "No."

He said, "What is lowering it like that, Joe?"

Joe said, "It's the rats that are lowering it like that."

"Mais," li dit, "les rats! Mais jamais. Les rats apé manger maïs même. Ça même," li dit. Li dit, "Ça c'est une chose mo comprends pas!"

Li dit, "To peux croire ça m'apé dit toi. Mo vois gros rat à peu près haut comme ça."

"Mais," li dit, "pourquoi to pas appélé moi, Joe?"

Li dit, "Mo pas voulu réveillé toi. Mo eu peur."

Li dit, "A quelle heure to vois ça, Joe?"

Li dit, "Une heure après minuit."

"Mais," li dit, "Joe, to apé pas dormi encore?"

"Mais," Joe dit, "Quand mo entend le train, mo couri guetter."

Li dit, "Ta vieille voit ça?"

Joe dit, "Non."

Li dit, "Pourquoi to pas réveillé la vieille? To sé gain témoin de ça."

Li dit, "Non, mo pas voulu réveiller ma vieille. C'est juste mo qui vois ça."

Li dit, "Okay, Joe." Li dit, "Mo fini avec ça, ouais, Joe." Lit dit, "Laisse yé manger toujours, Joe."

Ça to crois li fait? Li té gain un ces grosses trappes-là, aussi gros qu'il y avait moyen. Joe té gain un trou. Quand vieux n-homme t'apé dormi, li té couri là, li té prendre tout le maïs que li té oulé. Li t'apé vendre tout le voisinage maïs. Mieux que ça, li t'apé fini vieux n-homme-là. C'est li qui té gain toutes les clefs.

Li dit à sa vieille, "Well, well,

"But," he said, "rats! Hardly. Rats eating the corn. Imagine," he said. He said, "That's something I don't understand!

He said, "You can believe what I'm telling you. I saw a big rat about this big."

"Well," he said, "why didn't you call me, Joe?"

He said, "I didn't want to wake you. I was afraid."

He said, "At what time did you see this, Joe?"

He said, "One hour after midnight."

"Well," he said, "Joe, you weren't sleeping?"

"Well," he said, "when I heard the noise, I ran to look."

He said, "Did your wife see this?"

Joe said, "No."

He said, "Why didn't you wake your wife? You would have a witness to this."

He said, "No, I didn't want to wake my wife. Only I saw this."

He said, "Okay, Joe." He said, "I'm done with this, Joe." He said, "Let them go on eating, Joe."

What do you think he did? He had one of those big traps, the biggest around. Joe had a hole. When the old man was sleeping, he would go there, and he would take all the corn he wanted. He was selling corn to the entire neighborhood. Better still, he was ruining the old man. He had all the keys.

He said to his wife, "Well, well,

m'aller connaître ça qu'apé prendre mon maïs." Li met cette grosse trappe droite dans le trou. Une heure après minuit, Joe té là avec tous ses hommes qui té vend maïs. Joe fourré sa main dans le trou. To entends, Kabô! Joe commencé héler les cris.

La vieille a dit, "Hé! M'apé entendre des cris au magasin."

Li dit, "Non, non. Laisse li héler jusqu'à jour." Li dit, "m'a connaître qui c'est ça il est. Mo pas aller dans la nuit."

La vieille dit, "Va donc voir ça qu'apé héler les cris. L'apé héler à tous les saints pour mander Bon Dieu pour aider li, qui li pris dans la trappe."

Li dit, "Non!"

Li laissé le jour ouvert sûr, pour tout le monde voir qui c'est li est. Quand li arrivé, li regardé Joe té là avec son bras pris dans le magasin, dans le trou, avec cinq maïs. Li dit, "Joe, mo té gain confiance en toi, Joe." Li dit, "Regarde ça to fais mo, Joe. Il y a longtemps t'apé ruiner moi comme ça, Joe." Li dit, "Mo crois m'aller quitter toi pour quelque temps encore."

La femme dit, "Jules, ôte donc li là, s'il toi plaît." La trappe té gain son bras près coupé.

Li dit, "Joe, c'est honteux pour toi. Mo payé toi, Joe. Regarde to gain moi." Li dit, "M'a lâcher toi. Mo pas oulé voir toi sur ma place du tout!"

I'm going to find out what's taking my corn." He put that big trap right inside the hole. One hour after midnight, Joe was there with all his men who sold corn. Joe stuck his hand in the hole. You heard, *Kabo!* Joe started yelling.

The old woman said, "Hey! I hear cries from the store."

He said, "No, no. Let him yell until dawn." He said, "I want to know who he is. I'm not going in the night."

The old woman said, "Please go see who is yelling. He's yelling to all the saints to ask God to help him who is caught in the trap."

He said, "No!"

He waited until the sun was up, for all to see who it was. When he arrived, he saw that Joe was there with his arm stuck in the store, in the hole with five ears of corn. He said, "Joe, I trusted you, Joe." He said, "Look at what you've done to me, Joe. You've been ruining me for a long time, Joe." He said, "I think I'll leave you there for a while longer."

The woman said, "Jules, take him out of there, please." The trap had almost cut his arm off.

He said, "Joe, it's a shame for you. I paid you, Joe. Look at where you've gotten me." He said, "I'm letting you go. I don't want to see you on my land at all!"

Bel Abbey: Koasati Stories

ELTON, JEFFERSON DAVIS PARISH

*Introduced by C. Renée Harvison
and Maida Owens*

Northof Elton off of Highway 190, about three miles down a country road, lies the Koasati (or Coushatta) community. The Koasati are one of Louisiana's larger Native American groups, numbering about four hundred persons. Their ties to Louisiana date back to the late eighteenth century, when the tribe came from Alabama and crossed the Mississippi River to settle in villages near the present Arkansas-Louisiana border. By the middle of the nineteenth century they had made several settlements in Louisiana and Texas. Today the Koasati are concentrated in an area near Beaumont, in East Texas, and in southwest Louisiana near Elton, in Allen Parish. Although long and close contacts with European Americans have influenced their culture significantly, the Koasati still strongly retain many of their native traditions, including their foodways, crafts, native tongue, and stories.

Bel Abbey was one who clearly maintained his identity, but not at the expense of separating himself or his family from outsiders. Until his death on January 21, 1992, Bel and his family shared their culture with anyone willing to watch and listen. They participated in several of the state's festivals and worked closely with the Louisiana Folklife Program. Two of Bel's daughters, Myrna Wilson and Marjorie Batisse, continue to make two popular Koasati dishes, frybread and corn soup, and to demonstrate their basketry. Bel demonstrated the woodworking skills he learned from his elders by making blowguns (used to shoot birds and small game) for adults and toys for children. He said that the toys he made helped him relate to the children. "I enjoy to play with the children," Bel said. "I like it." And both the children and their parents enjoyed him as well. He was a soft-spoken, gentle man with a warm demeanor that touched people and drew them to him.

Often, once Bel had caught his audience's attention with a toy or other woodcraft he was making, he would tell them a story. He said, "That's what the important thing [is], the stories. A lot of people like the stories." Because his native language was not English but Koasati, his English was awkward at times. But neither Bel nor his audience let this language gap prevent the enjoyment of his stories. Just as he learned woodworking from the older people, Bel learned many stories from his

Bel Abbey, Koasati taleteller from Elton. Photo: Jerry Devillier.

elders, who he said would get together and tell each other tales. He said that as a boy he would stay near them and listen all the time. It is from them that he learned the traditional animal tales, such as the turtle and the trickster rabbit running a race, the bear teaching the Indians about resin's medicinal qualities, and how the Indians first met Europeans. Bel also told his own personal experience hunting stories, in which he nearly always mixed human and animal characters, with the animals outsmarting the human, namely, Bel. Before his age slowed him down, he frequently hunted and fished. During these outings he tangled with many creatures of the forest, including ducks, owls, rabbits, and even lost cows.

At the conclusion of each of his tales, whether a traditional Koasati story or one of his own, Bel always said, tafhiyám, *and then spit in order to avert evil. The belief is if a story is not concluded in that manner, the teller will get a humpback or crooked back. "You'll have something coming up your humpback or something wrong," Bel explained. "You've got to say* tafhiyám *and you've got to spit one time."*

Bel was born in 1916 in the Koasati community near Elton, where he lived his life, out in the country. Behind his house on the other side of a large field are the woods to which he often referred in his hunting stories. He worked with students at Tulane

University in New Orleans, the University of Southwestern Louisiana in Lafayette, and Northwestern State University in Natchitoches. He also participated at the Festival of American Folklife in Washington, D.C. Bel continued to give demonstrations at festivals across Louisiana. In 1991, he completed an apprenticeship with his nephew Timothy Langley, in which he taught Timothy his traditional skills and stories. Bel was glad that his nephew wanted to learn from him because he felt it important to hand down the Koasati ways; as he said, "how we get it, where we get it, how they do it, the way they used to do." Perhaps, like Bel, Timothy will, in turn, continue to share his special culture with interested outsiders.

37. Learning from the Bear

Recorded September 22, 1990, at the St. Francisville Heritage Festival, West Feliciana Parish.

Two young men decided to go hunt in the woods, along the river. They went in that woods, and they went off with a bow and arrow and tomahawk, all that stuff. They find a trail along the river bank. They find a bear. A big black bear in there. It was starting rooting, something in the bushes. Said, "Look at that bear. Let's kill that bear."

Other said, "How we going to kill it? That big bear?" "It's a big one," they said. Said, "Who's going to shoot it first?"

"You going to shoot it first!" he said. "Let's kill it," they said.

"All right, you shoot him first, and if you don't kill it for the first time, I'll get ready for the second one."

Said, "All right." So they creep on it. So he shot the bear. He shot the bear, and the bear still there. The second shot, he shot him again. After a while, the bear still alive and still walking, looking for what shot, what shoot. After a while, get ready for second, get arrows, both get ready for him. After that, the bear stand up. Full of blood on it. Stand up, look around for where the arrow come from.

After a while he find a man standing by. He run after the man. But the man was running under the pine trees—they got a lot of big log trees— big black bear run after the man. They was running away from him, go around the trees. The bear was running after him all that time, and the man got tired. Can't hardly go no more. [Breathes heavily.] Can't hardly run no more. One man stay hide back behind the pine trees. He motion, "Pass right close by me right here," he said. But they get ready for it. You got to be careful is what I'm talking. After a while, he motion for him to pass by right close. So they pass by right close back of that tree, hide back of that tree.

When he pass by, they shot him again. They hit [the bear] but it don't fall down. It got the blood come out, but the bear is too strong and too big. He don't come down. He turned around and run after the one that shot him. So the one got tired, got to rest back of that tree again. They do that again when the other man got tired. They motion again. "Come right here, pass by right close to me," he said.

When he pass by right close, they shot him again. He got full of blood. The bear got so much blood on him. Can't hardly go no more. He stop running after the man. Went back of the pine tree, start digging up under the pine tree on the roots. He start digging up by the roots.

"What we going to do? We going to shoot him?" He said, "No, we got to wait." "What we going to do?" he said. He bite that root, they scratch on it. The resin comes out in there. "Let's watch what he going to do with that." So they watch him, and the bear starts scraping up and the resin comes out. Where the blood comes out, they put it on there, where they got the holes there. Stop up the blood with that resin.

"Let's watch what he's going to do with that." They was waiting for him. He stopped the blood up. He start doctoring himself. That's what the bear did. After a while, the man said, "Let's don't kill him, let's watch him again." He keep on doing that, all the time, all the time. "Okay, let's let him go. We learn something from the bear."

If it be something happen on the foot, the shoulder, if we got a cut, we use that resin. We going to learn from the bear. We learn how to use medicine from the bear. After that, we learn how to be medicine men; we learn from the bear. So they went back home.

38. The Turtle and the Rabbit Run a Race

The following four stories were recorded at the 1989 Louisiana Folklife Festival in Eunice, St. Landry Parish, November 16–19.

I'm going to tell you about the story about the Rabbit and the Turtle running a race. They were going to run a race one time. And Rabbit run so fast one time. He liked to run all the time. You know how the rabbit are. He jumped and he run fast and quick, and the turtle can't hardly run, can't hardly move out. They go after the insects, and that's the only time he run fast, I guess.

After a while, he said, "Okay."

But the Rabbit begging to run a race with the Turtle. Turtle said, "No, I can't run now. You're too fast for me. But you can't beat me because I'm running pretty fast all the time." And he said, "Okay, we put that when you're going to run a race."

He said, "All right. Let me know right away." He said, "Let me know right away."

He said, "All right. We'll talk to our people, and we're going to let you know tomorrow morning."

He said, "All right."

And after a while, turtles all get together. Turtles all get together and talk how they going to cheat with the Rabbit. They said, "You know, let's run. We'll run, and go a little ways. They got what they call hill. But it's no hill around here. It's low swamp in here. It's low flat; there's no hills in it. It's called a little mound. We're going to run over the mound and on top of the hill, on the mound. That's where we going to run the race, till there," they said.

Rabbit says, "Okay."

But the turtles talk to themselves, each other. They pick out four turtles. "You start it off first, and hide a little ways out there. And I come out and run a little ways and this one hide. But they're going to come out. And for the last go round, you run first over there in that line." They got four turtles, and they wanted to cheat that rabbit.

When they started off running, the Rabbit jumped and leaped and went off with it. But they find onions and cabbage plants, cabbage farms and onion places. That's where they stopped. They find a good place to eat. So they stop and start eating in there. But the other one had come out. That's where they hide. They come out and started off.

The Rabbit went over there and said, "Where you coming from?"

He said, "Oh, I'm still running. I'm still running."

So the Rabbit passed the second one. After a while, they find mustards, mustard plants. They stop again and start eating. And the other one comes out. The third one comes out. After a while, the Rabbit is through eating, and they start running. Drink water, and he starts running again. He find that Turtle ahead, way ahead. He was way ahead of him. After a while he said, "Oh, how did you pass me?"

He said, "Oh, I'm still running."

After a while, the last one. The last one when they was eating in there, the last one come out first. On the line, they sit down, waiting for the Rabbit. The Rabbit ran over there where there's supposed to be a line in there. And he ran over there, but it's too late. Turtle goes over there first. Rabbit got mad at him. He said, "How did you get here?"

He said, "I run over here."

He said, "No, you don't. You don't pass me."

"I will," he said. Keep arguing, and the Rabbit got mad. He got a stick like this and start beating on top of the back of shell. Break him all up. He tore it all up on the back. That's what you see there now, that's where the marks in there. On the back, the little skulls in there on the back. That's what that's for. They beat him up and they left.

The Turtle was all beat up, broken back, and they laying down. But they calling for help. "Help! Help! I need help!"

What you call it? An ant. An ant heard him. He said, "Somebody need help. Somebody need help somewheres."

"Where?" one said.

"Back in there somewheres," he said.

"Let's go meet him," they said. They all get together and line up, and they all went over to where they needed help. They went over there, and the turtle got hurt. He got beat up.

The third one said, "What you want?"

"I need help. I got beat up. My back is broken. I need somebody help me throw it over. But you eat my fat. I got a little fat in there. That's what I'm going to pay with."

So the ant start eating the fat in there, the blood in there, start sewing him up. Pinch him all together. After that, they got well. That's why the turtle got spots all over him. That's the end of my story. That's my story.

39. Bel's Encounter with a Wise Owl

We got all kind of owls where I come from. I live in the piney woods, along the creeks, small creeks. Got a lot of trees, lot of pine trees; that's where the owl likes to stay in there. They run after, like me, they go after animals all, too. I go after animals, too, like squirrels and rabbit. But the owls are very violent on the animals, like rats, like the birds, and all those small rabbits. They kill anything, and I do the same thing, too. We try to make a living together.

One time, it was so bad, I can't kill nothing in one day. I go look for it and I can't kill nothing. No bird or nothing. I ain't got no food to eat that night. So one night, I went. But I don't have no flashlight. So I cut me a pine stump, a pitch pine stump, about that long in there. I split it up, and I light the end. I go at night because I know where—they call it a brown thrasher— they got the bush in there, that's where they go roost at night. I go at night because I can't kill that day. I go at night with my blow gun. I go with my blow gun in there, and every time I see him—his breast was white when I see it, not too far from the bush—when I see it, I aim with my blow gun.

After a while, that pitch pine was burning, and resin was jumping my hand like this here. I jumped off, and I missed. That's what made me mad—it burned my hand. The resin fall on my hand. And after that, I shoot him again, and I aim it. I shoot it, I hit it, but I don't kill it. I got the dart in that brown thrasher, and the brown thrasher said, when I hit it. [Makes a bird noise.] He wanted to get away from me! After a while, he start running, and the owl somewhere back in there said. [Makes an owl noise twice.] I hit it—it tried to get away from me, and start running with my dart in it. After a while, the big old owl catch it first. He get it with my dart. He get my brown thrasher and went off with it. So I come home without a bird again. That's the end of my story about the owl.

40. Bel's Encounter with the Rabbit and the Cow

I'll tell you different from the rabbit this time. What I did one time. I was camping in the woods. I went hunting. I was hunting in the woods. I was camping. Rest of us was camping in the woods, too. We camping in the woods, and we looking for something to eat like a bird or squirrel or rabbit or duck. We found all that stuff in there. After a while, it got a flood in there. Big flood in it. So we chased a rabbit along the flood in there.

After a while, when we find it, we jumped it and it jumped in the high flood and starts swimming. We can't catch it. We can't catch it. It went off. It went off. I was waiting and waiting and can't catch it. The rabbit jumped where the stream was running and the log was floating. After a while, I jumped the rabbit. They jumped in the water and take off with it. I wait. I thought they'd come back. But it went in the water, and they find an old log. They find a big old log that was floating. That's when the rabbit jumped in the log and start floating and went off. He said, "Goodbye."

So I can't catch it. But I was waiting in there. It was late. I was along the river until late. But the storm getting bad. Look to me like it was hurricane or something like that. Bad storm coming in there. Dark clouds in there. It was coming. But I look at it—I was waiting in there. It coming so bad, it was kind of dark. It was late. I thought I was running back home. I thought I was going back home. Got nothing but a trail in the woods. Nothing but a cow trail in the woods.

So I was coming back home in the woods. I was looking up here, just look at the weather. Lightning, thunder, lightning and thunder. I just keep looking up. I start walking the trail. I don't know what's in the ground—I stumble with the logs. Get up, stumble with the logs. I thought it was a log in there. But they got a bunch of cattles in there, laying on the trail. The cattle was laying down there. I was crawling, I thought I was crawling over logs. After a while, big old black cow was laying along the trail there. I thought it was logs. The cow come up. Start looking at me and throw me off! He throw me down in there! I was scared after that. I was really scared after that, when they throw me down. I thought I was going thataway, coming towards home. But when they throw me down, when I get up, I get to same place where I come from. I got lost. That's the end of it!

41. A Duck Hunting Story

I went duck hunting, too, one time. Cold. I don't have no rubber boots. I just wear shoes. It was rainy day, and I went. I went out. I went in the morning and I went afternoon. I kill in the morning, and I want to go back and kill again in afternoon. And I went back. Got a swamp, a big swamp in there. It's late in the afternoon—all the ducks comes in that swamp. I got twelve-gauge, double-barrel shotgun. I got my bow, too, but I can't hardly hit them with the bow, so I want to make sure to bring every duck back with the twelve-gauge double barrel shotgun.

I brought it over there, and I shot it. The limit's supposed to be four that time. But I killed over four. But I keep shooting. After that, I went out shoot it. When they were flying up, I shoot it. They come down like this on the water, on top of the water. The water was running. But they was falling there, and their head was under the water. I start to go get it. I was walking in the water. It's deep and deep all the time when I start walking in there. It's cold, too. It's coming here, almost to here. I try to raise up like that. But it's cold. But I want the duck so bad. I just went in there. I had to go get the ducks because their heads were in the water like this.

When I get over there where the duck is, I can't hardly reach it. But I touch the back of the duck like this here. And the duck jump out and fly away from me. I come back. I come out and go home! That's all! That's it!

42. How the Buzzard Got a Pierced Nose

The following two stories were told to Pat Mire, June 7, 1991, at Bel's home when he was interviewed for the Imperial Calcasieu Folklife Survey. Bel first heard this story when he was about twelve. In this story, the Rabbit, the Koasati trickster, is himself tricked by Vulture. An important theme in this story is the excessive pride of

Rabbit, who tries to imitate Bear's way of providing food, even though he is unable to do so.

The Bear and the Rabbit are two friends, two friends. They like each other. They go see each other all the time. Talk to each other. Stay together most of the time, the Rabbit and the Bear. One time the Rabbit went over to the Bear and visit over there. "Okay, come on, sit down," [Bear] says. They sit down and talking and talking. Build a fire.

"Well, just about ready to go back home," he says. That's what Rabbit says.

The Bear asks him, says, "No, you could stay here till I cook and [you] eat with me and you go home."

The Rabbit says, "All right," and sits down and wait. After a while, the Bear went over there and look for something to cook, but he don't have nothing to cook. He look for it, but can't find nothing, nothing cooking. After a while, he says, "Okay." The Bear so fat, you know, so he get the knife and put a little side in there. [Makes motion like he is cutting the side of his body.] He start cooking to feed the Rabbit. The Rabbit eat some and went back home.

[The Rabbit said], "You come over and I cook some, too," he said.

"All right," and the Bear will stay a while there. After a while, the Bear says, "I'm going to go see the Rabbit." Went over there to Rabbit's.

"Come on in. Let's talk, sit down and talk." Have a friend talking to each other. After a while, the Bear is just about leave over there, too.

"No, I am going to cook, too, you know. You going to eat with me. You going to have a dinner with me."

And the Bear says, "All right." After a while, you know, [Rabbit] wants to do like the Bear did. He went over there and looked for something to eat. He don't know what the Bear was eating. He look around and look around, you know. He ain't got nothing to eat, because he eats a little grass, a little green grass, like a cabbage. But he don't have it. So he look around. He do the same way, too, you know. He pulled a side in there, used the knife in there. [Makes motion like he is cutting the side of his body.] But the Bear was fat, you know. But the Rabbit was skinny. He don't have much in it. But they pull it anyhow. And they cut it open and the guts was falling out.

The Rabbit says, "Oh, I got hurt! I got hurt!" he says. He called the Bear, "I got hurt. I got hurt," he says.

"Okay." He runs over there and looked at it, you know. Got a big cut in there. Guts was hanging out, you know, so he don't know what to do.

He says, "I'm going to town. I need some help." That's what Rabbit says.

"Okay, I'll go get you a doctor. I'll find you a doctor and be right back." The Bear left, on a trail. Went walking on a trail. And after a while, he says, "Help, I need a help. My friend got hurt. I need a help."

And one old Buzzard was heard about it, on top of the thing, sitting on top of the thing. "Oh, I need a help. My friend got hurt."

"Hey, what do you want me to do?" [Buzzard] says. "I'm a doctor," he says. The old Buzzard says.

"Okay, okay, my friend got hurt. I want you to come and doctor for me."

He says, "Okay. Show where they at."

"Okay." The Bear run back to tent to where the Rabbit at. And the Buzzard followed all the way over there.

"Okay, now what you want me to do?," he said. "Cut you a lot of palmetto, you know." They cut it and pinch it up all the way around. So disease won't get in there, he says. [Makes motions to build a small palmetto shelter.] So they cut it and they pinch it all in there. Because the Rabbit was laying down. They pinch it all in there. The Buzzard flies in there. [Makes a shooshing noise.] Says, "What happened?" Oh he got hurt really bad. But they don't see because it's all pinched in, you know. Really bad.

After a while the Rabbit says, "*Whah, whah, whah.*" The Bear was outside. "What happened, What happened?" he said.

"Oh, he got hurt so bad. But he don't want to take my medicine," he says. "Don't want to take my medicine," he says.

After a while he said, "*Whah, whah, whah.*" He stop, he stop making noises. Then that's it, no more noise. But the Buzzard, you know, he kill him, he eat him in there. He killed the Rabbit. And he eat the Rabbit, eat the Rabbit. That's why he don't make no noise in there.

"Hey, what happened? What's the matter in there?"

"He so hurt, he don't want to take my medicine," he says. That's what Buzzard says. "He don't take my medicine." But he eat it up, you know. He kill him and eat him. The Buzzard eat him up, eat him up. Just a lot of bones in there, you know, when he finish it up. "Okay. Okay, now you can come in there to see him." But the Buzzard's ready to fly off. Fly off to the limb over there. Fly to the limb over there. "Now you can go in there and see it," he said.

The Bear was walked in there. Look at it. He can't find the Rabbit. All the bones was there. Look around in there. Look around in there. He says he can't find it. Thought he would take it [Rabbit] up there, too. He looked at it, nothing in there. But the Rabbit bones was there. He found out he was killing him and eating him up, you know. The Bear got so mad, you know. He don't know what to do. He mad. Mad at that Buzzard, you know. So after a while, you know, the big Bear got up, got a knife on the side in there. The Buzzard was up there. He got this knife, you know, and throw it at that Buzzard. And he pierced in that nose right here. [Points to the bridge of his nose.] It stuck him through and through. Stuck it through and through in there. And Buzzard jumped out and pulled the knife out and throwed it off and fly away. He almost kill him, but it was just through in his nose. And the Buzzard just took the knife and throw it away and fly off. And after that, you know, and today, you can see all the buzzards' noses are speared all the time. All the birds got speared in there. [Points to his nose.] But you see, birds went through and through there. That's what had happened. That's the end of my story. That's a *tafhiyám*. [Spits.]

43. Rabbit Rolls into a Ball

Pat Mire: Do you know a story about a rabbit that rolls up into a ball? Curls up.

Bel Abbey: Yeah, Yeah. Oh, I been telling that story, how long I don't know. Because I see it myself—and I make it do that with my dog and all, too, you know. I was living [near] right here. One day I decided to go hunt, and I got my twelve-gauge shotgun, you know, and I call up my dog, you know. I got one dog, you know. He followed me back over here, you know, not too far from here. We got some gullies and some bushes and all the trees in there. That's where I used to go hunting. So I carried my dog over there. And after a while, you know, I loaded up my gun, and I was waiting for it, you know. I wait for my dog. And the dog was all in the bushes in there looking for a rabbit. Now, I used to kill a lot of rabbit and eat it, you know. I used to like it. But, you know, that's my sport, that's my living and all too, you know. I used to do that a lot. I liked it, too.

But sometime I don't get none at all in one day. I went back in here and after a while, the dog was chasing. All the bushes in there. Come out in there. After a while, *yowh!* [Makes sound of a hound.] Jumped up the rabbit. I started shooting in there, but the dog was right at him, you know. I don't shoot him cause I might hurt my dog, you know. Because I might hurt my dog. So I don't shoot it. I just wait for him, you know. But the dog almost [caught him], was about that far apart. I thought he was going to catch it. The dog was run after it, and I thought he was going to catch it.

After a while—keep it closer, closer all the time. I was standing up watch, but with my shotgun, you know. After a while, you know, that little rabbit, I think, I think when they almost catch it, you know. I thought he going to give up. But you know what thing did? That little old thing is smart, here. So he's got long ears like that. He folded up. He's got two front legs and he folded up like that. And two hind legs. They jump and rolled up like that. He just rolled. And my dog was almost catch it when he started rolling like that. And dog was jump over the rock. He thought it was a rock, you know. The dog would jump over the rock. [Sound of a yelping hound trailing a rabbit.] He went through. He drove about a quarter of a mile in there, way back over there. Rabbit rolled and rolled, and it stopped over there. He stopped rolling.

And they get up, come back to where the same tracks is. He went back where the same place. But I was waiting for him, you know, with my shotgun. I said, "No." It's safe because he smart. I tell him to let him go. I don't even shoot him, neither. So they went back to the bushes and went back through there and went off somewhere. I wait for my dog. After a while, he goes a long way. They barked way back over there. I said, "No, the rabbit was over here."

Pat Mire: He fooled the dog.

Bel Abbey: Yeah. The dog was barking over there, but they turned around and come back and meet me over here. I said, "Okay, that's enough. Let's go home." I said, "We'll come back home without a rabbit." They beat us one time. But that's good.

44. The Deer and the Wildcat

The following story was recorded at the Natchitoches Folklife Festival in 1981. H. F. "Pete" Gregory and Joe Dillard interviewed Bel on the festival's narrative stage about his storytelling. This story features animals that are totems for two of the seven clans or kinship groups among the Koasati, the deer and the wildcat. It is also an example of a story used to teach children the lesson to be careful when hunting and to know their own level of skill.

The same way the Indian hunter learned from the other animals. But like if you sleep too much in the wood, you can understand what makes the noise in the woods. Like animals' noise. Animals' holler. Like a cow what bellow. You can understand what that means.

So, they got a few deer around there where we at now. But the old-timers said, old-timers said that's the way he used to kill, they said. You know, some of that big tigers and leopards, I think Leopard now. That one that used to stay down there, they said. But you know, when the trail, they have a trail for the deer trail. They always—follow the trail, each other. And—like those bobcats, wildcats I mean. Some like that, you know, they was stay on top of the land and waiting for them, they said. Waiting for the animals pass by.

But the deer was pass first. One of those Tiger still on top of the land. When they pass by, the Tiger was jump over the deer neck and caught it by its claws in it. They hold it down. After a while they run a little ways. That Tiger was so heavy, so he—leaning on one side like this. And the deer was running, but he can't hardly go no much, turned over like this. Then they killed the deer. Panther jumped on it and killed it. That's why they used to say. That's what Wildcat used to say that, how they kill it like that.

And the Wildcat says, "I'm going to do the same way, too," he says. "I'm going to kill the same way, too." And [he] was climb up on top of the limb and waiting for the animal. And [he] got a big deer that passed through under the trail, under the limb and all. So the Wildcat was too small, just like a little cat, you know. So [he] jumped on it, on his back, you know. And the deer was running so much, so fast, on that little trail, you know. And the Wildcat, he thought he could lean him on one side, you know. Anyhow, [he] put on his back like that. Deer still running, you know, but the cat is not heavy enough. So they running up that little trail.

After a while, you know, they pass close to that tree. And [he] hit [his] head over like this here. And turned over. The cat was running over the deer. Running away from him. And the Wildcat don't know what happened when [he] get up. [He] was unconscious, and [he] got dirt on. And I think [he] was out of breath and all too. [Laughter.] Okay that's the end of my story.

45. Thátkak ilá:ci:fó:kok (The First Meeting of the Indians and the Europeans)

Geoffrey Kimball, a linguist at Tulane Unversity, recorded, transcribed, and translated this story told by Bel Abbey in February 1982. After fourteen years of research, Kimball published the first Koasati/Coushatta grammar in 1991. In order to emphasize that the original story was told in Koasati, the Koasati version of the prologue and Scene 1 is included. Reading the translation from Koasati helps convey how Bel Abbey expressed himself in his native narrative tradition.

Prologue

Athómmak i:sáhcotohon,
yá:li ihá:nifa i:sáhcotohon
Thátkak ilá:ci:fó:kok,
thátkak ilá:ci:fó:k,
ná:hotoho:limpahcok,
athómmak illónkat
intółkamá:min sobayáhlok.

Mántik, athómmak i:sáhcotohon,
athómmak yá:li í:sat ilanawíhlit
ná:so:t í:bit, í:pat, i:sáhcotohon.

Scene 1: The Meeting and Flight

Thátkak kotałá naksofón
yomahlihcómmit ilá:ci:fó:k,
himá:k afánka mán ómmot ómmit.

Himá:k ilá:cin
món itto:tamálit iláhcok.
Thátkak ilá:ci:fó:k,
piłón áłkat sto:wilá:ci:fó:kon,
athómmak í:satohok
híhcok intółkatoho:limpáhcok.
Intółka:fó:kon,
intółkafók afáłhíkkon.
"Ná:sommo:lí ʔsá? Sámmin intółkó?"
ká:hatoho:limpáhcok thátkak.

Prologue

The Indians once were dwelling,
here in this land they dwelt.
When the white people arrived,
after the white people came,
they existed, so it is said,
and they knew that the Indians might
run and hide from them.

But, to change the subject for
a moment, the Indians were
dwelling,
the Indians dwelt here, and they
hunted for game,
and lived by killing and eating various
sorts of things.

Scene 1: The Meeting and Flight

Wherever the white people were
going about on our side of the
ocean when they arrived,
It seems to also have been the first
meeting.
On first arriving, they also came to
trade with them.

When the white people arrived,
when within a boat they arrived over
the water,
the Indians dwelling there, on seeing
them, ran from them, so it is said.
When they ran from them,
after they ran from them, they did
not meet them.
"Whatever could it be? Why must
they run off?" the white people
said, so it is reported.
And then, they kept on fleeing from
them so,

Má:min intółkat akkánt í:san,
naksásimmi:pintółkaná:nan
  illónkaná:nan.
Athómmak immałáhlik ómmitohok,
akkó á:tik ná:si akkámmin
ikhí:comáhco:lisk.
Immałáhlik ómmitoho:limpáhcok.
Intółkat í:san.

sometimes they all ran from them, at
  other times they all hid from them.
The Indians were afraid of them,
  because they had never seen such
  people as those.
It is said that they were afraid of
  them.
They kept on fleeing from them.

Scene 2: The Dilemma of the Europeans
Then the white people said,
"How can we get to know them before we speak to them?"
as they all ran hiding from them.
If they looked into their dwelling,
(those they had were somewhat sunken in the earth),
they who were the openers of their houses,
that those others dwelt in,
if the white people looked into the Indians' own dwellings;
people's own dwelling were looked into,
but contrary to expectation, there were no Indians of any kind,
they had gone out and run and hidden from them and disappeared.
And then, "How ever would it be possible for us to meet and speak with
them?"
they kept on thinking.
It was impossible; the white people did not know how they might do it.

Scene 3: The Leaving of the Whiskey
They [the white people] went around with liquor, they carried whiskey with
them.
They brought over one keg and went and laid it down for them, so it is said.
When they laid it down for them, as for the drinking glass, if it were not
such,
it was more or less like a coffee cup, but I don't know.
How many they laid down for them I don't know,
but having laid them down for them, they returned [to their ship], so it is
said.

Scene 4: The Return and Debate of the Indians
And then, the Indians who had gone off,
these Indians returned and came arriving,

and when they saw it, the Indians kept on returning.

There were many Indians there.

Having returned and arrived back, they who said it [the keg] lying with it [the liquor],

upon seeing the one keg lying there,

when they saw it, they said, "What is it?

No! Do ye not approach it!

Whatever it is will hurt you!

Whatever it is will kill ye!" they said,

forbidding the rest, so it is reported.

But then, contrary to expectation, they kept on turning and looking at it, turning and looking at it,

and they kept on so—so it is said, they kept on so;

thereupon [one said], "What is it?"

"I do not know, but it is lying there with it [the liquor] just like that," said another.

Thereupon, when one person said, "Let me test it by drinking!"

"No! Do not drink it! It is bad by nature!"

"As it is a bad thing, upon your drinking it, you will die," the other said.

Scene 5: The Intervention of the Orphan

Thereupon, "I shall be the one!

I shall be the one!" said the orphaned man who was passing by, so it is reported.

Being without living relatives,

he was completely and utterly alone.

He used to live by joining up with people;

his relatives were no more.

It is as an orphan that he lived.

"Well, I will be the one!"

When he said, "I might just drink it,"

"Nay!" said another. "Do not drink it!"

As it is something bad by nature, you will die¡'

When he said this, the orphan man would not quit begging to try drinking it, so it is said.

"But all the same, let it be drunk,

because my relatives no longer exist,

no one at all can feel sorry about anything.

Nothing will sadden anyone.

Because I have been habitually alone,
no one sorrows for me.
It will be a good thing if I err in drinking it.
I want to know and tell you how it is," he said.

The leader said, "Nay!
Please do not drink even a little bit.
You as well deserve to live."
When he forbade him, the other did not listen, and just did not quit pleading.
"All right, drink it then," he said, and the other left off [begging].
"Take a drink of it that you might tell us how it is," he said.

Scene 6: The Results of Drinking
Thereupon, having left off with him,
the orphan man filled up a container and drank, so it is said.
He drank, and continued to drink,
and now, when he was completely dizzy, it is said that he was insensible.
He was in a state of insensibility, as it is reported.
Thereupon, when he was completely dizzy,
now also, he made noise
and what he said was unintelligible,
but he went on, so it is said.
Now also they said, "Drinking does so to us!"
"Listen! That is completely and utterly what will happen to ye!"
Now you see it," they said.
It is said that he was in a state of insensibility.
He drank, went on drinking, and became drunk.
Thereupon, they watched him as he drank, got drunk, fell down, and lay down on the ground;
they all were really keeping on watching him.
"He is almost dead.
He will die,
he is dying on us;
such is the case, he is going to die," they said.
On watching him, they kept on waiting for it, so it is said.
Thereupon, they kept on watching him in the same way;
he was lying on the ground, so it is said.
He really lay there;

I do not know how long he lay there before he regained consciousness,
but he just lay there, and he awoke;
he just lay there, woke up, and moved.
"Look! Lo! He is about to awaken!"
He was continuing to rub himself as he was awakening
Thereupon, as he was awakening, it is said that they asked him,
"How is it?
What is it like?
How was it for you?
How are you?" they said.
Then, this one here, contrary to expectation said, "It was a very good soporific.
It was an extremely good soporific.
This being so, drink ye it!
If we were to drink it,
it would be a very good soporific.
I liked it very, very much;
it was an extremely good sleep," he said.

Scene 7: The Drinking Bout
Thereupon, the remainder of them,
thinking it to be the truth,
some drank
and others drank;
each lay about on the ground
drinking, as it is reported.

Thereupon, as they were doing so,
as the Indians were doing so,
the Indians were lying on the ground,
they did so and lay on the ground.

Scene 8: The Return of the Europeans and Capture of the Indians
The aforementioned white people, upon arriving,
came and caught some of them, about two in number.
They caught them, returned with them and
getting over there to the boat put them into it.
After they regained consciousness,
when the other spoke to them,

they tried to run away,
but because they could tell that they were on the water, they were unable to do so.
Their having given up [trying to escape],
now they spoke to them and taught them.
They spoke to them, and dressed them in things such as clothing;
they would have dressed them completely.
The rest also would tell them nothing more than,
"Belt on the clothing and so forth that we made and gave you."
Having spoken to each other, all the white people went along accompanying the Indians.
They gave them things such as clothing and made friends with them with it [clothing].
As liquor was with them, and having met them with it,
[the Indians] were now habitual drinkers.

46. The First Meeting of the Indians and the Europeans

The following story was recorded by Maida Owens, July 5, 1990, at Bel's home just outside of Elton in Allen Parish. This story was told by Bel in English after some discussion on storytelling among the Koasati. He said the old-timers would tell these stories, but he didn't know if any of them were true. Bel told this story about the influence of the white man after Maida inquired about it. It is one he heard among the elders as a child. He personalized it, however, by tying it in with his extensive experience with folklife festivals. Comparing the version told in English with the Koasati version translated above (#45), gives the reader a sense of the difficulty that the teller has in shifting back and forth between languages. The two versions also illustrate the importance of modifying a story to suit different audiences.

The Indian don't have nothing [alcoholic] to drink, don't have none, no drink. But he don't wear no clothes, he wears a towel. That's when he used to lay in here, for the first time he comes around here somewhere. After that he got a dancing place and camping place. That's why he stays in there all the time, in this area. It's a good place to stay.

But the white people want to come see what he's doing in there. The white people come along in there and every time he start, try and come meet the Indians. And the Indians got afraid of the white people. Well, you see, they start walking, come toward them and they all run and hide. They hide all the time. Run away from them. They hide all the time. The white people can't get friends with the Indians. The white people want to be friends, talk to him, want to ask him a few questions. Want to get along with him. But the Indians run and hide all the time, all the time.

After a while, the white people think about it, how to get to him and talk to him. After a while the white people find a barrel of whiskey. Try and trap him. "Let's trap him." "How we going to trap him?" "Let's take a barrel of whiskey and let's put it in the hunting ground." That's where they dance and play, right there." "All right, let's do that." And they bring a barrel, a keg, I don't know how big. They bring it over here to the place and set it up. They set it up and put a little cup in it. After that they come back and they left, went back.

All the Indians come out to see what's in there. When they come back, they look around, they open it up. They open it up and smell it, say, "Hmmm, that's strong. Smells strong."

One orphan boy was with the bunch. But the leader said, "Don't drink it. It might be some kind of poison. We going to get killed. Everyone going to be killed. Going to kill us everyone."

Orphan boy said, "I'm by myself. I don't have no daddy, no mama, I don't have no kinfolk. It don't matter if I die. If I drink, I die."

"No, we need you. We need you to stay with us."

But he keep begging all the time, he want to drink so bad. But they don't let him drink. He begging so much, they said, "All right. Go ahead and drink and tell us what happen to you. What it do to you."

They open it up, get the little cup in there. Start drinking. After a while, make him feel good. Put another cup in. Feeling good, talking, moving around, jump up and down. Dancing and all, too. So happy. After a while, get him another cup, gets dead drunk. Fall down drunk.

Leader said, "Now, tell you what's going to happen. He's going to die. Good thing we don't drink it because I think he's going to die." They all gather around where he laying down; they all get scared and watch him, what he do. He's laying down asleep. Sleeping all the time. Four hours. If he dies they going to bury him. But don't drink that. Then he starts moving. "Looks like he's going to get up." After a while he get up and sit down on the ground. "What it do to you? What happen to you?" they said.

"Oh, that thing make me feel good, go to sleep," he said. "Medicine to sleep with. I sleep well. I sleep well. I don't know. It make me sleep good." Everyone gets his cup and start drinking, drinking, drinking. They all got drunk. They finish it up. They all lying down on the ground. And the white people stopped in there and said, "Everyone laying down on the ground."

They picked up two of them, bring them over there, put them in jail or some kind of a cage, put them in there. They woke up. They were caught, in a different place. Different man, white people talking. They don't understand what they talking about because they don't speak English. After a while, white people be friend to us. Said, "Okay we got some extra clothes, we going to let you have it." We put the trousers on, pants. Put the shirt on, put some shoes on. After that, give them a hat to wear. "Yeah, it looks good. Now, go tell the others over there. Tell them to come back over here and get some clothes."

So they all come back to the camp over there and tell him, "Go over there if you want this kind of clothes." Everyone back over there and wear the clothes now.

Now I warned you, we'd wear the good clothes. Take the diapers off and wear the good clothes. Shirt and all that stuff. Now we use that kind. If it don't be for that we'd have not clothes. We can't hardly go to no festival, like that without the clothes on! That's what I thought about. I think that's it, you know. That's what they say.

47. Hacinmánkalá:himá:m (A Man Loses His Breechcloth to a Bull)

Recorded in May 1987, this story was also recorded by Geoffrey Kimball as part of his research to produce the first dictionary of Koasati. Again, the first two scenes are provided in Koasati to give the reader some sense of how Bel narrated in his native tongue.

Scene 1: Two Men are Out in the Woods

Áá:tik a :yácitoholimpaáhcok.
Łopohlíhcok,
naksó:n atłací hcommíhchok,
inko:p, ilanawíhcot ómmit.
Ittohayó ayá:cit.
Wa:ka małáhlik í:san,
hícat łopóhlit ayá:cit.

Scene 1: Two Men are Out in the Woods
It is said that two people were going about.
They were passing through,
it was the case that the two of them were going somewhere, or if not, they must have been hunting.
The two of them were going about in the forest.
The wild cattle that were dwelling there,
the two of them saw them as they were passing by.

Scene 2: They Come Across Wild
   Cattle
Wá:kak małáhlotoho:limpáhcok,
wá:kak małáhlotoho:limpáhcok
   ittohayó isá.
Mó:tohok,
wakná:nik lapó:t hobáskit,
wá:ka lapí hobáskit o:láhcotohok,
   i:sáhcotohok.
Có:ba małáhli mók malmámmit
   ístoho:liyon,
ittohayó a:yá:cit łopóhli:fó:k,
hínosok atí:yatohon,
hínosi ałłá:ci:k,
ayá:ci:fó:kap,
wá:kak mathí:catoholimpáhcok.

Scene 2: They Come Across Wild Cattle
It is said that the cattle were indeed
   wild,
it is said that cattle which were indeed
   wild were dwelling in the forest.
Then,
the bulls had long horns,
the long horned cattle were lowing,
as they were standing there.
Wild horses also lived in just the same
   way,
but as the two of them were passing
   by,
the path went that way,
when the two of them were going on
   the path,
when they were going about,
it is said that the cattle saw them from
   afar.

Scene 3, Part 1: An Ill-Tempered Bull Chases the Men
Then,
an ill-tempered bull that was dwelling with them,
after he saw them.
well, it is said,
it is said that he ran at them from afar.
Thereupon,
he was coming,
after he kept on coming,
it is said that they ran from him.
When they ran from the bull . . .

[Interpolation: How the Men Were Dressed]
Now long ago,
shoes at that time did not exist,
and as for trousers, it is said that they went about wearing short breechcloths.
They wore short breechcloths,
shoes at that time did not exist,
they carried bows with them,

and contrary to what one might think, they were like that,
people went about so.

Scene 3, Part 2: The Ill-Tempered Scene Bull Chases the Men
These two who were going about,
they were going about,
and a bull, catching sight of them, came running,
it is the case he was chasing them.
Now it is the case that he is chasing them;
"Let us run from him!" they said.

Scene 4: One Loses his Breechcloth
Then,
there were a few trees that were standing there,
when it was running from afar,
one man ran and climbed up away from him,
when the other was beginning to get himself to climb,
it is said that the bull was upon him in chasing him.
When the bull was almost upon him,
he really ran more than him,
and there was a bent tree standing there,
and he ran straight there;
when he was just getting there,
the bull was almost upon him,
when he jumped and was hanging from a branch,
when he jumped and was hanging,
"I shall be gored," he thought,
and after he gored at him,
as he was hanging from the tree,
he gored only his breechcloth,
he took it from him, went past with it and ran off with it;
he ran with it hanging from his horn,
and it is said he disappeared.

Scene 5: The Men Return to Camp
Thereupon,
the men merely jumped down,
the two of them went jumping,
and they went back running, so it is said.
Thereupon,

one came back with his breechcloth,
he came back and they said,
"What in the world?"
"There was an ill-tempered bull, a—
and he took my breechcloth off of me," he said,
and it said that they told the story at the campfire.
There sitting by the fire,
when he came returning,
and so they stayed;
they were cautious;
it is said that they were afraid of those bulls.

Scene 6: Epilogue
Just like that,
in the forest long ago,
it is said that life was excessively difficult.
Just like that
as they lived an uncivilized life at that time,
because bulls chased after people,
thus it is said a man had his breechcloth taken off of him.
Just so much is what I am ready to tell you.
Tafhiyám!
The end.

48. A Man Loses His Breechcloth to a Bull

This story was also told to Maida Owens, July 5, 1990, at Bel's home. Bel doubted that this story, and many others that he told, were accurate depictions of actual events. He said, "That's just the way they talk. Might be just a story, might be true or not." Linguist Geoffrey Kimball commented that Bel had some trouble translating the Koasati word "iboskí," or "breechcloth." He used the word "diaper" as the closest English parallel because it resembles a breech cloth in form and wearing.

They have some bulls, some cows. Wild cows. Wild ones. And mean. They run after people. One or two hunters was hunting along the trail in the woods. They followed the trails. But they followed cow tracks. But the bulls was wild, cows was wild. Long horns, maybe.

But old timers, he wears the diaper [breechcloth].

Maida Owens: What's the word for that? You're using the word "diaper."

Bel Abbey: Some kind of a tan hide wrapped around.

Maida Owens: Leather?

Bel Abbey: Leather, maybe. They go hunting, and they get something to eat. Every day they get up to go and look for it, something to eat. They go to the woods one day, and they look for it and look for a few deer trails. Look for it. But they got one of those cows in there. Find wild cows and some wild bull when they start walking back there. The wild bull look at him. Horns and everything. Stand there and look at him. Start walking. Somehow, he don't know what it is, I guess. He come run after him. The bull come after him.

Got bows and arrows on his back. After a while the man start running. He run away from him. The bull come so fast, come closer to him. He turned around and looked and closer and closer. They find a tree, a low one. The bull almost catches him. He jump up on a limb. He hangs up. The bull is too close and picked his diaper [breechcloth] off. He was naked in there. And the bull went off with it hanging on his horn. He run off with it.

He jumped down. He had to come back home. I don't know if he tiptoed, I don't know. I don't know how he did it, but he come back!

Enola Matthews:
A Creole and Irish Family Tradition

JENNINGS, JEFFERSON DAVIS PARISH

Introduced by Annette Huval

Des autres fois quand on veillait, on faisait des pralines, et les tac-tac et grillait des pistaches dans le foyer. Notre grand-père nous contait des contes, pauvre vieille bête. Et ceux-là qui connaissaient en contaient" *[In the old days, when people got together at night to tell stories, they made pralines and popcorn, and roasted peanuts in the fireplace. Our grandfather, poor old guy, told us stories. And those who knew stories, told them.]—Enola Matthews.*

Enola Matthews, a black Creole now living in Jennings, was born and raised near Durald. Her grandfather Arsen "Blanco" McIntire came to New Orleans from Ireland at the age of five. He and his family brought with them from the old country wonderful magic tales with which he entertained his grandchildren on evenings before bedtime. Matthews was only ten years old when her grandfather passed away, but at age seventy-eight, she somehow still retained these precious jewels. On April 2, 1993, I was fortunate enough to be present as the stories returned to life.

I visited with Mme. Matthews because I had been informed that she knew something about jurés, group religious chants once widely performed by Louisiana Creoles. During our visit I discovered that she had also taken part in storytelling traditions. Mme. Matthews was very surprised that a student like myself would be interested in anything she had to say, but at the same time she was excited and willing to help. She began to recount stories as her grandfather had when she was a young girl. At times she would apologize for getting the stories mixed up, but for the most part she surprised herself with how much she had retained. It was the first time in sixty-eight years that she had attempted to tell her grandfather's stories. And, in her words and in her mind, these stories still belonged to her grandfather. She would begin a tale by saying, "Mon grand-père contait que. . . ." [my grandfather told a story that went].

After the second and third visits, I began to notice that these stories were becoming her own. She wasn't just relating them as she remembered them, she was performing them. By taking control, she was able to add new life and style to her tales.

Enola Matthews at her home in Jennings. Photo: Maida Owens.

She manipulated them by using vocabulary and phrasing that was comfortable for her, throwing in a few words of Creole and English.

Today, when visiting with family and friends, Enola Matthews spends much of her time sharing her wonderful tales. She always has two or three new ones when I visit. She recognizes her unique talent and wants to make sure her stories live on. Although these stories were missing from her repertoire for many years, they have returned. Mme. Matthews has kept alive many of the traditions she learned in her childhood, including the skills of Creole quilting and lye soapmaking. Now she is actively revitalizing her family's storytelling art.

49. Bouki, Lapin, et Rat de Bois (Bouki, Rabbit, and Possum)

Il y avait Bouki et Lapin et Rat de Bois. And Lapin était canaille. Et Bouki et Lapin et eux autres, ça	There were Bouki and Lapin and Possum. And Lapin was naughty. And Bouki and Lapin and the others, they

travaillait. Ça fait, ils avaient plus d'eau.

Ça fait, Bouki et Rat de Bois, dit à Lapin (that is your [word for] "rabbit"), *"Allons fouiller un puits d'eau."*

"O," Lapin dit, "Moi," il dit, "Je vis sur la rosée."

Quand ils fouillaient le puits— mais le soir, quand ça allait le lendemain matin, le puits était sec. Lapin allait le soir, il volait l'eau.

Ça fait, Bouki dit à Rat de Bois, il dit, "O, je vas faire une dame en goudron. "Et," il dit, "Je vas la mettre là." Il dit, "Je connais c'est Lapin qui vient prendre l'eau et il aime beaucoup les filles."

Ça se fait, il a fait la catin en goudron puis il l'a mis au ras du puits. Quand Lapin a arrivé avec ses baquets d'eau, il a vu la fille.

"Bonjour, petite mamselle," il dit. Elle disait pas de rien.

"Bonjour, petite mamselle." Elle disait pas de rien.

Ça fait il l'a touchée. Well, *il l'a touchée et il a resté* stuck.

Il dit, "Petite mamselle, lâchez-moi." Elle lâchait pas.

Il dit, "Mo vas cogner vous, oui." Ça fait il l'a foutu la tape. Sa main, ça a resté collée.

Il dit, "Petite mamselle, m'a foutre vous un coup de pied." Elle le lâchait pas. Il l'a foutu un coup de pied. Il a resté collé.

Quand il a revenu, il dit, "Mon

were working. It happened that they ran out of water.

So Bouki and Possum say to Lapin (that means "rabbit"), "Let's dig a water well."

"Oh," Lapin says, "I," he says, "live on dew."

While they were digging the well . . . that night—when they came the next morning, the well was dry. Lapin went in the night and stole the water.

So Bouki says to Possum, he says, "Oh, I'm going to make a woman out of tar. And," he said, "I'm going to put her there." He says, "I know that it's Lapin who comes to take the water—and he loves girls."

So he made the doll from tar and he put it near the well. When Lapin came with his water buckets, he saw the girl.

"Bonjour, little miss," he says.
She said nothing.
"Bonjour, little miss."
She said nothing.

So he touched her. Well, he touched her and he got stuck.

He says, "Little miss, let me go." She didn't let go.

He says, "I'm going to hit you for sure." So he gave her a hit. His hand got stuck.

He says, "Little miss, I'm going to give you a kick." She didn't let go. He gave her a kick. He got stuck.

When he revived, he says, "I have

*gain un autre pied oui." Il l'a foutu
l'autre coup de pied. Il a resté* trap,
*c'était du goudron. Il pouvait pas
s'échapper.*

   *Ça fait quand Bouki et Rat de
Bois s'a élevé, ça dit, "O c'est toi, le
coquin qui venait voler notre eau."*

   *"Non, mais," il dit, "c'était la
première fois moi t'apé vini pour
l'eau. Mo vois petite mamselle, elle
veut pas me lâcher."*

   *Ça fait il l'a ramassé. Et force
Lapin était canaille, il dit, "Jette-moi
dans l'eau. Jette-moi dans le feu.
Mais," il dit, "Jette pas moi dans les
éronces. Parce que," il dit, "les éronces
va tout gratter ma peau." Il dit, "Tu
peux me jeter dans l'eau, n'importe
d'autres choses, dans le feu, mais,"
il dit, "Jette pas moi"—parce qu'il
connaissait ils l'auraient jeté dans les
éronces. C'est là où il voulait aller.
Ça fait quand il a été, "O mais," il
dit, "c'est là où je veux être mettre."
Quand ils l'ont tiré dans la talle
d'éronces, il dit, "Ehhh," il dit, "je
suis dans mon pays." Il dit, "C'est
là où je voulais tu me mets." Il les a
toujours embêtés.*

another foot for sure." He gave
her another kick. He was trapped,
trapped by the tar. He couldn't
escape.

   So when Bouki and Possum got
up, they said, "Oh, you're the rascal
who came to steal our water."

   "No," he says, "this was the first
time that I've come for water. I saw
the little miss, and now she doesn't
want to let go of me."

   So they seized him. And because
Lapin was naughty, he says, "Throw
me in the water. Throw me in the
fire. But"—he says—"don't throw me
in the briars. Because," he says, "the
briars will scratch my skin all up." He
says, "You can throw me in the water
or in the fire, but," he says, "don't
throw me"—because he knew that
they would throw him in the briars.
That's where he wanted to go. When
he was [in the briars], "But, oh," he
says, "that's where I want to be put."
When they had thrown him in the
briar patch, he says, "Ehhh," he says,
"I'm in my home." He says, "That's
where I wanted you to put me." He
always made fools of them.

50. Grandes Oreilles (Long Ears)

   *Un homme qui s'appelait Grandes
Oreilles—il avait des grandes oreilles.
Ça se fait quand il partait, n'importe
qui il avait besoin, il avait pas de
couteau, il usait ses oreilles. Fait, il
allait dans le bois et il coupait son
bois avec ses oreilles. Il coupait son*

   There was a man named Long
Ears. He had long ears. So when
he wandered, no matter what he
needed, if he didn't have a knife,
he used his ears. So he went into
the woods and he cut his wood with
his ears. He cut his tree down and

*arbre et il amenait son bois. C'était ses
oreilles qui étaient sa hache.*

*(Moi et mon petit frère auraient
dit, "Mais Pépère, ses oreilles doit
traîner par terre." "Oh," il dit, "il
avait des grandes oreilles.")*

*Ça fait, il allait dans les bois. Il
coupait son bois. Il l'amenait. Et si
il voulait de la viande, il lavait son
oreille. Il coupait le cou d'un veau.
Puis il usait ses oreilles pour couper
ça il voulait.*

*Là il avait parti. Quand il a parti
le chemin, il a rejoint deux hommes
qui étaient après se battre. Il les a
demandé d'arrêter. Ça voulait pas.
Ça se fait, il a passé son oreille et il
a coupé le cou de les deux. Il les a
arrêtés.*

*Et il a continué. Ayoù il passait,
dans son chemin, si c'était dans le
bois ou dans les cannes, il prenait son
oreille et il coupait comme ça.*

*Et il a été jusqu'à il a arrivé à
la montagne. Quand il a arrivé, il
a tombé dans un bas fond. Et là il
y avait des eagles. Là où les petits
eagles étaient. Et il a pris à jouer
avec les petits aigles. La vieille aigle
était pas là. Quand elle, elle a arrivé,
elle dit, "Quoi c'est que t'es après
faire?"*

*"Mais," il dit, "Je suis après jouer
avec les petits eagles."*

*Elle dit, "C'est mes petits ça." Elle
dit, "Tu connais pas je peux t'attraper
et puis aller te jeter en dedans un
autre trou."*

Là il a dit, "Je peux pas sortir." Il

he took his wood. His ears were
his axe.

(I and my little brother would have
said [at this point], "But, Grandpa,
his ears must drag the ground." "Oh,
he said, "he had long ears.")

So he went into the woods. He
cut his wood. He gathered it. And if
he wanted meat, he washed an ear.
He'd cut the throat of a calf. Then
he used his ear to slice off what he
wanted.

Then he wandered on. As he
traveled down the road, he met two
men who were fighting each other.
He told them to stop. They didn't
want to. So, he flashed his ear and he
cut both their throats. He stopped
them.

And he went on. Wherever he
went along his path, whether it was in
the woods or in the sugar cane, he
took his ear and cut like that.

And he went on until he come to
the mountains. When he got there,
he fell into a deep ravine. And there
were eagles there. That's where the
little eagles were. And he started
playing with the little eagles. The old
[mother] eagle wasn't there. When
she—she came, she said, "What are
you doing?"

"Well," he said, "I'm playing with
the little eagles."

She says, "Those are my children."
She says, "You know, I could take you
and throw you in another pit."

Then he says, "I can't get out." He

dit, *"Comment ça ferait pour tu me mets dessus ton dos et puis me fly en haut."*

"Well," elle dit, *"Pour moi faire ça faudrait j'aie de la viande pour moi manger."*

Ça fait, il a été. Je connais pas éyoù les moutons étaient. Il a été, il a tué deux moutons puis il a revenu.

"Ça sera assez, ça?"

Elle dit, "Je crois ça."

Puis il a parti. Il a monté sur son dos puis elle volait. Et elle a dit, "Donne-moi un morceau de viande chaque fois je vas dire 'Quauk.'"

Chaque fois elle disait "Quauk," *il lui jetait le morceau de viande.*

Chaque fois elle disait "Quauk," *il lui jetait le morceau de viande.*

Chaque fois, puis ça s'en allait. Quand c'est venu pour proche arriver, la viande a manqué. Quand elle a dit, "Quauk," *il a passé son oreille et il a coupé la graisse de la cuisse. Et puis il lui a donné. Quand il a mis son pied sur la butte,* "Quauk," *il a coupé l'autre quartier; il lui a donné. Ça fait, elle l'a mis en haut. Elle s'a retournée et lui il était en haut.*

says, "What if you put me on your back and flew me up?"

"Well," she says, "For me to do that, I'd have to have some meat to eat."

So he went—I don't know where the sheep were. He went, he killed two sheep, and then he came back.

"Will that be enough?"

She says, "I think so."

Then he went. He climbed on her back and she flew. And she said, "Give me a piece of meat each time I say, 'Quauk.'"

Each time she said, *"Quauk,"* he threw her the piece of meat.

Each time she said, *"Quauk,"* he threw her the piece of meat.

Each time—and they went on. When they had almost gotten there, the meat was gone. When she said, *"Quauk,"* he swished his ear and he cut some fat from his thigh. And then he gave it to her. When he put his foot on the hilltop: *"Quauk."* He cut the other thigh. He gave it to her. Then she put him on top. She went back and he was on top.

51. Les trois jobs (The Three Jobs)

Il y avait un homme qu'avait une jolie fille. (C'est toujours dans les filles. Ça m'a revenu dans la tête.) Il a demandé à le vieux homme pour marier sa fille. Ça fait il a dit, "Avant tu maries ma fille," il dit, "J'ai trois jobs pour toi faire. Et si tu fais ces

There was a man who had a pretty daughter. (The girls are always pretty in these tales; I remember that.) [A man] asked the old man if he could marry his daughter. Then [the old man] said, "Before you marry my daughter," he says, "I have three jobs *trois jobs là,* " *il dit,* "*Je vas te la donner.*"

Il dit, "*Qui c'est?*"
Il dit, "*Je veux que tu prends un bassin qui était plein de trous. Et je veux que tu vas à la rivière et*" —à peu près, lui il disait deux arpents, *that must have been* éyoù il restait—"*aller chercher l'eau avec ce bassin qui coule et remplir le carçon.*"

Et chaque fois il attrapait l'eau, ça tombait.

La fille a été le rejoindre. Elle avait une baguette. Et elle a dit à l'homme, elle dit, "*Cogne trois coups par terre et trois coups sur la rivière et dit à la rivière qu'elle va remplir le baril, le carçon.*"

Ça fait il a cogné trois coups par terre et il a cogné trois coups sur la rivière. Il dit, "*Va et remplis le baril là plein d'eau.*"

Il a été, il dit, "*Well, j'ai fini mon* job cil-là là."

"*O,*" *il dit,* "*Tu l'as rempli d'eau.*"

"*Oui.*"

"*Bien,*" *il dit.* "*L'autre, ça je veux que tu fais, et il dit,* "*Je veux que tu vas séparer l'eau et la rivière.*" *Il dit,* "*Je veux que tu sèches la rivière pour moi passer.*"

La fille a entendu, elle a fait le tour. Elle a dit, "*Va cogner ma baguette par terre. Trois coups par terre et trois coups sur le côte de la rivière et dit à l'eau de sortir, que l'eau s'en va.*" *Puis il a été, il a fait ça.*

for you to do. And if you do these three jobs," he says, "I am going to give her to you."

He asks, "What are they?"

[The old man] says, "I want you to take a bucket that is full of holes. And I want you to go to the river and—about two arpents away, that must have been, from where he lived—to go for water with that leaky bucket and fill the cistern."

And every time he got the water, it leaked out.

The girl went to meet him. She had a wand. And she said to the man, she said, "Strike the ground three times and the river three times and tell the river to go fill the barrel, the cistern."

So he struck the ground three times and he struck the river three times. He says, "Go and fill that barrel full of water."

He went. He says, "Well, I finished that job."

"Oh," [the old man] says, "you've filled it with water."

"Yes."

"Good," he says. "The next thing that I want you to do," he says, "I want you to go and take the water out of the river." He says, "I want you to dry up the river so I can cross it."

The girl heard this, she went there. She said, "Go strike my wand on the ground. Three strokes on the ground and three strokes on the river bank, and tell the water to go out. Have the water go away." Then he

Il a ouvert la rivière. La terre était sec. Il a été. Il dit, "Asteur je crois mon job est fini."

Ça fait il a été. O, la rivière était sec.

"Là," il dit, "Le job je veux que tu fais." Il y avait un arbre en glace. C'était tout de la glace. C'était haut. Il dit, "Je veux que tu vas attraper les deux oeufs en or qui est en haut."

La fille a fait le tour. Elle a été le rejoindre. Elle dit, "Qui tu fais?"

Il lui a dit, il dit, "Ton père veux je vas monter dans cet arbre là, attraper ces trois oeufs d'or (golden egg) *qu'est là-bas en haut et je peux pas grimper ça," il dit. "J'essaie et je glisse, chaque fois j'essaie et je glisse."*

"O mais," elle dit, "C'est pas rien." Elle dit, "Souffle trois fois sur moi." Et elle dit, "Je vas tomber. Je vas mourir." Là, elle dit, "Prends tous mes ossailles." Et puis elle dit, "Tu les colles. Ça va coller. Ça va faire ton échelle pour toi monter." Là, elle dit, "Quand tu vas revenir, tu vas ramener mes ossailles et tu vas me les remettre. Et souffle trois fois sur moi, je vas revenir."

So il a fait ça. Il a monté en haut. Il a attrapé les oeufs et il a revenu. Là il a attrapé les ossailles et puis il a remis. Mais il a oublié le petit doigt en haut. L'ossaille du petit doigt.

Ça fait, là il s'a mis à brailler

did that, he did that. He drained the river. The river bed was dry. He went. He says, "Now I believe my job is done."

So he went. Oh, the river was dry.

"There," [the father] says. "The job I want you to do." There was an ice tree. It was made completely of ice. It was tall. He says, "I want you to get the two golden eggs that are up at the top."

The girl went over there. She met the man. She says, "What are you doing?"

He told her; he says, "Your father wants me to go climb that tree, get the three golden eggs that are up there on top—and I can't climb that," he says. "I try and I slide down; each time I try and I slide down."

"Oh," she says, "that's nothing." She says, "Breathe on me three times." And she says, "I'm going to fall down. I'm going to die." Then she says, "Take all my bones." And then she says, "You stick them together. They will stick together. They will make a ladder for you to climb on." Then, she says, "When you come back, gather up my little bones and put them back in me. And breathe three times on me; I will revive."

So he did that. He climbed up high. He got the eggs and he came back. Then he got the bones and then he put them back. But he forgot the little finger, he left it on top. The bone of the little finger.

So he began to cry, but then she

mais elle a parlé. Elle dit, "Je suis all right." *Elle dit, "T'as quitté l'ossaille de mon petit doigt en haut dans la tête. Faudra tu retournes."*

Ça fait, faut il reprend ses ossailles de la fille encore et il a grimpé pour aller chercher le petit finger *qu'avait resté. Ça se fait, il est revenu. Il a mis les ossailles et il a soufflé trois fois sur elle et elle a revenu.*

Ça fait, sa mère lui a demandé, elle dit, "Mais qui t'as fait aussi longtemps? Eyoù tu sors?"

"O," elle dit, "J'ai été marché regarder les fleurs farouches dans la savane."

Ça fait, il a venu apporter les oeufs à son maître. Et il dit, "J'ai été les attraper et je les ai apportés." Ça fait, le maître a jamais pu comprendre comment que le garçon faisait. "Bien," il dit, "tiens prends-là. Je te la donne." Il lui a donné sa fille.

spoke. She says, "I am all right." She says, "You've left the bone of my little finger up there at the top of the tree. You must go back."

So he took the girl's bones back and he climbed up to go look for the little finger that remained. So then he came back. He put the bones down and he breathed three times on her and she revived.

Then her mother asked her, she says, "Well, what have you been doing for such a long time? Where have you been?"

"Oh," she says, "I have been out walking to look at the wildflowers on the prairie."

So he came to bring the eggs to his master. And he says, "I went to get them and brought them here." So the master couldn't understand how the boy had done that. "Well," he says, "come take her. I give her to you." He gave his daughter to him.

52. Les trois couillons (The Three Fools)

La fille s'est mariée. Le dimanche, ils ont été faire le dîner. Et la vieille a dit, "Je vas aller chercher du sirop dans le baril." Ça fait, elle a été cherché du sirop mais elle est plus revenue. Elle braillait.

Ça fait, vieux homme dit, "Laisse moi aller voir qui la vieille est après faire. Elle revient plus."

Vieux homme va. Il la trouve après brailler. Et il dit, "Quoi faire tu brailles?"

The girl got married. On Sunday they went to prepare lunch. And the old woman said, "I'm going to get some cane syrup from the barrel." Then she went to get the syrup but she didn't come back. She was crying.

Then the old man says, "Let me go see what the old woman is doing. She hasn't come back."

The old man goes. He finds her crying. And he says, "Why are you crying?"

*"Mais," elle dit, "J'étais après
jongler à ma chère petite fille quand
j'étais venu ici chercher du sirop pour
elle manger."*

Vieux homme se met à brailler.

*Ça fait, elle et son mari étaient
assis. "Well," elle dit à son mari, "Ça
revient plus. Laisse-moi aller voir qui
Pop et Mom après faire."*

*Ça fait, elle va là-bas, les trouve
après brailler. Elle dit, "Quoi faire
vous autres brailles? Qui il y a?"*

*"Mais chère, on était après jongler
quand on venait ici chercher du sirop
pour toi manger quand t'étais petite."*

*Elle elle se met à brailler avec eux
autres. Ça fait, les trois braillaient.*

*Là, le garçon était assis à la table
là-bas. "Well," il dit, "Laisse-moi
aller voir qui ça fait."*

*Lui il arrive là-bas. Il les trouve
après brailler pour leur chère petite
fille qui a autant été chercher du
sirop. Et elle était mariée et elle était
plus avec eux autres.*

*"Well," il dit, "Je vas m'en aller."
Et il dit, "Garde ta petite fille et,"
il dit, "si je trouve trois couillons
comme vous autres là, je vas revenir
et remarier ta fille."*

*Ça fait, là il a parti et il rejoint
celui-là qu'avait une paire de culottes.*

*Ça fait, il dit, "Qui t'es après
faire?"*

*"Je suis après essayer de mettre mes
pantalons. Après essayer de mettre mes
pantalons."*

*Et chaque fois il la mettait, il
mettait les deux jambes dans le même*

"Well," she says, "I was thinking
about my dear little girl; I came to
get the syrup for her to eat."

The old man starts crying.

Then, the girl and her husband
were sitting at the table. "Well," she
says to her husband, "They haven't
come back. Let me go see what Pop
and Mom are doing."

Then she goes over there and
finds them crying. She says, "Why are
you crying? What's wrong?"

"Well, darling, we were thinking
about the times that we came here
to get syrup for you to eat when you
were little."

And she starts crying with the
others. Then all three were crying.

Then, the young man was seated
at the table there. "Well," he says, "let
me go see what's going on."

He arrives there. He finds them
crying for their dear little girl who
had so often gone to find syrup. And
she was married and she wasn't with
them any more.

"Well," he says, "I'm going away."
And he says, "Keep your little girl,
and," he says, "if I find three fools
like you, I'll come back and remarry
your daughter."

So he left, and he met a man with
a pair of trousers.

Then he says, "What are you
doing?"

"I am trying to put on my pants.
Trying to put on my pants."

And each time he put them on, he
put two legs in the same hole.

canon. Ça fait, il essayait. Il a planté deux piquets puis il a monté sur la maison et il se tirait dedans et il mettait ses deux pieds toujours dans le même canon. Ça se fait sa femme a été pour l'aider. Ça pouvait pas.

Ça fait, l'autre qui cherchait pour les couillons, il a été, il dit, "Laisse-moi mettre tes pantalons." Il a mis ses pantalons. Okay ça c'est bon. Ça il dit, "Ça c'est une."

Fait, il a gone et rejoint la femme qui courrait dans la savane avec une baille. Il dit, "Qui elle est après faire?"

Quand elle allait dans sa maison puis elle sortait la course encore. Il dit, "Qui il y a? Qui t'es après faire?"

Elle dit, "J'ai froubi ma cuisine et puis je suis après essayer m'attraper du soleil pour aller lâcher dans ma maison pour la sécher." Et elle dit, "Quand j'arrive ma baille est vide." (Elle était après essayer d'attraper du soleil.)

Ça fait, il a dit, "Ça, c'est deux."

Il a gone. Là il a rejoint Jean Sot. Jean Sot a été et les gypsies lui a donné une aiguille. Ça fait, il a mis l'aiguille dans son wagon avec son bois. Ça fait, il s'a retourné, il déchargeait son bois tout doucement.

Ça fait, sa Mémère dit, "Qui il y a, Jean Sot?"

Et il dit, "Les gypsies m'a donné une aiguille et puis," il dit, "Je l'ai mis dans le wagon."

"Mais," elle dit, "Cher, quand ça te donne quelque comme chose ça, t'attaches ça après toi."

So he tried. He tried two more times, and then he put down two sticks and he climbed up on the house and he jumped down, but he always put his two feet in the same hole. So his wife went to help him. They couldn't do it.

Then the man who was looking for fools, he said, "Let me put your pants on." He put on his pants. Okay, that's good. Then he says, "There, that's one [fool]."

Then he left and met a woman who was running through the prairie with a bucket. He says, "What is she doing?"

Then she went in the house and then she went out and did it again. He says, "What's wrong? What are you doing?"

She says, "I've mopped my kitchen and now I'm trying to catch some sunlight and get it into my kitchen to dry it out." And she says, "When I come back my bucket is empty." (She was trying to catch sunlight [with it].)

Then he said, "There, that's the second one."

He left. Then he met Jean Sot. Jean Sot went, and the gypsies had given him a needle. And he put the needle in his wagon with his wood. Then he went back, gently unloading his wood.

Then his mother says, "What's wrong, Jean Sot?"

And he says, "Then gypsies gave me a needle and," he says, "I put it in my wagon."

*Ça fait, il a retourné. C'est là
ils lui ont donné la charrue. Une
charrue. Il a essayé, il a essayé de
l'attacher, il a essayé de l'attacher.
Mais quelque manière il est arrivé,
son linge était tout déchiré avec la
charrue.*

*Sa mère dit, "Mais qu'il y a? Qu'il
y a?"*

*"Bien, mais," il dit, "J'ai pas pu
attacher ça après moi!"*

*Elle dit, "Imbécile, quand ça te
donne quelque chose comme ça," elle
dit, "Tu mets ça dans le wagon."*

Ça se fait quand il s'a retourné
back, *il a passé et les gypsies lui a
donné la taure. Ça fait, il a mis
la taure dans le wagon et la taure
sautait par terre. Il a mis la taure
dans le wagon et la taure sautait par
terre.*

*Puis il a été et il a dit a sa maman,
il dit, "Ils m'ont donné une taure."
Il dit, "Je l'ai mis dans le wagon,
elle saute par terre. Et je peux pas la
garder."*

*"Mais," elle dit, "Quand ça te
donne quelque chose comme ça," elle
dit, "Faut tu la pousses en avant toi
avec un petit fouet'" elle dit, "Puis tu
l'amènes à la maison."*

*Ça fait, il a retourné encore. Ils lui
ont donné une grande chaudière à
laver. Une grande chaudière. Ça fait,
il cognait la chaudière. Fouettait la
chaudière pour la faire marcher. La
chaudière pouvait pas marcher.*

*Ça se fait, là, il dit à sa Maman, il
dit, "Ils m'ont donné une chaudière.*

"Well," she says, "Dear, when
someone gives you something like
that, stick it to your shirt."

So he went back. Then they gave
him a plow. A plow. He tried, he tried
to attach it to his shirt. But no matter
what he did, his clothes were torn up
by the plow.

His mother said, "Well what's
wrong? What's wrong?"

"Well," he says, "I can't attach it to
my shirt."

She says, "Imbecile! When some
gives you something like that," she
says, "you put it in the wagon."

So when he went back, the gypsies
gave him a heifer. So he put the
heifer in the wagon, and the heifer
jumped out on the ground. He put
the heifer in the wagon, and the
heifer jumped out on the ground.

So he went and he said to his
mother, he says, "They gave me a
heifer." He says, "I put her in the
wagon; she jumps out. And I can't
keep her in."

"Well," she says, "when they give
you something like that," she says,
"you must drive it ahead of you with a
little whip," she says, "and then you
drive it to the house."

So he went back again. They gave
him a big washtub. A big tub. So
he was hitting the tub—whipping it
to make it walk. The tub couldn't
move.

So then he said to his mother,
he says, "They gave me a tub.

Elle veut pas marcher en avant de moi."

"Mais," elle dit, "Quand ça te donne quelque chose comme ça," elle dit, "Faut tu mets ça sur ta tête ou bien le mettre dans le wagon."

Fait, là, il a été, ils lui ont donné le mouton. Ça fait, là, il mettait le mouton sur sa tête. Et le mouton le cognait à coup de pieds et tout ça. Mais il a arrivé à la maison.

Ça fait le bougre était après le guetter. "Well," il dit, "Tout ça-là," il dit, "il a jamais compris qui fallait il fait."

Ça fait, là, il a parti. Ça c'était ses trois couillons. Mais il s'a retourné marer la fille encore.

It wouldn't move ahead of me."

"Well," she says, "when they give you something like that," she says, "you have to carry it on your head, put it in the wagon."

So then when he went there, they gave him a sheep. Then he put the sheep on his head. And the sheep kicked him and all that. But he made it to the house.

Then the guy [with the silly wife] was watching. "Well," he says, "with all that," he says, "he never understood what he was supposed to do."

So he left. He had his three fools. So he went back and married the girl again.

53. Jean Sot, la Vache, les chiens, et sa petite soeur (Jean Sot, the Cow, the Dogs, and Little Sister)

The following tale relies on the double meanings of words. Foolish John is asked to "milk" [tirer] the cow, but he takes these orders as commands to "shoot" [tirer] the cow. And when he is to tap [cogner] the chair to make the baby sleep, he uses the baby to hit [cogner] the chair and put her to sleep forever.

Ça fait, la maman a dit à Jean Sot, elle dit, "Je suis gone travailler dans le clos." Et elle avait un petit, un petit bébé. Elle dit, "Tu vas faire dormir ta petite soeur."

Il dit, "Comment?" Ils avient pas jamais de berceuse.

Elle dit, "Tu cognes la chaise."

Là, elle dit, "Tu vas tirer la vache et," elle dit, "Mets du persil et des onions dans le gombo."

Ça fait, il a été, il a attrapé le fusil. Elle a dit, "Tire la vache." Ça fait, il a attrapé le fusil, il a tiré la vache.

So the mother said to Jean Sot, she says, "I'm going to work in the field." And she had a little one, a little baby. She says, "You're going to put your little sister to bed."

He says, "How?" (They didn't have a crib.)

She says, "You rock [hit] the chair." Then, she says, "You're going to milk [shoot] the cow, and," she says, "put parsley and onions in the gumbo."

So he went, he got the gun. (She said, "milk [shoot] the cow.") so he

(Elle a mean *tirer* [milk] *la vache.) Mais lui, il l'a tiré au fusil. Il a tiré la vache.*

Et il a attrapé les deux petits chiens qui s'appelaient Persil et Onions, et il les a mis dans la chaudière. Et puis il s'a assis dessus pour les tenir.

Là il a pris sa petite soeur et il l'a cognée après la chaise. Et puis il l'a jetée dans le lit. Elle s'a plus réveillée.

Ça fait, quand sa maman est venu, elle dit, "T'as tiré la vache?"

"O, oui," il dit, "Elle est par terre."

Et elle dit, "T'as fait dormir ta petite soeur?"

"Oui," il dit, "Un coup-là, elle a dormi." Il dit, "Je l'ai mis dans le lit, elle s'a jamais réveillée."

"Et," elle dit, "T'as mis du persil et des onions dans la chaudière?"

Il dit, "Oui." Puis il dit, "Fallait je m'assis dessus. Parce que," il dit, "Ça voulait pas rester." Quand elle a ouvert sa chaudière, ses deux chiens étaient bouillis dans le gombo.

got the gun, he shot the cow. (She meant "milk" the cow.) But he shot it with a gun. He shot the cow.

And he got the two little dogs that were named Parsley and Onions, and he put them in the pot. And then he sat down on it to keep them in.

Then he took his little sister and hit her on the chair. And then he threw her in the bed. And she never woke up again.

So when his mother came, she said, "Did you milk [shoot] the cow?"

"Oh, yes," he said, "she's on the ground."

And she says, "Did you get your little sister to sleep?"

"Yes," he says, "One blow, then she slept." He said, "I put her in the bed, and she never woke up."

"And," she says, "Did you put parsley and onions in the gumbo?"

He says, "Yes." Then he says, "I had to sit on the pot. Because," he says, "they didn't want to stay in there." When she opened the pot, the two dogs were boiled in the gumbo.

54. La fille du Roi (The King's Daughter)

Le Roi voulait pas qu'il marie sa fille. Il allait quand même. Le Roi voulait pas, mais il allait quand même. Et la fille, elle l'aimaissait. Ça se fait, le Roi l'a attrapé puis l'a mis dans une cage. Et il dit, "Je vas aller te jeter dans la rivière. Je vas te noyer." Là il dit, "Tu viendras plus."

[There was a man;] the King didn't want him to marry his daughter. But he went, anyway. The King didn't want this, but [the man] went anyway. And the girl, she loved him. So the King got the man and put him in a cage. And he says, "I'm going to throw you in the river. I'm going to drown you." Then, he says,

Ça se fait, il l'a amené. Quand il a arrivé à la rivière il a mis la cage là, et il a été comme plus loin pour faire quelque chose. Et il était après brailler en dedans. Mais il y avait un autre. Un de ses camarades qui venait qu'il connaissait qui poussait des moutons à cheval.

Il arrivait, mais il dit, "Qui tu fais là, un tel?"

Mais il dit, "Le Roi veut je marie sa fille, et moi, je veux pas."

"O," il dit, "Moi, je vas la marier."

"Bien," il dit, "Ôte-moi ici dans et prends ma place," il dit.

Il l'a ôté et il a monté dessus le cheval et gone *avec les moutons.*

Et le vieux Roi est revenu. Quand il l'a attrapé, il a dit, "O," il dit, "non, Monsieur Roi. Jetez pas moi dans la rivière. Je vas marier votre fille."

"O," il dit, "Tu vas marier ma fille?" Mais il dit, "Oui, je vas te jeter."

Il l'a tiré dans la rivière là-bas.

Ça fait, ça a resté trois ou quatre jours. Tiens, il voit le même qu'il voulait jeter dans la rivière venir. Mais il dit, "Mais regarde donc un tel. Mais je croyais je t'avais jeté dans la rivière, toi, et te noyé."

"Oh non," il dit, "Là où vous m'as jeté," il dit, "j'ai juste trouvé

"You'll never come back."

So [the king] took him. When he came to the river he put the cage there, and he went away to do something. And the man [in the cage] was crying in there. But there was another man, one of his two comrades, a man that he knew, who was coming on horseback, driving sheep.

He came, and he said, "What are you doing there?"

And he says, "The King wants me to marry his daughter, and I don't want to."

"Oh," he says, "then I'll marry her."

"Well," he says, "get me out of here and take my place."

He lifted him out, and the man mounted the horse and left with the sheep.

And the old King came back. When [the King] took the cage, [the man inside] says, "Oh," he says, "no, Mr. King. Don't throw me in the river. I'll marry your daughter."

"Oh," he says, "you're going to marry my daughter?" Well, he says, "Yes, I'm going to toss you."

He threw him into the river.

So three or four days went by. Then the King sees coming the same man that he wanted to throw in the river. Well, he says, "Would you look at that. But I thought that I'd thrown you in the river and drowned you."

"Oh, no," he says, "the place where you threw me," he says, "I only found

le cheval et les moutons." Il dit,
"Si vous m'aurais eu jeté plus loin,
j'aurais trouvé de l'argent, et de l'or
et j'aurais eu des bêtes et tout quelque
chose. Mais," il dit, "C'est juste là
où vous m'a mis là, c'est ça j'ai
trouvé."

"O," il dit, "Moi, je veux aller."

"Bien, mais" il dit, "Je peux vous
jeter, vous, là-bas."

Ça fait, il dit, "Oui, viens me
jeter."

Ça se fait, il l'a pris. Il a été là-bas
et puis il a tiré le Roi en dans la
rivière dans une cage aussi.

Ça se fait, s'en aller, s'en aller.
Son monde était après guetter. Ça dit,
"Qui il dit?"

Ça entendait, "Gloupe, gloupe."

"Oh mais," il dit, "Il est après
trouver les bêtes et l'argent et l'or
asteur."

a horse and sheep." He says, "If you'd thrown me a little farther, I would have found silver, and gold, and I would have had livestock and everything. But," he says, "I just found what there was in the place where you threw me."

"Oh," [the King] says, "I want to go."

"Well, then," he says, "I can throw you there."

So he says, "Yes, come throw me."

So he took [the King]. He went over there and then he threw the King in the river—in a cage, too.

So [the king] went away, he went away. His people were watching. They say, "What is he saying?"

They heard: "Gloop, gloop."

"Well," [the young man] says, "he's finding the animals and the silver and the gold now."

55. Séparer le maïs dans le cimitière (Dividing Corn in the Cemetery)

Quand ça disait "compter," ça
mettait une pour moi, une pour toi.
Comme si on aurait pour séparer
une piastre. Ça dirait un cinq sous
pour moi, un cinq sous pour toi. Ça,
ça se séparait quand ç'arrivait à la
moitié.

Ça fait, il y avait un clos de
maïs. Des jolis grands maïs. Il
y a deux hommes qu'a décidé,
c'était pas loin du cimitière. Ils
ont décidé, ils ont été snap du

What we meant when we said "counting" was: we would divide things up and say, "One for me, one for you." This was the way we would divide up a dollar. We would say, "one nickel for me, one nickel for you." It would all be divided up when we got to the middle.

So there was a cornfield. Big, beautiful corn stalks. There are two men who decided—they weren't very far from the cemetery. They decided, they went to pick corn at night.

maïs le soir. Ils ont été voler du maïs.

Ça fait, quand ils ont arrivé à la porte. Il dit, "Comment un tas de maïs on a dans le sac?" "Well," il dit, "On va se les séparer."

Ça fait, il disait, "Un pour toi, un pour moi. Un pour toi, un pour moi."

Eux autres estiont après séparer le maïs dans le cimitière. Là il y avait deux hommes qui étaient après passer. Ils les entendaient. Il dit, "Une pour toi, une pour moi. Une pour toi, une pour moi."

L'autre dit, "Hé, arrête, toi!" Il dit, "Écoute ce que j'entends."

"Un pour toi, un pour moi."

"O," il dit, "le Bon Dieu et le diable après séparer les morts."

Ils ont baissé à se sauver. Ils ont été là-bas, ils ont dit à les autres, ça dit, "On a passé au cimetière. On a attendu le Bon Dieu et le diable après séparer les morts." Et il dit, "Un pour toi, un pour moi. Un pour toi, un pour moi."

Puis c'était les hommes qui étaient après séparer le maïs ils avaient volé.

"Mais," il dit, "Le diable et le Bon Dieu étaient après séparer les morts."

They went to steal corn.

So when they got to the gate. One says, "How much corn do we have in the sack? Well," he says, "we're going to divide it up."

So he was saying, "One for you, one for me. One for you, one for me."

They were dividing up the corn in the cemetery. Then there were two men passing by. They heard them saying, "one for you, one for me. One for you, one for me."

One man say, "Hey, stop." He says, "Listen to what I hear."

"One for you, one for me."

"Oh," he says, "The Good Lord and the devil are dividing the dead."

They took off at a dead run. And they went away, and told other people, they said, "We passed by the cemetery. We heard the Good Lord and the devil dividing the dead." And he says, "One for you, one for me. One for you, one for me."

(It was really people who were dividing the corn that they'd stolen.)

But he says, "The devil and the Good Lord were dividing the dead."

Alfred Anderson:
Master Teacher of a Family Tradition

DONALDSONVILLE, ASCENSION PARISH

Introduced by Carl Lindahl

Folklore favors the extrovert. Seeking to coax stories from a strange community, the collector inevitably finds the loudest talkers but not always the best. Some of the great storytellers in Louisiana, as elsewhere, are those whose art stays home.

Alfred Anderson is a case in point. He never sat on a stage. He was not interested in sharing his stories beyond his family circle. Yet he was an absolutely masterful storyteller, the best I've been privileged to hear.

Only because his daughter, Debra, was a student in my folklore class was I able to hear Alfred Anderson. After reading several tales from a textbook, she told me that her father knew similar stories. At my request she prodded him to share his art. Since 1982, when he taped seven of his favorite tales in one sitting, hundreds of my students have been moved by the voice of this unassuming man who never left his home to tell a tale.

One of eleven children brought up near Donaldsonville, Alfred became in turn the father of fifteen. As a child he learned stories from his father, and as a father he passed them on to his children. Although people of all ages admire his artistry, he reserved these tales solely for young listeners. They are products of a time when parents, and not TV or radio, provided home entertainment.

Anderson's stories belong to a worldwide body of fantasy narrative and possess analogues in such international classics as Grimms' fairy tales. "The Girls and the Alligator," for example, is extremely close in plot to "The Wolf and the Kids" as rendered by the Grimms; both are classified by folklorists as belonging to the same tale type, AT 123. But far from being a rubber stamp of the Grimm tale, "The Girls and the Alligator" has been flavored by Alfred Anderson's environment, the Louisiana bayous. This is the only published version of AT 123 that features an alligator as the villain. For Alfred and his listeners, the reference to a killer alligator was no mere fantasy. It was part of safety education. Anderson ends his story: "I got out of there, because that alligator was terrible."

Anderson blends a world of rich imagination with lessons of common sense survival. He works himself into his stories, hinting that he was present when the

Alfred Anderson before his brother's funeral in 1989. Photo: Courtesy of Debra Anderson Forney.

events of the tale unfolded. He ends many of his tales with the formula, "I stepped on a wire, and the wire bent. . . ." In one sense, this phrase—like "they lived happily ever after"—is merely a convenient way of closing a story. Yet, in another sense, it implies that the tale is not entirely make-believe—that it possesses an impact and a use in the day-to-day world in which it is told.

And that is exactly the way in which Alfred Anderson's children understand his stories. Their father was their finest teacher, and his stories were their most effective learning tool. He told the story of "Skullbone"—of the man who died trying to share the secret of a talking skull—as a warning against tattling. To this day Debra and her brothers and sisters consider "Skullbone" a model lesson in how—and why—one keeps a secret.

Alfred Anderson's heroines and heroes are resourceful people valiantly struggling to succeed in a dangerous world. Although the stories are filled with magical features—talking animals, for example—there are no kings and queens. The characters reflect the South Louisiana African-American culture that shaped these tales. Children use their wits to save themselves from danger—but they do not marry princes or princesses. Intelligence and loyalty are their greatest strengths, and simple survival,

*rather than a magic kingdom, is their reward. The successful characters are smart.
In "The Lazy Sisters and the Smart Sister," intelligence and virtue go hand in hand:
to be smart is to be fair, hardworking, and caring. In "Brer Bear Meets Man," Brer
Rabbit is "a smart fellow" who manages to avoid the blast of the shotgun, though he
cannot convince the stupid bear to follow his example.*

*No oral performance translates perfectly to print, but Alfred Anderson's tales
suffer more than most from the disruption. His stories relied on vocal flourishes that
cannot be rendered on paper. He used high-pitched tones to impersonate women and
children and adopted an ominous low tone when depicting the alligator. Singing
enlivened his stories: the bird in "My Mama Killed Me," the boy in "The Toodling
Horn," and the alligator in "The Girls and the Alligator" all have musical roles. Like
other great African-American narrators, Anderson was a master mimic who enriched
his tales with sounds that imitate the noises of nature. An Anderson alligator does
not merely lie in the sun, it traps flies in its jaws. To depict this action, Anderson
would make a clicking sound with his mouth. The sound of a huge animal feeding
contentedly on a tiny victim entertains the audience but also adds to the plot, because
it underlines the central action: the alligator's swallowing the baby girl.*

*With Alfred Anderson's death at age sixty-four in February 1991, Louisiana
lost one of its most modest and one of its great storytelling teachers. But his children
and grandchildren still have these tales as reminders of how much he taught them.*

56. The Girls and the Alligator

So—they had a lady. She used to work. And she had three daughters.
So she told the little girl, she said, "I'm going to work." She said, "I want
you all to stay upstairs until I come back." Because they had a big alligator—
right outside of the house, they had a big *pond* down there. Big Alligator
stayed there. So the mom and the daddy was working. And she told her
three daughters, "I want you to go upstairs. And you stay up there till I *call*
for you. And this is the way I'm going to call: [clears throat, then, in a low,
chanting tone] "*Ma-ma-li-to, dee-tunk, dee-tunk, dee-tum.*"

Says, "When you hear that, you come down."

But the alligator was *listening*. And he heard what the lady said. So he
was trying to make his voice sound like the little children's mother. And he
practiced on that word. Alligator went [in a very deep voice, parodying the
mother's voice], "*Ma-ma-li-to, dee-wump, dee-wump, dee-wump.*"

He said, "No, that's not it. Try it again: *Ma-ma-li-to, dee-dum, dee-dum,
dee- dum.*"

He say, "Oh, no, that don't *sound* right." So he finally got it almost like the mother: "*Ma-ma-li-to, dee-dum, dee-dum, dee-dum.*"

So after the lady went to work, it was *dark* down there. You couldn't see nothing. That old alligator waited till the mother and they got away from the house—almost around time for the mother to come home. Then he goes trying to fool the little girls downstairs, so he could eat them. He goes to the bottom of the stairs, and he called, almost like the mother:

"*Ma-ma-li-to, dee-dum, dee-dum, dee-dum.*"

The little baby girl said [high voice], "Oh, that's mother, that's mother. I'm going downstairs."

The oldest sister said, "No. Don't go. That's not mother. That's that alligator."

"No. That's my mother calling. I'm going."

So the two sisters were trying to hold the little girl, but she got away from them. And she *ran* down the stairs—right in the mouth of that alligator. And he swallowed her. After he swallowed the little girl, that old alligator dragged on back out to the pond, laid on the bank of the pond, sunning himself, with his mouth wide open, catching flies [sound of jaws snapping]— *dunk*. Every time he gets a mouthful of flies—*dunk*—take them. *Dunk*. Mouth wide open. *Dunk*. Yep.

Mother came home. So she went to call her children. She wanted to get them as fast as she can. Say, "*Ma-ma-li-to, dee-tum, dee-tum, dee-tum.*"

The girls go, "Oh, that's mother, that's mother." So they came downstairs, the two oldest sisters. And when they got down there, the mother say, "Oh, where's my baby?"

Say, "*Mama,* something terrible happened! The *alligator* got little sister."

"*Say, What!*"

"Alligator got little sister. The alligator came and called, *almost* like you. We *told* little sister not to go downstairs. But she came down anyway and she ran right in the mouth of that alligator, and he done swallowed little sister."

[High, piercing voice] "Oh, my *baby!* Alligator got my baby. My *poor* little *baby!*" Mama went to crying and hollering for her baby.

So here come the daddy. He heard the mama crying and carrying on. So he said, "What's the matter? What happened?"

She said, "Oh, alligator got little sister. The alligator ate my little baby."

He said, "*What!*" Took his pocket knife out into his mouth and opened the blade with his teeth and ran down to that pond. That old big alligator was still laying down on the bank, just catching flies. *Dunk. Dunk.* Mouth wide open. And that man ran down and he jumped on that alligator with his pocket knife. He went to cutting that alligator, cut him, and turned that alligator over, and split his guts open, and opened them up. And the little girl jumped out.

And he grabbed the little girl. And the mother hugged her. She grabbed her and kissed her and said [high, excited voice], "Oh, my *baby, baby*!" And then went in the house and they all were so happy they had got that little girl back.

And I stepped on the wire, and that wire bent, and I left there. Because that alligator was terrible. And that's the end of that story.

57. The Toodling Horn

And they had a little boy . . . He had four dogs. And every day . . . he had to go take his daddy his toodling horn. His daddy was working way back in the woods. So one morning he got ready to go take his daddy his toodling horn. He went to his mama. He said to his mama, "Mama, if you see the dogs raring against the chains," he said, "turn them loose."

Mama said, "All right, son."

So he starting out walking through the woods. First thing he did, he met Brer Rabbit.

Brer Rabbit say, "Where you going, little boy?"

"Oh," he say, "I'm going in the woods to carry my papa his toodling horn."

He say, "How about blow me a little something for me before you go?"

Boy say, "All right [in a melodic voice, imitating a horn]: *Toodle-loo, toodle loodle loodle loo.*"

Brer Rabbit say, "Boy, that sounds good." He said, "Play a little when you meet Brer Possum back there."

He walked a little further down the road—he met Brer Possum. Brer Possum say, "Where you going, little boy?"

He said, "I'm going to the woods to carry my papa his toodling horn."

He said, "Well, boy, why don't you blow me a little something for me before you go?"

Boy say, "All right: *Toodle-loo, toodle loodle loodle loo.*"

"Say, oh, that sound pretty good. Play it for old Brer Fox sitting back there."

Walks on a little further, he meets Brer Fox.

Brer Fox say, "Where you going, little boy?"

He say, "I'm going to the woods to take my papa his toodling horn."

Say, "How about blowing a little something for me?"

Boy say, "All right: *Toodle-loo, toodle loodle loodle loo.*"

"Oh, that sounds all right," he said. "But look. You going to meet old Brer Bear back there," he say. "Old Bear kind of hungry," he say. "He's a little angry this morning. He may eat you up."

Little Boy say, "Okay." Little boy walked on a little further down the road. Till he met Brer Bear. Brer Bear say, "Where you going, little boy?"

He say, "I'm going to the woods to carry my papa his toodling horn."

"Hey, blow a little something for me before you go."

Boy say, "*Toodle-loo, toodle loodle loodle loo.*"

Bear say, "Oh! Boy, that thing sound good. I tell you what. Come a little closer and blow that horn."

So the boy got a little closer to him: "*Toodle-loo, toodle loodle loodle loo.*"

"Oh boy," he say. "That sound *real good.*" Says, "I tell you what." He say, "Come up a little *closer* to me—and blow that horn."

Little boy got a little closer to the bear. He begin to get a little worried. He said, "*Toodle-loo, toodle loodle loodle loo.*"

Bear says, "Oh boy, that thing sounds too good. I tell you what. Why not stand on my *hip* and blow it?"

Little boy say, "Well, do you mind if I say a prayer?"

Bear said, "No. Go ahead."

Boy said, [singing] "Here, Ro-ver,

Counsel-lo,

Daddy-o,

And Jim—

Don't you hear your master calling you?" And, boy, the dogs went to—looking. But his *mama* was in the house sleeping.

Bear says, "Oh, boy, that thing sounds so good." He says, "I tell you what. Come up a little higher on my *back* and blow it."

"Here, Ro-ver,

Counsel-lo,

Daddy-o,

And Jim—

Don't you hear your master calling you?" And the dogs start to raring against the chain and barking: "*Ooh-woo, ooh-woo.*" And Mama, she's still sleeping.

Bear says, "Boy, sounds so good," he says. "I tell you what. Come up a little higher and blow it."

And the boy walked up a little higher on his back and said,

"Here, Ro-ver,
Counsel-lo,
Daddy-o,
and Jim—
Don't you hear your master calling you?"

And those four dogs went to raring on the chain and hollering and barking, and finally the mama heard it. She *jumped* up out of the bed, said, "Oh," she said, "these old dogs is raring against the chain! Little Brother must be calling." And she went out in the yard and she untied those four dogs. And they laid out into the woods.

And that bear told that boy, say, "Boy, that sounds so good." Said, "I tell you what." Said, "Stand on my shoulder and blow that horn."

So the little boy got on his shoulder; he began to getting worried, *scared*. Then his voice started trembling [in a trembling voice]:

"Here Ro-ver,
Counsel-lo,
Daddy-o,
And Jim—
Don't you hear your master calling you?"

That bear say, "*Ooh, ooh*. That sound *so good*." Says, "I tell you *what*. Why don't you stand on my *head*—and blow that horn."

Little boy start to worry. He start to crying. *Tears* running down his face. His voice got in a tremble. He said, [as if crying]:

"Here Ro-ver—*sniff, sniff*—
Counsel-lo—*sniff, sniff*—
Daddy-o—*sniff, sniff*—
and Jim—
Don't you hear your master calling you?"

He says, "*Oh!* That sound *beau*tiful." Says, "I tell you what. Get on my *lip* and blow that."

The little boy got on his lip:

"Here Ro-ver—*sniff, sniff*—
Counsel-lo—*sniff, sniff*—
Daddy-o—*sniff, sniff*—
And Jim—*sniff, sniff*—
Don't you hear your master calling you?"

And those four dogs was running and barking like mad. And that old bear said, "*Boy*, I tell you what. That sound *so good*, I want you to stand on my *tongue* and blow that horn."

Well, the boy got on his *tongue*:

"*Sniff, sniff*—Here Ro-ver—*sniff, sniff*—

[in a softer voice] Counsel-lo,

Daddy-o,

And Jim—

Don't you hear your master calling you?"

Just at that time, that bear swallowed him. And just as he swallowed that little boy, those four dogs was coming around the corner. And they jumped on that bear, and they ripped that bear apart. And they tore that bear open, and that little boy jumped out, and say, "I'm going in the woods and carry my papa his toodling horn: *Toodle-loo, toodle loodle loodle loo.*"

And I stepped on the wire, and the wire bent, and I left. And that's the end of that story. Because I didn't want those four dogs to get me.

58. My Mama Killed Me, My Papa Ate Me

I'll tell you about the one story about the little girl and little boy. And the mother didn't have too much to *eat* at the house. They were poor. So the mama said—she called the little brother and the little sister home—she said, "I want you two to go get me a sack of chips. And the first one to come back, I'll bake them a cake."

So the little boy and the little sister went out to get some chips for the mother to make a fire in the stove to cook. And he was thinking to get back, because when he got back, the mother would make him a big cake. So Little Brother, he came back first. And when he came back home first, the mother grabbed him. She was sharpening on a big knife, and she grabbed the little boy, and she—*Swussh*—cut off his head. She said, "Hah, I shall eat you today."

And she cut up Little Brother and she put him in a pot to cook him. And Little Brother just kept jumping out of the pot, jumping out of the pot. And the mother just kept saying, "You can jump, but I shall *eat you* today." So finally she cooked Little Brother, and when she went to fix dinner, Little Sister was *suspicious*. She said, "Mother, I don't want to eat anything." She asked—then she asked, "Mother, where is Little Brother?"

She said, "Oh, Little Brother went over there by *Commère* to play."

Little girl goes over there by *Commère*, looks for Little Brother; Little

Brother wasn't there. She came back and she say, "Mother," she say, "Little Brother is not by *Commère.*"

She said, "Little Brother went by *Compère* to play." Little Girl go over by *Compère*'s house, and Little Brother wasn't there. And everywhere the mother sent the little girl to look for Little Brother, Little Brother wasn't there.

So, when she went to fix dinner—the little girl wouldn't—you know, she fixed the dinner. But the little girl say, "Mother, don't fix me nothing. I don't want to eat."

So the daddy was coming home. So when he got to the house, he asked the same question, said, "Where's Little Brother?" Say, "Little Brother usually come *meet* me every day. This time I didn't see him."

Mother say, "Oh, Little Brother went *way* over, way over by *Compère,* to *play*. He ain't come back yet."

Little Girl didn't say nothing.

So when they set the table to *eat*, Little Girl say to her daddy, she say, "I don't want to eat, but—all the little bones—I want you to save the little bones."

And she spread her little silk pocket handkerchief. And when he eat, he put the bones into the handkerchief. And after he got through eating, the little girl took the pocket handkerchief with the bones, and went out, and she buried them under a *marble* stone.

So after they got through eating, the daddy was sitting down in a rocking chair with his pipe in his mouth, sitting down a-rocking. And a little *bird* flew in the window. Said, [singing]

"My *ma*-ma killed me,
My *pa*-pa ate me,
And my little sister buried my bones
Under a *mar*-ble stone."

And Daddy looked around, and he said, "Hah! That little bird's a-singing a song!" He flew out a way, then flew back to the window again:

"My *ma*-ma killed me,
My *pa*-pa ate me,
And my little sister buried my bones
Under a *mar*-ble stone."

Dad say, "There's something *funny* going on over here—something strange." He said, "I wonder what's happening. What's that? That *bird* is singing a song!"

And that bird flew out the window, and he flew *back* into the window *again.* He said,

"My *ma*-ma killed me,

My *pa*-pa ate me,

And my little sister buried my bones

Under a *mar*-ble stone."

He said, "Wait a minute. Something strange here." He said, "Mama, say, *where is* Little Brother?"

She said, "I ate, we ate—you just got through eating Little Brother."

He said, "*What!*" So he grabbed her. He cut *her* head off. Yeah, then he had her hanging up—meat like a hog—the way you'd kill and hang a hog or something.

Here come *Commère* a-saying [shrill, high voice], "*Compère,* where's *Commère?*"

He says, "Oh, *Commère*—she went out to visit her people. She ain't come back yet."

She say [same high voice]: "What all that meat hanging up there? You kill that hog and *Commère* not here?" She say, "Give me some of that meat."

He said, "Go ahead. Help yourself."

She went along, she got some of that meat. She go home, she cook. She had four dogs—she fed her dogs.

Next day she came by the house again. She said [shrilly], "*Commère, Commère!* Ain't she back yet?"

He said, "No."

She said, "I sure could use some more of that meat."

He said, "Well, go ahead, *Commère,* help yourself."

She got some more of the meat, and, so, she cook it and fed her and her dogs. And she did that until all of *Commère* was gone. She ate *Commère.* And the last piece of *Commère* she had, she went back to the house.

She said, "*Compère! Commère* hasn't come back yet?"

He said, "No. You just ate the last of *Commère.*"

And she said [screaming]: "*What!*" [Audience laughs.]

He said, "You just ate the last of *Commère.*"

She went home; she called her dogs [Wildly, in a high-pitched voice]:

"Here, Rover!

"Here, Rounder!

"Here, Fido!

"Here, Spot! [Children laugh.]

"Come on." And all the dogs came a-running.

She puked, made her four dogs puke. She took a long iron rod, she ran it down all the dogs' throats, and she ran it down her own throat. She almost killed herself.

And [laughing] I stepped on the wire, girl. And the wire bent. And I left. [In a whispering, mysterious voice:] Because *Compère* might have caught me. And that's the end of that story.

59. The Lazy Sisters and the Smart Sister

Once upon a time there was three girls—three little girls. And their daddy used to work in the woods. So Daddy got ready to work one morning, and told his wife, he said, "Look," he said, "I'm going to work," he said. "I want the oldest girl to bring me my lunch."

So the mother said, "How will she find you?"

He said, "I'm going to the store and buy a big bag of corn." He said, "Wherever I go, I'm going to drop corn." He say, "Just follow the corn. That's where I'll be working."

The next morning he went on out, just started walking, dropped corn all the way, and as he dropped the corn, the birds came along and picked the corn up. So the little girl started walking. She went out in the woods. She couldn't find her pa. She got lost. She couldn't come out.

So the night got *dark*. She was way back in the woods. She didn't know where she was. And she looked across. Over there she saw a *light*. She went over by the house where the light was and she knocked at the door, saw an old lady there.

She said, "Ma'am," she said, "I'm lost," she said. "Would you mind showing me the way out of the woods," she said. "I came to bring my father his lunch and I got *lost*."

So the lady said, "All right," she said. "Tomorrow morning, if you do everything I tell you to do *tonight*," she said, "tomorrow morning I will take you to the edge of the woods and show you the way back home."

She said, "Thank you."

"But first thing," she say, "you have to do, you have to go in there and cook supper."

Little girl went in the house. She cooked supper.

The old lady said, "Now you've got to fix *my* supper, your supper, the bull supper, the cat supper, and the dog supper." So the girl goes in there, and she fixes her supper, the old lady supper; she fix the cat supper, and the dog supper. But she didn't fix the bull supper.

The old lady said, "Now, go upstairs and fix the *beds*. Said, "Fix my bed, your bed, the cat's bed, the dog's bed and—the *cow* bed."

So the girl goes up there, upstairs. She fix her a bed, the old lady bed, the cat bed, the dog a bed—but she didn't fix the *cow* a bed.

So the next morning she got up. The old lady said, "Now you've got to go fix breakfast." The girl cooked the breakfast. She said, "Now fix my breakfast, your breakfast, the cat breakfast, the dog breakfast, and the bull breakfast."

The girl fixed her breakfast, the old lady's breakfast, the cat breakfast, the dog breakfast, but she wouldn't fix the bull breakfast.

So what the old lady did, she put her in, let her out in a *trap* door, in a *dark* room. She wouldn't show her the way out. She put her into a dark room.

The next day the daddy was going to work again, so he told his wife to send the *next* oldest girl. He said, "I'm going to the store and buy some *rice*. And I'm going to drop the rice along, and as she walks, just follow that little string of rice."

He goes to the store, he buy a big bag of rice, start walking, going into the woods, and as he'd go along, he dropped *rice*. And in the morning the birds came along and picked up the rice. So when the girl started walking, got up in the woods, she got *lost*. And it got dark. And then she looked across, she saw the light; she goes over by that old house, and she asks the lady, she says, "Miss, would you mind showing me my way *out* of here?"

The old lady say, "Well, yeah," she say, "but you got a few things to *do*. You have to cook supper: fix my supper, your supper, the cat's supper, the dog's supper, and the bull's supper." The girl goes up there, she fixes her supper, the old lady's supper, the cat's supper, the dog's supper, but she didn't fix the bull's supper. . . .

She sits up there, and *she* said, "Fix the *beds*. Fix my bed, your bed, the cat bed, the dog bed, and the bull bed." So—the girl goes up there, she fix her bed, the old lady bed, the cat bed, the dog bed—she wouldn't fix the *bull bed*.

And the next morning she got up to fix breakfast: the old lady had told her, she had to fix her breakfast, the old lady's breakfast, the cat's breakfast, the dog's breakfast, and the bull's breakfast.

Girl got up, she fixed her breakfast, the old lady breakfast, the cat breakfast, the dog breakfast—but she would not feed the bull breakfast.

So the old lady let *her* down the trap door into the dark room. Wouldn't show her the way out.

So the next day—they say they had one more little girl left, the baby girl. And the man says, "Well, I'm going to the store and buy some *grains*— and do the same thing. Little girl followed the grains. The baby girl. She goes out into the woods. The birds had picked up all the grain. The little girl in the wood—she got lost. Night caught her back there. She looked across, and she saw the big light—in an old house. She walked over to the old house, and she knocks. She asks the old lady, she say, "Miss, I'm lost; you wouldn't mind showing me the way out of the woods¿'

"Oh," she say, "well—if you do everything I ask you to do, tomorrow morning I will show you the way out."

So the little girl say, "Okay."

She goes in and she tells the little girl the same thing that she said to the other two. "Cook my supper, your supper, the cat's supper, the dog's supper, and the bull's supper."

The little girl did just that. She fixed her supper, the old lady supper, the cat's supper, the dog's supper, and the bull's supper. Pretty smart.

The old lady said, "Now go upstairs. Fix my bed, your bed, the cat's bed, the dog's bed, and the bull's bed."

The girl goes upstairs. She fix her bed, the old lady's bed, the cat's bed, the dog's bed, and the *bull's* bed.

The next morning, she got up, and she cooked *breakfast*. She fixed her breakfast, the old lady's breakfast, the cat's breakfast, the dog's breakfast, and the *bull's* breakfast.

The lady sit there and said, "Oh, you're a *smart* little girl. Since you are so smart," she said, "now I'm going to take you out and show you the way back home."

The little girl said, "I had two sisters came back here. And got lost. They haven't found them."

She said, "Since you've been such a nice little girl, I'm going to give you back your two little sisters and take you out to the edge of the woods and point you home."

And the next day, the old lady did just that. She give her her two little sisters, walked them out to the edge of the woods, and stood up and point to the house.

"Now, there's your house over there." She said, "Just walk straight ahead."

And they went home. And they was happy. But it pays to be *smart*. The other two girls were *lazy*, and they disobeyed orders, and they wouldn't do what the old lady said to do. And she punished them for not doing everything she asked them to do. But the little smart sister was *smart,* and she saved her other two sisters. So, you see, it pays to be smart—and not lazy. It pays off at the end. And that's the end of that story.

60. The Old Coon

Once upon a time, there's a man named John. He was supposed to be a *smart* fellow. He worked for this boss, and every night John had the habit of going to the boss's house to eavesdrop. So tonight the boss was talking to his wife; he said, "You know, tomorrow morning," he said, "that piece of black ground over on the east side of the field—I think I'll get John to plow that and chop it up." John got out and went, took up his mule and went out to the field, plowed that piece of ground and chopped it up. Next morning the boss made the round to go to work. He said, "John, you see that piece of black ground over there on the east side of the field?" He said, "I want you to go there, and plow it, and chop it up."

John says, "Oh, Boss, I done did that already."

"Well, John, how did you know I wanted that piece of ground chopped?"

"Oh, Boss," he say, "John know everything."

The next night, John go back to the Boss's house again, get under the house and eavesdrop on the Boss and his wife's conversation. The Boss told his wife, "Do you know?" he said. "Tomorrow—that piece of ground what John chopped up today—I think I'm going to let him go over there tomorrow and plant some *corn.*" So John got out there at night and drove down, took up his mules, to go on down to the field and plant the corn.

Next morning, the Boss go round to go to work. He say—"John, you know that piece of ground you chopped last night?" He said, "I want you to go out there today and plant some corn."

John say, "Oh, Boss, I done did that already."

He said, "John, you mean to tell me that you went out there and plant corn?"

John say, "Yes."

He said, "How'd you know I wanted that corn planted there?"

"Boss," he said, "John know everything."

So, a week or two later, there was a circus came to town, and they had a lot of people out there. About thirty thousand people, at the fair. And the fair boss had a *box* in his hand. And he said, "Anybody who can tell me what in this box—I will give them thirty thousand dollars." And nobody in the circus knowed what was in that box.

So John's Boss was out there. He said to the fair boss, say, "I tell you what," he say, "I got a fellow work for me—by the name of John." He say, "John'll tell you what in that box.

He said, "Well, you go get John. [If] John tell me what's in this box, I'll give him thirty thousand dollars."

So John's boss went out there and he got John, and he brought John back to the circus. He said, "John," he said, "they got—the circus boss out there got a box, and he want somebody to tell him what in the box—and he will give them thirty thousand dollars." He said, "I want you to go out there and tell him what he's got in that box."

So John and his boss go on out to the circus. And they walk around out there, saw the man, just riding around on his horse, with a big box, holding it up—and asking: "Anybody can tell me what's in this box, I will give him thirty thousand dollars."

So John's boss looked at him and said, "John," he said, "tell him what's in that box." John looked at the box, looked at his Boss. "Go ahead, John, *tell him* what's in that box!"

John looked at his Boss—and said, "Well, Boss, you got the old coon at last." And *that* was in the box: a coon. But John was calling *himself* a "coon" because the boss had caught up with his tricks. So that's the end of that story.

61. Skullbone

So they had another fellow by the name of John, worked for another man. And John used to go out in the woods, to cut *wood*. So one day John went *way* back into the woods to cut some wood. And there was the Skullbone. . . . John looked at the skullbone. He says, "Skullbone, what you doing here?"

Skullbone said, "Tongue brought me here, and tongue going to bring *you* here."

He say, "What?"

Skullbone said, "Tongue brought me here, and tongue going to bring you here."

"Oh," he say, "I'm going to go and tell Master: Skullbone can talk." John run back up to the big house, he say, "Master, Master," he say, "Skull-bone can talk!"

"Oh, John," he say, "Skullbone can't talk."

He says, "Yes, Sir. Skullbone can talk." He says, " I just went in the woods and I saw Skullbone, and Skullbone talked to me."

He says, "Oh, John." He says, "Skullbone can't talk."

John says, "Master, say, I tell you what I'll do. I'll bet you my neck on the *chopping block* against five dollars that Skullbone can *talk*."

Master said, "Oh, John," he said, "no such thing as Skullbone can talk."

And John insisted that Skullbone could talk.

So the master told him, he said, "Well, I tell you what. If you hitch up my buggy, get my horse and hitch it to the buggy, put my axe and the chopping block in there, we going to the woods and hear Skullbone talk."

So he goes on out the woods, and there was Skullbone. John got out and called. John said, "Skullbone—what you doing here, Skullbone?"

Skullbone don't answer.

He said, "Skullbone, what are you doing here?"

Skullbone don't answer.

So John begin to getting worried. He said, "Skullbone—you talked once, why can't you talk twice? Skullbone, what are you doing here?"

Skullbone don't say nothing.

So John's Boss say, "Oh, John," he say, "Skullbone can't talk." He say, "Look, I got to go. I can't stay here all day—to wait for Skullbone to talk."

He say, "Wait, Boss." He say, "Skullbone can talk."

"Try it again."

He say, "Skullbone, *please*. You talked once. Why can't you talk twice?"

Skullbone don't say nothing.

So John's Boss told him, he say, "Well, all right, John, Skullbone can't talk. Go ahead, you lost the bet—put your head on that chopping block. I have to chop it off, because *that* was the bet."

So John laid his head on the chopping block, Boss took his axe— *sshup!*—off went John's head. Throwed his axe in his buggy, his block—goes on back up to the big house.

And about time the boss had got out of sight, Skullbone looked over at John, and say, "I *told* you, tongue brought me here, and tongue was going to bring you here."

So—I stepped on a wire, and the wire bent—and I left.

62. Brer Bear Meets Man

You know, Brer Rabbit was a pretty smart fellow.

And Brer Bear had never seen *Man*. So Brer Bear asked Brer Rabbit, he said, "Brer Rabbit, you're a pretty smart fellow in these woods, and you know a lot of things. I've been hearing talk of *Man,* but I have never seen Man." He said, "What is Man? What Man look like?"

So Brer Rabbit said to Brer Bear, he said, "You don't know Man?"

He said, "No."

He said, "Oh, you don't want to meet Man." He said, "Man is a terrible fellow."

So Brer Bear said, "I would like to see Man. I've been hearing talk of Man," said, "I have never seen Man."

So Brer Rabbit say, "So you want to meet Man," he said. "All right, I tell you what. Tomorrow," he said, "we'll go walk down that road a spell. We going to meet Man," he said. "But I tell you what," he said. "I'm going to stay on the side of the road in the grass, and *you* walk out in the road. And every time you see something coming, you let me know. And I will tell you when it's *Man.*"

So the next day Brer Rabbit and Brer Bear started walking out to the woods, come a walking up the road to meet Man. So the first thing, they saw a little boy coming up the road, you know, with a stick in his hand, batting rocks. So Brer Bear say, "*Brer Rabbit, Brer Rabbit!*" he say. "Look here!" he say, "Is *this* Man?"

Brer Rabbit peeked out from the grass where he was. He said, "Oh, no." He said, "That's *Going-To-Be-Man.*"

"Boy," he said. "I want to see *Man.* I've heard so much, so much talk about Man. I want to see Man—what Man look like."

They walked a little further, and he met another little boy, a little bigger than the first one. He said, "Brer Rabbit, is *this* Man?"

Brer Rabbit looked and he said, "No. That's not Man."

So he walked down the road a little further. He met a big boy with a stick, batting rocks. Brer Bear said, "Brer Rabbit," he said, "here comes something else!" He said, "What is this? *This* is Man?"

Brer Rabbit peeked out, and he said, "No. That's *Soon-Will-Be-Man.* That's not Man. But that'll soon be Man. That's a *big* boy."

They walked on a little further up the road, and here comes an *old* man with a walking stick, bent over. He can hardly walk. Brer Bear said, "Brer Rabbit! Come out and see. Is *this* Man?"

Brer Rabbit came out and looked. He said, "*Oohh, noo.*" He said, "That *Has-Been-Man.*" That's not man. That *Was-Man.*" He goes on back in the grass again.

Bear starts walking up the road. Way, after a while, here come Man.

Double barrel shotgun on his shoulder. Brer Bear says [in a whisper], "Brer Rabbit. Looky here. What is this?"

Brer Rabbit walked out and looked. Said, "Ohh-hh, yes-ss. That's *Man*. That's *Man*, coming there." He said, "Brer Bear, if I was you, I'd turn around right now." He said, "You don't want to meet Man—face-to-face." He said, "Let's go back to the woods. Now you've seen Man, let's go back."

Brer Bear said, "No. I want to meet man face-to-face. I want to see what Man look like."

Brer Rabbit said, "If you know him like I know him, you'd turn around now," he said. "Because Man is a terrible fellow. You don't want to meet him face-to-face."

Brer Bear says, "Oh, yes. I want to see what man *looks* like. I want to get *close* to him."

Brer Rabbit say, "Well, I tell you what. I'm going on back to the woods. You go ahead and meet Man. If you're lucky, when you get back in the woods, you tell me how you made out." So Brer Rabbit was *smart*. Brer Rabbit turned around and went on back to the woods.

Brer Bear walked on until he got close up to man—and man got in gun range of him—and he opened up on Brer Bear—*Boom!*—with the shotgun.

Brer Bear turned around—and he unloaded the other barrel. *Boom!*

And, boy [laughing] to the woods Brer Bear ran. A-running. [Teller and audience laugh.] And Brer Bear went to the woods. And Brer Rabbit's way back in the woods, waiting when he got there.

Brer Rabbit say, "Brer Bear, how you made out?"

He said, "Ohhh-hh." Man don't say nothing. He say, "I finally met Man. I never want to see Man no more." He said, "You right, Brer Rabbit. Man is a *terrible fellow*."

Brer Rabbit say, "What happened? What happened?"

He says, "Well, *Man*"—he says. "*Man* is a *terrible fellow*. He *thundered* and *lightninged* in my face and stuck splinters all in my behind." [Audience laughs.]

He never would meet man no more. Oh, no.

[More laughter.]

PART II

Tales from the Everyday World

Family Life, Memories, and Pranks

George Lezu

HOLDEN, LIVINGSTON PARISH

The following two stories were recorded at the Livingston Parish Fair on October 13, 1990, from George Lezu, age sixty-five. Lezu is a first-generation Hungarian-American who was raised in Hungarian Settlement outside of Albany. As a young boy, he was nicknamed "Mockingbird" because he thought the birds were calling him. He explained, "When the mockingbird sings, it calls my Hungarian name, Gyuri." Lezu is a dancer with the Arpadhon Hungarian Cultural Association in Albany.

63. Following His Father's Example

When we were growing up around there, everybody helped everybody back in those days. When somebody needed help, all you had to do was call. I got loaned out quite a bit. It's just like I was a tool or something, you see? There was an old couple that lived close to where we were. It was Janos *bacsi* [Mr. John]; I'm not sure if you all remember him. But he was old when I was living. He was really old. You know how kids always think of anyone grown up as old. But this man was old. He could barely walk already.

He had a horse named Cola. A white horse named Cola. And I don't know who got used to whom, but Cola would walk only about ten steps and it would stop with the plow because Mr. John just couldn't go more than ten steps at a time.

Anyway, they had a corn patch that they wanted tilled up one Saturday. Mrs. Helen, she came over and asked my daddy if they could borrow George. Didn't ask me if I wanted to be borrowed! So they loaned me. I was, at that time, about the age where girls began to interest me. This was a Saturday. I knew if I plowed with Cola, it would take me about a week to plow that corn. So I asked Daddy if I could borrow Pityu [pronounced *Pea-chew*], which was our horse.

Daddy said, "No, we're going to plow with Pityu."

So then I was trying to figure out, "How am I going to finish that patch before Saturday night?"

So I remembered the story that Daddy told when he was in Hungary. [When] he was in Hungary, they had community pastures. They drove cows

Quilting bees are a traditional setting for women to swap stories. Here Doris Ellzey, Dovie Flores, Opal Clower, and Ivy Solis, also known as the Los Adais Quilters, demonstrate their skills at the Sabine Parish Fair, September 18, 1990. Photo: Dayna Lee.

Barbershops and beauty parlors offer additional contexts for storytelling. Here Harry Lee Leger of Eunice works in his shop where he tells many of his stories [see story #68]. Photo: Maida Owens.

home to the village every day. My daddy was a little cowboy. He drove the cows out from the village out to the pasture every day and watched them all day. He drove them back in the evening. Daddy told me the story [of] when he had some lazy cows that didn't want to move. They had in Hungary a nettle, which was probably very similar to our stinging nettle over here. So he said he would take a piece of that nettle and raised the cow's tail and put it under his tail. And they would move.

So we didn't have any stinging nettles in Albany that I knew of. I've never seen any. So what I did, I took some of Mama's black pepper, wrapped the black pepper in a rag, and I moistened it. And I went over there and hitched up old Cola. I got to plowing, and after about ten steps when Cola stopped working. When Mr. John and Mrs. Helen couldn't see me, I went over there and raised Cola's tail up and put that black pepper under its tail. We finished that whole patch in a couple of hours!

Old Cola was so hurried to get through, when I unhitched him, he sat down and rubbed himself in that dust. He looked at me with bloodshot eyes and ran off! [Audience laughs.]

64. High Road to China

Can I tell my favorite story? When I was going to school, it was in the early years, I don't remember what grade, maybe the third at most. The teacher was telling about a strange land, about China, about all the customs in China. I'd hardly accepted that I'd learned English already, and here's the teacher talking about the Chinese. I didn't quite believe all of that. She told us that the only way you could get to China, the closest way, the quickest way, would be to go straight down. It was right down on the other side of the earth. The only other way would be by ship.

So I kept thinking. I was a kid, and I was thinking like a kid. I kept thinking about it. I decided I was going to build a highway to China. I was a kid, and I thought like a kid. I incorporated two sisters and a brother. I had Ida [his sister] digging, a brother, Frank, and Irene. The two girls, Frank, and I did all the digging. What we did, I convinced them that in the cornfield would be the best place. The corn was high enough where the parents couldn't see us out there—what we were doing.

So right in the middle of the cornfield, good sandy soil. I talked them into it. I was able to talk them into anything. Not my biggest brother [Andy]. I wouldn't tell him anything. I convinced them to dig that big hole. Frank and I did the digging. The hole got so big we had to put it in buckets and the girls would pull it out. We dug all summer. It was a huge hole for a field, you know. All summer we dug.

School started, and we had to go back to school. It came corn shucking time—judgment day. So we started shucking, and we knew it would be just a matter of time before we got to the China highway. Andy, my oldest brother, he had a nature call. So he went a few rows ahead over there. He saw that big hole over there. He said, "Daddy, would you just come here, please?"

And Daddy went over there, and Hungarians, when they were angry, they would spit. It was a dramatic spit. It went like this—[spits dramatically]. When a Hungarian did that, you better tow your line. Anyway, Daddy looked at that big hole. He didn't ask who did it. He said, "George! Frank!"

We went over there, and I said, "Well, I'll be doggone, a big hole!"

He was too angry to whip us, so he told us to go to the house and get a couple of shovels. He said, "I don't want to see you boys until there's no more hole there."

So sure enough, we went to the house and got the shovels, and we filled the hole up. A whole summer's work, we filled up before the day was over. We finished shucking the corn and everything, and we took the corn stalks over and put down the bottom of the row and threw dirt on top of it to plow for the strawberries.

We did all that, and it had rained over this spot where the big hole was. Daddy sent Andy out there to harrow the land, smooth it down. Andy went out there with it, harrowing, and when he come to the spot where we had the China highway, the horse went in there and it started sinking.

Andy said, "Whoa!"

Of course, Pityu couldn't whoa. Pityu just sank. It was like quicksand. Pityu just sank all the way down in there. Andy threw the rope down there. Pityu finally went on the other side and crawled out the hole. Of course, [the horse] refused to work that day. That was the end of the day. That piece of real estate, that horse would never cross. It never crossed that piece again!

Alex Bartus

HUNGARIAN SETTLEMENT, LIVINGSTON PARISH

The following story was recorded at the Livingston Parish Fair, October 13, 1990, from Alex Bartus, who died in the summer of 1991. He was the son of Reverend Alexander Bartus, the well-remembered minister of the Hungarian Presbyterian Church. Alex Bartus left the settlement for many years, during which time he received an education and enjoyed a thirty-six-year career with IBM. He returned to Hungarian Settlement in the early 1980s, where he lived until his death.

65. A First Job

I had quite a few experiences growing up. We worked on the farm, and we worked from sunup to sundown, and as I say, we were enough of us to where we could farm without a lot of mechanical things we farm with today. And many times I would be out in the field, and I'd say, "If I can ever get off this farm, I will never come back."

I was determined that I would get off the farm and, really, anything away from the farm was fine. Dad came home one day and told me, "Alex, I've got a job for you."

I said, "Fine."

Whenever that came up, I said, "Where is the job?"

He said, "In Albany."

I said, "What kind of work am I going to be doing?"

He said, "Pumping gas, fixing flat tires, greasing cars, washing cars, and so forth."

And I said, "When do I start?"

He said, "Tomorrow."

Now, remember that my dad was the minister of the Hungarian Presbyterian Church, and every Sunday we went to Sunday school and to church. But in this particular time, he told me that I wouldn't have to work on the farm, wouldn't have to go to church and to Sunday school, so I said, "That's great."

I went to the place and started working ten, twelve, fourteen hours. I'd start at six in the morning and get off at eight, ten o'clock at night. I delivered ice, and then I'd pump gas and everything in the afternoon. I never did ask my dad how much money I was getting. I never did ask him. You didn't ask my dad anything like that. He'd volunteer some information, but you never challenged or questioned him. Whenever I got my first pay, it was in cash. The fellow reached over and gave me my money. Then I gave it back to him.

He said, "What's that for?"

I said, "That's to put on the gas bill." Because my dad farmed me off to pay off a gas bill. When I gave him that money back, he said, "Is this the arrangement you and your dad had?"

I said, "Yes sir, it is."

He told me, he said, "I tell you what, I'm going to raise your pay 25 percent, provided you keep three dollars of it."

So he raised my pay from seven days a week, twelve, fourteen hours a day, and I was getting twelve dollars for the entire week. So he raised my pay to fifteen dollars, I'd give him back twelve dollars, and I would keep three. I'll remember that forever and ever.

Max Greig

ST. MARTINVILLE, ST. MARTIN PARISH

Recorded by C. Renée Harvison, August 20, 1990, from Max Greig, eighty, a Cajun. In this story, Greig alludes to the Cajun tradition of Saturday night bals à maison (or "house dances"), at which families would gather at a neighbor's home to pass the night in dancing. Older boys and girls courted while the oldest generations minded the infants, and a grandparent would often sing a fais do do (lullabye) to soothe young children to sleep. Hence the Saturday night dance was often called a fais do do.

66. He Got the Pig and the Girl

There's one thing I'd like to tell you about that is very interesting. It's one of the stories I tell on my storytelling ventures.

A country dance at an old widow woman's. She had a big house and had a *fais do do* every Saturday night. I used to go there. It was walking distance from the end of our street, three or four blocks. They'd take all of the furniture down in the two front rooms. They'd put two or three beds together in one of the rear rooms. The older women would have the job of taking care of the babies when [the] mama came in to dance. The music had already started. She'd rock her baby to sleep. She was anxious to start dancing. She'd sing a little French lullaby, *"Fais do do, Minette, pour Papa, Fais do do pour Mama"* [Go to sleep, little one, for Papa, go to sleep for Mama]. That's where the word *fais do do* was born.

After the baby was asleep, she'd take him and put him in the back room with the rest of the babies. The old ladies would look after them periodically. The rest of the old ladies, all around the place where they danced, they had benches. These old women would sit there and watch their daughter[s]. They didn't want the boys to hold them too tight, so they kept an eye on them.

There was one old gal that I had an eye on. She was pretty as heck. Built like a Coca-Cola bottle. But she didn't trust me too much.

So, I went to a voodoo woman and told that to that voodoo woman. That voodoo woman's name was Marie Louise. She fixed me a magic powder. She told me, said, "Put that in her lemonade. She's got to take it in."

So I bought her a hamburger, and I put a little bit of that powder on the hamburger. But she was very suspicious. So, when I wasn't watching, she threw it out of the window. The pig ate it. When I left that dancehall, that pig followed me all the way to the house, squealing! But, you know, I finally married that old gal. I've been married fifty-eight years.

Harry Lee Leger

EUNICE, ST. LANDRY PARISH

Harry Leger was videotaped at Leger Barber Shop in Eunice on November 13, 1992, by Pat Mire and Maida Owens during production for the video documentary, Swapping Stories. *As he often does, Leger, a Cajun, told this story while cutting hair.*

67. I'm Going to Leave You, Chère

[There was this] guy that . . . was always telling . . . his old lady, he said, "I'm going to leave you, *chère*," he said. "One day," he said, "I'm going to leave." Oh, and it went and it went and it went. So, one day, he just jumped in the pirogue, and he started going down the bayou.

She said, "*Cher* Pierre," she said. "Where you going?" she said.

He said, "I *told* you was going to leave you."

She said, "That's it?"

He said, "I'm going, and that's all."

Mais, she said, "Pierre," she said, "what about the house?"

He said, "I don't care," he said. "You can give it away, you can sell. You can do what you want." He said, "That's it."

Mais, she said, "Pierre," she said, "what about the kids?"

He said, "You can do the same thing. You can keep them, you can give them away, you can do what you want." He said, "I'm going. I *told* you that."

Oh, . . . all at once, she raised up her dress. She said, "Pierre," she said, "What we going to do with that—"

"Yeah, see my baby," he said. "One day, I'm going to *leave* you, yeah, *chère*." [Audience laughs.]

Sidna Coughlin

BATON ROUGE, EAST BATON ROUGE PARISH

Recorded at a monthly Pokeno game on May 25, 1993, by Pat Mire and Maida Owens for the video documentary, Swapping Stories. *Pokeno, a bingo-style card game, requires twelve players, who provide a ready-made audience for the players' stories about their lives.*

68. Down the Wrong Hill

Sidna Coughlin: This was—this was a long time ago. But we went to Squaw Valley and went skiing.

Patty Fraser: You and David, or you and David and the kids?

Sidna Coughlin: Well, David and I and the kids, and my sister and brother-in-law. And my brother-in-law had been on skis a couple of times. David had never been on skis. I mean, he doesn't even know how to *spell* it. [Laughs.] And so he gets on the skis—we're on the bunny slope, you know, you ski and you fall down, you ski and you fall down.

Well, they decide they're going to go up on the lift to the next level. So, the bunny slope is right there by the parking lot, you know? So he goes up there and he gets off of the thing—can't see him, it's that high up. He gets up there, and here they come down, [laughing] down the slopes, through the parking lot, up the roof of the restaurant

[Teller and audience laugh together. Several say, "Oh, God."]

—and we're standing there, saying, "Oh, my God!"—[He] didn't know how to stop.

It was a very steep roof on that restaurant. [Laughs.] He's lucky he didn't go over the side.

Kathy Boudet: That's the first thing I wanted to learn was how to stop.

Another Pokeno player: Can you teach me how to stop before I—

Sidna Coughlin: You sit down.

Yet another Pokeno player: No, you turn your skis up.

Sidna Coughlin: I know.

Robert Albritton

RUSTON, LINCOLN PARISH

The following two stories were recorded September 16, 1993, by Pat Mire and Maida Owens for the video documentary, Swapping Stories. *Robert Albritton and his wife,*

Sarah, African Americans, took a break from working at their restaurant, Sarah's Kitchen, to tell stories.

69. Leaving Mississippi

This one you never heard either, you know. Way back, long years ago, you know, it used to be kind of rough on black people in Mississippi. You know. And this sharecropper, you know, and his family, they sharecropped down in Mississippi. And end of every year, when it was time to settle up, sharecropper didn't have nothing coming, you know?

So, he told his wife one Saturday night, he said, "Old Lady," he said. "We're going to go ahead and die here." He said, "What you do," he said, "you pack up all our belongings [and get out of here] tonight. We're going to leave Mississippi. We going move out. We got to leave in my old car."

They packed up, loaded up. Got his family and car, and down the road they go. Head out of Mississippi, going north, okay? They got pretty good piece up the road there, and after a while, here come this big rattlesnake out from under the seat. [Laughs.]

And this guy jumped up on the seat, said, "Pass me the pistol out the glove compartment over there." He said, "There's a rattlesnake back here."

The rattlesnake jumped over and said, "Mister," he said, "please don't shoot me." He said, "I ain't going to bite you." He's going, "They been rough on me down here too, so I'm trying to get out of Mississippi too." [Laughs.]

70. You Think I'm Working, But I Ain't

Then I got another one. This is a true one. . . .

This guy, he was working on this farm for this guy, you know? And, they had what you call a big house. And this is where they kept all the farm tools—in the big house, okay? So, he had to get up every morning and go to the big house, and he'd hook up the mule and the old plow and he'd go out in the field and work, plow for them.

He had him a big old shade tree down there in the field, you know, and every morning he'd hook [his mule] up. Boss Man thinking he's going to work. He'd go out and get under that shade tree; he had a guitar with him out there. His guitar, his back up against the tree, get to singing a little song about [sings] "You think I'm working, but I ain't"—oh, he did that for I don't know how long.

One of the Boss Man's [laughs] neighbors passed by one evening and heard him out there. So, he goes down and he tells the guy, "Well, you're just paying him for nothing," he said. "Because he ain't working," he said, "He's sitting under the tree, singing."

So [the Boss] said, "Well, that's all right. I'll catch him."

Next morning before day, he got up, Boss Man did, went out there and got up in the tree.

Workman hooked up the mule, plow, then he comes by. Ties the mule up. Get right by that tree in back, he starts [playing] his guitar, [sings] "You think I'm working, but I ain't—" he says about two or three times.

Then the Boss Man fell out the tree, "Um-hm." He said, [sings] "And you think I'm going to pay you, but I ain't." [Laughs.] Yeah.

Rodney Cook

ARCADIA, BIENVILLE PARISH

The following four stories were recorded by C. Renée Harvison, July 20, 1990, from Rodney Cook, a British-American resident of Arcadia, Bienville Parish. Cook is employed in the oil and gas industry, but in his extra time writes a column, "The Arcadia Agitator." He is also a woodcarver.

71. Those Drivers Were No Dummies

We pulled tires. We were one of the first boys to do that. The first thing we tried, we made a dummy of a person. There was no interstate then. Highway 80 was your main highway from California to the East Coast, the one that comes through downtown. We got out there and laid this dummy down, like a person laying there. Nobody would stop.

I said, "I know what it is."

I got a bucket of water and threw it out on the road, to make it look like somebody had really been hit or something. We got tired of doing it, so we picked the dummy up and came back to town. Then we went back and put it back. We kept noticing people pulling into the grocery store. What had happened, the time we went to town, a lot of people had reported this dead person laying on the road. We didn't have an ambulance service then so they'd called the state police. They had sent two ambulances out from Minden.

So we hadn't been out there long that second time, looked like the president was coming, there were so many red lights flashing. We took off! They got our dummy and carried it over to the courthouse.

72. Pulling Tires

But then we branched off into tires. Tires used to come wrapped. New tires had paper wrapped around them. On Saturdays, we'd take an old tire and go down to the filling station, unwrap a new tire, and wrap an old one. We'd put a wire, punch a hole in tire and put a wire in there and tie it to something so it wouldn't come out. We'd run that wire thirty or forty yards off in the bushes. We'd go off on the side of the road and sit that tire on the side of the road.

Everybody that'd come along would stop and try to pick up that new tire. We'd even let them sit it in the back seat. Set it in there, and all at once there'd be this tire coming out of there! We did that when I was about fourteen or fifteen. We were in a place, too, where trucks couldn't stop. They'd have to go 150 yards or so and there'd be a big place where they could pull off. A lot of them were trucks hauling watermelons. We'd have some people up there. When the driver went to get the tire, we'd get a few melons off the truck. If it was a cold drink truck, we'd get a case of cold drinks! Highway robbery, I guess.

73. Highway Robbery

I remember one time, the watermelons hadn't even sprouted good around here. We were sitting downtown, and we saw a watermelon truck come through. It was hauling from Florida or something. We knew that when he got to the corner up there, he'd go ninety degrees, one block, and then there's a light. That light catches you all the time. Well, when he slowed down there for that corner, two of us got on the truck. Started handing watermelons off as he went up the hill. When he stopped, we got off. We were always doing stuff like that.

74. Dentist or Proctologist?

We had a dentist here we were always picking at. One Halloween we went and searched until we found a big outhouse. Right after dark, it took fifteen of us to pick it up. And we loaded it up on a truck and brought it downtown. His office was on the second floor of a building.

Well, our outhouse barely would fit between the sidewalks and the awnings. We stuck the outhouse out there. Even the law held back traffic for us until we could get it unloaded. Put a big sign out there. Had a chair for the waiting room. Then, to make sure it stayed there a good while, the town had a truck they hauled trash in. We went and took all the valves out of the tires and let the air out of all the trash trucks. The next morning, the dentist wouldn't come to work until they moved it. The town marshall said he couldn't move it, because his trucks had flats. Some people were taking pictures and passing them around. The next year, he sent word that if we would leave him alone for Halloween, that he'd buy basketball uniforms for the church team we played on. We were always doing something like that.

Harry Methvin

HARGROVE SETTLEMENT, CALCASIEU PARISH

Recorded June 30, 1990, from Harry Methvin, a British American, by C. Renée Harvison.

75. On Top of Old Smoky

Living here on this corner was Bronson Dickerson. Now, Bronson had a son-in-law named Ralph Myers, and Ralph's wife's name was Betty Lou. Ralph bought him a horse, and he didn't have any place to keep his horse, so his father-in-law, Bronson, agreed he could keep his horse in his pasture. And Ralph would have to come over every afternoon and pack up the buckets of water to fill up the number three tub with fresh water everyday.

And the horse was getting to be more trouble than he was worth, but he loved the old horse. The horse was named Smoky. But [Ralph] decided he was going to blow him a water hole in the middle of Bronson's pasture. If he could get him a stick of dynamite to blow one big hole—and it would be full of water—he'd never have to water his horse again. He only needed half a stick.

So he went to—I don't know, maybe Pete Bennett—and he got him a stick of dynamite, half a stick, but Pete was a generous sort, said, "No, just take the whole stick." So he gave him a fuse, everything he needed to blow a hole.

So on a Saturday morning, Sunday morning maybe it was, Ralph came over to blow the water hole. And he went out to the middle of the field, and he found a crawfish hole. He got the hoe handle, and he kind of wallowed it out.

He said, "I'll never need the rest of this dynamite." So he decided to use the whole stick. He stuck a hole in the end of the dynamite. You put the fuse inside the stick of dynamite, then you fray the ends with your pocketknife where it'll burn better. You put the cap on the end, and you clinch it on before you put it into the dynamite.

He did all those steps properly, stuck it into the crawfish hole. He lit the fuse and ran for the shelter of Bronson's barn, because dynamite is a very powerful explosive. And he got to the barn, holding his ears, and he turned around and looked back, and his horse, old Smoky, had gone up to find out what all that smoke was from. And Smoky was over there smelling the smoke.

And then the dynamite exploded, and old Smoky went probably eight-five or ninety feet into the air and Ralph said, "Oh my God!" He ran and got there just about the time that Smoky came back down. He thought—and Arliss Van Winkle told me this, I know it's true—he thought that he had blown Smoky's guts out.

He walked over there to that limp body and he rubbed it, and it was just mud that had blowed up all over Smoky's belly. Smoky was not dead. Smoky was just dazed temporarily. So Ralph knelt on the ground beside Smoky, and he rubbed his neck, and he tried to give him artificial respiration.

Finally, Smoky started to regain consciousness, and Ralph ran to the barn and got a rope and he tied it around Smoky's neck. Finally, he got Betty Lou out, and they managed to get Smoky up on his feet. And Betty Lou got in the back and pushed, and Ralph got in the front and pulled, and they got Smoky into the barn.

Smoky was still very wobbly. He could hardly stand up. Ralph stood out there with that horse for hours, because he loved that horse. He rubbed his neck, and he leaned over on its back, and Smoky was beginning to get some strength back. So Ralph just leaned across the back, rubbing [him], and Betty Lou was holding the rope. Ralph crawled up on the back to see if Smoky could support him, because Smoky seemed to be okay now.

Ralph was sitting up on the back of old Smoky, and not thinking, Betty Lou reached into her pocket and got out her pack of Camels. She got one of the kitchen matches and flicked it on the back of her jeans and lit the match. When Smoky saw that smoke, Smoky broke through the north wall of Bronson's barn, and Ralph was hanging on around his neck! Smoky went through the woods where Shorty Van Winkle's living room now sits. That's the last Betty Lou saw of Ralph and Smoky.

Betty Lou was worried sick. She was over there alone. She walked just as far as she could. She saw some broken limbs where they had been. But she never saw Smoky and Ralph.

She finally returned home, but there was no one else, no neighbor where she could go to that was home. She worried and worried and walked the floor. Then she went outside and sat under the cedar tree. She had a bushel of peas, and she went out there to shell the peas and wait on Ralph, to hear from Ralph and Smoky. She was shelling the peas, and she was sobbing and crying. She didn't even have to salt the peas when she cooked them, she cried so much. All the tears, salt tears.

It was almost dark. She looked up, she saw a cloud of dust, and it was Earl Talley. Earl Talley made hot tamales and [sold] peanuts. He was also the dispatcher for the local police. Earl got out of the car, approached the gate, and he came inside. She said, "Earl! Earl! Something terrible has happened to Ralph!"

And Earl said, "Betty Lou, relax, I got some news from Ralph." She said, "Tell me, tell me! Please tell me! Where is Ralph?"

He said, "I don't know any details, Betty Lou. All I can tell you is what I wrote down when Ralph called." He said, "Ralph called and said to tell you he's in Rosepine. That he is okay. They tried to stop him for speeding in Singer, but they couldn't catch him. They put up a road block in Rosepine, and they finally got old Smoky stopped! He said to tell you that as soon as he hung up the phone with me, he was going to get back on old Smoky, and there was some guy there that was going to light a cigarette for him. He said to open the barn doors, and put on supper because, he thinks he'll be home by dark!"

And sure enough, it all worked to perfection because just about dark, right after supper was ready, here come Ralph and old Smoky right as they had gone, right through the north door of the barn. Ralph came in looking not much worse for the wear, and he visited with Betty Lou a while and told her about his exploits and what Rosepine was like because they'd never been to Rosepine.

They started to get ready for bed. Ralph said, "Betty Lou, I've been thinking. In the morning, soon as I wake up, I'm going to go out there and put the harness on old Smoky." Except he called him Dynamite. He'd changed his name from Smoky to Dynamite.

He said, "I'm going to put the harness on Dynamite." Said, "I want you to load up all the kids. Put them in the back of the wagon." Said, "You know that cigar I got in my dresser drawer?" Said, "I want you to get that cigar, and I'm not going to ask you to do this anymore." He said, "When you get the kids loaded, and I'm sitting in that seat," said, "I want you to just stand in front of Smoky." He said, "Take one puff on that cigar because I want to go see my brother in Shreveport!"

That's true, too. He did blow up the horse with dynamite. That part is true.

Bill Cox

RUSTON, LINCOLN PARISH

The following story was recorded at the Ruston Peach Festival, Lincoln Parish, June 16, 1990, from Bill Cox, a British American. Cox is the director of athletic facilities at Louisiana Tech University.

76. For Sale: One Tractor in Mint Condition

Joe Hinton had an International Cub tractor. He was crazy about that tractor. Joe was probably a good school teacher, but mechanically, he was—a nitwit. And everything mechanical he touched, he broke. The tractor was no exception.

He wanted to sell his tractor, so he brought it down to my place. We set it out; the first week there was a car accident out there. The car hit the tractor—did enough damage that he got more than the tractor was worth! But it broke the starter on it. It'd no longer start. To start the tractor, you'd have to pull it with a truck, to start it. But he still wanted to sell his tractor.

So early one Saturday morning, it was probably about five-thirty in the morning, nothing was going on. It was quiet, and a man from Mississippi came through. He was with the Red Fox Tobacco Company. He got to asking about the tractor down there. I asked him, did he want to buy it?

He said, "Oh no, I don't want to buy it, I was just making conversation. I just want to drink a Coke, buy some gas, and I'll be on my way."

I said, "Do you want to have some fun this morning?"

He said, "Oh, yeah."

I said, "I'll call the fellow who owns that thing, and we'll have some fun."

Well, I always kept some of these bombs. I called them bombs. You put them on the motor of a car, and when you start that thing up, it starts making funny noises, a lot of smoke, and then it'll explode. Well, I called Joe's house, and the phone rang maybe ten times. He was sound asleep. So finally he answered the phone, and I said, "Doc, are you up?"

He said, "Oh, yes, I've been up all morning."

I said, "Listen, I didn't want to bother you, but there's a gentleman here from Mississippi; he's traveling through, and he wants to buy this tractor." I said, "He does not know how to start it." I said, "If you could come down, I'll have it all tied onto the truck, we'll start it, and I think he'll buy it." By that time, several people came up, I told them what was going to happen, and they went around behind the building to hide and watch.

Well, in a few minutes, I heard him coming. You know everywhere he went, he was in a big hurry. At that time, he had a white Pontiac, and he'd inadvertantly knocked a hole in the muffler. Pulled the whole bottom off the muffler. You could hear him coming. Well, he topped the hill, and we were watching for him, and it was just kind of hitting the ground every once and a while. He got there, and he jumped out of his car. Now, you know Joe is flat-footed. His feet are as flat as a duck's feet. No arch at all. He had no shoes on, he had no shirt on, and his hair had not been combed. It looked like maybe birds had been in it or maybe dynamite had gone off in it, or something. He had a pair of cut-off blue jeans on and that was it.

He got out, and I introduced him to the man. The man gave him a Red Fox cap, had a Red Fox chewing tobacco logo on the front. He put that on his head—his hair was all out from under it—and he told the man, "This tractor runs like a top. You just barely bump it, and it starts right up. It'll run good."

So he climbs up on it, and he says, "Let her go!"

Well, I just eased off. He popped the clutch and it started. Well, when it started, that thing says, "*Eeeeeeeee!*" Started squealing, very, very loud. Smoke started rolling out from under the hood. I can still see it. He put that one old flat foot on that brake, and it just wrapped around it. He put the other one on the clutch, and it just wrapped around it. He said, "*Whoa!*"

Well, about that time, it reached the end of its cycle and it exploded: "*Bloooey!*" And a lot of blue smoke came out then. I saw it. He pushed it into gear, he hit the ignition switch, and he jumped! Now, if you know Joe Hinton, he can jump further on one leg than most people can on two. He's just that athletic. He jumped one time, hit the ground, one more time, and he was about thirty feet from that tractor. By this time, he looked around at these other people, might have been fifteen there by then. They were all watching. And they gave him a standing ovation! He never said a word. He got in his car and he left!

Tommy Grafton

BERNICE, UNION PARISH

Recorded at Bernice's Corney Creek Festival, June 2, 1990, from Tommy Grafton, fifty-one, a British American. Grafton is an instructor in Ruston in Louisiana Tech University's Health and Physical Education Department.

77. That's One Tourist Who'll Never Come Back

You brought up a character a little while ago that probably had an imprint on all of our lives, and that was Mr. Stone Harris. Since I started riding that school bus. . . . The best story that came out about Mr. Stone was when he worked down there with Mr. Joe Leonard and Mr. Taft Burns.

All of you all remember when these air hoses came out that they blew your car out with. Gosh, it blew dust all over everything in the car, but at least it wasn't in the car anymore! But Mr. Stone couldn't hear very well because we had yelled in his ear so much on the school bus.

This lady from out of state drove up there one day, and she just skidded in there one day. Mr. Stone, being the conscientious guy that he was, rushed out there to help the lady, and she said—she kind of had a funny accent—she asked him did they have a restroom. He said, "Ma'am?"

"Do you have a restroom?"

He thought she said, "Do you have a whisk broom?" He said, "No ma'am, but if you just back that car out a little bit, we'll blow it out for you!"

I'm going to tell you something, people! There may still be rubber marks down there in front of Taft Burns' station. I'm telling you, she didn't ever come back to Bernice! I can assure you.

Harry Cook

BERNICE, UNION PARISH

Recorded at the Corney Creek Festival in Bernice, June 2, 1990, from Harry Cook, a British American.

78. That Darn Cat

I was thinking a while ago about Corney Creek. It has a memory to all of us. I remember Stone Harris. Stone said that he was coming up from Barnes' Bridge one day. It was in the middle of the summer, and it was real hot. He got up to Mr. Grafton's house, and he needed a drink of water. So he asked Mr. Grafton could he have a drink of water.

He said, "Yep. Go ahead and help yourself" in typical Bernice-fashion, open-handed approach. So he dropped the bucket in the well and drew up a bucket full of water, and it was a big black cat in the bucket when he pulled it up. And he said, "Mr. Grafton! Here's a cat in this well!"

Mr. Grafton never quit rocking in that chair." He said, "You know. I've been missing that old cat for about two weeks." He said, "Glad we finally found him and everything."

A. J. Smith

LAKE CHARLES, CALCASIEU PARISH

Recorded November 14, 1992, by Pat Mire and Maida Owens for the video documentary, Swapping Stories. *A. J. Smith, a Cajun humorist, was performing on stage at the Liberty Theater during the weekly* Rendez-vous des Cajuns *radio program.*

79. Big Red

He was driving along one day, like that, shaking his head. And out the corner of his eye, . . . he thought he saw a red rooster there . . . wearing red longjohns. Standing on a fencepost. "*Gol,* man," he said. "Something's going on, now." So, he went on up, and he went to the farmer's house there. Asked him, he said, "Is that true? I just saw a rooster back on your fence—got some red longjohns."

And the farmer say, "Yeah, yeah. That's my rooster, Big Red."

"Oh," but he say, "Well, what's the deal with the longjohns?"

"Oh," he said, "The other day, see I was back in my pasture, bushhogging. Red, him, he was running down a hen. Wasn't paying no attention where he was going and ran right up into that bushhog. Spun him around, spit him out. Man, didn't have no feathers left on him. [Laughs.] My wife saw him, just sitting there the next morning, just shivering in that cold morning air. You know, felt sorry for him. [Laughs.] Made him them little red longjohns to keep him warm [laughs] till his feathers grow back.

"Well," he say, "Man, that's the funniest thing I ever saw."

"Oh," he say, "*Mais,* you think that's funny, you ought to see Red hold that hen down with one foot, get them longjohns off with the other foot." [Audience laughs.]

A. J. Smith shares a story with Dave Petitjean and friends at a backyard barbeque at David Bertrand's home in Elton during taping for the video program, Swapping Stories *[see story #80]. Photo: Maida Owens.*

Dave Petitjean and A. J. Smith

CROWLEY, ACADIA PARISH, AND
LAKE CHARLES, CALCASIEU PARISH

Recorded September 18, 1993, by Pat Mire and Maida Owens for the video production, Swapping Stories, *during a barbeque at the home of David and Lorraine Bertrand in Elton, Jefferson Davis Parish. The following exchange, featuring two expert Cajun humorists, presents a full-blown story session. Tale follows tale in quick succession, as one man picks up on a theme or a phrase from the other's joke, using one-liners and brief exclamations to help craft a chain of stories. This story swap contains at least eight jokes on several topics—cooking, domineering wives, and psychologists—as well as innumerable gags.*

80. Swapping Stories

Dave Petitjean: All Cajuns love to cook. I know you do.

A. J. Smith: And I love to eat.

Dave Petitjean: Oh yeah. But they always say, you know, when you go somewhere [far away], they always say to make Cajun food, it got to be hot.

But how you tell when it's too hot? Well, when you get bald-headed, it'll be a lot easier. . . . Because I can tell when I eat some food, and you know the little beads break out [pointing to his head] right there? It's just right.

A. J. Smith: Falvey [A. J.'s wife] cooks, I swear, she tries that Cajun cooking, but that woman don't have the commitment.

Dave Petitjean: What you mean . . . ?

A. J. Smith: Well, you heard they got blackened fish, blackened this—all I get is darkened. [All laugh.] She says, "I can't bring myself to burn it."

How's about that blackened toast? I get blackened toast now and again.

Dave Petitjean: Audrey asked me the other day. Because, I got the same problem. Audrey's a Cajun girl. Cleans the house spic and span. . . . She washes the bananas—everything. When we first got married, I got up one night, went to the kitchen, made me a sandwich; when I come back, she'd already made the bed. [Audience laughs].

One day, she said, "Dave, I want to go someplace I ain't *never* been in my life.

Oh, I said, "Good. Why you don't try the kitchen?" [Audience laughs.] The toast—the toast you talking about? . . . One day, she asked me, she says, "Dave, you think the toast is done?"

I said, "I won't be able to tell you until the smoke clears out the window."

I been eating blackened eggs for thirty years.

A. J. Smith: I'll tell you the truth. You don't want to let the wife hear you talk like that.

Dave Petitjean: Why not?

A. J. Smith: Well, I was fussing like that the other day. And out the back room—I didn't know she could hear me. I heard her in the back room,

"Yeah, and if you want a hot meal, you can turn off the air conditioning, too!" [Audience laughs.]

Dave Petitjean: Now look. I know that. I know that. I'm kidding. I get so far in the doghouse sometime—for this kind of stuff . . . [that if] you come to my house, I don't know if I ought to shake your hand or lick it. [Audience laughs.] Oh, no. It gets bad.

A. J. Smith: When you get that far back in the doghouse, they got to feed you with a slingshot, man—[Audience laughs].

Dave Petitjean: I don't got to tell you. We get in little discussions.

A. J. Smith: Okay, that's what you all call them?

Dave Petitjean: No, most people call them fights—but we call that discussion.

A. J. Smith: Uh-huh?

Dave Petitjean: Now, *wa-a-ait* a minute. At my house, I rule the roost.

A. J. Smith: Uh-huh?

Dave Petitjean: Course, she rules the rooster. [Laughter.] That's true, by God.

Now, let me tell you. Course, watch the Cajun girls. I want to tell everybody, watch them, because one night, I come home, and I was messing up some way, and she said, "Dave, I want to you know something. You have been the light of my life." She say, "But if you don't straighten out, I'm going change the bulb." [Audience laughs.] . . . Now, before you all jump too fast. *I'm* the boss.

A. J. Smith: *Come on,* Dave.

Dave Petitjean: I wouldn't lie with *you.*

A. J. Smith: Well-l-l-l.

Dave Petitjean: No, *wa-a-ait.* I'm going to prove it. The other night, we was having one of the little discussions at my house. I had that woman on her knees.

A. J. Smith: On her knees! Come on.

Dave Petitjean: On her *knees!* . . . She was there. There she was, saying, "Come out from under that bed, you coward." [Audience laughs.] You don't have trouble like that.

A. J. Smith: No, and I'm going to tell you what. I got a special bed. That—

Dave Petitjean: Should I ask you what *that* is?

A. J. Smith: Yeah, you can ask me, because I'm going to tell you anyhow, Dave. [Audience laughs.] . . . There was this psychological problem I had.

Dave Petitjean: A what?

A. J. Smith: A psychological problem.

Dave Petitjean: All right.

A. J. Smith: That's one where your brain ain't working good, no.

Dave Petitjean: Okay. Well, I got that too.

A. J. Smith: Because it's on the blink. Always on the blink. Always on a skip or something. I don't know what it was, but I could not sleep. I was afraid someone was under the bed. All the time, I'd wake up in the middle of the night. I couldn't get my night's rest sleep. [Calls out] *"Someone's under the bed!"* And I was too scared to see.

Dave Petitjean: Gosh, that's bad.

A. J. Smith: I went to the psychiatrist. He want to charge me seventy-five dollars a visit, and he take about fifty visits to cure me with that.

Dave Petitjean: *Shoom!*

A. J. Smith: I said, "I got to think about it." Because, I tell you what. . . . I . . . couldn't sleep, couldn't sleep. I ran into him one day at the K-Mart's there, like that.

He said, "Man, I remember you was in my office." He said, "You had the trouble sleeping." He said, "Did you all think about taking the treatment?"

I said, "Hey, I'm cured."

He said, "You're *cured?*"

I said, "Hebert cured me."

He said, "Hebert—Hebert—Dr. Hebert?" he said, "Is he a psychiatrist?"

I said, "No, *Hebert.* He's a carpenter. He cut the legs off the bed. 'Nobody's under the bed now, man.' " [Audience laughs.]

Dave Petitjean: Special bed!

A. J. Smith: Well, I can't hide under it. . . . You got a place you can go. I don't—I got to go to the doghouse.

Dave Petitjean: I got a Badon Hebert from Gueydon. I thought you [were talking about him]. . . . He's one of them—psychological doctors, you know? You go lay on the couch, you know—for thirty minutes. And he sits. He take your fifty dollars and you leave.

Well, Madame Boudreaux been going there for five years. Lay down, get her money, never did nothing. Huh? She walk in one day, she said, "Now Badon"—she knew him since she was a little kid, you know? "That's enough. I ain't paying you no more money. I been five years giving you fifty dollars every week. That's it—I want to know what's the matter with me."

Well, he said, "Okay." He said, "I'm going to tell you what's the matter with you: you're crazy!" [Laughs.]

Yeah! Ooh, but she back off like that. She said, "*Mais,* I never been so insulted in all my life." She said, "I ain't going to accept that." She said, "I want a second opinion."

He said, "All right." He say, "You ugly too." [Audience laughs.]

A. J. Smith: Yeah, yeah, I'll tell you what—Dave talk about Badon there—that sound like when . . . that woman . . . [had] to take [have] a bad operation. And she was telling her neighbor across the back fence, "Yeah, the doctor had told me, 'This is a pretty serious operation you got to take.' "

And the neighbor said, "Well, you didn't get a second opinion?"

And, she said, "*Mais,* no. I didn't think about that. I'm going to do that." Sure enough.

Then, next day, she was talking with the neighbor across the fence. [The neighbor] said, "Say," she said, "did you get that second opinion?"

She said, "Yeah, I sure did. I had my husband call the doctor. The doctor told him the same thing he told me." [All laugh.]

Louisiana Politics:
The Longs and Their Cousins

"They take their politics seriously here in Louisiana. I think Louisiana is where politics was born in the United States of America. I think we have the best politics in the world."

Max Greig, St. Martinville

Hiram Wright

WINNFIELD, WINN PARISH

T*he first eight stories of this political section were collected on June 19, 1990, by C. Renée Harvison from the Honorable Hiram J. Wright, a retired judge. Dayna Lee, formerly with the Louisiana Folklife Center in Natchitoches, told Renée about Judge Wright and his political stories. When Renée let Dayna know that she was going to follow through with her recommendation and pay Wright a visit, Dayna warned her not to let his soft-spoken, judgelike nature fool her. "He's full of some wonderful stories," she said. Dayna was right. About thirty minutes into the conversation, after some talk about his ordeal as a prisoner of war, the judge gradually led into stories of happier times in his life—those centering around his experiences in the courtroom and with such Winn Parish characters as Julius Long, an older brother of Huey and Earl.*

Wright was born and raised in Jonesville, Catahoula Parish, but moved with his family to Baton Rouge in 1939, when his father became the executive secretary of the Louisiana Teachers Association. It was during this time that Wright began to get a taste of Louisiana politics through his father's position, first with Sam Jones and then with Earl Long. Most of Wright's stories focus on political shenanigans in Winn Parish, the hometown of the Long family.

Before entering law school, Wright fought in World War II. He was captured by the Germans on July 7, 1944, a month after D-Day, in Normandy, France, and became a prisoner of war until his escape about eight months later. After returning home from the war in April 1945, Wright completed his undergraduate studies at Louisiana State University and then soon entered its law school. He began practicing law in Winnfield in 1948, became a city judge in 1969, and in 1973 became district judge. Although Wright is now retired, on occasion he still serves in some judicial

Neighborhood gathering spots such as the corner grocery are often sites for storytelling. Photo: Nicholas R. Spitzer.

capacity. Most recently the Louisiana Supreme Court assigned him to the Eleventh Judicial District Court. With every new character he meets in the courtroom, he's still picking up stories.

81. Earl's Grave

At Earl Long Park here, on the east side of town, they'd buried Earl right there and put a lot of concrete over his grave to hold up the statue of Earl that's on top of his grave. The cement man had poured all that cement there and was out there one day finishing the cement, smoothing it. A local Presbyterian pastor walked by, saw all that cement on top of that grave and said, "You know, I don't believe I'd want all that cement on top of my grave come Judgment Day."

The old cement finisher didn't even look up. He just spit that tobacco juice out there on the grave, said, "Don't worry about that, Preacher, he ain't going that way."

82. Funeral Approval

Another story that was related to me [about an old lawyer]—Squire Kidd was his name. When Huey Long was shot, of course, all the country people supported Huey Long, practically. In every parish in North Louisiana, they gathered up in towns.

Here, they gathered up at the courthouse to get rides to Baton Rouge. They were running school buses down there. Anybody that had a car and was going down to Baton Rouge would stop at the courthouse to pick up some people to go if they didn't have a ride. Highways weren't the same then. It wasn't easy to get to Baton Rouge from Winnfield or anywhere else in North Louisiana. The roads are now much better because of what Huey had done.

But anyway, Squire showed up that morning. Brand new linen suit. New shirt, new tie, new shoes, new straw hat—looking great. Everybody was amazed at how good Squire looked. One of them said, "Squire, you going to the funeral?"

He said, "Hell, no, but I approve of it."

83. Just Don't Watch Wagon Train in His House

Another story I told is about a good friend of mine who lived up in the northern part of the parish. He was in court on a charge of "drunk and disturbing the peace" for an incident that happened in his home in Ward 10. And, of course, he didn't have a lawyer in those days, and he was defending himself. His wife had had him arrested for this disturbance that occurred in his home.

And so he got up, and this was his story to the judge: He said, "Your Honor, I work real hard." Said, "I work with surveying crews and highway crews, and I work real hard for my money. I own the only TV in Ward 10 in Winn Parish." And he said, "Every Wednesday night, I go home from work and there's not a bite of food in my house, and everybody in Ward 10 is gathered up there watching *Wagon Train*." Said, "I got home that night," and said, "I'll admit I'd stopped and had a few beers on the way home." Said, "I brought a six-pack home with me."

"When I walked in, I came in through the kitchen door and set them down on the counter." He said, "I also had a dozen eggs in my other hand." Said, "There wasn't a bite of food in that kitchen. And I looked in the living room, and everybody in Ward 10 was gathered up in there watching *Wagon*

Train on my TV." He said, "Your Honor, I picked up that [TV] and threw it right out through that living room window."

I said, "*Wagon Train* had rolled through Ward 10 for its last time!"

The judge said, "Well, how did the eggs get on the ceiling?"

He said, "Your Honor, I guess I just dropped them."

84. He Was Definitely Out

I have a story here about Julius Long. Julius was [Huey's] older brother who practiced law in Shreveport. Julius and I were great friends. He used to come to Winnfield, and in the building I was in, there was a dentist down at the far end of the hall. And Julius and that dentist had grown up together.

And Julius used to come down and come up to my office and tell my secretary to go get the dentist. He'd just walk in and take my whole office over, all day. And they'd sit in there and tell old stories about growing up in Winnfield.

One of the ones he told, Julius told, was that they had—back in the old days every town in North Louisiana had a semi-pro baseball team. Lot of them were just local people; some of them were guys who would come in here, and they may get on jobs and make $50.00 a month playing baseball. Of course, they divided the money from the baseball [games].

And then most of these North Louisiana towns, including Winnfield—I found out after I got here, and Jonesville was the same way—owned slot machines. The baseball teams owned the slot machines and got all the proceeds from the slot machines. And that's the way the sport of semi-pro baseball was.

But anyway, the story was that they went to an old town north of here—small town, much smaller than Winnfield—to play a baseball game. Rode up there in wagons. This was in the early 1900s.

And they had a manager [and] a managing coach from here, and he was a big fellow. Much larger than I am. Big chest. He later went to Shreveport and became quite wealthy, this lawyer did.

But anyway, they went up there to this little town to play that ball game, and along after nine innings, score was nothing-nothing. Winnfield came to bat at the top of the ninth, and one of the Winnfield players hit a long ball to the outfield and made it all the way to third base and just stopped. Was standing there on the bag, and the ball was thrown to the third baseman. The third baseman caught the ball and reached over and touched him.

Well, the coach of that team, that small town team, was also umpire. He was a little, short, slender man. And the umpire says, "You're out!"

And this big manager from Winnfield sailed up there and stuck that stomach out in his face and said, "What did you say?"

That umpire pulled a pistol out from under his coat and said, "I say he was out."

The manager turned around and said, "Well, hell yeah, you're out! What are you standing up there delaying the game for?!"

Julius swore that was a true story.

85. How to Save on Heating Costs

I used to have a friend here who had a habit of, when cold weather came, he'd turn off his utilities and get drunk. And we had a judge then that believed in giving thirty-day jail sentences if you'd been up there that many times being drunk.

He'd get out in the middle of the street, and if the police didn't come get him out there—drunk and in that cold weather—he'd walk down to the police station or flag down a police officer.

Of course, they'd bring him in, arrest him, and put him in jail, and bring him to court. The judge would give him thirty days in jail. He'd spend thirty days, and while all his utilities were off, he was warm in jail.

But anyway, the old judge in those days liked to kind of lecture you along. I used to tell my clients, "When you go over there for sentencing, if he starts out, 'I knew your old mammy and your pappy and your grandmammy and grandpappy, and I want to help you out,' " I said, "You better grab onto something because his idea of helping you out is putting you in jail in the penitentiary for as long as he can put you there!"

But I said, "If he just starts out, 'I sentence you,' relax, it's not going to be bad."

So this fellow came up before the old judge, and the judge began to tell him, "I knew your mammy and your pappy—"

And he said, "Forget it, Judge. Don't give me none of them expended sentences. I'm ready to board mine out right here."

86. Who's on Trial?

I heard this story from old lawyers. This involved a man who used to live in a town in another parish years ago. Highly reputable man. Real friendly, real nice, deacon in the church. Everybody just loved him. All the kids. He'd always give kids money to buy ice cream, and that was something during the Depression. He'd been married many years, great reputation.

Another man was charged with killing a man and was being tried. He called this old gentleman as a character witness for him. He knew this man could influence a jury by testifying on behalf of the defendant. Of course, he testified that he'd known the man for many years, had a reputation for being a peaceful, honest, law-abiding citizen.

Then the District Attorney began to cross-examine this elderly man. This man in his early days, at twenty-one or twenty-two, had gotten into a squabble with another fellow over some girl they were both trying to go with. There'd been a shooting scrape between them, and he'd killed this man. They charged him for killing him, but he'd been acquitted.

Anyway, the District Attorney said, "You've been charged with murder once yourself, haven't you?"

The witness said, "Yes, and I will be again if this line of questioning continues!"

They didn't ask him any more questions.

87. 20/20 Vision

I was trying an accident suit many years ago. I represented a plaintiff in an accident suit many years ago. The accident had happened on one of the then-gravel roads in Winn Parish, going south.

My client told me they were going south on that road, and they were on their side of the road and this other vehicle came around a curve on the wrong side of the road and never straightened out—just ran into them.

And I had gone down there, checked the scene, and there was a house about a quarter of a mile back from where the accident had happened. An elderly black man lived there. I had gone by and talked to him and asked him if he'd seen the accident. He had and gave his description, just like my client had, that that fellow was on the wrong side of the road and run head on into my client.

So the trial came up, and I put this black man, who was seventy-four, I think, on the stand. He testified that she was going down the road in her lane, and a fellow came around a curve on the wrong side of the road and just ran into her.

So the defense lawyer began questioning, "How old are you?"

"Seventy-four."

There's no question that he could've seen the accident if he'd been on the porch of his house where he said he was. The lawyer said, "Can you see very well?"

He said, "Yeah, I can see pretty good." Kept on about how well he could see.

Finally, the lawyer said, "Well, how far can you see?"

The witness said, "I can see the moon, how far is that?"

88. His Client Was Saved

I'm going to tell you a story about a lawyer friend of mine, and I'm not going to call any names of the judge or the lawyer, either. But I had a lawyer years ago, when I first started practicing, tell me that when I went to these small towns, if they had a beer joint there, stop by when I started to leave town—not coming into town but when I started to leave—and stop by, go in, shake hands with everybody, and buy everybody a beer.

He said, "In the first place, they might get to know you, and you might get some cases out of it. And in the second place, you might get one of them on a jury one day when you need a friend."

So this lawyer in this other town called me. He was representing a woman who had killed her husband. She was charged with murder. She had married a man that would come in and beat her up every night.

One night she hid a rifle under the covers, and when he started that with her, she shot him and killed him. And course, he wanted some time on [the trial]. In those days, we just had jury trials, criminal term, one in February and one in October. That was it. If you could get by in one week in February, then you could put that thing off until October. He wanted some time.

Those days, too, if you'd ever had a charge filed against you by the district attorney and you hadn't been tried and found not guilty, and the district attorney hadn't dismissed it, it was still pending. If you tried to try him on it, he had a right to plead lapse of time and have it dismissed. But it hadn't been dismissed; it was still pending.

A grand juror, who had a charge pending against him, was not eligible to serve on a grand jury if he had a charge pending against him. The theory was that the D.A. could use it to put pressure on him and make him vote for something he might not want to vote for.

So I went to this town, and I checked every member on the grand jury against the criminal list, all the way back as long as any of them had lived. I didn't find anything.

On the way out of town, I stopped at this bar. I always did at beer joints. Went in, shook hands, bought everybody a beer, and somebody said, "What are you doing down here?"

I said, "I've been checking to see if any of the grand jurors had any charges against them."

One of them said, "Well, old so-and-so comes up in federal court next week for killing too many ducks and . . . all kinds of game violation charges against him." Of course, I bought everybody a beer, and I left, drove to Alec [Alexandria], got a copy of the charge, certified it, came back and filed my motion. Judge had to sustain it, and by doing that, the charge is dismissed. Then they had to wait for the fall to get another grand jury, get her reindicted, and then she'd be tried.

Along about the first part of September, I hadn't heard anything. This district judge in that district also did a little bit of preaching at some country church. I hadn't heard from this lawyer anymore, either. I went to arrange my schedule for the fall, because I had some trials here I was going to tend to, and so I called him, this lawyer. I said, "What about our woman client down there? We're going to have to get together on that and do some work on it."

He said, "Oh, it's all over with."

I said, "What do you mean, 'it's over with'?"

He said, "The judge came down here, [to] this little old country church down here, holding a revival this summer, she joined the church, I plead her guilty, and he gave her a suspended sentence!"

Eck Bozeman

WINNFIELD, WINN PARISH

The following two stories were collected June 18, 1990, by C. Renée Harvison from Eck Bozeman, eighty-three when interviewed but now deceased, a British American who was hired by Huey Long to drive his father, Hugh. Hugh, according to Eck, was "something else." Eck drove him for sixteen months and said that Huey instructed him, "Drive Papa wherever he wants to go, but don't let him come to Baton Rouge, don't bring him to any of my speeches."

For the most part, Eck followed these orders and took Hugh wherever he wanted. It was from this time as Hugh Long's driver that Eck gets his stories.

89. Hugh Goes Courting

One morning, he called me about four. He said he wanted to go to Urania. This was when we didn't have any gravel roads, let alone paved ones. And so he wanted me to pick him up.

So I picked him up about seven that morning, and we started out. About twenty miles east of here, there was a Mr. and Mrs. McCartney who lived over there. The man had died about a month before. We was going up the hill, and he says, "When you get up to the top of the hill, I want you to stop. I want to go in that house."

He went in, knocked on the door [Eck knocks on the table], the lady came to the door, and he says, "I'm Hugh Long," says, "I understand you lost your husband recently."

She says, "Yes sir."

He says, "Well, do you want to get married?"

She said, "Just a minute." She went back in the house and got a shotgun, and she told him, "I'm going to count to five and you better be in that car moving."

90. For Better or for Worse

The old man remarried. He married a woman from down here, Dry Prong . . . I didn't even know her. I didn't know he had remarried.

And it was on a Saturday, and he got me that morning to come up and take him somewhere. He had a niece—her husband ran a cafe up there, the American Cafe. So he had me put him out at the American Cafe; he wanted to eat dinner.

But he wanted me to pick him up. He wanted me to take him somewhere that evening. So I came back and got him. I thought he was wanting to go home. I thought he was wanting to go home to Earl's house.

He said, "No. I want to go down to Dry Prong. I want to go home." He had left home!

We got down there and [she] was out there chopping wood, and he made a move to get out of the car.

She looked at him, and she began to say, "Where have you been? Where in the world have you been? You been gone six months, and not a postcard!"

He stood there and leaned on the car door about fifteen minutes, and finally he said, "Is that old spotted calf come up yet?"

That's all he said to her! He left and came back to Winnfield.

John T. Campbell

MINDEN, WEBSTER PARISH

The following three stories were recorded May 12, 1990, at the Minden Germantown Festival from John T. Campbell, a British American resident of Minden, Webster Parish, now deceased.

91. He Knew How to Get Votes

I first knew Huey, knew of him—I knew of him before I knew him, when I was running for Railroad Commissioner—1918, I think it was.

The first story I heard about Huey was that . . . before he was Railroad Commissioner, before he was a lawyer even—he had been a traveling salesman traveling in a buggy, peddling Codline Oil. And he went down to Bienville, a town down there where I lived, and went in the store there. Pulled up in his buggy, jumped out, and went in the store there to try and make a sale.

When he came back out, Uncle Nick . . . who was the town marshall of Bienville, was standing there holding his horse. And he said, "Young man, we have a law against leaving horses unhitched."

So he took Huey down to the mayor, and they fined him three bucks for leaving his buggy standing out there with the reins dropped and his horse [unhitched].

So Huey came back there running for the Railroad Commissioner, and he got out and he drove up in front of the store. A bunch of the old-timers were sitting out there whittling as they do—cuss the government, talk about politics, what have you. He was driving an old Model T automobile, and he got out, didn't say a word, opened the back door, took out a manila rope, a two-inch manila rope, tied it to the axle. Then he went up and tied it to the hitching post. Then he went up to where this group of people were. He said, "The last time I was in this damn town, they fined me for not hitching my horse! By God, they ain't going to get me for that this time!"

Well, they said Huey got every vote in Bienville in that race. He was elected Public Service Commissioner. Then, up until that time, Public Service Commissioner, it wasn't the Public Service Commissioner, it was Railroad Commissioner back in those days. It was just a—didn't amount to anything, tell you the truth. It was a few old-time political hacks got elected to it. Never did anything but maybe meet once in a while. When Huey went on that commission, things changed. Fact, that's what happened every time

Huey came on the scene, things changed. So he revitalized the Railroad Commission and made it a vital organization.

92. They Couldn't Fool a Polecat

Huey was the most outstanding individual I've ever known. He's the most brilliant man I've ever known. He was—in every field—he was brilliant. He was the best politician that I ever saw. He could be a statesman among statesmen. He could get down with the lowest people in the world. Or he could be an s.o.b. among s.o.b.'s. He got along with everybody and he was always out front. He was smarter than any of them.

He was the most unique politician I ever saw. He talked about his program, whatever he was going to do, very little. When others would stand up there and hammer and hammer about "what I'm going to do, and what I'm going to do" and all these promises, he'd talk about his a few minutes, and then he lit in to whoever was the big shot in the parish where he was speaking. He ran parish by parish. He didn't run by the state. He'd tell you a little bit about what he planned to do, but then he would light into whoever the big boys were, running the parish. It appeared to me that his idea was that he wanted to be the big man in every parish. I've said many times: he reminded me of the new kid coming in wanting to be the bully of the school. And to be the bully of the school, he had to whip the bully. He tore into everybody. He had somebody in each parish who was his whipping boy.

When he went to Shreveport, he had three that was the big people over there. That was Andrew Querbes, who was the president of the First National Bank; L. E. Thomas, who was the mayor of Shreveport; and John Ewing. John Ewing was the publisher of the *Shreveport Times*. His dad was the publisher of the *New Orleans States*. They were big politicians. Well, Huey belittled them in every shape, form, and fashion. He never called John Ewing anything but "Squirt"—Squirt Ewing. And Andrew Querbes, he wouldn't say "Andrew"— he'd say "Andy"—Old Andy. And L. E. Thomas, one of the stories he'd tell, he said that they got into a contest. They got into an argument about which one of them could stay in the room with a skunk—he didn't call it a skunk, he called it a polecat—which one of them could stay in a room with a polecat the longest.

So they got together there, and he said Little Squirt Ewing took a deep breath and grabbed his nose and went in the room with the polecat. Stayed two minutes, had to come out. Then old Andy rared back, took a great big breath, and grabbed his nose, went in. He stayed three minutes and had to come out. L. E. Thomas, he was a brustly type of fellow. He grabbed his nose, he goes in, stays a minute and the polecat comes out! [Huey] had a lot of good stories he liked to tell.

93. Coon Chasers and Possum Watchers

One thing when he got to be the governor, one of the things he was going to do, he was going to fire all these, as he called them, "Coon Chasers and Possum Watchers." They were working for the conservation people. All these game wardens, he was going to get rid of them.

But he said he found that was harder to do than he thought it was. He said, "Boy, a guy got himself a political job, he was hard to shake!" Says it reminded him of a fellow down there in Winn Parish who was going through the woods, and he could hear somebody screaming out in the woods. He kept listening, and he could tell it was a woman screaming. Well, he went out there to look and see what the problem was. After he got about a half a mile out in the woods, here come this woman, hair flying in the wind, clothes torn about half off, briar scratches all over, running just as hard as she could run. Right behind her was an old boy about fourteen years old. He was digging in after her. This guy jumped out and he grabbed this kid. He said, "What do you think you're doing chasing that woman out here? You lost your mind?"

The old boy rared back, and he said, "You turn me a loose! That's my Ma! She thinks she's going to wean me, but she's not!"

[Huey] said that's what he was facing with these Coon Chasers and Possum Watchers. They were just a little difficult to wean, but he was going to get rid of them one way or another.

Jimmie Davis

JONESBORO, JACKSON PARISH

Recorded July 7, 1990, by Monty Brown at Jonesboro's Kraft Paper Festival of the South from a former governor of Louisiana, Jimmie H. Davis. Davis is a native of Jonesboro but now resides in Baton Rouge. He was twice governor of Louisiana, once in the 1940s and again in the early 1960s. But Davis's fame is not simply linked to politics. To outsiders, he's probably better known for the widely popular song, "You Are My Sunshine." He also appeared in movies, most notably Louisiana, *in which he had the leading role, and* Mississippi Gambler.

Davis follows in a long line of silver-tongued Louisiana politicians. Even though he is not in political office anymore, his oratorical skills remain sharp, and he can still tell a doozy of a story without so much as blinking an eye.

94. Bull Talk

Gov. Davis: This is kind of new to me. I don't know if they want me to tell lies or what.

Monty Brown: Anything you want to tell.

Gov. Davis: Oh, I don't want to tell lies! [Audience laughs.] That reminds me, a few years ago, I was up on an engagement in North Carolina. And it's about fifty miles from where a good friend of mine lives. He used to hold office here in this state. But he went up there, since his boy was there; he's a judge.

I went over there, and he said, "I'm glad you're here." Said, "They're having a fair here in town. Let's ride around a little bit." And he said, "Oh yeah, the teenagers are having a lying contest. And the one who tell the biggest lie gets an eighteen-month-old, white-faced, registered Hereford bull."

I said, "Let's go by there and hear them."

Went by there, he introduced me, they said, "Gov. Davis, we know you not a teenager, and you're a visitor here. So we'll just put you in on this too. You can tell, and if you tell the biggest lie, then you can win the bull, too."

I said, "That's great." And I said, "This is kind of tough for me, though. I've never been to something like this. In the fact of the business, down there where I came from in Louisiana, people don't tell lies."

He said, "Governor Davis, you just won the bull!" [Audience claps and laughs.]

95. Walking on Water

Monty Brown: Somebody leaned over and said to me that you had a story about walking on the water.

Gov. Davis: I guess they're talking about maybe—see, I live right next door to the [Governor's] Mansion. There's a lake there. . . . Across the lake is the capitol. And my wife and I were out in the backyard one morning. Knocked down a wasp's nest, dirt daubers, killing snakes, lizards, everything else running around there. And she said, "Well, Edwards!"

Governor Edwards was coming down, going walking toward the water. She said, "I believe he's going to walk on the water!"

I said, "No, I don't think he can walk the water!" [Audience laughs.]

But I was wrong! [Audience laughs harder.] He took off, went across there, just prancing like Edwards does, you know! [Audience laughs.] Prancing. Got about halfway, down he went! Sunk. I ran on out there, picked him up, and walked him on across! [Audience laughs and claps.]

And that's the truth! I couldn't win the bull on that being the truth.

96. It's a Dirty Game

Monty Brown: One of the things I've noticed about your political campaigns is that you always ran what you might call a positive campaign. That seems to have changed a lot these days. People now spend most of their time putting the opposition down, whereas you just talked about the positive side of electing you.

Gov. Davis: I didn't talk about anybody. I guess I'd been as bad as the rest of them.

Monty Brown: But they talked about you.

Gov. Davis: Oh, they worked me over good! Everybody got on to me. But I think they might have made me the underdog. Sometimes the underdog might become an advantage.

You can expect anything in politics. As the law is now, you can say anything about a politician, anything you want. It doesn't make any difference how bad it is. You can sue, they can sue, but they can't get a dime. You not in politics; that's a different story.

Most anybody ever won was a case over in Bastrop, Louisiana. A man running for judge, they accused him of doing everything that a man shouldn't do. Said some terrible things. When he sued, he won. He got seven thousand, five hundred dollars. Today he wouldn't get a penny because the Supreme Court has held that—maybe they didn't term it just like this. Pappy [R. L. "Pappy" Triche, an active politician in Louisiana who was floor leader during Davis's last term as governor] would know. But they said, "Politicians are free game. Shoot them anywhere you want them!"

97. Bedtime for the Governor

The first time I was in [the Governor's Mansion], we had hotdogs and hamburgers and sardines that day for lunch. We had a big, big feed, you know. And soda pop. At night at the mansion, after that, I was really tired. About as tired as I was last night. I said, "I'm getting ready to go to bed."

And they had a man and a woman come take charge of me to put me to bed! I never had been put to bed by a man and a woman—that you've never seen! Well, they got me, and they had some red, white, blue, and green, yellow, and purple pajamas. Well, I never have had on a pair of pajamas; I'm a gown man!

They got me all fixed up. And the pajamas was as slippery as they could be. Finally they said, "In the bed you go."

I run and jumped in, and I slid all the way out in the hall! I got back, got in that big gown, had a wonderful night's sleep. I said, "You all just let me alone. I'll handle my own bed-going, you hear?"

98. Wedding Special at the Barbershop

While I was up here, I've been visiting around some of the places all around, Quitman and Hodge, Clay, Ansley, back over to Weston here. I was just riding around, seeing a few people I know. I was riding around and got to thinking about one time when I was a young man.

I was in Quitman one Saturday morning. And Hardy Brooks had a barbershop in there, in the back end of the feed store. I went in there to get a haircut. He said, "I've got to go back out to my house." It was about three miles, and he always came to town in a buggy. He said, "You stay here while I'm gone. Tell them I'll be back."

I said, "I'll stay here. You go ahead. I'll be here."

He hadn't no more than got going good till a long, tall boy came in there. I said, "What can I do for you?" I wasn't a barber.

He said, "I want a haircut."

I said, "What kind of haircut would you want?"

He said, "Well, I'm getting married tomorrow."

Well, I said, "We got a wedding special on today." [Audience laughs.]

He said, "Well, I'm ready to go with it."

He got in the chair. You had those manual clippers then. You didn't have electric. I got to going on his hair. I get it too high over here, too high over there. I finally wound up, I had cut it all off! I said, "I better quit somewhere." Had a patch on top about the size of a saucer. He said, "How am I looking?"

I said, "You looking great." I said, "Now what you got to have is a shampoo."

He said, "What's that?" I said, "Well, it's where you wash your hair and get it all cleaned up."

Did that and dried him out. Said, "Now you need a tonic."

He said, "I don't need that. I take [a chill tonic] every morning."

I said, "This is not [a chill] tonic. This is tonic for your head. You got to not only look good, you got to smell good." Put that perfume in there. Got that fixed up.

Back in those days, I don't know whether they ever do that now or not. But they had a stick there, like a match, about as long as a pencil and half as big as a pencil. You take that and light that, some of you have seen that I'm sure, and you go around the edge of the hair, singeing the edge of the hair.

He said, "What is that for? You going to burn my hair off."

I said, "No, I'm not going to burn your hair off." Said, "You got all this perfume in here, and you want to smell good. And you going to be ready."

So he did. Got him all fixed up. Went to pay me, and I said, "No, wedding haircuts are free." And he took off for the wedding the next day.

I saw him in town about a month or two later. I saw him, and I went behind the building because I didn't want to meet him. I knew he'd kill me! [Audience laughs.] Some months later, one morning, ran into him face to face. He said, "Hello, barber."

I said, "What you say there, John? How was the wedding?"

He said, "We didn't have it."

I said, "What's the matter?"

He said, "When she saw my haircut, she just balked. She wouldn't move. Couldn't get married."

I said, "That's bad."

He said, "No, it was good. If a woman is that cranky and doesn't appreciate a good haircut, well then I didn't want her, because she would've given me a lot of trouble." [Audience laughs and claps.]

Mazie Hardy

ST. MARTINVILLE, ST. MARTIN PARISH

Recorded at Le Grand Boucherie des Cajuns, February 25, 1990, from Mazie Hardy, a Cajun resident of St. Martinville. The following is a dialogue between Hardy and her daughter, Lona, who said that she can remember from her childhood her mother's loyalty to Sam Jones—a loyalty that remains today.

99. She Was a Loyal Sam Jones Follower

Lona Bernard: Did you always vote the way your husband voted?

Mazie Hardy: Oh no. But it was supposed to be that wives voted like their husbands. But I wasn't a wife like that! [Audience laughs.] I had my own opinion. If I did not think that was the right man to be elected, I did not vote for him—*anyhow* my husband voted. [Audience claps.]

Lona Bernard: A woman before her time. Tell us a little bit about that. I'm sure that at one point or another, you must have convinced him to vote like you.

Mazie Hardy: When Earl Long was running, my husband had been an Earl Long [man] all his life. And he was running against Sam Jones. And Sam Jones was my man. So my husband, at the time, had a partnership cafe with [a man named] Martin from Arnaudville. I have to think a little bit. I'm not getting any younger, you know.

Lona Bernard: Let me clue you in a little bit. Daddy and Martin were in partnership, and Daddy was for Earl Long. But you didn't like Earl Long. He was a good man! Why you didn't like Earl Long too much? He was a good man.

Mazie Hardy: Well, maybe he was, but I didn't think so. Well, anyhow, they had a meeting at the . . . bar. And he came in there sloppy drunk, falling all over. So I decided, "Oh no. I can't believe that Daddy is going to vote for that man." And he spit all over. He smoked, and he just threw his cigarettes around. In other words, I just didn't like the way that he acted.

So after the meeting, after [we] were home, I told my husband, I says, "Now, are you going to support him?" I says, "After all he's done?"

He says, "Well, no, I'll go along with you. I'll vote for Sam Jones."

Well we did, and Sam Jones won that year.

Lona Bernard: What did you all do when he won?

Mazie Hardy: Oh, we celebrated! Naturally! We had parades, and all the ones we knew that had voted for the opposite party, well, we'd stop by their house or store, and we'd celebrate and naturally make them very angry. But my turn did come.

Lona Bernard: When was that?

Mazie Hardy: Well, a few years after Sam Jones ran again, against Earl. And naturally I was still for Sam Jones. And Sam Jones lost that time! Well, honey, the people hadn't forgotten of the years before. People from Breaux Bridge, St. Martinville, Cecilia, Arnaudville. They all got together in trucks and what have you.

After the election, I heard all this noise. I told my mama, "I bet you they're celebrating." I says, "And they'll come here and tease me."

Mama says, "Well, just smile. That's all you can do."

I says, "I will."

Lona Bernard: How did you smile? Through your teeth?

Mazie Hardy: I'd just do like this [demonstrates], you know! And I'd curse them for all I could.

But anyhow, they did come. And I went on the porch and I waved to them and I cursed them under my breath, you know. And I went along.

But this isn't the funny part. It was that night, after we were in bed. Well, here comes a bunch of cars. They drove in my yard. And an old school bus. I recognized the school bus. That was [Mr.] Wiltz. That night, I didn't know who the man that was dressed like a priest. I didn't know then who he was. But he happened to be . . . your uncle! [Audience laughs.]

So they were tooting horns and hitting on buckets and what have you. So I told Mama, "Let's get up and see what's going on."

Well, I did. We had shades, and we watched through. I says, "Oh Mama," I says, "that's the gang from Bayou Portage and Coteau. . . ." I says, "I recognize the bus."

So we went out. And this priest, well, we didn't have our gate yet. So we had put just a board across. Well, they'd come to bury Sam Jones at my step. The priest went over that board. [Audience laughs.] Well, that was just too much. I just couldn't take it anymore. So I went back in the house, and I got my gun. And I shot two shots in the air, and I'm telling you, in five minutes there wasn't a soul left.

But the priest forgot all about that board, you know? And poor thing, he just rapped himself up and fell over the board. [Audience laughs.] They had to bring him to the doctor that night! Nearly broke his two legs. But anyhow, I still didn't know who it was. I had recognized some of the others. They nearly broke my bench trying to back out. As if I'd have shot anybody, but I got rid of them. The next day, it was all over town that the priest that nearly broke his leg was [my uncle].

Lona Bernard: How did they bury Sam Jones?

Mazie Hardy: Oh, that evening, they had stuffed a dummy. And they had him hanging from his feet down. And they'd holler at me, "Look at your man! Look at your man!" Oh, I could have killed them.

Stephen Dart

ST. FRANCISVILLE, WEST FELICIANA PARISH

Recorded March 15, 1990, at St. Francisville's Heritage Days from lawyer Stephen Dart, fifty-seven, a British American.

100. You Never Know When Your Ass Is Going to Be in a Box Like Mine

Judge Lewis was the lawyer for the Yazoo and Mississippi Railroad, which was taken over by the Illinois Central. He had a case involving a cow that was killed right near the Mississippi state line. The Mississippi state line is only about eight miles north of us. The lady who owned the cow got a Natchez, Mississippi lawyer to handle it. And he wrote to the railroad, and the railroad turned it over to Judge Lewis, and Judge Lewis corresponded with him. They wrote back and forth, back and forth, and after a year, which is our prescriptive period—the statute of limitations, if you will, ran out.

After the year had run, Judge Lewis wrote to this lawyer in Natchez and he said, "I've really enjoyed our correspondence, but the question is now moot since the statute has run. I'm going to close my file."

So he got this frantic letter back from the lawyer in Natchez, after explaining that the statute in Mississippi was six years, and it said, "Judge, I want to tell you a story. There was a man who had a pet jackass, and he wanted to ship the jackass from here to there. It was over a three-day period. He worried about what he would do to be certain his jackass would be taken care of. And he thought and he thought and finally, he said, 'I think what I'll do is put him in a crate. Then I'll put this sign on the crate that says, "Please, I am helpless. Please feed me and water me and take care of me because you never know when your ass is going to be in a box like mine!"' "

The judge wrote back, and he said he thought it was a marvelous story, but he had no choice but to close the case.

Roy Inabnett

MINDEN, WEBSTER PARISH

Recorded May 12, 1990, at Minden's Germantown Festival from Roy Inabnet, a British American. This story is well known around Minden, where Roy first heard it from her father; she is not certain about some historical details.

101. Chaffee's Bull

It was soon after the Civil War, I guess, and a man was running for the mayor of Minden. He was a newcomer; probably many people thought he was a carpetbagger and didn't belong here. The man who was running against him *died* before the election. The man had nobody running against him. There was no way he could be defeated for mayor. So there were a lot of people in Minden who didn't want that to happen. So they wrote in on the ballot. They had a candidate, and it was a bull that belonged to Mr. Chaffee in his pasture out here west of town. And you know the bull got more votes than the man did! The man served as mayor, but my father said they called him Bull Jones the rest of his life.

Virgil E. Callender, Sr.

BOGALUSA, WASHINGTON PARISH

Recorded at Bogalusa's Storytelling in the Park, June 29, 1990, from Virgil E. Callender, Sr., seventy, a British American.

102. And He Knows His State Capitals Too

We want to tell the people how smart our officials are here in Bogalusa. This was years ago, we had this chief of police. He was going down the road there, and he saw this big Cadillac driving by, and it come—skidded the wheels when it stopped. Now he walked up there and he said, "Where do you think you're from?"

[The driver] said, "Chicago."

He said, "Well, then how and the hell you got them Illinois license plates on your car?"

That is our politicians. Our hired officials.

Hubert L. "Anatoo" Clement, Sr.

EVANGELINE, ACADIA PARISH

Recorded November 3, 1990, at the Louisiana Folklife Festival from Hubert L. "Anatoo" Clement, Sr., sixty-two, a retired custodian, who is also a Cajun humorist and musician.

Clement's tale appears in two versions. The first is transcribed according to the style rules that the editors have applied generally (see the section titled "The Texts of the Tales," preceding the first story in this book). The second version was provided by Clement. After seeing the editors' transcription, he stated that the flavor of his story would be lost unless he could make changes to convey the comic Cajun dialect that he uses when performing. He then wrote a version of his story to indicate how a comedian's Cajun accent "looks" to him.

103. The Politician Gets His

I'll tell you a little story—it won't take long. I got a opponent what run against me for governor. . . . I was worried about him, but I don't have to worry no more. He's all finished. You see, he was working on his roof, and he make a platform, and he start speech against me up there. He got in a big high, "throw mud" [campaign] . . . against me, and he fall off of there. He hurt his self bad on the head.

And they put him in the bed, and they put his little girl sit by him. And she's there watching him, and his wife was in the kitchen. She was cooking in the kitchen, and the little girl looked at him and she said, "Papa," she said, "are you dead?"

"No, *chère*, not yet."

So she waited a little while, and she said, "Hey, Papa, you dead now?"

"No, *chère*, I'm still hanging on. What smells so good?"

She said, "Well, Mama in the kitchen. She's making some gumbo."

"Oh, *chère*," he said, "That's my best thing. Before I die, go in there and ask Mama to send me just a little bit in a cup. I going to eat that one more time before I die."

So she said, "Okay."

So she went in the kitchen, and she stayed a while. Then she came back in there, and he [look] dead. She said, "Hey, Papa, you dead now?"

He said, "Hey [in a wheezing voice], not yet. Did you brought me some gumbo?"

She said, "No."

"*Mais*," he said, "*Chère*, why you didn't brought Daddy just a little bit of gumbo, so he can eat one more time some gumbo?"

She said, "Because Mama said, 'No.' "

He said, "Why your mama said, 'No,' *chère*?"

She said, "Because Mama said that's for the funeral tomorrow."

I thank you please!

The Politician Gets His

I gonna tole y'all a lil story—it won't took long. I got a opponent what run againtz me for governor to the state of Louisiana. I was worry abot dat "sone-be-gone," but I don't had to worry abot ham no more. Heez all fanish. You see, he was work on heez roof an he make a platform up dare an he start to speech againtz me up dare. He got in a high "chromud" campaign againtz me and he fall off of dare an hurt heezsef bad on heez head.

An day put ham in de bed an day put heez lil girl sit side by ham. An she's dare watching ham an heez wife was in de ketchen. She was in dare cooking. An de lil girl look at ham an she say, "Papa," she say, "you are dead?"

"No, che're, notyet," he say.

So she wait a lil while an she say agane, "Hey, Papa, you dead now?"

He say, "No, che're, I'm still handging on. What smell so good?"

She say, "Well, Mama in de ketchen, she make some gumbo."

"Oh, che're!" he say, "datz my bess ting! Before I die, go een dare and ax Mama to san me juss a lil bit in a cup. I gonna eat dat one more time before I die."

So she say, "Okay, Papa." So she waynt in de ketchen an she stay a while. Den she cam back een dare an he look dead—he have turn green. She say, "Hey, Papa, you dead now, anh?"

He say [in a wheezing voice], "Notyet, che're. Did you brought me some gumbo?"

An she say, "No, Papa."

"Mais," he say, "che're! Why you don't brought Papa juss a lil bit of gumbo, so he can eat one more time some gumbo before he die?"

She say, "Becuz Mama say 'no'!"

He say, "Why yore mama say 'no,' che're?"

An she say, "Because Mama say datz for de funeral tomorrow!"

I tank you please!

Joseph Aaron

IOWA, CALCASIEU PARISH

Recorded at the Lake Charles Spring Arts Fest, April 22, 1990, from Joseph Aaron, a Cajun.

104. Huey Long and the Importance of Sticking Together

I was in Iowa High School. [Huey Long] was elected. . . . governor in 1928. But he had already taken over the senate post in Washington, and he was a senator then. But he was touring the state of Louisiana around this area with his candidates. He wanted to get all his ticket elected to public office. So he spoke at the school that day. . . . Iowa had never seen that many people before—when Huey Long came to Iowa to talk! They kept us on the school buses that day after school, and they came from Homewood, Hayes,

Bell City. Came on horseback, wagons, buggies, you name it. And I can still remember it. We had a stile in those days that went over the fence. Kids today don't even know what a stile is. We didn't have steps; you crossed over the fence. And it was high.

So I can still see Huey Long up there waving his hands, talking. I can still see it like today. And he made a talk there on something, I'll never forget. I told his son, Russell Long, in later years about that. And he made me write it down exactly like Huey Long said.

Huey Long said, "Now, listen folks, you all stick with me." He said, "The other day, I went fishing with this friend of mine. He fell out of the boat." He said, "I reached over the boat to pick him up, and his hand come off. So I threw his hand in the boat. I reached over and caught him by the leg and his leg come off!" He said, "I looked down at my friend, and I said, 'How in the hell can I save you if you don't stick together?' You all stick with me, and I'll save all of you all!"

I'll never forget that for as long as I live.

Crawford Vincent

LAKE CHARLES, CALCASIEU PARISH

Recorded at the Lake Charles Spring Arts Fest, April 22, 1990, from Crawford Vincent, a Cajun and a member of the Hackberry Ramblers, who play Cajun swing, Western swing, and country music.

105. Huey Long and the Pink Silk Pajama Episode

This big high German officer come to New Orleans. That was back there—he was assassinated in September of 1935—so it must have been long about 1933 or 1934. This German officer, boy, he was a big dog in the German army. They tied up at New Orleans in some great big German ship over there. They said he said that he wanted to talk to Senator Long from Louisiana. They knew him from all over the world.

But, anyhow, he come to the old Heidelburg Hotel in New Orleans. Huey Long met him at the door in a pair of pink pajamas. This German officer thought Huey should've met him in a tuxedo or something. He was highly offended, and I can't use the language today that Huey Long told him! He said, "You can go, So-and-so, back to your ship, friend. We don't need you over here!" That actually happened.

Max Greig

ST. MARTINVILLE, ST. MARTIN PARISH

Recorded August 20, 1990, by C. Renée Harvison from Max Greig, a Cajun.

106. Huey Let Him Sing

I was here when Huey Long made one of his first stops. They had a big truck, flatbed truck. First time he ran for governor. He got up on the stand and started talking. They had a drunken troubadour that was strumming the guitar.

So the chief of police was Claude Thomas. He rode a horse. Never had a gun or anything. He controlled this town perfectly. He went over there and arrested that old boy. This boy was strumming his guitar and disturbing Huey Long's speech. So the chief of police went over there and arrested the man.

Now, Long is a smart cookie. Smart as they come. He stopped. He said, "Now, Chief, what goes on?"

He said, "Well, this man is disturbing the peace. I'm going to lock him up."

"No! Don't lock him up."

The chief of police said, "Yeah, he's drunk."

Long said, "He's not drunk! As long as he can throw his head up and take another drink! Bring him over here."

So they put him a chair on the stand. Told him to sit there. Said, "I'll put you on as soon as I get through with my speech. Sit there and be quiet." So the man sat there and listened to Huey give his speech.

After he talked, Huey introduced him. He said, "Now, you play something."

So the guy starts strumming a song. Sings, "You know you belong to Huey P. Long. So why don't you leave Simpson alone?" [Huey] was running against O. H. Simpson.

Sarah Kent

GREENSBURG, ST. HELENA PARISH

The following three stories were collected by C. Renée Harvison, September 29, 1990, from Sarah Kent and Dorothy Peroyea, both British Americans from Greensburg, St. Helena Parish. The first two stories are Kent's, the third is Peroyea's. Politics are like religion to St. Helena residents, although no famous politicians have ever come from the area. As Kent explained, "St. Helena always had sense enough to know that the people that controlled the politicians had more power than the politicians themselves!"

107. Aunt Dora's Death and Aunt Tot's Vote

I'll start off with Aunt Dora. Aunt Dora was sort of the family matriarch. She was an old maid school teacher and was pretty well respected in the family. It was during the thirties that she died. She died in March, and they were having a bad snow storm at the time. During the storm, she was sitting in front of the fireplace in a little old straight-back chair, eating [the last of the Christmas] fruitcake. They said Aunt Dora was sitting there, laughing, talking.

And I think it was when John [Harvin and Babe Morga were] running in the [assessor's] race. It was a tied race. They were talking about the sheriff's race and wondering how it would come out. All excited, and all of a sudden Aunt Dora just died. Well, everybody was terribly upset! There she was talking. They knew she wasn't doing well, but she just died unexpectedly. Snow was on the ground, and they were in a dither.

Well, as they got to thinking about it more, somebody said, "Oh my goodness! We have lost the election. Not only have we lost Aunt Dora, we've lost the election!" So then they got doubly upset. Well . . . later on they were looking through her belongings. In her purse, my daddy found eight dollars. My daddy said, "I know what to do with eight dollars. I can buy a vote!" [Laughs.] And what better way to spend Aunt Dora's last eight dollars than to cover her vote!

So he went out and bought a vote with her last eight dollars. This is true! Only in St. Helena. He bought a vote with her last eight dollars.

Then, come election day, everybody was excited. There was parties all over the parish. We get excited about elections. Tension was running high. Well, Aunt Tot and Uncle Walt got up early in the morning and voted down in the fifth ward. She came on up here, the party had started, and everybody was excited. And she went into town with the women, and as they were coming home and riding on out, she said, "Oh! My Lord, I have voted [twice]!"

The women said, "Shut up! They'll never believe that that was an accident. The men will all be killed if you say anything about it. Nobody will ever believe that. So you just shut up, and we'll go on home."

They shut up and went on home. They won the election by about two or three votes! That's true, too! This was the same election. Aunt Dora died, and we lost that vote. But we bought that vote back. We covered that vote! It would've been a tie, but Aunt Tot voted twice!

108. Guarding the Ballot Box

This was a story I heard about . . . when they had the black boxes, the election boxes. And Judge Reed was anti-Long, and my daddy was anti-Long, and the sheriff at that time, J. D. Redmond, was pro-Long. So there was the ballot box that was the actual ballot box, and then the Long ballot box that they already had prevoted. And the order of the day was to get the real ballot box to Baton Rouge. They had to get the ballot box to Baton Rouge.

Judge Reed had hidden a gun under the judge's podium for them to use. He was with them in trying to get the ballot box over there. And Uncle Paul, who was a huge man and didn't usually get involved in politics, was there. M. J. was there. Several other people. They were going to get the ballot box, and J. D. Redmond was sheriff, and he broke a bottle over the edge of the podium. He cut Pa. You know that scar that Pa had on his forehead when he died? That's where J. D. Redmond cut him with the broken bottle. He was trying to keep him there. The other side was taking the already-voted ballot box, and they were taking the actual ballot box. They were trying to stop them. Anyway . . . J. D. was a huge man himself. They say that Uncle Paul just got him by the waist and pulled him in until he just sort of collapsed. Then they skedaddled. They got out with the ballot box! But you had to have bodyguards, in the sixth ward, to go in to get the ballot boxes.

[Later on, J. D. and Pa became the best of friends. When Pa got sick and died, nobody was better to us than Mr. J. D.]

Dorothy Peroyea

GREENSBURG, ST. HELENA PARISH

109. Remembering the Day Huey Was Shot

Uncle Clyde was overweight. And he was always wiping his brow, perspiring. They lived in a big old house, and they called it Pike's Peak. It was his father's house, and Grandpa Holland had been to Pike's Peak. Said that you could tickle the angel's feet. So he came back home and said, "My house is high on a hill. I believe I can tickle that angel's feet." So he named the house Pike's Peak. Anyway, that's a different story.

The house had a swing. Uncle Clyde, every night, would sit in that swing. He'd strip down to whatever was decent or indecent. The family never quite told to what extent! But he was big on sharing news. If he heard anything, he just had to tell somebody.

And Mr. Charlie lived up on the hill. Charlie had a big job under Huey Long. He was on his staff. Somebody had been out on a date, and they came back and told Uncle Clyde that Huey Long had been shot. He said, "Oh, let me get my clothes on!" He wanted to go tell the next neighbor.

Mr. Charlie used to tell that he heard Uncle Clyde talking loud. His voice just carried. He came down the hill to see what was going on. He said, "Charlie! They got Huey!" That's how he remembers that Huey Long was killed: when Uncle Clyde said, "They got Huey."

Anyway, that tells you how news got around. The news came by telephone to Hammond. This person had been on a date in Hammond. News had spread around in Hammond, then they came back and told Greensburg. I guess what was so bad about this story is that everybody that heard in Greensburg that Huey Long was shot, told, "Clyde had to go get his clothes on so that he could go tell Charlie. Charlie got excited so Clyde just yelled to him from the bedroom window and said, 'I don't have my clothes on yet, but they got Huey!'" So then Charlie did go and call people and said, "Clyde didn't have his clothes on, so I don't know everything, but they got Huey."

Aunt Birdie [Clyde's wife] was just mortified that everywhere she went, of course Huey Long's death was big news. Every time she heard it—she was very prim and proper—she'd get embarrassed. She was a preacher's daughter, Sunday school teacher, the pillar of the church. There sat Uncle Clyde without his clothes on!

Religious Humor:
Personal Narratives and Jokes

Max Greig

ST. MARTINVILLE, ST. MARTIN PARISH

Recorded August 20, 1990, by C. Renée Harvison from Max Greig, a Cajun. Greig, a retired salesman, speaks French, English, and some Spanish and Italian. He is Catholic.

110. The Cajun and the Minister

I tell a little story about a Cajun boy from Catahoula. He was hiking a ride to St. Martinville. He couldn't hardly get a ride and directly here comes a preacher—in an old, beat up Model A Ford. He stops. Told him, "Son, get in."

So they started toward St. Martinville. He said, "Son, are you a Christian?"

He said, "No, I'm a Cajun!"

He said, "If you not a Christian, how in the heck you going to get to heaven?"

He said, "Man, don't kid me. I can't get to St. Martinville. How in the hell am I going to get to heaven!"

Clarence John Broussard

LAFAYETTE, LAFAYETTE PARISH

The following two anecdotes were recorded September 16, 1990, at Lafayette's Festivals Acadiens, from Clarence John Broussard, a Creole, now deceased.

111. Dammit to Hell! The Fun Is All Over!

I want to tell you all a little story. They had a place in the middle of nowhere, they call that. People growing over there like wild, not exactly wild but not civilized, I call that. I say they didn't have no school, no church, no

Weddings are often the setting for both young and old to exchange stories.
Here families and friends entertain at a wedding in the Cane River Creole
community of Isle Brevelle. Photo: Joseph Moran.

nothing. But after awhile, the Diocese or the Bishop decide, "Let's go put a church back there."

So they decide to do that. So they put a church there, and at the same time they put a church and a priest and some sisters! But at one time, they couldn't keep a priest there. People were so rough, the priests get away from there.

But they had a priest from somewhere, heard about that. He say, "Well, they got a beautiful church over there with some sisters, but no priest. But I'm going there. But I'm going there to stay." That's the words of the priest.

So at that time they didn't have no cars, nothing. He just saddled his horse, put all his belongings, and rode on to the church. But the people where he was going knew he was coming. They knew that he was coming.

So he passed by a country store. "I'm going over there. I'm going to act as a priest and act like a cowboy. The people so rough over there, I got to buy me some handguns, like a pistol." That's right, the people are so rough! So he passed by a country store, and he was able to buy some guns, one on each side.

When he got to the place, he introduced himself, "Hi, I'm Father So-and-so. I heard you all need a priest, but you all can't keep no priest. But I'm here to stay." So he unwrapped his guns and put his guns on the altar there! And everybody could see the pistols right there.

"So we going to begin mass. Everything understood? It's time to start mass. And when I start mass, I want everybody to sing! Not just the sisters! Everybody going to sing!"

So they start singing. [Laughs.] He starts singing, "Glory, glory the fun is all over! Dammit to hell! The fun is all over! Dammit to hell, the fun is all over! Look, I said! Everybody sing!"

Nobody was singing! Even the sisters wasn't singing!

He say, "I'm going to try it one more time! Dammit to hell, the fun is all over!" He took his gun, he fire two or three shots, *bam! bam!* "Now, I want you all to sing!" The sisters sing [in a high-pitched voice], "Dammit it to hell! The fun is all over! Dammit to hell! The fun is all over!" [Audience laughs.]

112. Trying to Get to Heaven

They had a man, he was going somewhere. And he had a old car. Every once in a while, you know, the tires wasn't as good as they are today. He went a little piece, and he caught a flat tire. He start fixing his tire, but the jack was no good on that car. He jack it up to a certain height—*blam!* It fall down.

There comes another car. It happened to be a priest, a Catholic priest. The priest got out, "Can I be a help to you, my son?"—or "my friend"—whatever it is.

"Yes, Father, I'm trying to jack up my car. But it seems like my jack don't want to hold up."

"My friend, it happens I got no jack. But we going to try yours."

Keep on trying—*blam!*—*blam!* A certain height, it fall down again. Now, the man, the owner of the car, kind of, you know, he kind of got all mad. He said some curse words. The priest said, "Don't use them curse words." He said, "You not a Catholic?"

He said, "Oh, no, Father, I'm a Boudreaux, not a Catholic!"

He keep on, "You not going to go to heaven!"

He said, "Father, I'm not going to heaven. I'm going to Ville Platte this time." [Audience laughs.]

Évélia Boudreaux

CARENCRO, LAFAYETTE PARISH

The following three anecdotes were recorded September 16, 1990, at Lafayette's Festivals Acadiens, from Évélia Boudreaux, a Cajun, celebrated for her storytelling skills.

113. The Man Who Stole Lumber

This man went to confession. And when he went to confession, he said, "Father, I stole some lumber!"

"Oh," he said, "Well, how much lumber have you stolen?"

He says, "Well, Father, I made a dog house."

"Oh," he said. "For your penance, you'll say two or three Hail Marys and two or three Our Fathers."

He said, "Father, that's not all."

"Well," he said, "What else?"

He said, "I built one of those little outdoor houses."

He said, "Yes? Well," he said, "for that you'll say a whole decade, ten Hail Marys and two Our Fathers."

He said, "Father, that's not all."

"Well," he said. "What else did you build?"

He said, "I built a house."

He said, "How big was your house?"

"It was a very big house," he said.

"Well," he says, "then I think you'll have to say the whole rosary."

He said, "Father, that's not all." He said, "I built a barn!"

"My God!" the priest said. "Well, you'll have to say two rosaries."

He said, "Father, that's not all." He said, "There's still some lumber left."

"Well," he said, "then in that case, I think you'll have to make a novena."

He says, "Father, I'm all excited." He said, "If you have the blueprint, I think I have enough lumber to make it."

114. Bless Me, Father

Well, I've heard a story at Vermilionville. It was the priest saying mass. And he said, "Before we start mass, I think I'll put everybody at ease, and I'll say a joke or two."

So he said that there was this old lady that had come to confession. And of course, he knew her background most probably. He could also smell, as you will later understand. So he said, "Well, now, when we want to go to communion, we don't eat anything after midnight until after communion."

She said, "Yes, Father, I know that."

He said, "We don't drink water after midnight, until after communion."

She said, "Yes, Father, I know that."

And he said, "No liquor also."

"Yes, Father, I know that."

And he says, "No coffee, either."

She says, "Father, you smell my coffee." She says, "I just soaked my teeth in coffee before coming to confession!"

115. Curing Corpses

Then, he went on to say, when he was a little boy, he'd like to go to funerals. He said, "Of course, I was small, and I didn't realize the sadness it brought to the family." He said, "Regardless, I would enjoy going to the funeral."

He said, "So one morning Mama calls. She said, 'Let's go to the funeral. Come get ready.' "

He says, "Mama, will they smoke him? Will they smoke him, Mama?"

He said, that's why I would like to go to the funeral—to see them use incense—to see incense burning! He said, "Mama, will they smoke him before they bury him?"

Autrey "Chank" Baudoin

LAFAYETTE, LAFAYETTE PARISH

Recorded at Lafayette's Festivals Acadiens, September 16, 1990, from Autry "Chank" Baudoin, Catholic, a Cajun.

116. Don't Cuss in Church

I know about a priest. [Audience laughs.] A Catholic priest. It's not a bad one. But he had a neighbor he made friends with. And the fellow wouldn't go to mass. The fellow wouldn't attend mass. He said, "Joe, come to mass."

"No, no, Father, I don't believe in that."

He says, "Come to mass and I'll come to lunch with you after." He said, "Come listen to me!" He said, "We're friends! It can't hurt you!"

"Okay, I'll come."

So the next time he goes to mass, naturally the priest put on a show. He talked good for his neighbor. Mass was over, Joe goes up to the altar, he said, "Dammit." He cussed all the time, wouldn't go to church. He said, "Damn, Father, you did good!"

He said, "Don't cuss, son." He says, "You can't cuss in church. Catholic church, that don't go."

"All right," but he said, "but dammit, you made a good sermon!"

"Don't cuss," he says. Says, "You not supposed to cuss."

"Oh, but dammit," he says, "I can't help it, Father!"

He says, "Don't cuss, son!"

He says, "I was so impressed." He says, "When they pass the basket, I put a hundred bucks!"

The priest said, "Dammit! Did you?" [Audience laughs.]

James "Podge" White

MONROE, OUACHITA PARISH

Recorded at Monroe's Storytelling Jamboree, April 23, 1990, from James "Podge" White, British American, a retired farmer in his late seventies. Originally from Bastrop, White, a Protestant, now resides in Monroe. Here, White playfully works the moderator of the storytelling session, Dr. George C. Brian, into the jest.

117. The Persimmoned Parson

The events I am about to tell you actually happened in an area not far from here. For reasons you will see, I cannot call any names of the individuals concerned. [Audience laughs.] In a small, rural church one Sunday morning, they were discussing, making plans for communion, observing the Lord's Supper the following Sunday. Us good Baptists always have to get down to the basics, so the ones who believed in using wine because it was scriptural were very adamant that we had to have wine. The Holy Bible said so; we were a scriptural church. The ones who—the teetotalers—said, "No way. We're Baptists. We cannot have alcoholic beverages in our church. We are not going to be a party to it." So back and forth like a yo-yo.

Finally, one fine young deacon got tired of it, and he told his mother, in a loud enough voice where everyone else could hear, "Mother, if we are a New Testament church and are going to do exactly like the scripture says, there's everybody go home, pack our suitcases, go to the Holy Land and get baptized in the River Jordan like our Savior did." Well, they did what most congregations do. They put it on the back of the preacher. After all, they paid his salary, why not? So, the following Sunday, after the appropriate religious services, the minister said, "We will now observe the ordinances of the Lord's Supper."

The deacons passed out the unleavened bread, poured the beverage in the little communion cups. But unbeknownst to the deacons and the minister and everybody but one person, one young person had slipped into the parsonage one night preceding, found a bottle of sacramental wine, drunk it all up, refilled the bottle out of his jug—his fruit jar—of green persimmon wine. Put the stopper on it and went his way.

So at the proper time, the minister said, "Partake." They chewed the unleavened bread, attempted to wash it down with the sacramental beverage, and it was the time, of course, for the minister to say the proper scriptural passages. His mouth was so puckered he couldn't speak.

So he gave the dismissal sign to the choir to sing a dismissal hymn. Their mouths were so puckered they couldn't sing. So they whistled the "Old Rugged Cross" and marched out. I'm not going to say who that young person was. Nobody can make me tell it. United States Marines can't make me tell it! Rev. Dr. George Brian, may I borrow your recipe for Green Persimmon Wine?

Jerry Bunch

CLINTON, EAST FELICIANA PARISH

Recorded at the Clinton Peach Festival, June 24, 1990, from Jerry Bunch, a British American. Bunch, a Baptist, is a salesman.

118. Brother Jimmy Walks on Water

We had a preacher down there, Jimmy Robertson, one time. He was nineteen years old. Jimmy Robertson, down at Bluff Creek Baptist Church. He was nineteen and come in there. It was me and Harry and all of us—Dorman, Phillip—it was all us old Bluff Creek boys. We got to going with

Jimmy pretty strong. And oh, the people around there, the deacons and all of them, said, "Oh, look how good this young preacher's doing getting all these young boys in. Just doing so well." He didn't know we had a deal going with Jimmy. Every time we'd say "Amen," we got fifty cents.

So one night, he was just a-preaching. He done got hot. He was getting hot, just beating on that thing, Jimmy Robertson was. So Harry, every few minutes, "Amen!" Here's Dorman over there [in a deep voice], "Amen."

After a while, Jimmy said, "Whoa, boys. You all just got to slow down back there." He said, "Dorman and Harry and Phillip's playing dice." He said, "Bound to be." He said, "Dorman's done bound won the pot. He's done said it six times. Too much commission." So it was a baptizing coming along there. Jimmy had never baptized. Now you all think I'm lying. If I'm lying, I'm dying. I'm telling the truth! It was a baptizing coming along there. Jimmy had never baptized nobody. We was out on the back porch. And Mama, she was always putting food out there. And she'd say, "Harry, Jimmy's going to practice baptizing Harry. Harry, get serious."

Daddy was sitting over there. He said, "Now straighten up, boys. You all try and do something right. Jimmy's trying to practice. Learn!" So Jimmy was trying to put Harry down on the floor and baptize him. Wouldn't work. Harry's feet would keep slipping. You know, barefooted, his feet would keep slipping.

Daddy said, "Get out in that pond, boys. Practice in that pond." We had a light out there on the pond that we fed the ducks at night. We'd plug it up, and the ducks would eat the bugs and all. The mosquitoes would stay off the porch that way, where we could sit out there and shoot the bull at night. Didn't have no TV's in that day, no radios, we'd just shoot the bull. So Jimmy Robertson got out there with Harry. There was a light bulb handy, hanging right there. I hollered back to Phillip, I said, "Phillip, when they get out there, if Harry and them get in the water, I'm going to holler to you or Watty and you all plug that light up just a little bit, and I'm going to throw it in the water."

Now, people, I got out there. There he was. Jimmy had done memorized his thing, his little testimony. He was down doing it. He was dipping old Harry. And just about the time he got ready to dip Harry again, I took that light bulb and I chunked it. I said, "Ready, Watty!" And he plugged it in! And you talk about a preacher walking on water—he walked on water!

Harry Methvin

HARGROVE SETTLEMENT, CALCASIEU PARISH

Recorded by C. Renée Harvison, June 30, 1990, from Harry Methvin, British American, forty-five. Methvin, a Protestant, is a high-school teacher.

119. God Works in Mysterious Ways

Sister Lily was a big woman. She was Luther's wife, and they lived right across from the Baptist church. And on one Sunday morning the preacher, Jack Bell, Reverend Jack Bell, who also worked in a lumber yard during the week in Westlake, and he was the pastor here, too. He was in the pulpit preaching after Sunday school.

We were into the preaching hour, and as I recall, his subject that day was the rapture of the church. We, of course, were enraptured. Everybody was attentive and still, and all was quiet. And I remember the preacher saying, "And in a moment, in the twinkling of an eye, at the sound of the last trump," and when he said, "the last trump," we heard, "*Heeeyyyy, ohhhhhh.*"

And he stopped in the pulpit, motionless. Everybody in their pews just kind of froze. And we heard this giant collision outside on the double doors in front of the church. And there was renewed silence. Then the two doors of the vestibule swung open. And as they were pulled open, it created a vacuum in the church. And there was a great rushing wind that swept over the congregation that had to be like the day of Pentecost, you know, a great rushing wind, and there stood Sister Lily in all of her glory. Sister Lily was standing in the doors of the vestibule.

Everybody was enraptured, and everybody turned in their pews, and Sister Lily hollered, "Brother Jack, Brother Jack, Aunt Rosie's house is on fire!"

You see, we didn't have a fire department, and she figured the best authority on fire would be the Baptist preacher. I mean he preaches about it every other Sunday, hellfire and brimstone. So she went to Brother Jack and interrupted his message.

And Brother Jack, being calm, cool, and collected as he was, said, "Would some of you men please go and help remove the furnishings from the home?"

And we did. But the funny thing about that was that when she hit those double doors and yelled, everybody thought it was the rapture! On that Sunday morning we had fourteen rededications and seven conversions! Yeah! All because of Sister Lily. And I'm always amazed how God works in mysterious ways. Just because of Sister Lily.

We did salvage some things from Aunt Rose's house, so it was a good Sunday. There were a lot of things saved because of Aunt Rose's house that day. People were saved. The refrigerator was saved. I mean, we saved it all. Brother Jack had some divine intervention, and his subject was most fitting. Sister had to be an instrument of God. It made people think seriously about the rapture. That's true. That's real.

Sarah Albritton

RUSTON, LINCOLN PARISH

Recorded September 16, 1993, by Pat Mire and Maida Owens for the video documentary, Swapping Stories. *Sarah, an African American, took a break from working at her restaurant, Sarah's Kitchen, to tell stories.*

120. The Reverend Gets the Possum

We have a story about two guys—wanted to go possum hunting. They sit down, and they discussed it, and in each family, they needed more than one possum. So, they went to hunting, and they hunted all night, and they killed one possum between the two of them. And they couldn't decide which one would take the possum.

So they decided to have a lying contest: the one told the biggest lie would get the possum. So they lied and lied, and every time, they would have a draw. And they lied till daylight. And they were sitting there, and the pastor came riding up—he was a Baptist minister on his mule. And he says, "Hello, brethren. What are you all doing?"

And they said, "Rev, we just having a lying contest. We killed one possum last night—and there's two of us—and the one tells the biggest lie gets the possum."

So Rev says, "*Ha*-ha. That's funny. Never told a lie in my life."

They said, "Here, Rev, you take the possum."

A. J. Smith and Barry Jean Ancelet

LAKE CHARLES, CALCASIEU PARISH,

AND SCOTT, LAFAYETTE PARISH

The following three stories were videotaped November 14, 1992, by Pat Mire and Maida Owens for the video documentary, Swapping Stories. *The first two were told to stage crew and performers backstage between A. J. Smith's two performances on stage at the Liberty Theater. The third was told on stage by A. J. Smith, a Cajun humorist. Barry Ancelet, the emcee of the weekly* Rendez-vous des Cajuns *radio show, is a Cajun and folklorist.*

121. Too Strong a Penance

A. J. Smith: The woman in confession confessed she hadn't been to church like she should have. And the priest asked her how come, and she said [laughs] she worked with the circus. Always with the circus, she's on the road. She can't go to church like she should, you know. And the priest said, "Well, what is it you do with the circus?"

And she said, "I'm a contortionist."

"Ah," he said, "a contortionist." He said, "I haven't seen that since I was a young man. My daddy would bring me at the circus, you know. I wonder—after church—would you mind, [giving] me a demonstration of that?"

She said, "No problem." So, after church, she get out on the side lot, sit down on the ground, take one foot and put that behind her head. Take the other foot, put that behind the head too. So, one hand go up on top of her head like this. The other hand on top of her head. She turned her head about halfway around.

About that time, Miss Hebert and Miss Thibodeaux coming up the road like that. "Look at that, Miss Thibodeaux." She say, "I don't think I'm going to church. That priest give too strong a penance!"

122. Not Dressed to Confess

Barry Ancelet: You know, I heard a story like the one that you told me about the too strong a penance?

A. J. Smith: Yeah.

Barry Ancelet: There's the two old ladies were going to confession, and—and there was a little girl. It was basically the same story. The little girl was in the confessional, and [the priest] said, "Well, what do you do?" you know?

She said, "I'm a high school cheerleader."

He said, "Oh yeah? Well, what you have a specialty?"

She said, "I cut the flips, you know. I go all the way across the stage."

He said, "I'd like to see that. I haven't seen that for years." So, he went out and took a look at that. And he went out to—to look at her, and she was cutting flips all over the church yard in the front. You know, the two little old ladies saw that, and they said, "Ooh, I can't go to confession today. I'm not wearing no panties." [Laughs.]

123. A Priest with a Small Parish

A. J. Smith: There was a fellow that was playing golf. And he went to drive a long drive down the fairway like that. But at the last minute, hooked off into the woods. Well, he went looking in the woods, and there was an old woman in there, stirring this pot.

He say, "Excuse me." He said, "Did you see my ball come through there?"

And she pick up the ladle, and say, "Yeah, it's over there."

Well, he went and got his ball, come back, he say, "By the way, what you making there, anyway, *hanh?*"

She said, "Oh, that's a potion."

He say, "A potion. What kind of potion is that?"

Well, she said, "That's a special potion. Anybody that drink that can have any wish they want."

"Huh," he say. "It sounds pretty good."

"Yeah," but she say, "I got to tell you. That's going to have an adverse effect on their sex life."

"Oh," but he said, "Give me some, anyhow."

Man, he drank that, and she said, "What's your wish?"

He say, "I want to be the greatest golfer in the world."

"No problem," she said. "You got it."

Well, about a year later, playing the same golf course. Gets to the same hole. Noticed them woods. He say, "I wonder if that woman's still there." Man, he go and look [laughs], and sure enough, still stirring that same pot, there she is. [Chuckles.] Well, he say, "Hey," he say, "You remember me?"

She said, "Yeah, you wanted to be the greatest golfer in the world." She said, "Well, how did it work?"

"Great, wonderful," he say, "I can shoot any score I want at will."

"Well, good." She say, "How your sex life?"

"Oh," he said. "Not too bad."

"Well, how many times you had sex in the last year?"

Well, he told her, "Let's see. About three times."

[Laughs.] She said, "Three times in a year? That's not too bad?"

"Well," he said, "no." He said, "Not for a priest with a small parish."

Fishing and Hunting: Personal Narratives and Tall Tales

Jerry Bunch

CLINTON, EAST FELICIANA PARISH

Recorded from Jerry Bunch, a British American, at the Clinton Peach Festival, June 24, 1990.

124. The Possum Gets Jerry

I want to tell you why I don't hunt. Well, back in the days, Watty and R. T. Carter and Robert Carter, they had some dogs. Watty had old Blue. I was a little old bitty yearling boy. Harry was down to there. We'd beg Watty to go hunting with him, and Watty'd say, "No, you two kids got to stay. You'll slow us down."

Now, old Blue was a good dog. Now, baby, you talk about a good dog—he was. If I'm lying, I'm dying, but I'm going to tell you the truth—he was a good one. We asked Robert if we could go. Watty wouldn't let us go. He'd say no. He said, "No, Robert, they'll just slow us down."

But we went. Well, Watty got his old lantern, and we always carried us a couple of pine knots. So we started out down there in the back. Old Blue was ready and old Red was ready. Robert turned old Red loose; he was a young pup, but Watty turned old Blue loose and down in the swamps he went. He went way on down there, and he got him a coon up that tree. *Yap yap yap.* That's a long ways, too, that's a good four miles. But on down there we went.

Me and that Harry, we was trying to get through those briars. Watty would say, "See, Robert, they holding us up. I got to get to that dog. Got to get to that dog before he jumps that tree."

See, a coon jumps trees. Watty would say, "I got to get to him." All we had was a .22 rifle. That's all we could afford back then. That was a little old semishot, too. Remember that Watty? Boy, when you got that automatic, you thought you was something else, didn't you?

But we went on down there, and let me tell you something, when we got down to them woods, there he was. Robert said, "Hey, you want to knock him out and let's have us a dog fight!"

Tall tales and legends run rampant in hunter's retreats such as the Eagle Claw Hunting Club off Highway 71. Photo: Nicholas R. Spitzer.

Watty said, "No, he's a bit too high. We going to wait until we get on down the woods a little further. We'll get us another one after awhile in a smaller tree and knock him out."

So that was the deal. Watty—*ping*—shot him out of there. So I had to pack the sack, because Harry was too little. Harry said, "Put him in Baby's sack, in Baby's sack." So they put him in Baby's sack.

I got that coon, and we were going on down through the woods. After a while, that dog treed a coon down by Mr. Jude Martin's. That was another four miles, down through them woods. Watty and Robert still going. Watty said, "See, Robert, I told you, them boys going to run out. We going to have to pack them out of here."

So, we got over there, another durn coon. Same thing—big tree, shot him out, put him in Baby's sack! Got on over there. About two minutes, old Red hit a lick. Watty said, "That dog's lying. Ain't no use going to that tree. Red's lying. Ain't nothing there. Blue ain't that smart."

After a while, Blue went, *Yip, yip.*

Watty said, "Oh, that's got to be a possum."

Robert said, "I hope so. If it is, I'm going to shake him out of that tree and let Red fight that possum."

Well, sure enough, he got over there and there it was, a little old possum in a persimmon tree. Shook him out of that tree. Red went in there and started fighting. Watty was holding Blue back. They got that possum a bloody nose. Hit him and knocked him in the nose. Robert said, "Put him in the sack."

He said, "Ants'll be on him tomorrow morning." So, we turned Blue loose. Blue went to get him a train. Now, you think I'm lying, darling, but I'm telling you the truth. If I'm lying, I'm dying.

After a while, that possum come to in my sack when Blue was down there by the railroad track. He bit me in the back! That's why I hate a possum today! I said, "Oh my God!"

Watty said, "Ain't nothing wrong with him. He's putting on. He wants somebody to pack that sack."

I said, "Oh, Lord, get him off!" And I was down in that ground, just scratching. I mean, just eating up. That possum was still eating on me. And look, they tried to get him loose! . . . He'd sulled in my back. Watty got a knot, and he hit on him.

Robert said, "Shoot him! Shoot him!"

Watty said, "Don't shoot! You'll kill Baby! You'll kill Baby!" That's true! That happened for the truth, darling.

Bill Cox

RUSTON, LINCOLN PARISH

Recorded at the Ruston Peach Festival, Lincoln Parish, June 16, 1990, from Bill Cox and his straight man, Dr. Edwin Davis, both British Americans. Cox is the director of athletic facilities at Louisiana Tech University. Davis is a local Ruston veterinarian and former track star at Tech.

125. They Could Coach, but They Couldn't Fish

Edwin Davis: Tell us about the football coaches going to catch a mess of fish out at the pond.

Bill Cox: Out at your pond! You know, through the years, I've always been very active in fundraisers and whatnot for Louisiana Tech. It was about August. It was hot. It was as hot as it is today. It was not a breeze stirring anywhere. We were going to have an alumni dinner at my house. Someone suggested we have a fish fry. Dr. Davis came by, and I was talking about it, and he said, "Well, don't buy the fish. Come out to the house, and you can catch them. I got a catfish pond."

I said, "We're talking about two hundred, two hundred fifty people."

"No problem, we can catch them."

I said, "I don't believe this, but I'll come out, and we going to look at it." So we went out there and Edwin got a five gallon bucket of feed, and we walked down there, and boy, the most beautiful catfish! They were this long [gestures]. Just churning the water, just churning the water.

I said, "Hey, we'll catch all we need here in a little while."

He said, "No problem."

I said, "Edwin, you know this would be a great opportunity to have some fun. You know, we could get some of these football coaches"—he had another little pond about one-fifty, two hundred feet from the other one. Wasn't even a crawfish in that pond. Nothing, not even a minnow. It was water—I said, "Wouldn't it be great if we told them we've got to catch the fish; they're depending on us. We bring them out here, and they go over and they go catch fish over in this pond where there are no fish."

He said, "That'd be great. We need to get that on film!" He said, "I got a VCR camera. We need somebody to operate it."

So we called Sammy Riser. Now, Sammy has all this camouflage stuff, and we go out there, and we make us a blind about thirty feet from where the fishing's going to take place. Sammy puts his camouflage stuff on, and it's hot, folks—as hot as it is today. All you can see is just his eyes. And he's all in this blind, and he's got the camera. Grass is mowed down at the right pond. We get to the other pond, we make them crawl through fences, wade through blackberry briars, wade through sage grass, crawl over other fences. We tell them to bring a lot of stuff. They got tote sacks, they got ice chests, they've got five gallon buckets, they've got three or four tackle boxes, they've got rods and reels, cane poles, big dipping nets. They could barely walk. Coach has his daughter with him. Sammy goes out there early, and he gets in there, and Edwin gets five gallons of feed, and I'm telling you, it is hot by the time we get there! Everybody is just panting it's so hot.

Edwin says, "Well, I'll throw the feed out and they'll come right up." They start baiting their hooks, he throws a five gallon bucket of feed out there, and nothing happens. I mean, not a ripple. They all throw their bait in; I get my pole and throw mine in. Edwin just standing there, not saying a word.

I said, "Edwin, what do you think?"

He says, "I don't know, they've never done this before."

Well, Billy says, "I have heard that when the sun's real bright, fish won't come up. It hurts their eyes." I said, "Well, that sun's bright. That ought to do it."

I'm thinking, "Boy, Sammy, you getting all this?"

A.L. said, "Well, you know—when it's real hot—if there's not enough oxygen in the water, they won't move around. They won't even bite!"

[The coach's daughter is fishing.] Then, her cork wiggles just a little bit. Just a little wiggle. I think it's that one old crawfish maybe. Every one of them throws their hooks in right on top of it! Well, they stand there a little while, and by then it's about three o'clock. The fish fry is at six-thirty. We hadn't caught a fish, nothing.

And they start grumbling, "We better go buy some fish."

Then Edwin says, "You know, we've got one other little old pond over here we haven't fished in in years, but we might try it."

Billy says, "I don't want to try it. I've had all this I can stand."

I said, "We gotta do something. Let's go over there and try it."

We've got to go through more briars and everything. I looked back, and Sammy's coming out, wringing wet with sweat. We were going to show this video at the alumni gathering that night. He's right in behind us. He leads us right through the thickest thicket he could go through. The poles are snapping and bending, and they get down there. You could tell Laird didn't want to. He just underhands one, and it hits and it never slows up. He sets a hook, it breaks his line, *ping*! Right on out there. They miss about the first five or six. They settle down, they catch a beautiful bunch, we go back up to Edwin's, we dress them, we go out there that night. Well, that's not the funny part. We get the TV all ready; we're going to show the video. Sammy Riser never had it turned on. He did not get an inch of any of it! None of it!

Glenn Demoulin

CLINTON, EAST FELICIANA PARISH

Recorded at the Clinton Peach Festival, June 24, 1990. Demoulin, a research technician, is forty-three. The place he refers to in this story, Toledo Bend, is a 186,000-acre artificial lake on the Louisiana-Texas border and a mecca for sportsmen.

126. That Squirrel Could Really Fish

I'd like to tell you a story about hunting. I am not a fisherman. My wife is. My wife loves to fish. She got me up to Toledo Bend a couple of years ago to meet my cousin and his wife. We were all going to go fishing. Well, I went along for the trip. I like to camp, sit around the campfire, cook out, things like that. I knew she'd enjoy the fishing, so we all went and we were all going to go fishing.

They thought they'd play a cute little joke because I don't fish very much. They caught a squirrel somewhere up at the campground, and they put that squirrel in my tackle box. Well, we get out in the boat. Well, but that morning, we were preparing, and I said I was going to rig up my gear and get everything going. They said, "No, no, no, no. Let's wait until we get out on the water." They did not want me to open that tackle box.

Well, we get out on the water. We're only about fifty yards offshore, not real far. I decided it was time to rig up the pole and start fishing. I opened up that tackle box. That squirrel had gotten tangled up in every bit of fishing line, every lure in that box, every sinker, everything, pliers—everything in that box, that squirrel was tangled up in it. Well he was so happy for freedom, when he saw daylight when I opened that box, he jumped overboard and hit the water. Well, he hit the water splashing and kicking and swimming just as hard as he could go. He was making so much noise kicking around that water, them lures and them silver spoons was a shining and clinking and making noise splashing that water. When he hit the shore, he had seven big bass on those lines. I got to shore to go after that squirrel, [and] the game warden was there. I hadn't got my line rigged up, and I got ticketed for being three fish over the limit.

Harry Methvin

HARGROVE SETTLEMENT, CALCASIEU PARISH

Recorded June 30, 1990, by C. Renée Harvison from Harry Methvin, British American.

127. Mosquitoes Save a Life

There was an old fellow who lived over here, Elbert Cooley, who was telling me about this guy he knew who went squirrel hunting. And he got lost in the woods. And he was bitten by a rattlesnake. And it was almost dark.

But he made his way to the edge of the woods, and he collapsed in the ditch. And he lay there dying.

During the night they sent out a search party, and by daybreak the next morning, they found the guy. They thought the guy was dead. But on closer examination, they found out he was still alive. They looked beside him, and there was a giant pile of mosquitoes.

What had happened was the mosquitoes had sucked all the poison blood out of his body during the course of the night, and the old man lived to tell the story. That's true.

Hugh McGee

BERNICE, UNION PARISH

Recorded at the Corney Creek Festival, June 2, 1990, from Hugh McGee, a British American.

128. Looks Can Kill

There's a little squirrel hunting joke I've got to tell you all. About two or three days before the squirrel season opened, the game warden decided he'd just ride off down Corney Creek bottom and look around. And while he was down there, he heard an old pickup truck come rattling down through the old rough road, coming down through the woods. He said, "Well, I'm going to check this fellow."

And he got behind a tree. Old fellow stopped his truck, had his wife in the truck with him. Got out, got his gun, his shot sack, went slipping out through the woods. Well, the game warden stayed out of his sight, wouldn't let him see him. The old fellow, he found him a squirrel. And when he did, he just jumped out from behind the tree where the squirrel could see him real quick. He startled that old squirrel so bad he just fell off that limb and just dead as could be. Hit the ground. And the fellow walked over there and just picked him up. He didn't fire a shot. Picked the old squirrel up, just as unconcerned, put him in his bag, his sack, and started easing on through the woods, looking for another one.

Well, that game warden, he didn't know what to think about that. He'd never seen nothing like that before in his life. He said, "I just got to see what's going on here. I just got to see what this fellow is doing."

So he watched him. Old fellow did the same thing. Found another little old squirrel, jumped out where he could see him, old squirrel looked down at him and just died of fright. Just had a heart attack. Just hit the ground. That old game warden said, "I can't stand this no longer. I got to find out what's going on here." So he got out from behind the tree and he says, "Hey, fellow!"

Fellow says, "Hey!"

"I caught you hunting out of season."

"Yes sir. Yes sir, you did. You caught me, you sure did."

Game warden told him, "But I'll tell you one thing, if you'll just tell me how you're killing those squirrels like that, I won't even write you up a ticket."

He said, "Yes sir, yes sir, I sure will tell you." He said, "If you'll notice, I am so ugly until if I can get that squirrel's attention, and if he sees me, he'll just have a heart attack and die right there."

The old game warden said, "Well, well, I never heard of that before. See your wife out there in the truck. She ever hunt with you?"

He said, "Dat blame, no! She tears them up too bad!"

Sarah Kent

GREENSBURG, ST. HELENA PARISH

Recorded by C. Renée Harvison, September 29, 1990, from Sarah Kent, British American.

129. A Tale about a Catfish

My poor old Uncle Paul. He was the biggest storyteller. I have to tell this. Uncle Paul was the [outlaw] of the family, and he was a big tall tale teller. And a huge man he was. With all of his meanness, people forgave him. That's one of the nice things about St. Helena, people go on and like one another. But he was maybe just six one or six two [in height], but his ankles were like that [gestures], and his wrists were like that [gestures]. He told big tall tales.

Anyway, he was in town one day. Cal Bankston told me this story. He told me he heard Uncle Paul tell it. Somebody had a catfish. It was a huge catfish, maybe twenty-four, twenty-five pounds. He was looking at it, and he said, "Well, that's a big fish. But I tell you, it's not as big as a fish I saw the other day."

He said that he and his mule were walking in from logging and thought it was a cloud over the river. He saw this black shape. He looked up, and it wasn't any clouds. He got to looking, and he said, "That's a big fish down there!"

He got to looking, and he decided that he would lasso [that fish. He did, and] he and the mule started pulling, pulling on the fish. And he had to let go. He said, "Well, folks, I never did see that fish. But I think it was bigger than this one." Said, "It pulled my mule in the river and drowned it!"

A. J. Smith

LAKE CHARLES, CALCASIEU PARISH

Recorded November 14, 1992, by Pat Mire and Maida Owens for the video documentary, Swapping Stories. *A. J. Smith, a Cajun humorist, was performing at the Liberty Theater during the weekly* Rendez-vous des Cajuns *radio program.*

130. Does He Drive, Too?

You know, Fond de Culotte was my uncle. That was the best man I ever knew. Used to bring me everywhere. Brought me fishing when I was a little boy. We were out fishing. Man, we hooked into the biggest fish. It felt like a freight train. Man, we was fighting, and it was going everywhere. And, finally, it snagged up. You could pull and pull, and it wouldn't go nowhere, you know. He said, "Boy, here's a good lesson." He say, "You follow that line, down under the water. When you find out what it's hang up on," he say, "get it loose. We going get the fish."

"Well," I said, "okay, I'm going to do it." So, I followed the string, down the water like that, you know? After a while, I came up. I said, "Fond de Culotte, cut the string, man, cut the string."

He say, "How come?"

"Well," I say, "you got about a fifty-three-pound catfish down there. In the back seat of a '57 Buick."

"Well," he said, "Pull him out! Pull him out!"

I said, "I tried. But he put the window up on me!"

[Audience laughs.]

Dave Petitjean

CROWLEY, ACADIA PARISH

The following three stories were collected September 19, 1993, by Pat Mire and Maida Owens for the video documentary, Swapping Stories. *Dave Petitjean, a Cajun*

Storytelling is a regular feature at the weekly Rendez-vous des Cajuns *radio program in the Liberty Theater in Eunice. Cajun humorist Dave Petitjean is often featured. Photo: Maida Owens.*

humorist, entranced guests at a barbeque at David and Lorraine Bertrand's home in Elton.

131. A Well-Dressed Deer

Let me tell you, it got bad. When he hunted deer every day, every day, every day. He hunted. And his wife was kind of tired of that, you know. She said, "Look, what's going on with you?"

"I'm just passing a good time."

She said, "Look, I'm going to find out about that."

He said, "Well, look. You don't even know how to shoot a gun."

She said, "I don't care, you taught me how."

So, he brought her out to the gun range, you know, showed her how to shoot that thirty-aught-six and everything. Brought her out to the deer stand, and he said, "Now, look. I've got your gun loaded. Put it down here. I'm going to go drop the other guys off. I'm going to come back and get you." All right.

So, he goes. He's coming back, right before he gets to the stand, *Pow, pow, pow!* He says, "Oh, my God, she killed herself."

He gets there, but she hadn't killed herself—she had her gun. And across the clearing, they had another man with his hands in the air, like that.

He said, "Okay, Lady. That's your deer. I don't want that deer. I *know* you shot that deer. You can *have* the deer. All I'm asking you is let me take my saddle off of it."

[Laughs from his audience.]

132. Fish or Talk

I had a friend. He used dynamite [for fishing]. Yeah, you've heard of that. I can throw the dynamite—*p-p-p-p—Boom!* They come right to the top. And he didn't care *payonc* about what people thought. And his best friend was the game warden. Took him out fishing. So, they get in the boat. Didn't have no rods and reels or nothing. But they caught a lot of fish, you know.

So, they're getting on and the game warden says, "What're we going to do?"

He said, "Hold yourself. I'll show you what I'm going to do."

So, they go out there to the middle of the lake. So, reaches under the seat and got him a stick of dynamite, had him a cigar—*shhhh* [imitating the sound of a lit fuse]— threw it over—*p-p-p-p—Boom!* Fish come up, scoop them up.

He says, "*Man*, I can't believe you're doing that." He said, "Here, I'm a game warden, and you're doing that over here?"

He reached under the seat, got him another stick. He threw it to the game warden, said, "You want to fish or talk?"

133. The Dog That Walked on Water

In the following tale, Dave Petitjean relies heavily on onomatopoeic sounds depicting the dog as it walks on water. He also uses a number of malapropisms (for example, saying "laboratory receiver" instead of "Labrador retriever") and gestures to entertain his large audience.

Clay's my other friend. He loves to hunt ducks. But, he was getting kind of old, you know? Kind of like Jean over here. [Chuckles from his audience.]

But he's going to hunt them ducks, you know? And you know. . . . So, he write off, and they him sent him back a big black dog, big like that, you know? So, he said, well, I'm going to see if I got—I paid a lot of money for that.

So, he go out the duck blind. And a duck come out of the bunch all by himself. Oh, yeah, man, he jump up, *Pa-tchoom!* Killed that stone dead. [Claps his hands.] He said, "Got him, Boy. Go see if it worked." And that dog didn't go in the water, no. He jumped right on top the water. *Tu-tu-tu-tu-tu-tu-tu* [mimicking the dog's footsteps on water]—he picked that up—*Tu-tu-tu-tu*—he brought that back. "Ooh," he said. "I can't believe I saw *that*." [Laughs and exclamations of disbelief.]

Oh yeah! "Oh," he said, "Oh, man, yeah. I'm going to try that again, me!"

So, he waited for some more ducks to come in high like that. He jumped—*Pa-tchoom!* He say, "Got them, Boy." [Claps hands together to indicate impact.] Right on top the water. *Tu-tu-tu-tu-tu-tu.* He picked that up. *Tu-tu-tu-tu.* He goes, "Ah-ho" [claps hands]—like that.

"I got to show Sosthene about that." He said, "I have never seen a dog like that in my life." So, he said, "Sosthene, come on. We going to go hunt them ducks tomorrow, man." Then he said, "I got me a new dog—I am going to show you how that work."

"All right."

So, then, next morning, they get out in the blind, and they sitting down, and the big, black dog's there. He said, "Well, Sos [Sosthene], how you like my dog?" He said, "That thing costs high, but it's full bleed" ["full blooded," a pure breed].

He said, "*Mais,* what they call that?"

"Oh," he said, "they call that a laboratory receiver." [Laughs from his audience.]

So, they get in the blind. He didn't said nothing, you know, about that. So, he get in the blind, a duck come out and ma—*Pat-tchoom*—he bust that. He said, "Got him, Boy." There he goes, right on top the water. *Tu-tu-tu-tu-tu-tu.* He picked that up. *Tu-tu-tu.* He brought that back.

Clay looked. Sosthene didn't say nothing. Well, he say maybe he didn't saw that. So, they wait some more. Another duck come—*Patchoom!* They bust that [claps hands]. He said "Got him, Boy." *Tu-tu-tu-tu-tu. Tu-tu-tu-tu.*

Then looked at Sosthene—[who] didn't say nothing. Well, Clay is kind of getting his mad off [pissed off], you know? He said, "Well, Sos, how you like my dog? Boy, he catch them ducks pretty good, *unh?*"

"Well, yeah, yeah," he said. "He catch them pretty them pretty good." But he said, "You better get your money back, yeah." He said, "That dog can't swim!" [Laughs from the audience.]

Pierre Daigle

CHURCH POINT, ACADIA PARISH

The following two tales were collected on July 3, 1990, by C. Renée Harvison from Pierre Daigle, a Cajun. Until his memory was prompted by a collecting session, he had forgotten about the stories that he had heard as a young boy from his grandfather. Like most tall tale tellers, Pierre narrated in the first person. Pierre explained that his grandfather often used this technique before telling his tall tales: "He would always tell his tall tale, any tall tale, in the first person, as if he'd experienced it."

134. The Alligator Peach Tree

My grandfather told a lot of tall tales, and we had an uncle who would come. He was a bum. He traveled all over. He lived here a while until they kicked him out and then he'd go somewhere else. And he'd spend several nights at the house during the wintertime. I was very happy to see him because he was my television set long before television was invented. We'd stay up all night and tell stories about buried treasure and that kind of thing. Those were not folktales. They were just lies he made up.

Tall tales—we had several. My grandfather used to tell one to all the grandkids, and that one stuck to my mind. He said—this was all said in French, but I'll tell it to you in English. "One morning, I'd gone hunting." Of course he had an old musket, muzzle-loading musket.

And he said, "I had my horn, my powder horn hanging from my belt, and my lead ball pouch hanging on the other side." And he said, "I was way out there in the forest, and I shot something." And he said, "When I came to reload, I noticed the pouch had broken open and all the lead balls had fallen out. There I was way in the forest, plenty of powder and caps to load the gun, but no lead balls."

So he said, "I started back home. I came to this small lake in the forest. On the bank of that lake was the biggest alligator"—which makes me think this one originated here because alligators were not called alligators, they called them *cocodrie*. They thought they were crocodiles. Anyway, he said, "The biggest alligator was sleeping on the banks. Boy, I sure would like to kill that alligator for the skin! I could skin it and sell the skin." He said, "I started thinking what I could use for musket balls. That morning, before going hunting, I passed by a peach tree, and I'd plucked some peaches and I'd eaten them, but I'd put the seeds in my pocket when I came back." He said, "I decided, maybe a peach seed. I packed that powder in, put a peach stone, I packed it in, went right up to that sleeping alligator and shot it right between the eyes. That thing pulled up, rolled over, crawled back in the lake and disappeared. Well, I didn't get him."

He said, "Five years later, I went hunting in that same place. Right on the banks of this lake there was a beautiful peach tree growing. It was loaded with peaches. When I ran out to grab a peach, it swam out in the middle." He said that peach [stone] had sprouted in that alligator's head and made a beautiful peach tree!

135. All His Ducks in a Row

He went hunting one morning, and there were live ducks around a round pond. A lot of ducks, they were all in a row. But he thought, "If I shoot just one, all I'll get is one duck." He said, "I disguised myself with straw, and I went up there, and I swam under the water until I got to the middle of the pond." Then he said, "I took my gun barrel and bent it. When I shot, the bullet went all around." He got all the ducks!

Tommy Sanches

JACKSON, EAST FELICIANA PARISH

Recorded June 24, 1990, at the Clinton Peach Festival as told by Tommy Sanches, a Spanish American.

136. A Frog Gigging Story

When I was living in Calcasieu Parish, I really honed my skills catching frogs. There's a lot of frogs in southwest Louisiana. Again, my friends told me, "You're coming to East Feliciana Parish—they have some of the nicest, biggest frogs in some of these East Feliciana ponds."

Well, when I got here, sure enough, I bought a piece of property and we had a pond on our place. For several nights, I could hear this big bullfrog. And he'd bellow. Of course, you can tell how big frogs are by the way they bellow. I also figured out in my years of frog hunting that when you shine a light on them, you can pretty well tell how they're sitting on the pond. If you see two half-moon eyes, that means the frog is looking toward you. If the frog is sitting to the left or sitting to the right, you can only see one eye and it looks like a full moon. But if a frog is sitting away from you, you see quarter-moons. You see the back of his eyes. So I pretty well knew just how to catch frogs until I ran across this frog on my property in this East Feliciana pond.

It seemed like that every night I'd try and go catch him, he'd always be on the deep end of the pond. Every time I'd wade out in the pond, he'd just kind of sink. He was old and he was wise. That frog must've weighed probably—shoot—a good ten or fifteen pounds. Now for a second there, I thought he might be one of them South American frogs somebody had imported into East Feliciana Parish. Well, a ten- or fifteen-pound frog, each leg would've weighed about two and a half pounds. Now that's some good frog legs if you're a connoisseur of frogs.

Anyway, every night . . . I'd go out there, and he'd be sitting on the deep end of the pond. Every time I'd step off into the water, he'd just kind of sink. Well, one night, I caught that sucker on the shallow end of the pond. The water was too shallow for him to sink. I caught him looking right at me. I knew if I waded up on him, if he jumped toward the deep end of the pond, he'd have to jump right past me, and I'd catch him. As I stepped off into the pond and waded toward him and shined my light toward him, I could see two half moons. So I knew he was sitting toward me. I shined my light around the pond to make sure there were no snakes around because I always like to do that as I approached a frog. Well, when I shined my light back toward the end of the pond, I didn't see any eyes at all. I knew that there's no way that frog could've gone under water, because he was so big and the water so shallow. I looked for half-moons—I didn't see any eyes. I looked for a full moon—I thought maybe he'd changed positions on me. But he didn't. I thought maybe he'd even turned his head to look the other way, so I couldn't see his eyes. But I knew how to look at a frog. I'd look for these little quarter-moons.

Well, I didn't even see a quarter-moon shining. So as I waded on down the pond and kept looking for snakes and that frog, I knew that frog . . . he was somewhere. All I had to do was find him. As I got a little closer, . . . that frog was still sitting towards me, facing the deep end of the pond. But what that sucker had done, he'd taken those little hands, like this [places his finger over his eyes], and he put them over his eyes like this. Every now and then, he'd open his toes like this [spreads his fingers] and he'd look around to see where I was. That sucker was so smart, I decided to leave him in the pond. If you're a frog hunter, you can try and catch that sucker.

Ray Robinson

GRAY, TERREBONNE PARISH

Recorded July 5, 1990, by C. Renée Harvison from Ray Robinson, Cajun, sixty-five, a retired state trooper who has published a book, Tales of the Louisiana Bayous. *Robinson said that Tit Jean stories were often told by the Cajuns for humor but aren't heard as frequently nowadays.*

137. Tit Jean, the Greatest Liar of Them All

There was Tit Jean. He was the greatest liar of them all. He'd fall in the bayou. He'd catch more fish by falling into the bayou, and the fish would get into his pants. He'd go hunting, and he'd fall into the bayou, he was so goofy. When he'd come out, he always had a fish in his pocket. He was known as the greatest liar on the bayou. In fact, one time he was riding his horse down the bayou. And one of the men said, "Tell us a big lie. Can you tell us a big lie without stopping?"

He said, "I can't stop. I'm going to the priest. I'm going to tell him that your wife fell in the well and drowned."

He kept on going. The men were working on a house, so they threw their tools down, got on their horses, and beat it back to this man's house. But they found the man's wife rocking on the porch. The man was very angry.

He said, "That man lied to me."

Well, when he came back, he stopped the horse, grabbed the horse's bridle and told him, "I'm going to whip you for what you did. You lied to me."

So he told him, "You asked me to tell you a big lie without stopping. You got what you asked for—now, get out of my way."

That was told many times by the old people.

PART III

Legendary Louisiana

Outlaws, Heroes, and Local Characters

Clarence Faulk

The following four stories were collected from Clarence Faulk, British American, a retired newspaperman. Although Faulk shares his knowledge about the notorious Bonnie Parker and Clyde Barrow, he is emphatic that they were vicious killers, not heroes, and wants his listeners to understand that. Like others from that area who lived during the outlaws' reign of terror, Faulk would just as well let the memories lie. Recorded at Ruston's Piney Hills Kite and Art Festival, March 31, 1990.

138. The Terrorism of Bonnie and Clyde

Of course, they were not personal friends of mine, but they were a couple of killers. I guess today we would call them serial killers or something like that. I hear of serial killers today who kill a dozen or so people, and usually they appear to be doing it just for the hell of it, you might say, to see somebody die.

But back in 1934, this fellow Clyde Barrow and his girlfriend, Bonnie Parker, got together somewhere or another as youngsters. He was out starting his career, of course, stealing cars and breaking into stores, robbing banks. And he was caught and put in jail a number of times.

I have been so surprised in the years recently, in the last ten years, that there's been an effort made to make heroes out of these people. Well, that's entirely wrong. The people hated them. All the folks in North Louisiana were frightened of these people; they were afraid to go out at night. They were afraid they'd find them on the road. They were afraid to have anything to do with them because they often shot people in cold blood [and] because they got into . . . argument[s]. They'd go into a country store and want to buy some food and things, and try to walk out without paying for it. If the store owner tried to stop them, they'd just as soon shoot him down.

They would come here. They came here to Ruston. [Someone] tells the story about him working at a filling station. He filled the car up, and he

Tour guides frequently rely on local legends and tales
in their presentations. Here Ranger Wanda Lea Dickey
leads a tour in New Orleans for Jean Lafitte National
Historical Park and Preserve. Photo: Courtesy of Jean
Lafitte National Historical Park and Preserve.

noticed the backseat—there was a bunch of guns in it. He began looking
around there, and suddenly a fellow clapped his hand on his shoulder and
said, "Son, get away from there." Said, "You know who I am, don't you?"

He said, "No sir."

He said, "Well, this is Clyde Barrow, and you better get moving!"

So he ran down the street. The guy drove off and never paid for the
gas.

139. Bonnie and Clyde Almost Rob the Ruston State Bank

I was in front of the James Building one day, and looked. There was
a car parked there, and there was a woman sitting inside smoking a cigar.
Women look funny today smoking a cigar! 1934, a woman smoking a cigar
was something to look at!

So I went on down the street and went into the bank to probably fix an overdraft, and I said, "You want to see something funny, go down there, and you'll see this woman smoking a cigar!"

They said, "My goodness, that's Bonnie Parker!"

It could have been, very easily, because a week or so after that, I started down to the bank again—had to go there every day to kind of cover an overdraft. I got in there, and Mr. Howard Smith met me at the door. He said, "Man, what do you want in here!"

I said, "Well, I got to make a deposit in here."

He said, "Well, you get it over with in a hurry!"

I said, "What's the matter with you?"

He said, "We're going to be robbed!"

I said, "Who?"

He said, "Bonnie Parker! Clyde Barrow!"

I looked around and all over the bank. There was a little balcony at the old bank downtown, and there were fellows up there with automatic rifles looking at me. [They] said, "Hi, Clarence."

Got across the street where Mary Ann's book store is, and there was a car full of sheriffs and deputies, holding pistols and guns. I looked down the street the other way, and there was about six more guys with rifles. Nothing happened because somebody tipped them off, or they would have tried to rob the Ruston State Bank.

140. The Day Bonnie and Clyde Were Killed

Well, it wasn't a week or so after that, a policeman downtown said, "They done killed Bonnie and Clyde over in Arcadia."

I said, "Oh, man, no! We hear that all the time, that they got them captured or cornered or hemmed up somewhere."

The fellow said, "Yeah, that's true! I just talked to the sheriff's office over there."

So I went and told Louise I was going over to Arcadia, and she said, "I'm going with you."

If you knew her, there's no way to stop her. So she jumped in the car with me. We went over there. There was a huge crowd of people. They said there were twenty thousand people in the town. I think it may have been two thousand people there at that killing, but no more, I'm sure. But they were bringing the car with a wrecker. You could see it from uphill, south of Arcadia, coming in.

I said, "Well, you stay here on the sidewalk, and I'll see if the bodies are in the car." I thought maybe they had taken the bodies out somewhere, and they were just pulling the car in.

As I went on through the crowd and stepped up on the running board, as old cars had, and looked in there, the bodies were there. And Bonnie Parker, the girl, was bent over with a pistol in her hand. And Clyde Barrow, he was rared back with his feet this way, a pistol in his hand. And in the back seat, there were rifles and shotguns and pistols and ammunition and about a half-inch of blood all over the place.

So we sat around there a while, and I began to ask who was in the posse that killed them. One of these Texas rangers about this wide and about seven feet tall, pistol on each side, big boots and a hat. I said, "Sir, I'm with the paper over in Ruston. Can you tell me how this happened?"

He said, "Well, since you're with the paper, I'll tell you more about it."

He said that they got a tip that Bonnie and Clyde were going to spend the night over here on the road south of Gibsland. And they'd been trailing them, of course, for years around this country, always trying to hem them up. And they had offered a bribe of five thousand dollars to anybody who would give them information that led to the capture of those two people. And one of their relatives took the bribe. So the deal was that they were going to spend the night there that night in that country house. They were going out the next morning, I guess, to scout around the country. The fellow said that they were planning to rob the bank in Arcadia. That could have been true.

But anyway, this fellow said, "I'm going to go south of the road here a ways and pretend I've got a flat tire."

In those days you had to take the thing off, the inner tube, and pump it up. It was a long ordeal. So he said to Barrow, "You come on down here, I'm going to look at some timber to pedal today, and I want you to look at them with me."

So he says, "Fine."

So about eight-thirty, nine o'clock, they started going south. This fellow, sure enough, he had the wheel off his car, his car up on the jack, waving at Clyde. So they pull over in front of the car to stop. Right on both sides of the highway is a cut, about ten or fifteen feet high, that the road went through. The posse of the sheriff, the Texas rangers, the policemen from Shreveport and everywhere, were in there. The sheriff said in the paper here, it was the Arcadia paper, he called out to them to stop. Well, he may have. But there was no race or crash of any kind. The car just rolled up against it. The fenders were not bent. At any speed at all, the fenders of a car would have been crooked.

So turned the fire on them. They have what they called then machine guns and high-powered rifles and shotguns firing buckshot. Of course, they completely riddled that car with over a hundred or more pellets and killed them instantly. But they were ready, because when they first shot, both of them had pistols in their hands—and in their death grip; they closed in, and [Bonnie and Clyde's] pistols were held there.

Well, in a few minutes, the funeral home people came there and got the bodies on stretchers and carried them inside. There was such a demand from the people—there must have been a thousand people there in the street—they wanted to go see the bodies. They had to identify the bodies positively.

It seems that a year or two before that [Clyde Barrow] had been in a penitentiary in Texas. Cold weather, and they were out cutting the brush along the highway. He told him he wasn't going out in that cold weather anymore.

They said, "Well, yes you are, and don't give us any trouble or you'll be sorry."

He said, "Well, let me cut the little stalks with a sharp hatchet."

So he had a hatchet, and he'd sharpened it up real good. Just about the time they told him to come get in the bus to go clean the brush, he jumped off a chair and chopped off his big toe so he couldn't work. So to identify him, the man that pulled his socks off, his shoes and socks, there was his old foot up there with a stub for a big toe and the four toes.

Bonnie was laying on another table next to him with a pack of cigarettes up on her chest. He just had on a pair of blue jeans and a sweatshirt. We all filed past there and came on out to write the story. The newspapers had been notified that this setup was coming, and they had prewritten their story. So . . . they put out a special section, because everybody was just as scared as if there was a wild lion running through this country killing people. They said Clyde's car was speeding down the highway at sixty-five miles an hour and crashed into the embankment. Well, that wasn't true. But Clyde's father lived in Dallas, and they came over and got the body.

141. The Embalmer's Encounter with Bonnie and Clyde

There's another little story. You folks may have known Mr. H. D. Darby, the undertaker here at the time. About a year before this, right where the

Ruston State Bank's new building is, there was a family named Brooks lived there. And she ran a little room and boarding house. And I was eating lunch there; Mrs. Faulk was out of town.

I went over there to eat lunch, and Mr. Darby and I were walking up the steps of the house. And Ms. Sophie Stone at that time—she's Ms. Sophie Cook today, was the home-ec teacher at the high school—was sitting in the swing on the front porch waiting for Ms. Brooks to call her for lunch. Just as we got on the steps, she said, "Mr. Darby, look! Somebody's taking my car! Look at them! They're driving it off!"

He said, "Well, it's probably some crazy nut here pulling a prank on you. Jump in my car, and we'll go get them."

So they jumped in the car, chased out after them; they didn't know who it was. Went down through the roads around here, and about a half an hour later, they went down a country road, and the car stopped.

Fellow jumped out of there, and he said, "What do you want?"

This fellow Darby was a small, red-headed, freckle-faced guy, kind of bandy-legged—walked up there and said, "You a bunch of car thieves, stole this lady's car! What do you mean by that?"

This fellow reached in his back pocket and whopped him up side the head with a pistol in his hand! [Darby], for the next thirty years, had a headache twenty-four hours a day. Knocked him on the ground, and said, "Kill this so-and-so. If you don't kill him, they'll know who we are now. We'll have officers all over this country swarming us. Be dead by night."

Ms. Stone, of course, was in the back seat. She said, "Don't kill that man! What did he do to you?"

About that time, Bonnie Parker jumped out of the car, and she whopped her up side the head one way or another, knocked her out right there on the ground on top of him.

There was another couple in the car with them. He said, "You all ought not kill that poor fellow. He's just trying to help this poor lady find her car."

They said, "Yeah, but he knows who we are."

Said, "I don't care nothing about killing him. Look here, you want to shoot him first, shoot him!"

Well, somebody said, "No, don't do that!"

Finally he says, "Well, I don't know why not." Said, "What do you do, man, what do you do for a living?"

[Darby] said, "I'm an undertaker."

Everybody just hollered, fell out. Said, "Okay, we'll spare your life if you promise to embalm us when we get killed."

So he was glad to make that promise. They called up Mr. Darby here in Ruston and said, "We got Bonnie and Clyde stretched out over here in the morgue at the funeral home. You want to come by?"

"I'll be there!"

I saw Darby the next day or two, I said, "Did you go over there?"

He said, "That's the durndest job I've ever had in my life. Those people were so full of holes we couldn't put any embalming fluid in them!" That poor fellow.

There's no way these people could have been Robin Hoods or helped anybody or heroes. They were the worst criminals that we had in North Louisiana back in 1934. They deserved what they got, and you should have heard everybody shouting praise that the thing was over with.

Julienne Cole

ARCADIA, BIENVILLE PARISH

This anecdote, collected from Julienne Cole, a British American, is in response to the previous four stories told by Clarence Faulk at the Ruston Kite Festival on March 31, 1990.

142. A World-Renowned Town

I moved to Arcadia in 1960, and when anybody mentioned Bonnie and Clyde, it was just like somebody had clamped down on what was going on. No one wanted to discuss it. Like Mr. Faulk said, everybody thought that that was—you know, Hollywood does strange things. They tried to make heroes and heroines out of these two people, and they were kind of like mad dogs. I know the people who lived during that time didn't really want to talk about it. They purely did not. It was a very scary time.

But I'll tell you one thing, I was speaking to someone who works with me in Piney Hills, and he works for the state of Louisiana. He said he went to Japan last year seeking tourism and exchange of ideas with people in Japan. He said when he got through speaking, he said, "I'll take questions."

And he said the first question—the guy held his hand up and he said, "How far are you from where Bonnie and Clyde were killed?"

We're world-renowned, even if it's the wrong kind of renown.

J. Maxwell Kelley

WINNFIELD, WINN PARISH

The following three accounts were recorded by C. Renée Harvison from J. Maxwell Kelley, British American, on June 19, 1990. Kelley was the mayor of Winnfield for eight years, until the summer of 1990. He ran his hardware store, O'Kelley's, until his death in 1994. A native of Winnfield, he grew up hearing legends like these.

143. Winn Parish Night Riders

You ever heard about the night riders? Earlier I told you about this trail, Harrisonburg Road. There was a group of men back in the late 1860s, after the Civil War, mainly two families, the West family and the Kimbrell family. A guy by the name of John West and a guy by the name of Lars Kimbrell. They were mainly from the Montgomery area, which is in Grant Parish now, but at that time it was part of Winn Parish.

Anyway, they were Masons; they were respected people in the community. But they devised a scheme to take advantage of these disenfranchised people who were traveling the Harrisonburg Road going west. Their scheme was simply to murder them and take what they had.

They really ravaged that road for many, many years. They took what money they had. They took what valuable possessions they had, pianos or whatever. Right out here in Winn Parish! Besides Lafitte the Pirate, it's really the only other outlaw band that ever established a foothold in Louisiana.

This went on for many, many years. No telling how many people they killed all along the Harrisonburg Road. Their territory was like Vidalia, Louisiana, all the way to the Texas line. They used to call it No Man's Land in Sabine Parish, Zwolle, that area. They really ravaged that whole countryside. No one ever suspected these people. No one ever knew that it was them that was doing these atrocities. Like I said, they were Masons!

They had an outlet for the sale of all these goods. The person who was in the gang was a retail merchant, and they just sold these pianos or whatever came in. They got the cash and divvied up the cash.

Anyway, even Lars Kimbrell's mother was involved in this. She had a boarding house. They would kind of woo people in to stay with them, and they'd probably never walk back out the door. There's an account told of Ma Kimbrell, they called her, of even throwing an infant into the air and grabbing a butcher knife and letting the infant land on the butcher knife.

144. The Legend of Lying Horse Rock

There's a place in Winn Parish called Couchee Brake and it was kind of the hideout for the West and Kimbrell clan, the night riders. It's said that that's where they hid some of the gold. There's a rock there called Lying Horse Rock that's shaped like a horse lying down on its side. The old tale goes that that's where they buried all their gold.

Apparently, Lying Horse Rock is voodooed, whereby anyone who goes near it, something bad happens to them or a member of their family. We've had some people to say that old so-and-so died because he got too close to Lying Horse Rock. I don't put much faith in all that superstition, but apparently it was voodooed or had a hex put on it. This gang operated for many, many years, until finally the governor at that time had to call out the militia to clean it up. Down in Atlanta, Louisiana, which is only about eleven miles southwest of Winnfield, for many, many years—before we had a big tornado come through here about three or four years ago—there was always a sign that hung there that said, "John West hung here." There was a gigantic oak tree where they hung him. But the tree blew down. They were some kind of murderers.

145. The Traveling Salesman

This is a neat little story, and the significance of it is not so much the events that happened but the symbolism of it. The dove and the seven days and all those things have Biblical connotations. I don't know if it's true or not, but it's a neat little story that's been told around here a lot.

After the turn of the century, there was a family here called the Meltons, and the Meltons have been pretty prominent people here in Winn Parish. At the turn of the century, it was a very sparsely populated area—they had all these timber, lumber mills in operation, and the big companies from the Midwest and Northeast were coming in here and setting up mills, cutting up timber. But you had some people who'd been here for quite some time, and they'd subsisted off the land by farming cotton or that type thing, and the Melton family had been here for quite some time. They lived off the land like everyone else. For the most part, a lot of these people who settled Winn Parish early on were on their way to Texas, but ran out of money before they got there and wound up here.

You see, in southern Winn Parish, the connecting link between the Natchez Trace and the El Camino Real comes through Winn Parish. It's called the Harrisonburg Road; some call it the El Camino Real. Of course, in Texas, everything's the El Camino Real because all that means is the King's Highway. The connecting link, the Harrisonburg Road, came right through the very southern part of Winn Parish.

A lot of people who traveled this road—this was as far as they could make it so they ended up settling here. Not that they wanted to—it's just that they didn't have any more money. Some later found things to do here and maybe moved on. I think if you talk to a lot of people around here, you'll find that they have kinfolks who established themselves in East Texas.

Anyway, the Meltons were one of these families who happened to wind up in Winn Parish. They settled in the southern part of Winn Parish, in the Packton area, a railroad stop at one time many, many years ago. There was quite a large family of them, and there was a Mrs. Melton, a widow lady, and she lived in her house, and she had three sons who lived in her house with her.

Of course, this was in the horseback days, and the primary mode of transportation was the horse and the buggy. The boys were gone one day, and Mrs. Melton was there, and there was a salesman that called on her there at her house. His name was Plumber. He was a tombstone salesman. I don't think we have real tombstone salesmen today, people who'll knock on your door and show you their variety of granite stones.

But anyway, Mr. Plumber called on Mrs. Melton and started talking about his products and really kind of irritated her. Kind of scared her apparently. She got into an argument with him; she was by herself there.

Well, the salesman was a persistent salesman, apparently, and he was trying to make the sale like he couldn't leave that house without it. He got into an argument with her. This went on for a pretty good while.

As I understand it, the boys came riding back up on the horses and saw this argument that had been going on between their mother and the salesman. They didn't know who he was. They had guns; they got out, and they had an argument with him. One of the Meltons shot the tombstone salesman.

As the tombstone salesman was falling dead, he grabbed ahold of a tree branch with his hand as he was falling to the ground. He fell dead there on the ground.

Amazing thing about that tree branch was that his hand imprint was left in the branch. It was like it was burned into the branch, and to this day you can still see the imprint of the tombstone salesman's hand on the branch. And more amazing than that, a dove came and lit right there on that branch where his hand imprint was and stayed there for seven days and seven nights, never leaving. It's kind of a scary thing. The word got out about this dove being there. People in that day and time thought it was the return of Jesus Christ or something. They said that people packed up and came to this sight and viewed this dove from as far away as Alexandria, a fifty-mile trip.

That's the story of the tombstone salesman. It is documented in Winn Parish court records that the Melton boys were apprehended and arrested. But they were never tried for the crime.

Carl Bunch

CLINTON, EAST FELICIANA PARISH

Recorded at the Clinton Peach Festival, June 24, 1990, from Carl Bunch, a man who claims both British-American and Native American (Seminole) ancestors. Carl first learned of his outlaw relative when he was working in the fields with his father on a hot day and asked, "Daddy, isn't there something in the world we can do to make a living besides planting cotton?" His father replied, "Son, cotton has saved many lives and it's caused a lot of trouble. . . . Our cousin, cotton got him in bad trouble." When Carl pressed for information on Eugene, nobody in the family would give it to him. He finally learned of his cousin's exploits from a Texas historian.

146. Eugene Bunch, the Robin Hood of Southeast Louisiana

Eugene's daddy's name was James Bunch. James Bunch's father and my grandfather, my grandfather was Thomas Clarence Bunch and his daddy was Alexander H. Bunch. He's buried at Kentwood today and his wife, too. His wife was Martha R. Bunch. That's Alexander, my great-grandfather. This James Bunch is my great-grandfather's brother. He come from Tennessee years ago down into Mississippi. James, when he come into Mississippi— the Bunches loved women. I don't know why, but they always did—he met a girl by the name of Martha R. McDonald, a wealthy, wealthy farmer in Mississippi's daughter. He had a big plantation, and James married his daughter. James and Martha had these children. Eugene and T. C. was brothers.

In later years, when they sold out in Mississippi, the boll weevils eat them up, so they was hunting new territory. They come north of Bogalusa over here to Angie, Louisiana, and they bought another big farm. So he sent his kids through every school he could send them to at that time. James and his wife sent Eugene and Tom up here to the best schools. Like I said, he had ten kids, James did. And my grandfather, Tom Bunch, had ten kids. They liked a lot of help, I guess.

But anyway, to make it short, these boys went through school and finished school. When the Civil War started, they both volunteered. They got out of the service. T. C. went back and he run for clerk of court. He was clerk of court in Washington Parish—T. C. was, after the Civil War. And Eugene went back to teaching school. He was a schoolteacher in Washington Parish. He taught school for a good many years, and he had a lot of friends in Washington Parish. About all this same time, the railroad came through. It went right through the middle of his daddy's field. Cotton and all, they tore it up. Lord, did he hate the railroad. What's so sad about it is that it turned a well-educated man into the worst criminal the state of Louisiana has ever known.

He left there teaching school, and he started robbing trains. He pulled the biggest train robbery ever pulled in the state of Louisiana by himself— from New Orleans going up to around Angie and Bogalusa. By himself, he robbed it. What he did with the money, he'd go back into Honey Island and hide out. When the taxes on these people's property came due and they couldn't pay it, he'd pay their taxes. So the money started showing up in the sheriff's office.

One of his close friends, an old lady, was fixing to lose her place over there. She was a young girl, in her twenties; they were going to lose their property. Eugene went there and said, "I'm going to give you the money." She got the word to Eugene when [the sheriff] was coming. So that afternoon, when the sheriff got the money and gave her her receipt, on his way back to town, he robbed the sheriff. This is the God's truth, he robbed the sheriff! They couldn't arrest him in Washington Parish. He taught school in Washington and Tangipahoa Parish, and everybody loved him. And they'd hide him out and feed him. They got real hot after him.

He left Louisiana, they got so bad after him. He went to Texas. He was a newspaper editor in Texas. He went to Waco, Texas, and opened up his own newspaper. The people really liked him over there. They liked him so well, he run for clerk of court and won for three terms in a row. In Cook County in Texas.

But what happened to him, he started drinking some. They began to miss him in town and for a few days he'd be gone. He was the clerk of court at this time. He was robbing trains while he was clerk of court! He was recognized in a bar as Eugene Bunch. A Texas ranger recognized him as Eugene Bunch and walked up to him and said, "I'm going to arrest you."

And [Eugene] said, "And you fixing to die." He always had a pistol in his coat and he'd shoot right through his coat. He said, "You going to die. If you don't get up and get out of here, you going to die." So the ranger got up and left.

So that night, he left. The next they heard of him was four years later. He was pulling robberies in Colorado and Wyoming. He made it back to Honey Island, and he contacted some of his friends over there. He was really planning this big one that time. He was going to really get it. And he got it. This train robbery, this last one, he said, "I want to rob it with these detectives sitting on the train." He had ten detectives riding the train. He boarded the train at New Orleans. Colonel Hobgood had the horses. He had a man with him with the horses who was a colonel. He was up at this creek by Sheridan, Louisiana, with the horses hid. So Eugene goes to New Orleans and boards the train. When he got closer, he eased on up and got the engineer, went back to the express car, got all the money, which was forty-eight thousand dollars. The detectives never knew the robbery took place until he came out there and waved goodbye and jumped out the window with the forty-eight thousand dollars.

He hid out at Honey Island. They had implanted a man in his gang. They killed [Eugene] sleeping. In this country, we all knew Judge Horace Reeves. Judge Horace Reeves' daddy [known as R. R. Reeves] tried the man in the gang over at the courthouse in Franklin. . . . They tried the man that shot [Eugene]. And they had a seven-year-old boy for a witness, and it really turned into a long, drawn out trial. But they convicted the man. You had a lot of people who wanted to claim credit for killing him.

What was so funny, while he was in Cook County, they were remodeling the courthouse. They had to move the clerk's office down to the jail. They moved the clerk's office down to the jail and he was sitting down there. He told this friend of his, "You know, I should be behind bars, but this is the closest I'll ever become to be put in jail in my life." He never was arrested at all. His daddy owned a big plantation over in Mississippi. Cotton caused all this trouble.

James B. Rider

BASTROP, MOREHOUSE PARISH

Recorded by C. Renée Harvison from James B. Rider, sixty-five, a British American, on September 14, 1990. Rider, now deceased, was a writer about outdoor life for the Bastrop Enterprise *and did extensive collecting on Ben Lilly, the Mer Rouge legend.*

147. Ben Lilly, Strongman of Morehouse Parish

Ben Lilly, around Mer Rouge, was always entertaining people. He was supposedly a tremendously strong man. People that have been witnesses to the things he did—according to what's been written on him, he once stood on the sidewalks of Mer Rouge and got in a barrel. And without touching the barrel, just flat-footed, jumped out of the barrel onto the sidewalk.

They said it was many times that he could pick up a hundred pound steel anvil from the ground and just extend it out at arm's length and just hold it there.

They said that he once picked up a five-hundred-pound bale of cotton and walked off with it.

Lilly made his own knives. He once said that, he showed a knife to a fellow one time out West and said that he had killed, in so-called hand-to-hand combat, six bears with this knife. He held it up and showed that he had stabbed those bears to death. They weren't all black bears. One or two were supposed to be grizzlies. Pretty tough customers.

Ben Lilly would not do any kind of work on Sunday, no matter what. If his cows got out, he wouldn't let anybody herd those cows up. They might stay lost for days. On Monday morning he'd go hunt them, but not on Sunday. He read his Bible on Sunday. He tried to adhere to the Bible as near as he could.

Audience member: Mr. Rider, I have heard that he organized a hunting expedition for Roosevelt. For President Roosevelt. Is that true? Have you found that to be true in your research?

James B. Rider: That was Theodore Roosevelt. Teddy Roosevelt. Roosevelt came down to Tensas Parish, around Transylvania down there, and he wanted to kill a bear. So they hired Ben to come over with his dogs to run bear. And he hunted with Teddy.

Audience member: And I've also been told, since I'm a Mer Rouge resident, and because so many people enjoy talking about Ben Lilly, that he had such a keen since of smell and keen sense of hearing, they say he was more animal than human. But he could be a gentleman when the occasion arose. Didn't they say something about how he could lay on the ground and tell you how the grass was growing, he had such a keen sense of smell?

James B. Rider: He said that. He told that. He was, like you were talking about, he was a gentle man, too. When he did come back to Mer Rouge on one of his hunts, he'd play with the children. He just spent a lot of time playing with children, no matter whose they were.

He had all kind of idiosyncrasies. He believed if you got wet, naturally out in the rain, that nothing would happen to you if you just kept wearing your clothes till they dried. You might get sick if you took them off and took a bath and dried off real good and put on dry clothes. You'd probably get sick. So what he did, he'd even go to bed with his wet clothes on. If he come in wet, and he wanted to go to bed, he'd just crawl in bed and pull the covers up and sleep wet. He had a belief, he stuck with it.

Audience member: They say he believed in bathing. He'd even bathe in the snow!

James B. Rider: One time, him and another fellow had been out in the woods for a long time. They hadn't taken a bath in months. They decided they'd take a bath. Ben said, "Let's take a bath."

This guy said, "Well, you know, it's about thirty degrees." Only thing they had was this stream to take a bath in. He'd heard that Ben didn't mind. He'd pull off his clothes and wade on in, start taking a bath. This guy didn't want to do that. So Ben took his bath in that cold water. It didn't make him any matter. It was just like when he was tracking a bear or a cougar. He'd pull off everything but his pants. He'd take his rifle and knife and take off. No food, no nothing. He might hunt two days without a bite to eat. Sometimes when he'd eat, he would just go out in somebody's corn field and pull two ears of corn.

Wendell Lindsay

LAKE CHARLES, CALCASIEU PARISH

Recorded by C. Renée Harvison from Wendell Lindsay, a British American, on June 28, 1990. Lindsay, a local oral historian, lives on Bayou Sallier, which is said to be the location of Lafitte's headquarters in southwest Louisiana.

148. The Legend of the Brooch

In 1816, Lafitte's ship pulled in on the lower end of the lake front across from the Sallier home, on the lake, which is on the corner of Sallier and Front. The Indians—and there were many Indians in this territory at this time—went on out to meet Lafitte's ship. Of course, Lafitte always had trinkets and favors for the Indians, and they liked him very much. . . . Most people have never heard that Lafitte had a daughter.

His daughter was then sixteen years old. They went to the home, and Mrs. Sallier met them at the door. The home was a twenty-by-twenty cabin, right near the lake front, elevated about six and a half feet from the ground. They went into the home and met Mrs. Sallier, and she met Denise Lafitte. And she gave Mrs. Sallier a large, gold brooch. And [Denise] put it around her head, and they kissed each other. They asked her, "Where is Charles Sallier?"

Mrs. Sallier was pregnant, five months pregnant at the time. She . . . hadn't seen him for four months, that he'd left and hadn't come back. Thought it was an unusually long time.

In the course of all the talking, Lafitte suggested to Mrs. Sallier, "Why don't you come with us to Galveston? We will take care of you over there. And if your husband comes back"—[he] had close dealings with Lafitte all the time—"why, you can come on back. But come on with us."

About that time, Charles Sallier returned, and he walked to the cabin. His head just reached the floor level, and he heard the proposition, "Come with us to Galveston." And he didn't like it. I don't know who he blamed for the trouble, but anyway, he drew his pistol, drew it out, and instead of shooting Lafitte, he shot Mrs. Sallier. She fell to the floor. Without saying anything—he knew he'd killed his wife—he jumped on his horse and left. He was never heard of or seen again after that time.

But Mrs. Sallier wasn't dead. The brooch had absorbed the bullet and made a big dent on it. The family is still here in Lake Charles, and they have that brooch. Anyway, Lafitte left, Mrs. Sallier had the child, and the child's name was Denise, after Lafitte's daughter, Denise.

Arthur "Arturo" Pfister

NEW ORLEANS, ORLEANS PARISH

Recorded at the 1990 Louisiana Folklife Festival held in Kenner, Jefferson Parish, November 4, 1990, from Arthur "Arturo" Pfister, an African American. Pfister grew up in a New Orleans neighborhood rich in oral tradition, in which he and his friends typically spoke to each other in rhymes. He learned this toast in the oral tradition, which often includes risqué wording, but cleaned it up for the festival setting.

149. Shine and the Titanic

I'm a weaver of the word, not a maker of rhyme
But I'm going to tell you the story about my man, my main man
    Shine.
It was a helluva day in the merry month of May,

Shine was the stoker on the Titanic that day
When a big iceberg come a floatin' their way.

Shine said, "Cap'n Charley, Cap'n Charley, there's a big iceberg
    floatin' our way."
Cap'n said, "Shine, Shine, don't you be no clown,
I got ninety-nine pumps to pump the water down.
I got pumps made of pipes and chumps to pump.
I got a trillion dollar load I ain't going to dump."

Shine said, "Cap'n Charley, Cap'n Charley, if you look now,
There's a whole lot of ice comin' 'cross the bow.
I ain't never read a book, ain't never been to school,
But Louzeeanna Annie ain't never raised a fool."
Shine said that to himself.

Cap'n Charley said, "Shine, Shine don't you know my might?
Anything I say and do is right.
You work for Cap'n Charley when the sun comes up
You brings my favorite slippers and my coffee cup.
You work for Cap'n Charley, stokin' the coal.
You work for Cap'n Charley and I owns your soul.
You might be a Christian and pray to the Lord,
But on the Titanic, I outranks God."

[Pfister makes a sound to indicate that an iceberg hits the ship]
Then there was a loud, crashin', smashin' sound
God pulled rank.
Shine said, "You might be the Cap'n on the land and the sea,
You might run the engines, you might turn the key.
You might be Cap'n Charley, well all that's hip,
But I'm gettin' off of Cap'n's stinkin', sinkin' ship."

Jumped his black butt into the sea, he did.
He said, "I'm going to tell you one thing, and I don't mean maybe,
But I was long and grown when Father Time was a baby.
I done kilt a whole lot of men's way better than you.
Done kilt a thousand V.C. in Dien Bien Phu.
You can be Tarzan and Rambo and Jungle Jim,
But that's one iceberg that sure ain't slim.
Forked is your tongue, I done heard all the lies,
I'm going to ride with the water and make my own enterprise."

Just about then a beggar came on board cryin',
"Save me, save me, Shine, in the name of the Lord.
I gots money and dollars I can't even spend,
I owns a whole lot of people, got stock in the pen,
I give you fine black women and white ones, too,
because I gots more money than the U.S. Mint do.
I give you big pretty houses and Cadillac cars,
Give you fifty hotels and ninety-nine bars.
I runs all the drugs from Harlem to Watts,
I takes food from the mouths of the tiniest tots,
I buys all the missiles and guns for the planes,
I own ninety-nine ships and three hundred trains.
I give you all the money that a black boy needs,
Give you ten tons of coke and twenty tons of weed."

Shine thought for a while. . . .
"I'm the runner of the world,
The master in the Lord,
I'm going to please her with my Visa and my Bank Americard.
I'll give you money and power and fortune and fame,
Every fine black girl in the world going to know your name."
Shine said, "You can giggle from the weed, you can laugh from the
    coke,
But get your bootie in the water and cut your stroke.
You can have all your money, your friends and your foes,
You can finance your wars and your G.I. Joes.
You gots more money than a human had oughta,
So get your butt out here in this freezin' cold water.
You rich and you greedy, ain't never been broke,
So get your butt in the water and cut your stroke.
You can call on the mounties and the C.I.A.,
But they going to get their dry behinds wet today.
Sorry, Mr. Banker, I don't need your pain,
because I'll be sittin' with my baby just a listenin' to the Train.
I'm going to swim to New Orleans for some panne meat,
Going to do the Mississippi Mambo down on Claiborne Street.
Going to wear orange and gold and purple and green,
Go runnin' with the Injuns, eat all the red beans.
You might like Chaka, you might like Rufus,

Even Leon Spinks know you lying through your toofus."

Just then the banker's daughter floated by Shine.
She said, "Come over here, Shine.
Save some o'little ole mine.
I got a body like a ballard and cheeks like Gladys,
Butt like Bertha and hair like Alice.
I got legs like Tina and a chest like Dolly,
I can almost sing colored and lilac ollie."

He said, "I like my women's lips red and my crawfish burled
I like the mamas with the boom booms and their hair all curled.
I like hot filé gumbo and devilish eggs.
I like them Uptown girls with they big fine legs,
I like Downtown womens with they night dark eyes,
I like Backatown womens with they big brown thighs.
I done lived on the land and on ships in the sea,
And the ladies on land is the ladies for me."

And Shine swam on. . . .
Shine swam down past the Florida Keys,
He was trembling in the arms and weak in the knees.
While Shine was a'swimming, the ocean grew dark,
And he bumped right into a great, big shark,
A biiigggg black one.
The shark he was purty, with pearly white teeth,
He said, "Come over here, Shine, I'm a make you my meat.
You sure look good, swimming in my sea,
Gon' make a right mighty fine meal for me.
I ain't got no chilrens and I don't have a wife,
But one thing I got is your no-swimming life.
I'm a take you and eat you and swallow you whole,
Make you cuss the very day your mammy borned your soul.
I'm big and I'm strong, I takes what I like,
I done robbed Robin Givens and beat up Mike.
Yeah, Mr. Shine, Mack the Knife is sweet,
I can outswim a wave, and I like dark meat.
I rules all the waters, I'm King o'the sea,
Ain't ne'er whale or minnow can get past me.
All the fishes in the water gets outta my way,
From the Rock o'Gibraltar to Barataria Bay.

Ran into a whale, he thought he was slick,
Lil' minnow told me his name was Moby-Dick.
When I tore my teeth into that little ole whale,
I had to hang out a sign saying [high-pitched voice], 'Blubber for
  sale.'
I done wrote with Alex Haley and dunked with Kareem,
Hung with I. W. Harper, got drunk with Jim Beam.
I done ate up the bones o'Gunga Din,
Got Cap'n Bligh's blood on my chinnie, chin, chin.
I done ate up some pirate when they walked the plank,
I done lied with Nixon and sang with Frank.
I done ate German subs and planes full o'people,
Ate the rock from the Hudson and the bell from the steeple.
I done ate up the quail that was hiding in the bush,
Took your grandma to the mountain and gave her a push.
I'm a meeaann shark.
I done ate up Sally, I done ate up Sue,
Start choking, quit stroking, I'm a eat up you!"

Shine said, "Mr. Shark, I'm a tell you, and it ain't no lie,
I taught the Signifying Monkey how to signify.
I done taught Hank Aaron how to hit the ball,
I showed Barbie's mammy how to make a doll.
That ain't really nothing, cause I tell you what,
I done showed Big Bertha how to do the butt.
You might rule the water from London to Selma,
But you ain't no badder than J. J. and Thelma.
My daddy's a poet, my mama's a singer,
I got a uncle out West who's a baaadd gunslinger,
Kilt three white men and lived, he did.
If you wants you some bones and some flesh to tear,
There's a cap'n and a banker and his daughter out there.
If you might chance to think you can catch this man,
You might as well be a tuna in a tunafish can.
Who you out here call yo'self trying to warn?
All you sayin' ain't but talk behind the barn.
You mighta ate a lotta pirates when they walked the plank,
But I likes shark meat, don't you see my shank?
I like red, silky shirts, I done paid my dues,

I like black Cadillacs and shark-skin shoes.
You might rule the ocean, reign over the sea,
But you gotta grow new fins to outswim me.

And Shine swam on.
The Titanic sank and a lotta folk died,
Grandmamas was weepin' and little babies cried.
When the news hit shore about the Titanic that night,
Shine was in New Orleans, high as a kite!
He played him some music with Satcha-moe,
Went to a cemetery party with Marie Laveau.
He was the slickest and the quickest,
He was fine like wine.
He was wicked in the picket, my man, Shine.

They thought Shine was dead, somewhere down afar,
But Shine was in New Orleans,
Hankin' and a pankin'
Glidin' and a slidin'
Honkin' and a tonkin'
Dreamin' and a schemin'
Smackin' and a mackin'
Smokin' and a jokin'
Bammin' and a jammin'
Jumpin' and a bumpin'
Winkin' and a blinkin'
Coolin' and a schoolin'
Juicin' and a goosin'
Hangin' and a bangin'
Skinnin' and a grinnin'
Rappin' and a yappin'
Buggin' and a huggin'
Gigglin' and a wigglin'
Hobbin' and a knobbin'
Peepin' and a creepin'
Maxin' and relaxin'
Funkin' and a junkin'
Chillin' and a illin'
In the neighborhood bar.
Yeah, yeah, in the neighborhood bar—Shine.

A family dinner after a funeral is another setting for expressing special memories in story form. Here Eva Colvin and Corinne Anderson visit in Ruston. Photo: Susan Roach.

Mary Etta Scarborough Moody

ANGIE, WASHINGTON PARISH

The following story was recorded June 29, 1990, at Bogalusa's Storytelling in the Park, from Mary Etta Scarborough Moody, a British American native of Angie, who now lives in Poplarville, Mississippi.

150. Elvis Comes to Angie

This story is a story that happened to me when I was a little girl. Anybody in here five years old? I was about five when this happened. When I was a little girl, we had television and all, but we hadn't had electricity a long time because I lived up at Angie, way out in the woods. Out in the sticks is where I lived. We didn't have electricity until I was about five years old. When we got it, it was just wonderful. We'd turn them lights on. Flick them on. My daddy bought a TV set, and everybody in the community would come around and watch TV. They'd just stand there and stare. There wasn't really great programs on. It was Kate Smith and stuff like that. A man named Steve Allen was on.

Anyway, the funny thing was that at about this time, Mr. Elvis Presley, whom all of you've heard of, I'm sure, got famous. He was on the TV, but I really didn't know that people on the TV was real because my mama kept saying, "Them people in movies is not real, Mary Etta. That's not true."

So I didn't believe Elvis Presley was a real person. So I was not believing in Elvis. He was not real, he was just on TV.

One day, I was over at Mr. Murray Soams' [store] in Angie, Louisiana. . . . Now Uncle Earl Long was the governor of the State of Louisiana at this time. I'm sure you've heard a lot about Uncle Earl. But Uncle Earl was the only person we knew that had a Cadillac car, except the mortician. The mortician sure wouldn't drive no pink Cadillac.

So we thought Uncle Earl had come to Angie because we'd seen this great big, pink Cadillac sitting over at Mr. Henry McMillan's store. He had a gas store, a pumping station, whatever you want to call it, a gas station.

Anyway, we were sitting there in Mr. Murray's store and Tommy Soams, that was Mr. Murray's daughter, she said, "Mary Etta, Uncle Earl is over at Mr. Henry's in his Cadillac. There's his car."

We were just thrilled to death because none of us had ever met the governor of Louisiana, Uncle Earl. So Tommy and I got up enough courage—I was five years old—to walk across the road to Mr. Murray's to see Uncle Earl, we thought.

When we got over there, Uncle Earl wasn't over there in his pink Cadillac. It was Elvis Presley. Honey, he was sitting right there on a Coke case, drinking an RC Cola. And good-looking! He was the best looking man you ever saw in your life. I was just standing—I was five years old, a little bitty kid. I was standing there looking at him. He said to me, "Hello, little girl."

I just thought the world had come to an end. I just said, "Hi." I just said, "Hi" to Elvis. I mean, "Hi."

Anyway, Elvis bought me and Tommy a Coke. We sat there and drank that Coke and looked at Elvis Presley. I want to tell you one thing, that was the most unusual and thrilling day of my life, of my young life, was to see Elvis in Angie. When he left, he got in his pink Cadillac and got all of his men assembled in and hauled them all in. He waved goodbye and he said, "You all be good."

And we tried, Elvis, we really tried. But we're not too good, I'm afraid.

Vernie Gibson

JENA, LASALLE PARISH

The following anecdote by Vernie Gibson, a British American, was recorded June 21, 1990, by C. Renée Harvison.

151. Old Levi Loved His Goats

I'll tell you one about an old steamboat captain. Old Levi lived at the old Virgin place up here on Little River. This was about the time they's getting these logs out of here, and Levi had about two acres of goats. You couldn't talk to him ten minutes without him mentioning his goats.

So Captain Swayze and Captain McCarthey and Old Man Levi had a little old steamboat. And Captain Swayze and Captain McCarthey was brother-in-laws, and they come up here to get some timber. So Captain Swayze knew Levi. When they got to Levi's house, Captain Swayze bet Captain McCarthey ten dollars he couldn't talk to Levi thirty minutes without him mentioning his goats.

So he was talking to him, got him on the subject of the Bible. He figured if he could get him on the subject of the Bible, he could keep Levi from saying something about his goats. So they got to where Lot's wife turns into a pillar of salt, and Old Levi said, "Damn! I wish I had her for my goats to lick!"

Ray Robinson

GRAY, TERREBONNE PARISH

Recorded July 5, 1990, by C. Renée Harvison from Ray Robinson, Cajun, sixty-five, a retired state trooper who has published his own collection of stories, Tales of the Louisiana Bayous. Cournair *is a Cajun word for "cuckold."*

152. The Cournair

I was working for an oil company when I was a young man when I heard this one in an area back of, near Baton Rouge, on the Atchafalaya River. It was near a place they call Maringouin, Louisiana. It's a story of a *cournair,* a man who allows other men to see his wife, to visit his wife. The story is told that this man was a very handsome man and his wife was very

Memorial Day cemetery visitations bring together families and friends. Tulip Cemetery in Claiborne Parish is the site for this visitation. Photo: Susan Roach.

beautiful. But she was very headstrong and she became unfaithful to him, and he didn't have the strength to put a stop to it.

She had a boyfriend who was the bully of the community. This of course is supposed to be true, but whether it is, I don't know. It got to where, when the guy would come in and the boyfriend was visiting, he would order him around his own house. And the boyfriend was so self-confident that he took his favorite chair one day. He walked in and there was the boyfriend sitting in his favorite chair. And he asked him to get out. And the boyfriend wouldn't get out.

So he went in the other room and came out and pointed a shotgun at him. The boyfriend didn't believe he was going to shoot him, so the guy pulled the trigger, double-barrel shotgun loaded with buckshot, just about cut him in half. The bones supposedly, according to what the people told me, the bones hit the floor. Behind the backbone, the rib cage, parts of it hit the floor behind the chair. And that was the end of the *cournair.* He was no longer a *cournair,* he'd had enough of that.

Irvan Perez

POYDRAS, ST. BERNARD PARISH

The following four décimas were recorded on March 18, 1988, by Monty Brown and Dayna Bowker Lee, from Irvan Perez, a singer of traditional décimas and the foremost authority on Isleño language and folklore. In La vuelta del marido, *a man returns from war unrecognized and tests the fidelity of his wife.*

153. La Vuelta del marido (The Husband's Return)

—*Yo soy la recién casada,*
de mí nadie gozará.
Mi marído a la guerra,
a tomar su libertad.
Mi marído es alto y rubio
y un vestido le corté.
En las mangas de las espaldas,
lleva un letrero francés.
Mi marído está en su guerra,
con su vestido francés.
Yo me miro en el espejo:
"¡Qué guapa viuda no seré!"
—*Señora, si usted quiere,*
nos casaremos los dos.
Si es el gusto mío y tuyo
y la voluntad de Dios.
—*Hay seis años lo he esperado*
y seis más lo esperaré.
Si a los doce años él no viene,
contigo me casaré.
—*Yo tengo un vestido negro;*
tres sastres lo cortó.
—*¡Ay, mujer, usted está en luto,*
sin haberme muerto yo!

"I'm a recently married woman;
no one will enjoy my love.
My husband went to war
to look for his freedom.
My husband is tall and blond;
I made him his uniform.
On the sleeves of his jacket,
there is a French label.
My husband is off at war,
wearing his French suit.
I look at myself in the mirror:
'What a pretty widow I'll be!' "
"Madam, if you are willing,
we could both be married;
if you and I want to
and if it's God's will."
"I've waited six years for him
and I'll wait six years more.
If he doesn't come back in twelve,
then I'll marry you."
"I have a black dress;
three tailors made it for me."
"Wife, you're in mourning,
though I haven't even died."

154. La Vida de un jaibero (The Life of a Crab Fisherman)

This décima *responds with good-natured self-mockery to the misery of crab fishing, an activity to which, traditionally, the Isleños only resorted in case of dire need. The hardworking, ill-paid crabber, half frozen by February winds, becomes involved in various grotesque adventures and humorous mishaps, but typically—and in self-defense—the Isleños respond to their suffering with good humor. As Irvan Perez says: "It's all in fun."*

Irvan Perez: The only way the people would fish crabs, at this particular time—later on, it got to be a big industry—but the crabs weren't worth hardly nothing—twenty-five, thirty cents a basket—and the only time they would fish was when we'd have a storm or some type of high water of some kind, that would drive the rats out of the trapping areas. Then these people had to make a living for their families, so they went to crab fishing. And they would always say that they hate it so much they would say that crab fishing was about seven degrees below a hog. Which didn't speak too well for the industry, but, anyway, later on, of course, it made a big change. The crab went to twenty-one dollars a basket. Naturally, you're fishing for that price, and gladly. The song pertains to a fisherman fishing in February, which is a cold month. Anything that can happen to you usually happens. In order to basket a crab, you had to have either moss or hay, or grass, and they used to go ashore, and whenever they caught a basket of crabs, they'd go ashore and they'd pull the grass and basket the crabs this way. They never had no covers.

Yo me arrimé a la costa,	I went up close to shore,
buscándome el abriguito.	just looking for shelter.
Sentí una voz que decía:	I heard a voice saying:
—¡Y aquí estoy yo heladito!—	"Here I am all frozen."
Era un pobre jaibero,	It was a poor crab fisherman,
pescando en el mes de febrero.	fishing in the month of February.
Y salió calando	He went out to lay his lines
derecho para el otro lado	straight over to the other side
y se encontró otro jaibero,	and he met another crabber,
otro pobre desgraciado.	another unfortunate fellow.
Entonces dice el jaibero:	Then the crab fisherman says:
—¡Maldita sea el mes de febrero!—	"Damned be the month of February!"
Lo conchó a la costa	He ran his boat in to shore,
y donde estaba el batimiento.	where the tide was beating in.
Entonces dice el jaibero:	Then the crab fisherman says:
—¡Maldita sea tanto viento!—	"Damn all this wind!"
Era un pobre jaibero,	It was a poor crab fisherman,
pescando en el mes de febrero.	fishing in the month of February.

De una lata a la otra,	From one pole to another,
iba un pobre jaibero.	went a poor crab fisherman.
Se fue a tierra a cortar paja	He went on shore to cut straw
y le cayó un avispero.	and a bees' nest fell on him.
Entonces dice el jaibero:	Then the crab fisherman says:
—¡Maldita sea el mes de febrero!—	"Damned be the month of February!"
Tenía el pelo largo	His hair was all long
y se enredó en los mangles.	and got tangled in the mangroves.
No podía salir	He couldn't go out
a recorrer sus palangres.	to check on his lines.
Era un pobre jaibero,	It was a poor crab fisherman,
pescando en el mes de febrero.	fishing in the month of February.
Cuando se muere un jaibero,	When a crab fisherman dies,
que nadie le ponga luto,	no one should mourn for him,
porque se va a descansar	because that poor deceased fellow
ese pobrecito difunto.	is just going to his rest.
Era un pobre jaibero,	It was a poor crab fisherman,
pescando en el mes de febrero.	fishing in the month of February.

155. La pesca del camarón (Shrimp Fishing)

This song is typical of the satirical spirit and tall tale mockery of locally composed décimas.

Irvan Perez: This *décima* here was composed by Florito González, an old-time composer. He was from the Yscloskey area. And it's about Boy Molero, an old fisherman. It was a time when they fished with seines. You know? And he was a pretty good captain, but he always wanted to be a little higher or a little better than the other one. See? He was a man that liked competition. So this individual wrote a *décima* about it and made it so big and out of proportion, that it got to be funny: *Cuando Boy salió calando.* When Boy come out with his net, the net was so long it took a month and seven days to get to the other end. And when he finished his catch, he had so much shrimp; when they counted the barrels, he had over a million.

Boy Molero vino hasta la Isla,	Boy Molero came to the Island,
un hombre con su razón;	he's right about what he says;
vino buscando gente,	he came looking for people
para la pesca del camarón.	to go out fishing for shrimp.

En la Isla encontró veinte,
en Bencheque veintiuno;
solamente que en el Torno
no pudo econtrar ninguno.

—Tengo veinte en el Canal,
que me dieron la palabra.
Tengo veinte mejicanos
y veinte que vienen de España.

Y con eso yo pienso,
que ya tengo mi compaña.—

A las cuatro la mañana,
la compaña de Boy se presentó,
otro día a las seis,
no habían embarcado la gente.

—Y esta salida la doy,
para ver lo que termino
y mientras puede ser que alguno
venga de Placamino.—

Cuando Boy salió al lacre,
con tantos sombreros de hombre,
se creían los capitanes
que eran bocas de cañones.

Cuando el viejo salió arriba,
con las anclas en la mano:
—Esto parece la Revolución
de España y el mejicano.—

Cuando Boy quedó muy triste,
se remó a la banda
y le preguntó al viejo:
—¿Tú trajiste las tarrayas?—

—Tus tarrayas, Boy, las tengo,
pero no llegan a su cuenta.
Tu compaña necesita
cuatro mil y setecientas.—

Cuando Boy encendió las luces,
en el centro del mar,

He found twenty at Delacroix;
twenty-one at Reggio;
and only at the Bend
he didn't find a single one.

"I have twenty at Violet,
who promised me they'd go.
I have twenty from Mexico
and twenty who come from Spain.

So now I think I've got
enough people for my crew."

It was four in the morning;
all Boy's crew reported in;
at six the next day,
they still weren't all on board.

"I'm going to try this voyage,
just to see how it turns out;
and meanwhile maybe some folks
will come over from Plaquemines."

When Boy went out on the lake,
there were so many men's hats,
the captains were sure
they were all cannon mouths.

When the old man went topside,
with anchors on his hands:
"This looks like the Revolution
of Mexico against Spain."

When Boy became sad,
he rowed in to shore
and he asked the old man:
"Did you bring the nets?"

"I've got your nets, Boy,
but they're not half enough.
A crew like yours needs
four thousand seven hundred."

When Boy turns on the lights
way out on the sea,

se quedó todo alumbrado,
como la Calle Canal.

everything lights up,
as bright as Canal Street.

Cuando Boy salió calando,
a esa mancha camarón,
tuvo un mes y siete días
para encontrar el otro calón.
En la Punta Tresbayules,
él le dijo a los muchachos:
—Vayan a buscar la barca,
más allá de Bayu Plato.—

When Boy went out fishing
for that school of shrimp,
it took him five weeks
to bring together his nets.

At Three-Bayous Point,
there he told his boys:
"Go get the boat
beyond Shallow Bay."

Boy mandó hacer una barca,
con una buena largura:
¡Cuando la proa esté aquí,
la popa está en Tchoupitoulas!

Boy made himself a boat
and it was pretty long:
When the bow is here in Delacroix,
the stern is in Tchoupitoulas!

Y en el banco del medio,
tiene telegrama y su cencerro,
para ver a saber la popa,
cuando la proa está en tierra.

And on the bench in the middle,
there's a telegraph with its bell,
to inform the stern
that the bow has come to land.

Esta barca camarón
ya no tiene su pareja:
Cuando el último se baja,
el primero está en Tejas.

This shrimp boat has
no equal anywhere:
When the last sailor goes on shore,
the first one's already in Texas.

Cuando acabaron el lance,
midieron el camarón
y contaron los barriles:
pasaban más de un millón.

When they finished the trip,
they took count of all the shrimp.
They counted all the barrels:
There were more than a million.

156. Setecientos setentaisiete (Seventeen Seventy-Seven)

This décima was composed by Irvan Perez and his wife Louise in 1976, to commemorate the two hundredth anniversary of the Canary Islanders' voyage to Louisiana.

Setecientos setentaisiete,
varias familias dejaron las Islas
*   Canarias,*
para la costa de Cuba,
del sur de la Luisiana.

In seventeen seventy-seven,
some families left the Canary Islands,
for the shores of Cuba
and Southern Louisiana.

En sur de la Luisiana
y en tierra regalada,
se pusieron de jardineros,
para mantenerse estas familias.

Varios fueron de soldados;
pelearon por su libertad.
También salieron victoriosos
y encontra de Inglaterra.

¡Viva Espana y su bandera!
Que con todo mi corazón,
sé que somos americanos,
pero sangre de español.

Cuando el tiempo se les puso duro,
cuando no podían más,
se fueron de estas tierras
y con otros españoles,
se pusieron a la pesca.

Entre el pato y la rata,
entre las aguas y las plerías,
con la ayuda de las mujeres,
se buscaron la vida.

Con penas y tormentos
y la voluntad de Dios,
así se pobló la costa
de la Parroquia de San Bernardo.

¡Viva España y su bandera!
Que con todo mi corazón,
sé que somos americanos,
pero sangre de español.

In Southern Louisiana
and on land that was given to them,
they became farmers
to maintain their families.

Some became soldiers;
they fought for their freedom.
They were also victorious
fighting against England.

Long live Spain and her flag!
For with all my heart,
I know we're Americans,
but our blood is Spanish!

When times got tough for them
and they couldn't hold out,
they left their land,
and with other Spaniards,
they became fishermen.

What with ducks and muskrats,
with the water and the marsh,
with the help of the women,
they earned their living.

With sorrow and trouble,
and by the will of God,
that's how they settled
the towns of St. Bernard.

Long live Spain and her flag!
For with all my heart,
I know we're Americans,
but our blood is Spanish.

Buried Treasure

Pierre Daigle

CHURCH POINT, ACADIA PARISH

R*ecorded July 3, 1990, by C. Renée Harvison from Pierre Daigle, sixty-eight, a Cajun. Daigle, a retired schoolteacher, writes stories and composes songs, some of which have been performed by Cajun Gold, a contemporary Cajun band. He doesn't take much stock in buried money stories but believes this one was probably true.*

157. The Widow's Buried Gold

The man whose story I'm going to tell you, as far as I know, actually lived, because I played around his grave a lot. He was buried, still buried, where we lived. He was buried in the yard where I lived. They had built a cypress picket fence around it. By the time I was old enough to know anything, the picket fence was falling apart. But it was still intact, partially.

This was a guy by the name of Fisher, which is obviously not a Cajun name. Supposedly Fisher and his wife and Fisher's wife's son, whose name was Billy, came to live in that house. Where they came from, nobody knows. The story is—and this is rumor and speculation—that he was a bank robber. He had moved into that house to sort of disappear. He was a drunk. Every time he'd go to town, he'd get drunk. This would have been Church Point, the closest town. He'd go on horseback and go to town and come back drunk and beat up on Billy.

One afternoon he came back drunk, and Billy shot him. Killed him. His wife and Billy buried him right there. That night, as it was dark, they left in the buggy, supposedly with a lot of gold. They came up to Jean Jannise, Jr.'s house. . . . The house is still there, not the house but the place. When they got there, she looked upon Jean, Jr., as a reliable man. She stopped there right after dark.

It's always after dark! He told her, "If you try to cross this forest at night, you're going to be robbed. Why don't you stay here tonight and tomorrow you can go."

Supposedly she was returning to Mississippi. That night, supposedly, she buried her money on the other side of Jean, Jr.'s house, a lot of gold.

Storytellers often start young perfecting their skill. Luke Booker is known for his skill in entertaining friends during lunch at Baton Rouge High School. Photo: Rachel Delatte.

Tremendous amount of gold. She never returned, so the gold is still there. I had a friend of mine who told me that was true because all drunks have a lot of money to bury!

And that's my reaction to that story.

Wendell Lindsay

LAKE CHARLES, CALCASIEU PARISH

Recorded June 28, 1990, by C. Renée Harvison from Wendell Lindsay, seventy-seven, British American. Lindsay, educated in both social work and engineering, also excels in oral history, as seen in this story.

158. Buried Treasure Money Used to Build a Catholic Church

There was so much Lafitte activity here, then legend glorified it. Then Texas picked up on it at Galveston. There's a lot of stories. In the little town of Duson over near Lafayette, on Highway 90 near Lafayette, you'll notice there's a little Catholic church on the left side of the road when you're coming this way, just a little out of town. There's a man named Judice who was very active in public affairs. He had a man plowing his field, and the plow hit something. They opened it up, and it was a big chest full of jewels and gold coins. All of them had early dates, and there were French coins and early American coins. They were buried there. They said it was Lafitte. They don't know who it was. But this negro man who found this built the Catholic church and the school there with part of the money. Seven years later—I guess jealousy—it burned down. He rebuilt it. Seven years later, it burned down again. He rebuilt it again. How much he had left I don't know. That's one case, and there's well-established fact on it.

Luther Sandel

FLORIEN, SABINE PARISH

The following three stories were recorded July 23, 1990, by C. Renée Harvison from Luther Sandel, seventy-two, a British American. Sandel, a retired carpenter, is a local historian and has written a book on the history of Sabine Parish, The Free State of Sabine. *These stories, however, belong to his personal and family traditions.*

159. Family Misfortunes

Where Hodges Gardens now is, my dad was hauling pine knots. They used to fire these locomotives, these trains. The locomotives would pull the log engines. They fired them with pine knots. He was hauling that stuff and selling to the railroads. He was working oxen. He stopped at a little branch to water his oxen, saw something glittering in the water, went to pick it up and it was a gold brick. A gold brick.

Now, that was a bullion. These Mexicans would mine [gold] and make it into little bricks. Now, the way he described it—I was too young to remember it. I was a baby at the—he described it, like, it would have been like a small Hershey bar the way he described it.

Well, him and his brother, they went down the little branch digging and hunting to see if there was any more. But they never could find any more. He put it over the door facing, and he'd show it to everybody that came in. One day, he went to show it to someone and it was gone. Somebody had put it in their pocket while he wasn't looking, and he lost it.

Now, [his father] had a cousin that found a gold—it was not a bar; it was some kind of medallion. They said it was hexagon-shaped and had

Spanish writing on it. He did about the same thing. Some guy was going to send it off and see what it was worth, and that was the end of it. That's why I'm not a rich man today; my relatives didn't hang on to their money!

160. Found Silver

I was in Leesville one day, in the grocery store, and a man told me, said, "You ought to talk to my dad. He's got a very interesting story he can tell you."

I said, "I want to talk to him, by all means."

So I went to see him, and he is a man by the name of Smith. They own the Piggly Wiggly store in Leesville. There's two of the brothers. I don't know if it was John, who is a state representative, John Smith, or if it was his brother. One of them told me about it. One of them told me to go see their dad.

So Mr. Smith told me, he said that his grandfather, a man by the name of Brock, originally lived in Marthaville, Louisiana, in Natchitoches Parish. He had moved to the Rio Grande valley and was a farmer. This was along about 1912. There was a bandit by the name of Pancho Villa. He would come across the river and raid farms in Texas.

Finally, well, for years they were trying to get the federal government to do something about it. They were pretty slow to react to it. He finally went up to Columbus, New Mexico. Killed a lot of people up there and done a lot of damage. They sent General Pershing. Later on, he was a famous World War I general over in Europe. He never did catch Pancho Villa, but he got close enough for Pancho Villa to decide he better stay out of the United States. Run him back across the river.

But back to my story, he raided a farm next to Mr. Brock's. I suppose he probably killed some people, took what valuables they had, gold or stock. Scared Mr. Brock up pretty bad, and he decided he'd just leave. Get out of there if that's the way it was going to be.

So he was packing up to come back to Marthaville, and there was an old Mexican on his place. Come to him and says, "Mr. Brock, I'm going to give you a map where you can dig up some money when you get back to Louisiana."

Well, I stopped Mr. Smith right there, and I said, "Now, look, why didn't the Mexican go dig it up?"

He said, "Well, he was an alien. He was not an American citizen. In those days, a law officer would just shoot one down."

Mr. Brock came on back. In the spring of the year, he was making a crop. He had two grown boys to help him. They were after the old man, "Let's go dig up the money. Let's go dig up the money." He was afraid they wouldn't get the crop in.

But after the crop was laid by in the summertime, he said, "All right boys, we'll go see about it." So they went straight and dug up. There was a little cave. They dug the money up. It was twenty thousand dollars in silver. No gold.

Mr. Smith told me, "I took my grandfather back there several times. He wanted to go see where this money was dug up, so I took him there several times."

I asked him, "Well, would you take me and show me where it was?"

He said, "Well, I'll try. It's been a long time."

Understand that they have straightened that road out. It used to have terrible curves. So we got over there. We went up there. It got pretty close to the place, and he said, "It's somewhere. I know it's over here somewhere." We went about a mile or two and he said, "We went too far."

We never could locate just where it was, but he said, "It's right in here on this ridge." He said that these two uncles came in later and used dynamite, hoping to find some more. But they didn't find any more.

There was an outlaw by the name of West. I believe, the best I remember, he might have rode with Murrell. He might have been in Murrell's gang when he was young. I think he was a Civil War veteran. I think he fought in the war. But he built him up a good little gang. But they were terrible as far as being heartless. Throw people in wells! Just let them starve to death! Killing babies, all kinds of stuff. West was the outlaw that [buried the money], according to the Mexican. He was with West and remembered it well enough to draw that map.

161. Buried Money Near Highway 171

I'll tell another little story. A friend of mine [Doris Coburn] told me this story. She was raised down here on Toro Creek, just off of 171 Highway. . . . I knew that there was an old stage coach route that came through where Hodges Gardens is now, just west of this Toro Church we were talking about. I didn't know that they had an old stage station over there. Nobody ever told me that. If they did, I'd forgotten it.

But [Doris] said there was an old stage station right close to where they lived. It was just off the road going to Toro Church. She went to church there when she was a girl. She said one day, one Sunday, they were going to church. There was a bunch of guys in a car, stopped over there, [and they] had shovels with them and everything. [We] stopped and asked them if they had trouble and could [we] help them, [asking], "What are you doing in the country, on a country road?"

They told them . . . no, they had [had] car trouble, but they had it fixed. So [we] went on to church. When [we] came back after church, the kids went out to the old stage station. It was close to the road—that's where they had stopped. [My friend] said it was a big rock.

I asked her, "Was the rock part of the foundation of the building?"

She said, "I think it was more foundation for the chimney." She said that rock had been turned over, and there was a neat, little vault about eight inches square and maybe eight inches deep. There it was, a neat little vault with nothing in it. She figured they'd gotten gold or money out of it. That happened in the thirties.

Arthur Irwin

DEQUINCY, CALCASIEU PARISH

The following three stories were recorded June 28, 1990, by C. Renée Harvison from Arthur Irwin, seventy-six, a British American. Irwin, who has resided in DeQuincy since his twenties, is known for his mean homemade dewberry wine.

162. A Barrel of Money

Years ago . . . this family pooled all their money. They had it in a flour barrel. John Reed's great grandmother had it in her family and had a cloth over it.

One of the kin folks' children come over there one cold morning and didn't have any shoes. She took him aside about where his shoes were and all, and he said, "I just don't have any."

She said, "Well, I'm going to stop that."

She went in to the pantry where this flour barrel was. John Reed's grandmother went with her. She was just a little girl then. She said her grandmother, John Reed's great-grandmother, threw this cloth back and reached in there and got a piece of money and gave it to this little kid. Told him, "Now you tell your mother to buy you some shoes."

Well, while she was doing this, John's grandmother, she couldn't see into the barrel, but she reached over it and she could feel this money. There was that much money in there in this flour barrel. They had pooled all their money and put it together.

So later on, one of them, I don't know which one, was [given the responsibility of] taking this money and [a] couple of slaves. He headed west to buy land for the whole family. He was supposed to buy land. But he got down to where they call Big Woods, and he sickened and died.

Now, the slaves told the story that this money is buried in there. By the time they made their way back to Mississippi, they couldn't remember where it was. They had buried all this money he had. What it was in then, I don't know. It was probably in boxes. Evidently, this money was supposed to be buried there. That money, as far as anybody knows, has never been discovered. But that whole area has been dug up!

163. Buried Treasure of Jean Lafitte

One of the most famous stories here is after the War of 1812. Jean Lafitte, the pirate, was still active here. He helped the United States in the Battle of New Orleans when Jackson defeated the British. They let him go, and he went to Galveston. The city of Galveston was founded by Jean Lafitte. He moved, supposedly, all his operations and headquarters outside the jurisdiction of the United States. But his biggest market, of course, was New Orleans. He would ply his piracy and his trade there.

At night, they knew all these swamps and innerland that the U.S. didn't know, the Coast Guard didn't know. And he would slip his stuff in through Barataria Bay and peddle it to New Orleans. One time one of his sloops or ships was apprehended, almost apprehended, by the U.S. Coast Guard. When they got to what they thought was waters outside of the United States, they turned into Sabine Lake [on the Texas-Louisiana border]. But it wasn't at that time outside of the United States. The Coast Guard was so close behind them that they scuttled their ship and sank it. There's always been a claim that they buried whatever they had somewhere in that area. People still look for the money there.

Virgil E. Callender, Sr.

BOGALUSA, WASHINGTON PARISH

Recorded June 29, 1990, at Bogalusa's Storytelling in the Park, from Virgil E. Callender, Sr., a British American, seventy. Callendar is a retired shift engineer.

164. The Haint Took It

Have you all heard anything about hunting money? Well, that's the thing I'm going to get involved with here. I went on a hunting expedition. And people don't know what actually goes on. I was invited to go on this trip, and they explained to me what it was. I'd never heard of it before. That was news to me.

Okay, people a long time ago—they claimed they buried their money. That was back when they had the slaves and all that there. And they—this old slave owner—he'd have a lot of money to bury. Well, he'd take his most-trusted slave he had. His old slave. And he'd take him with him. Well, he'd go out, and he'd pick him out a spot where he wanted it.

And he'd tell the old slave, "Now, I want you to dig right here." And he'd put it about four or five foot deep. Well, the old slave'd be down there digging.

When he thought it was deep enough, the old slave owner'd tell him, "Now, look. I want you to promise me something. That you'll guard this money as long as you can."

And the old slave'd say, "Yeah, I'll do that, boss."

Well then, he would—he'd shoot him. Kill him. Well, then the owner'd cover the hole up. He was the only man that knew where it was. That slave down in there—the belief was, that the slave, his spirit, would continue to guard that money.

Well, these people decided how to get around that. Well, I went off on this trip with them. I saw things I thought I'd never see again. They told me when they went, they said, "You gotta be pure."

Now, these are grown men. These ain't little boys. They said, "You can't have any dealings with your wife for a week, at least seven days before this hunt."

Well, these guys hired a man from the other side of Houma to come over here. He was supposed to be a professional finder. Well, he done it for a fee. They had to pay him, his expenses, to come over here. He brought a guy with him, and the two of them drove from Houma over here. He had a forked rod. And that's the thing he used to hunt the money with there. They could find it.

Well, we went way out in the country to an old plantation deal there. They told us, they said, "Now, you all stay here. And if that money's within a mile of here, we can find it."

And he said, "We'll come back and get you all."

So he told them all that. Well, we sat there in the dark, and he told us, "Now don't talk loud. You all can just whisper." So it was weird. I mean I was sitting there, and I didn't know what was going on.

Well, in a little while, they come back. And the guy said, "We've located it." He said, "Now, this is what I want you all to do. When we start out to get it, they can't nobody say another word."

So, we trailed along behind them back through the woods. And it was dark. We was stumbling over roots and everything else. And we finally got to the point, the place there, and they had an old lantern. It was the only light we had, and they had it up in front. We was all in the back. And they got up there, and sure enough, there was that forked piece of metal sticking in the ground where they'd located it.

Well, they told us, and everybody, wasn't nobody saying a word. They was motioning, stand back and all that there. Well, all at once, this guy come out with a little old box. This was the part that was weird to me. He got that box, and he went in there and he had some white powder. I know it was flour. That's what it looked like. He went and made a big circle around the whole thing. That was to keep that spirit in there. In other words, to keep that spirit from getting that money and running with it. It was their belief that once you got that powder around it, he couldn't cross that powder. Well, they got there, and they got that all powdered up.

Then they started digging. And I mean they was going at it fast. Nobody wasn't saying a word; it was just strictly just everybody was working. I didn't know nothing about it. I did get in there and dig just a little bit, but I was—more or less—wanting to watch than anything else. Well, they dug a hole—I bet you, it was seven-foot deep. You could've buried a car in it. There was some of them fellers there, they wouldn't work in a pie factory. But boy they was at it with that digging.

Well, they was going at it and all at once, one of them fellers got a coughing spell. Well when he did, this guy that was supposed to be the professional, he just got up and said, "Boys, it's all over with." He said, "It's gone now." He said, "I told you, you can't make no noise of no kind!" He said, "Now you can dig all day, and they ain't no money there now."

And that wound the money hunting up. Since then, I've heard other people talk about going on trips, and they always blame it on something! Even one time, they got so mad with one of the guys, they thought he'd lied. . . . They thought he was lying. I never heard of nobody finding the money. But they're right close to it. Now, there's people right today that's still doing it. Here a while back, I heard a man down below his house there; he went to work one morning, and there was a hole there [at] the side of the field. He said he don't know when they dug that! It was some time during the night!

David Allen

HOMER, CLAIBORNE PARISH

Recorded by Monty Brown at the Ruston Peach Festival, June 16, 1990, from David Allen, an African American. Allen's traditional background is reflected not only in his ghost stories but also in his ornately carved walking sticks. He says that the ideas for his canes "just come to him" in his mind in the form of dreams or thoughts.

165. A Moaning Ghost and Buried Treasure

You know, some people believe in haints and some don't. Ghosts or whatever they call them. But it's something. Something that I couldn't explain now. I've seen things, heard things. A lot of people don't believe it. But I have seen things happen on different occasions, living in the country. It's unexplainable. I don't know why or what it was, but I've seen things that I just couldn't explain what it was.

I was trying to remember the time that three fellows came up and asked me to go with them and show them where I had seen, what they said, the haints, spirits. I actually seen it, and they said wherever you see something like that, well usually—treasure, money, buried around. These three fellows came up and asked me would I show them where I seen this spirit or whatever it was. I'm getting ahead.

What I really seen, must've been about nine, ten years old. About first dark one night, I was on my way home. First I heard something that sounded like singing, moaning a song or something. I stopped to see what it was, and then, when I did see it, it looked almost like them clouds out there. But it wasn't as big as that cloud; it was just like a vapor-like. But it was just floating through the air.

I couldn't make out what it was, and when I realized it wasn't real, when it passed by the chicken house, the chickens started cutting up. And it came in front of me, and went out . . . and just settled down. But it was still like it was singing. By that time, I done got up enough nerve in my feet to run. And I take on off to the house. Run in there and told my dad about it. And so he said, "Oh, it's just somebody out there trying to scare you." And he got up, got the shotgun, went outside. I told him, I went out to the porch and showed him where the last time I seen it was.

So he went on out that a-ways. I come on back in the house, waiting to hear the gun to go off. Few minutes, still hadn't heard the gun go off, I heard him coming back running! He said when he got out there, when he raised that gun up to where I had told him that thing was, said something got all over him and that gun. Man, he come back in that house. Said something was out there.

After that, these two men came along, must've been about twenty-five, thirty years later, wanting to know where did I see this at. And I told them. They asked me could they go back there. Well, the house had been torn down and all growed up out there now. So anyway, I'm taking them out there, and these fellows had one of these treasure things, like you hunt buried treasure with. He had one of those, and one of them had some other kind of little gimmick. Another had a little Testament, a New Testament.

I got to the place we was supposed to go. So this fellow with the little Bible, he went out and sat down on a log and started reading. Fellow with this treasure deal, he started moving it around on the ground. Finally this thing started making some kind of whining noise. Getting louder and louder. And so he said, "Something down here." We got a shovel and dug down in there. Kept in and dug a little more.

Finally didn't dig no more. We taking it out the hole, and that's where they found it. When we did find it, a fifty cents piece. Search and search, couldn't find nothing else. I said, "Well, this ain't where I seen the haint at. It's over here between these two cedar trees." We went over there. He got in between them trees, and I said, "It's closer to the one on the right." And so he went over that way, and that thing started making this whining noise and going on.

At this time, a great big—I say a blackbird. Looked like a blackbird to me, but it was real black. It looked like it was blue. But it had a real yellow beak, and two big orange eyes, and he lit up in that cedar tree, and he starts making croaking noise like a crow. Then another one, then another one. The more we searched, the more them big old birds get in that tree.

Finally, them birds, got so many got in that tree it look like it was just leaning backwards and forwards. This man told me, said, "I tell you what, something's been here. But somebody done found it now." Said, "We better go!"

He packed up his junk, we left. But I honestly believe they went back out after I had helped them locate where I thought [it was]. I didn't know what was there, but I believe they located something, and they went back after they got rid of me. Keep from dividing with me. If there was anything there, keep from dividing with me. It was near night, so they carried me back home, and I wasn't about to go back there by myself! But, anyway, that's what happened that particular night.

Tales of the Supernatural

Velma Duet

GALLIANO, LAFOURCHE PARISH

V*elma Duet is a Cajun businesswoman who owns a real estate agency. She grew up in Lafourche Parish, which borders the Gulf of Mexico, and is steeped in the Cajun lore of that area. She is aware of the scientific explanations of her culture's folk beliefs but has not allowed that to affect her attitude toward them; she maintains the traditions of her forebears. Although she does not tell any firsthand accounts of encounters with the supernatural, she gives vivid accounts that involved people she knew, including close family members. The following five stories were collected from Duet at the Holy Rosary Family Fun Festival in Lafourche Parish, May 13, 1990.*

166. Failure to Heed a Warning

Then there were things like the *avertissements,* which were warnings. For example, now this is a fact. It happened to my grandfather. My grandfather's name was Celestin, and he had a trawl boat. He had a good friend that was trawling with him. They were real good friends all through the years. One day they went trawling. Grandfather slept in the top part of the boat, and his friend slept in the bottom. The fumes from the boat overcame [his friend], and he died.

About three months after he had died, Grandfather was sleeping one night, and he heard his friend calling his name. When he heard "Celestin" after the third time, he went outside and he did see his friend. And his friend said, "Celestin, don't go back on the boat." And when you see a spirit, which a lot of people have seen in their lives, . . . you're not supposed to name him. It makes him go away. I'm sure Grandfather didn't know or didn't think of it, and he named him. He said, "Why are you telling me that?"

And he named him, and he went away, so he wasn't able to find out at that point why. But about a week after, Grandfather went back trawling. And he slept in the same place that his friend slept in and the same thing happened to him. Except they found him before he died. He did not die from it, but it impaired his speech. Until the day he died, he wasn't able to speak well. He stayed six months without saying a word. Then his speech was very, very slurred. He couldn't speak well until the day he died.

Storytelling is an intimate part of the experience of a pilgrimage. Visitors exchange stories about their personal experiences as well as legends about phenomena that have occurred at the pilgrimage site. Here, during the Feast of St. Ann, Joseph Schillace speaks to pilgrims at Our Lady of Tickfaw, sharing stories about apparitions of the Virgin Mary and the construction of shrines in commemoration of these miracles. Photo: Maida Owens.

167. Veiled Eyes

[My] husband's grandmother was prophetic. She was born with veiled eyes. When a person was born with veiled eyes, they were able to prophesy. This woman was born that way.

One day, they came to tell her that her grandson, whose name was Leon—my husband's brother—was killed in an accident. When they approached the house, she met them on the porch, and she said, "I know you came to tell me that Leon has died."

They asked, "Well, how did you know?"

She said, "I saw his face in my window last night, and I knew he was dead at that point."

So again, a lot of times this has happened where—in fact, I know a man who lives in Cut Off right now that was born with veiled eyes. He's able to tell anytime that somebody in his family is going to die. He knows before. He knows who it is. It's a thin lining that is born over the eyes when you are born. They have to cut it out so they can see. They call it a veil. It indicates prophecy. This person is able to prophecize.

168. The Rooster Knows

They believed that if a rooster crowed, it meant that you were going to have company. Well, my mother had such a rooster. He could crow in the yard all day long, and it was okay. But if he came up the back steps and looked into the kitchen and he crowed through the screen door, Mama would say, "Okay girls, let's straighten up the house, we're having company." And we did, too! It's a sixth sense, but it worked.

169. The Ghosts of Jean Lafitte's Pirates

Let me tell you about Jean Lafitte. It is said that his pirates are still guarding his treasures. He has treasures on a lot of these little offshore islands. And there's a man that lives in Golden Meadow, he's still alive; he had a little trawl boat. He went trawling one day, and there's this little island with a beautiful oak tree on it. Every now and then, he'd stop and he'd sit under the oak tree. Well one day, he did. He stopped his boat there, and he went to sit under that oak tree. But as he approached it, he saw one of Jean Lafitte's pirates. And the pirate told him to get off the island, now!

So he went back to his boat, but he panicked, he lost his mind. When they came and found him, he was all cringed in the corner of his boat. He was shaking, shaking. He'd totally lost his mind. He went to Jackson [the location of a mental hospital]. . . . And he stayed there a couple of years. He's still alive today, but that's what he told them when they found him— that there was a pirate under the tree. So it's very possible that it's true.

John Verret

THERIOT, TERREBONNE PARISH

The following four stories were recorded from John Verret, a Native American of the Houma culture, at the November 1989 Louisiana Folklife Festival in Eunice. The Houmas live along the bayous and marshes of the Louisiana coast, primarily in Terrebonne, Lafourche, Plaquemine, and Jefferson Parishes. Many speak French and maintain traditional lifestyles based on hunting, fishing, and trapping. He died following Hurricane Andrew in 1992.

170. A Brush with the Loup Garou

I'm John Verret, and I'm going to tell you all about what, really, I've heard about but didn't see myself. Except I seen a ghost already, but a *loup garou* is like a ghost. It's a ghost. And what happened is two of my uncles and one of my cousins—you've got to understand that a lot of people don't believe in religion. . . . You got two sides: you got God, and you got the devil. That's because I know. I believe in both of them. Two men—there was one my uncle and one my cousin, and so, okay. They . . . visited the neighbors down the road, you know. So they was coming back home at night, late at night, to go back home. They said the moon was bright. So you could see— we almost had daylight. Then there come that big dog that appears in front of them. The dog was going after them, you know! So they started running, trying to get away! Good thing they had a fence right close, so they went over the fence, jumped the fence.

They said when they got over on the other side, that big man come up there. And it appears there wasn't no more dog, it was the man right there. He said, "You all got scared, eh?"

They said, "Yeah, you scared us." So then, it was him.

But you've got to understand when something like that happens, you do something wrong, bad, then what happens, God turn His back on you. Then the devil take over. So that's the way I understand . . . what happened. So his wife, . . . my cousin, too, said that man could be sleeping in bed at night, and you could shake him and call him and shake him and you couldn't wake him up. The soul wasn't there. The soul was somewhere else. So as far as that's concerned, that's what I heard. That's all I know about it.

171. A Brief Encounter with a Ghost

But I seen a ghost myself. A lot of people say when you see something, you're scared. I'm not . . . the bravest one, but really I'm not that scared. And I know I seen a ghost. I had an aunt was dressed up like that one that I seen. Had a big deal on their head like the old timers used to wear, and tied up like a nun. They used to wear these; it dropped way back on their head. All dressed up in white—that cap was white, too. I went to the store. I went to the store that morning, and I was coming back from the store. I saw that person cross the road in front of me going to the bayou side. I had some corn planted there. The corn was all dried up, so there was no way you could have went in there and hide yourself. So when I passed there, I looked and I didn't see no one after that. That was that. They didn't come nowhere near to me. . . . Went to the bayou side in that corn, and that was it. I remember that! I don't think that was a *loup garou*. I think that was what you call a regular ghost. That's what they call your soul. That's a ghost.

172. Feu Follet

That's another thing, the *feu follet*. That's the bad angel, the *feu follet* what they call it. You got the God angel, and you got the devil angel. What you call a *feu follet*. One of my uncles was brave. Brave enough. They said you put a needle up like this, and that thing goes through that needle and comes out sparking on the other side, flies, fire flies. If you go somewhere, like you go on a lake like we used to do—a lot of times. . . .

A lot of times, you go across the water, and you going to see that light, like a star across the lake. You figure, "Well, that's where I got to go." So that light starts moving around. You find out, you go in the wrong place. You hit the bank, and you're not where you're supposed to go. That light's going to trick you. That's what you call a *feu follet*. That's what you call an angel, a bad angel.

I don't believe you could hold them. [My uncle] was brave enough to try. That thing passes there. It's like a big owl. It's about the size of an owl. That's another thing I didn't see, but somebody told me that. They was hunting alligator, and they were brave enough to use that needle and try it. They even shot at it. Take a gun and shoot at it. Didn't do no harm. The spark fly was still flying.

173. Two Mysteries of Bayou Go to Hell

They got a place down below Grand Caillou. People used to—you could tie your boat to the bank, and the next morning you'd be drifting in the bayou someplace else. They got a little track on that bank. It's clean. No grass. It's clean, clean. Some people was brave. They said, "I'm going to go tie my boat there, and I'll put my mattress there and sleep on that road that night."

So they did. They tried. He went there and had to use that old-time mosquito net to protect them from mosquitoes. So he had all that set up to sleep on that road. He went to sleep. He didn't hear nothing to scare him, so he went to sleep. But the next morning, he was not on that road. He was in the grass. On either side, he was in the grass. That road was clean. That's another one they say is true.

They call that place Bayou Go to Hell. It's somewhere in that area there. You couldn't tie your boat and stay there. You'd have been drifting, just like that man was brave enough to try and sleep on that road. He couldn't stay there. From that spot there, one of my uncles, he was a Lee. He went down there fishing. Coming back, there come the prettiest lady you could find, sit down on the back of that pirogue while he was paddling. When he saw that, he got kind of scared. He put some more speed to it, not talking, nothing! When he got to where he was staying, he got out, he turned around and looked, the lady was gone. That was somewhere around the same area as Bayou Go to Hell, below Grand Caillou.

Loulan Pitre

CUT OFF, LAFOURCHE PARISH

The following four stories were collected by Pat Mire and Maida Owens on September 20, 1993, for the video documentary, Swapping Stories. *Loulan Pitre and his son Glen are Cajuns.*

174. An Oyster-Culling Loup Garou

My father was an oyster fisherman because that was his means of a livelihood. And people from his time didn't have anything to do at night. They'd gather—well, it's a gathering of working men instead of old men— and they'd tell each other stories, and they probably told each other stories so often that they'd believe them. They'd actually come to believe them. And this particular story is really amazing.

I don't want to go into the mechanics of the oyster business, but it was a little complicated—not to them but to anyone you want to explain it to.

They used to *tong* oysters. There were no such things as dredges. *Tong*. And they had these oyster skiffs—were about twenty, twenty-four, twenty-six feet long and maybe ten feet wide. They'd tong oysters, oh, practically all day long and load them up. And that was shells and regular oysters in the rough. And at night, they'd congregate in some bayou. They usually had some little camps or little cabins with the particular fishermen. They didn't sleep on the boats because it was so darn hot—or either so darn cold when it was winter time. And they would gather in one cabin and tell each other stories.

And this particular story stuck in my memory because I actually believed it when they—when my father—related it to me. Anyway, they'd bring these skiffs and tie them up along a big pile of oyster shells. We call this *culling* oysters, not shucking. It's an entirely different system. *Culling* oysters means sitting down in that skiff on a little old bench with a mitten in your hand, with a little hatchet, and get all those oysters as *singles*—single oysters. Every one you had to pass in your hand: if it was too small, throw it away. And then the shells would pile up at your feet and you'd have to shovel those shells onto the big shell pile, so it wouldn't clog up the little stream you were in.

And my father used to say—they call them *loup garou*. They were a famous topic. The *loup garou*. They'd pull all kinds of capers. *Loups garoux* would, not the people.

And so it came about that one of these old oystermen would say, "I keep hearing something at night in our oysters." He said, "I keep hearing noises." And they'd listen. Naturally, they wouldn't hear anything. But after a while, another one said, "I hear a noise in our skiffs. Maybe it's a raccoon." And more and more, one and after the other kept hearing [it] and finally they decided the only noise it could be was someone culling the oysters and hitting those clusters with a hatchet.

All night long, this would go. All night long. Next morning, they'd go check out the oysters to get ready to work. And one fisherman would find his skiff: the oysters had all been culled. And none of the others. And, well, they believed in *loup garoux*. They took them for—their existence as a fact. They weren't afraid of them. And this lasted forever. Throughout the winter, and then the following winter, lo and behold, the thing was back again. You see, they just work oysters in the winter time then, when it cool. And so one guy says, "I'm going to stay. I'm going to hide behind a pile of shells and *see* what's doing that in the moonlight."

So, he was brave enough. He stayed up. And he could see the pile of shells diminishing in the skiff. But he could not see what was doing it. And he could hear the hatchet hitting the clusters. So he kind of went, sneaked over there, and he saw like a shadow, some kind of apparition there. So he took a pole—they used these long poles—that they used to . . . push the skiffs around. They didn't have any engines in them. And he sneaked up on this thing and *whapped* it across the back of this—more of a shadow than anything physical—and it disappeared. There was nothing. And that night on they never heard another noise, and nobody ever got another oyster culled. And that thing disappeared. And that was the story. . . . And they believed it. They actually got each other to believe it.

175. The Shadow Companion

This other story was the one related to me by my father, but it was prior to the 1893 storm. There was this old man. He was kind of a cripple. He limped a little, and every day he'd do some beachcombing. He'd go walking on Grand Isle or the beaches at Cheniere come clear to Fouchon with his stick, and one day he noticed that he wasn't alone. He stayed out a little later than he should have, and he saw this apparition, this *shadow*. He always claimed it was a monkey. I guess that was the only—or closest thing he could come to describe it. And he tried to chase it. The thing was fast. He tried to hit it with his stick. He couldn't do it. And day after day, he'd walk the beaches. . . . He found himself staying out a little later every day, so the thing would appear—it wouldn't show up in the daytime at all. And sometimes it would jump on his shoulder—this thing. No way but he—he could see it.

So, the years went by, and the old man got older and hobbled along, and he got *fond* of the thing. He talked to it, and the thing would never change its pace. . . .

So, one day this man, coming back about seven in the evening. . . . Some vines were growing in the sand—still do. And he *stumbled,* the old guy stumbled, and he had his *stick* in his hand, and when he stumbled, he did this [makes a thrusting motion with his hand, as if holding a stick]—to hold himself up. Then he . . . pierced the skin of this thing. Here. Pointed stick got it. And the thing was all gone in a flash. And he never saw it again.

And the old man went walking more and more, and everybody thought he had lost his marbles. Because he spent all his time walking the beaches, and he actually pined away for his companion. He had grown so fond of it that and he died shortly after. And they believed that too—that story.

Glen Pitre

LOCKPORT, LAFOURCHE PARISH

176. Loup Garou as Shadow Companion

Okay, this is a story I first heard when I must have been nine, ten years old. I remember the moment on the porch at my parents' house, and my *parrain*, my godfather—who was also an uncle—was the one who told it. But definitely he had heard it passed in his family.

And it was about days back, ooh, back even before the depression, and they were all oyster fisherman, because the family had been oyster fishermen for generations. And they would fish the oysters with big tongs, . . . like ice tongs. And they'd tong them into the boat. But that was only half the battle, because they'd be all grown together in clusters, and you had to break them up with a hatchet into single oysters, because that's the way they were sold. Which was a lot of work. And at night, the boats would all tie up together, and they'd stay in their fishing camp, this palmetto camp they had built and tell stories and pass the time and go to bed and slap the mosquitoes.

And it started happening that they'd come out in the morning and the oysters would be separated, and they'd be culled into singles for them. But also, half of them would be eaten. So you had a good thing—a lot of your work would be gone. But you'd had a bad thing that the oysters would be eaten. And course, it scared them. They didn't know who was doing this. They could tell no other boats had come. There was no other house for miles around. It was open water. And one of the young men who was braver than most said he was going to stay on the boat and find out who or what was doing it.

Well, he stayed, but he didn't quite make it through the whole night, because somewhere in the middle of the night—everybody had been waiting up, trying to see what would happen, but one by one they fell asleep. In the middle of the night they heard screaming, and he came running down the dock into the camp and just was frantic and could hardly explain what he had seen—this creature that was huge and hairy and moved very quickly. But that was the end of it. After that whatever it was stopped appearing on the boats, stopped breaking them into singles, stopped eating half of them.

Of course it was the end of it for everybody else, but the one brave guy—who started telling the others that whenever he was alone, this creature would come to him. It would sit on his shoulders with featherweight touch. And he'd lie on his bed and if he was in a house alone, he was alone in the bedroom—it would rest on the bed head. Never hurt him, but frightened him, because it haunted him. And time went on and people—I mean nobody really believed his stories, and more and more, they kind of avoided him, because he was obsessed with this thing. And he had been engaged to be married, and his fiancée—*elle a cassée la paille* [she broke it off]—you know, she didn't want anything to do with him. And he grew older and the young kids used to follow him around and sing songs after him to taunt him, because everybody thought he was a little nuts. And he talked to himself—

or so they thought—because actually he was talking to the *loup garou*—the creature—which never answered but sure seemed to listen real well.

And again, as time went on, he grew older until finally he became an old man and had to walk with a cane. And he'd still go and meet all the oyster boats when they'd come in, walking on those shells with that cane. The end of the cane would get kind of sharp. And one day, he fell. And that sharpened end of the cane went up and *cut* the *loup garou* and—if you know about the *loups garoux,* you know that one way to get rid of them—probably the only way to get rid of them—is to draw blood. And when he cut it, and it drew blood, that was the end.

And the old man realized he had just lost the only friend he had ever had. After spending years trying to get rid of the thing, he had gotten so used to it that nobody else would have anything to do with him, that it became his only friend and now—*click*—by accident he had killed his friend. And he suffered in loneliness for a while and then he died himself.

Loulan Pitre

CUT OFF, LAFOURCHE PARISH

The following tale is one of the many told in connection with the great hurricane of 1893, which had a devastating effect on South Louisiana. At least 1,500 people were killed in this storm, one of the worst in American history.

177. Lifesaving Sirens

Well, it's hilarious—it's funny. Although it was tragic then, it's funny now.

One man, he was about twenty-four. Not an old man. . . . Maybe younger than that. And he had been given up for lost. And this goes six, seven days after the storm. They'd just about accounted for everybody they'd hoped to find. And a lot of people had gone up on the rooftops into the Gulf a mile or so. But they got picked up. Or they floated back into the beach. But this fellow, no. And nobody had seen him during the storm. Lo and behold, about three weeks later, he comes in—in one of those freight boats that was hauling ice . . . and food to Grand Isle for these people that'd been hurt bad. He's a passenger and he makes his way back to Cheniere.

"Hey, what in the world happened to you?" [he was asked.]

"Well," he said, "I'll tell you what. I spent seven days on a door and a door frame, floating, lying on it."

"And, well, how did you survive?"

"Well, I kept hearing this singing." He said they had some mermaids or something singing all the time. "And it kept me alive."

And they laughed, you know?

And he said, "No, no, I saw them. They were singing just for me. They'd come there and swim around and sing."

And one day, he was semiconscious, and he heard some racket, and there was a bunch of Portuguese, and the little yard boat was picking him up. And it was a Portuguese sloop that had seen him on that door and stopped. And that sloop was loaded with salted pork going into New Orleans. And that's a "miracle" he got saved. And he couldn't believe his—

And my daddy said, when they tried to talk to him and really get the story out of him, all he'd remembered was the singing. That's all he'd want to talk about. Beautiful. Beautiful voices. And evidently, he lived a nice long life because he moved to Golden Meadow afterwards, bought land, and raised a big family, this fellow. But he never forgot his ordeal on that door.

Peter Gitz

MADISONVILLE, ST. TAMMANY PARISH

Recorded September 30, 1990, at the Wooden Boat Festival in Madisonville from Peter Gitz, fifty-six, mayor of Madisonville and a lifelong resident. Gitz, who is German by ancestry, grew up hearing various versions of the legend of the Silk Lady, and when he was a young boy, he first encountered the Silk Lady himself.

178. The Silk Lady

The story I'm about to tell is more or less a legend, a story. People have sighted what we call the Silk Lady. I'm going to try and describe the Silk Lady. There's a lot of versions of the Silk Lady, but the way we took it and what we thought we'd seen is like a glow of silk, long silk hair, the color of white silk. Her eyes were silky-looking. Her fingernails was long, about two inches long, and looked like silk. We've never seen her feet. It's always like she's had a white, silk gown on. And that's the description of the Silk Lady.

The area that we've seen her in, I need to tell you a little bit about that. Madisonville is located on almost an island. We need to go back and think about it two hundred years ago, surrounded by the Tchefuncte River on the east side, south side Lake Pontchartrain. . . . The north side is surrounded by Bayou Desire. On the west side is all swamp. Madisonville set almost like an island. Where Bayou Desire and the west side connected is only one little, narrow, high ground swamp land. We feel that in the past, the Natchez Trace, or the so-called Natchez Trace, a trail that comes from the west . . . had to come south to New Orleans—all the people before then had to travel this one little, two-hundred-foot wide little peninsula. On this two-hundred-foot wide peninsula, it's maybe a foot-and-a-half above sea level. A lot of times it was under water. Since then, before my time, say in [the] 1850s, it was called Palmetto Flat. Had nothing but palmettos and swamp land, gum trees, and very few pine trees. That trail led into Madisonville. Since then, it's Highway 22. Back in the thirties, they'd made a new highway, which is now Highway 22.

But all of the sightings was always right west of Madisonville in the area called Palmetto Flat. That's where the Silk Lady has supposedly been sighted. There's a lot of stories that I'm going to try to go back and relate that I've heard during my time. My father brought the stories up to me, his father told him, and his grandfather told him. That's how it was brought on through history. My great-grandfather, Frederick Gitz—seems that there was a story heard, that maybe only a few settlers in here—there was very few people here when he come here in the 1850s. He heard the story about the Silk Lady, and thought maybe they shouldn't build. Well, they did, and they were about two miles out of Madisonville on Black River Creek.

The Silk Lady stories go back years and years. We've heard all kind of stories. The one I'm going to tell you now is what my grandfather had told my dad about the first logging that was done close to Palmetto Flat. Fellow by the name of Tom Noll had an ox team that was doing the logging and getting some of the cypress out of the swamp. He could never keep his oxen in a pen at night. Normally, oxen won't stampede. But when they moved in to start the first timber harvest, in [the] area called Palmetto Flat, these oxen stampeded. . . . He'd come back, and he'd find that he couldn't even use them; they were completely wild. . . . Something was coming in there at night and always scaring the oxen. That was one story of the Silk Lady.

Another story was [of] Rudolf Galatas [who has] a road named after [him]. This was about the turn of the century. When he would come into Madisonville, he'd want a weekend to buy food and supplies. All this was travel with horse and wagon. Always the horse and wagons would stampede the Palmetto Flat area. Horses would stampede and about turn the carriages over. The horses would be afraid when they got there. They tell me that the horses' ears would stand straight, they'd whicker, back up, kick. They always felt that something was in the area, and they always said it had to be the Silk Lady.

Rudolf Galatas claims that he saw the Silk Lady and she was the image we'd always heard of. Just a lady floating, and she always did a screaming sound. He said his horse bucked, he held it back and he said he seen her. He said it looked like she was floating in the air. She grabbed ahold to the buggy seat. Said he pulled his knife out, and he thought he cut one of her fingers off. But he was too scared to go back and see. So what he done, he went back the next day, and he could not find her finger. But he swears that he had cut her little finger off of her right hand when she grabbed ahold of the carriage.

The Silk Lady is always seen at night, never in daytime. The reason I feel that I should tell the story is that I was born in a place [near] where the Silk Lady was supposed to have been—our old home was in about five hundred feet of Palmetto Flat. That's where I was born in 1935. And I heard the story of the Silk Lady. Believe it or not, I was always scared of the Silk Lady. My father was also a truck farmer, and our farm was just about a mile and a half from our house. We'd always walk from the farm to the house. It was a many an evening late, that I got close to Palmetto Flat, I'd run as fast as I could run all the way to my house. I was glad to get in. I was always scared of the Silk Lady.

When I was about twelve or fourteen years old, on Bayou Desire, I used to set traps. It was in the Palmetto Flat area. I was always leery of the Silk Lady. One day I was back there running my traps, and it was late in the evening. I'd always run late in the evening; I had mink traps, and I used to catch mink and coon and some small muskrat. But I [got] caught back there in the dark, and the moon was just coming up. And I tell you, I heard this sound that they always said that she done. I'll describe it. It seemed like a scream, like [makes a high-pitched moaning noise]. I tell you what, I burned that swamp up getting out.

Since then, I've heard it three times. The next time I heard the scream, I was coming from the farm, just about dark. I knew it was getting late. It was in the fall of the year, and the moon was just coming up. The Palmetto Flat was between my house and where I was coming from the farm. The moon was shining, and I could see in the swamps like a silk glow. I stopped. I was almost too afraid to run. The first time I've seen it. It looked like a glow. She was standing there and floating, with not a [foot] on the ground, just like she was floating. I'm talking about a hundred feet away from me. So I kept a looking at her. I just kept a walking slow. All at once she screamed again; she screamed [makes a high-pitched moaning noise]. All I could do was run.

I run home and I got in my house. My mother asked what was wrong.

I said, "I seen the Silk Lady."

She said, "You ain't seen the Silk Lady. There's no such thing as the Silk Lady."

But to this day I believe I've seen the Silk Lady.

The next time, I guess I was about twelve years old, and we used to keep a horse at the house that we used to plow. I had an old harness on the horse, and we was plowing at the house. I was coming back—the horse never has rared up with me on him—but he rared up, threw me off, stampeded to house with the harness on. And I heard the scream again, and I ran to the house. That was when I was about twelve years old.

The last time that I heard the Silk Lady was in about 1947. That was the year after the hurricane. All the trees was knocked down, we had high water, the swamp was covered with about four foot of water. Just when the water went down, I was coming again from the farm, and that's when I seen her. It looked like she was floating there among the palmettos. She was glowing. You could see her long fingernails. That's the closest I'd ever been to her. She had long, straight hair, just like silk. Her whole body glowed like white silk. I just kept on walking slow and she screamed at me again. She done the same scream [makes a high-pitched moaning noise], like she was trying to tell me something. I don't know if she was afraid that the storm had chased her out of the swamp or what. But I ran! And that was the last time that I seen the Silk Lady, and that was in 1947.

Mary Etta Scarborough Moody

ANGIE, WASHINGTON PARISH

Recorded at Bogalusa's Storytelling in the Park, June 29, 1990, from Mary Etta Scarborough Moody, British American, forty-two. Moody was raised ("not reared, but raised," she says, "like peas") in Angie, but lived in Bogalusa for a number of years. She now lives in Poplarville, Mississippi. Her story concerns an incident that occurred while she was in high school in Bogalusa.

179. The Red-Headed Witch of Bogalusa Creek

How many of you had heard of the woman that walks on the water here? The ghost? Lot of you have heard of the ghost of the lady that walks on the water here. This is a story of the red witch of the water.

When Bogalusa was first a city, there was a certain woman who lived here who was not a very nice person. In fact, she was a very un-nice person. Some people said she was a witch, but the men in the town had another name for her. She was well known by everybody. A young man, a very, very good-looking young man, happened to come into her sight. She was determined that she was going to trap him and make him hers.

Well, the young man, at first, found the red-headed woman very fascinating, very interesting. But after a while, he got tired of her, and he wasn't interested. He didn't like her anymore at all. He found a beautiful young girl, very attractive, very pretty, that he liked a lot better.

The old witch tried everything she knew to get that young man back, but she couldn't get him back at all. She was desperate. She was out of her mind. When all of a sudden, she decided she couldn't stand it any longer, she was going to kill herself. She had had a pact with the devil, and the pact with the devil said that she would always walk in Bogalusa. That she would always be here unless she could get somebody else to trade places with her.

She came out here to Cassidy Park, right out yonder, to where the water-processing plant used to be, where the concrete parts used to be. She flung herself into the great, square water-processing area. Flung herself in and killed herself. But remember the pact she had with the devil: she was going to forever walk in Bogalusa.

Well, lo and behold, not too long after that, people began to see a vision of a woman walking across the water here at Cassidy Park, walking across the water very, very slowly. Walking towards the edge of the water, beckoning the people to come. But nobody'd get near that woman.

Well, Cassidy Park didn't last a long time. They closed it down. When I was a kid like you all, it wasn't here. It was here, but nobody used it. Well, in the 1960s, one of the mayors decided it was being wasted. So he opened up Cassidy Park to the public, and they put these roads in here. The kids—I was in high school—we decided to have Volkswagen races out here. We'd come out here in our Volkswagens, and we'd race around the area. We weren't supposed to; it was against the law. But we did it anyway. Wasn't like doing some other things that are too bad. We'd get out here with our Volkswagens, and we'd race around. We had the best time you ever heard of, but we all knew about that woman in the park. Nobody would stay here after midnight because they knew she was going to be here.

Well, lo and behold, one night we were having the Volkswagen races, and we stayed a little late. Carol Cassidy and Carol Waltman and Carol

Bridges and Mildred Seales and I were all out here playing Volkswagen races. Lo and behold, one of the boys was Leslie Sibley, and he was always clowning around, and Doyle Holloway. They came running up, "That woman's out there! That woman's out there!" "What woman? What are you talking about?" "That woman that walks on the water. That ghost is out there."

Well, we went over to the side of the area, the creek, and lo and behold, there she was, coming out of the water processing plant, coming through the mist, coming towards us. Boy, did we run for those Volkswagens fast! We got there in nothing flat. And Carol Waltman and the others all took off. But me and Carol Cassidy were sitting there, and she couldn't get her Volkswagen cranked. That thing was coming right at us, I mean right at us—she was coming with her arms stretched out and that red hair flying in the mist. It was the awfulest looking sight you ever saw in your life. She had big holes for her eyes. What an awful, horrible looking woman! And slime was dripping from her hands. Awful-looking horrible creature coming right at us! Carol couldn't get her Volkswagen cranked. "Carol, get that Volkswagen cranked, fast!" She couldn't do it. It wouldn't crank. It wouldn't crank.

Finally, "*Roar! Roar!*" She got it! We took off and headed out for the Dairy Queen. We got there, and Carol Waltman said, "Well, it's about time you all got here. I thought the red-headed woman got you."

I said, "No, she didn't get us, Carol, but we saw her."

She said, "Yeah, wasn't that the awfulest-looking thing you ever saw?"

I said, "Yeah," and I started to get out of the Volkswagen. As I got out of the Volkswagen, I slammed the door. There on the handle of the door was the slime that had come off of the red-headed witch of the water. That's how close I came to being got by the red-headed witch of the water of Bogalusa Creek.

I'll tell you something, if you're ever down here at midnight at Bogalusa Creek and that red-headed woman comes after you, you get out of the way and you get out of the way fast! Because if she catches you, you take her place and she takes a rest.

Jack Holman

MINDEN, WEBSTER PARISH

Recorded at Minden's Germantown Festival, May 12, 1990, from Jack Holman, British American, a retired Boy Scouts of America executive.

180. The Hammering Ghost of Minden

Right here in Minden—we moved to Minden in 1972. Lived here longer than anywhere we've ever lived in our lives. We lived on the corner of East and West right back over here, and Sullivan Street. When we moved to town, there was an old, old haunted-looking house right across the street from us. Some people call it the Old Male Academy; other people call it the Old Female Academy. Reggie might be able to tell you which one it was. Best I can remember, it was the Old Female Academy, and I think they moved it from Academy Park. They moved it over here on the corner, right across the street from us on East and West. Faced East and West on one side, and on the other side, it faced Sullivan. We'd been living there two or three years. The old house was an eyesore. But when the wind would blow, you know, vandals had thrown rocks up there and knocked windows out. The curtains were still in there. There was a bunch of old furniture in there.

But when the wind would blow, that old house would kind of whistle. It'd go, *Shhhhh*. Whistling, kind of. And the curtains would fly, like there'd be some old haints in there or something. But we don't believe in haints, so there weren't any haints or haunts in there.

Sybil Bridges—Sybil Bell she became after Jack's death—called one morning. I was still doing a lot of Boy Scout work and typing reports and that kind of thing. Mickey and them were gone. Sybil says, "Jack, would you meet me in front of the house, like right now? There's something going on in the neighborhood."

So I said, "Yes." I went out our front door, which is on East and West Streets, and Sybil came across; she lived on Sullivan.

She said, "Be real quiet and just listen."

And I'd be real quiet and I'd just listen.

She said, "Do you hear anything unusual in the old house there?"

I said, "Well, Sybil, there's somebody building, hammering and nailing in that old house."

She said, "That's right. But there ain't nobody in that house."

The lady who owned this house was a peculiar individual. She had a bunch of old cats. She owned it, but she lived two houses or three houses down, on Sullivan. She was an elderly lady at that time. Like Reggie, she used a stick sometime to walk with. As Sybil and I talked about going in there, about the nailing and the hammering in that house, I began to use some common sense. I said, "Sybil, now this lady, the way she is in her old age, if I go in that house, and she's in there, she might get me for trespassing, or even trying to break in, entering without permission. And I don't have permission to go in there."

She said, "I guess you're right."

So I said, "I think I'll just call the police."

And she said, "That's a good idea."

In a little while, two policemen came. I don't believe in taking the law in your own hands. I believe in the law taking care of legal things. Two policemen and I went in on the west side, which would be on the Sullivan Street entrance. They heard the hammering, too. It was Sybil and me and two policemen—four grown, mature folks. Minden citizens that hear hammering. And you could hear the nails going in. *Blam, blam, blam.* We thought maybe the old lady had fallen in and was trying to hammer on the floor and get somebody's attention. That was really what we thought. As you go in, you take a left and there's a room there. There's old curtains that just flip and flop around, spider webs, and all this kind of stuff—ghostly looking stuff in there! Old furniture that was mildewed. The hammering sounded like it was in there. Three of us went in. Sybil stayed outside because she wanted to see if anybody ran out of the house. She was going to watch for that.

So us three, the three of us grown men, go into that room right there where we thought we heard the hammering. It stopped. Give us a few minutes, though, and the hammering starts in the next room. So we said, "Oh, it just sounded like it was in here." So we go to the next room, and when we all three of us got into that room, the hammering stopped. You don't believe this, ask Sybil. I've forgotten who the two policemen were. There's an old staircase; it's really creaky. Spider webs everywhere. Dead spiders, roaches [makes a crunching noise], all this kind of stuff on that staircase. Three grown men begin to hear some hammering upstairs. We said, "Somebody is staying ahead of us."

So we go up the stairs, enter into a big old bedroom up there, and the hammering stops. [Laughs.] Goes into the attic. They get out them big old flashlights, big beams. It was dark up there in that attic. Shine that light all around, nobody up there. We went through every room, every closet, everything about that old house. Until this day, though, we have not found anybody hammering on anything or a hammer.

Now, you tell me where four adults can hear hammering move from room to room, and, my friends, there's something going on. Each of us will swear to you on a stack of Bibles, cross our hearts and hope to die, that we heard this hammering move from room to room in that old house. We've never had it happen again or since then. Course, they tore the old house down. It's gone.

Paula Brown

MINDEN, WEBSTER PARISH

Recorded at the Germantown Festival, on May 12, 1990, from Paula Brown, a seven-year-old child.

181. Bloody Mary

The story's called "Bloody Mary" and Karen Smith told it to me at school after the lights went out at school. She said her big sister told it to her.

Well see, ten years ago, at our school, this girl, she said she was an alien from another planet. She was disguised in the human form of a body. And these two fifth graders didn't like her. And see, she was a fourth grader. And that day they had brought a knife to school and they took her in the bathroom and cut up her stomach and superglued it on her hands. They told the principal that she had died in a car wreck. Karen says, everytime the lights go out, that she comes out and haunts the schools.

Harriet Lewis

BENTON, BOSSIER PARISH

The following two stories are a dialogue between a daughter, Harriet Lewis, and her mother, Lucille Culbertson, both British Americans. The first story is told by Lewis. Recorded at Minden's Germantown Festival, May 12, 1990.

182. The Headless Man of Black Bayou

I got my lore on the area and began to learn, not from the books, but from being probably the only white child up and down that road for about six miles one way and three the other. Very restricted. Supposed to stay on my own forty acres. That didn't always happen.

Mama had a lady named Evie that came to help. She had to help Mama, supposedly, with the wash and with the housecleaning. But Mama had two very active children at the time she moved out there, and managed to have three more by the time we got me up to adulthood. So they were helping Mama in more than one way.

So Evie was out washing, right? Evie was somebody new on the place every now and then. So nothing would do but that I was going to talk to Evie, and Evie began to talk to me.

And it came about with little things she'd say like, "Ooh, there goes such-and-so down the road. It's getting late. I better get through with my work, too." And Evie was ever grateful when we'd drive her home from work because people back in those days walked up and down the roads. They walked to the jobs and walked home in the evenings. If you saw somebody out late in the evening walking down those dirt roads, you saw somebody in a hurry. They didn't want to get caught down there after dark, which makes sense in the country. But it also makes sense in another way, too.

My home was up on a hill. Down in the valley, the slope of that hill was Black Bayou, which has now been converted, part of it, into Black Bayou Lake. But then it was a bayou, and in those hills, it was nice and sunshiny on top of the hill, but down in the valleys, the trees hung over the roads and along the waterways. It was dark down on the bayou. No one wanted to walk down the hill, across that one, single-lane, gravel-roaded bridge and back up on the other side. They just didn't want to walk down on that bridge. Evie told me because there's things down there.

I said, "What kind of things?"

She said, "Now, now, you don't believe in ghosts, do you?"

I said, "No, Evie, I don't believe in ghosts."

She said, "You hadn't ever seen anything down there?"

"Uh uh, I hadn't seen anything down there. Come on, Evie, what happened? What's down there? What have you heard?"

She didn't want to put ideas into my head, and she was a little reluctant at first to tell me. But then Evie began to tell me things. Long time ago, down at that bridge, Evie told me, there was some men that had gotten very angry with some other man. They had gotten angry to the point that they had taken that man out and hung him on a limb.

[Whispering.] His body had hung out on a limb over that bayou. And, Evie told me, that ever since that time, there was occasionally somebody that walked across that bridge, real slow-like, right at dusk when you can't see well. And he would never say anything to anybody, he never bothered anybody, but if they just happened to look right as they were walking by, they'd noticed, he didn't have a head! So they were very reluctant to be caught down on the bayou right at dark. They didn't want to see that man!

Lucille Culbertson

BENTON, BOSSIER PARISH

183. Evie Sees the Headless Man

Harriet did not mention [that] Evie saw the headless man one time. Only once in all those years. It was quite late. She and her friend Katie had stayed a bit late, and they were on their way home. Katie could talk faster than any human I've ever seen in my life. You've heard a sewing machine go clattering away. The more excited Katie got, the faster she talked. I've never ceased to be amazed at her quick speech. They were going along, and [Evie] said, "We were just talking and we saw a man in work clothes coming up the other side of the hill. We were going down the hill, down towards that bridge." She said, "You don't really stare at people. That's just not good to do. But I noticed his feet. And I said, 'Kate, do you see somebody?'"

Katie was short, and Evie was tall and angular. And she said [very fast], "Yes Miss Evie, *IthinkIseehim!*"

And Evie said, "Well, is that anybody you know?"

She said, "I think I recognize his old—oh my!"

And she said, "Katie said for us to run!" And she said, "I outrun Katie because we looked at that man to see who he was, and he did not have a head. I saw it myself one time."

But she didn't tell me that for two years. She had to know me well before she admitted she'd seen the headless man herself.

Mildred Osborne

STONEWELL, DESOTO PARISH

Recorded at the Louisiana Blueberry Festival in Mansfield, June 16, 1990, from Mildred Osborne, who traces her family roots to England, Scotland, and Ireland. In keeping with the book's editorial policy, the editors tried to title this story "Who's Going to Sleep with Me?" But Mildred Osborne insisted, "My family would hardly recognize the story without 'Gon'na.' Generations of children have asked grandmas to tell 'Who's Gon'na Sleep with Me?'"

184. Who's Gon'na Sleep with Me?

Mama had a scary story she used to tell us, "Who's Gon'na Sleep with Me on This Long, Lonesome Night?" She used to tell us about this lady who lived in Stonewall, off Red Bluff Road. She lived way, way back in the woods.

This lady was real old, but all of her neighbors would come every day to check on her, and see if she was okay. Every evening, she'd cook dinner, and one of her neighbors would come and eat with her and then spend the night so that she didn't have to stay alone at night.

Well, this evening, the lady was cooking up some turnip greens and cornbread. They were almost done, so she stepped out on the front porch and said, "Who's gon'na sleep with me on this long, lonesome night?"

"I will," said a voice way down the road.

So she went back in and started getting the tea ready, the table ready, because she knew company would be there soon to eat with her and spend the night. Well, it's all done and it's time to put it on the table, but no one's in the house yet. So she went back to the door, she opened it up, stepped on the porch, and she said, "Who's gon'na sleep with me on this long, lonesome night?"

And a voice from the woods across the street said, "I will."

Now, she knows they're right by, so she went ahead and put supper on the table. She sat down, nobody knocked on the door. She waited and she waited, nobody came. She stepped back to the door, and by this time it was getting dark. She just peeped outside and said, "Who's gon'na sleep with me on this long, lonesome night?"

And a voice out at the barn said, "I will." Now, the lady didn't recognize this voice. She's never heard this person come and spend the night with her before, and she's beginning to get worried. But she knows she can't stay there by herself. Well, she waited and waited, nobody came. She went back to the door, opened it up a little bit and said, "Who's gon'na sleep with me on this long, lonesome night?"

"I will," said a voice in the yard.

She closed the door and waited by it to see who would come up on the porch. She didn't hear any footsteps. Nobody was there. So she opened the door a little bit, "Who's gon'na sleep with me on this long, lonesome night?"

And a voice right on the porch said, "Gotcha!"

Allen Babineaux

NEW IBERIA, IBERIA PARISH

Recorded September 15, 1990, at Lafayette's Festivals Acadiens, from Allen Babineaux, a Cajun formerly from New Iberia. Babineaux was the fire chief of the New Iberia Fire Department.

185. A Holy Tree

There is a story that is told about a holy tree. That intrigued me, and after some years I decided to try something. There had been a drought for several months. The farmers needed water badly for their crops. Well, I had been fishing in the lake, and on the way back, I decided to go by this holy tree to sprinkle water on this tree and ask the good Lord for rain. God, the farmers needed water badly.

So I did that. And that tree was only about a 150 feet from the boat landing. When I got to the boat landing, while pulling the boat up, and before I get the boat on the trailer, it started to pour down rain. Well, it hadn't rained hard in months. I said, "I can't believe that this thing is true."

The story of the beliefs of the holy tree is that, at some point many years ago a white man showed up. He was running away from the Attakpas tribe that wanted to kill him. He asked the Chitimacha for protection, to hide him from the Attakapas. They agreed to do that.

While he was living with them, he taught them how to raise . . . various crops. He taught them a lot of things to better their lives, about medicine and such.

But one day, the Attakapas finally found out that he was hiding among this small Chitimacha tribe. A scout came over and said, "They are on their way to get this man and kill him."

So [the white man] said, "Well, I'm not going to put you in jeopardy; I'm going to leave. But bring me over to this cypress tree."

So he went right opposite the chief's mound to this huge cypress tree on the banks of Bayou Portage, right across from the chief's mound. That man climbed the tree. Before getting to the top of the tree, he told them, "Anything you need, ask for it at this tree. And if you ask for something sincerely, and it is sincerely needed, I will grant it."

Supposedly the man climbed to the top of the tree and actually ascended, in front of their eyes, into heaven. So they believe that this indeed must have been God. And they revered this tree as a holy tree from then on and asked for favors when needed. They claim, through the years, many times they've gotten rain by asking for it at this tree.

So the first time I go by the tree and ask for rain after a dry period, it rained! I said, "Oh well, that's just one of those things." I'm not superstitious.

Well, sometime later, the same thing happened. There was a dry period, I happen to be fishing, I noticed the water's way down. We needed rain. Cane farmers sorely needed it. I said, "I'm going to do this again, just to see what happens."

And it happened again. I sprinkle water on that tree, I asked for rain. I said, "Lord, I'm not superstitious. I'm not worshipping any tree. But I'm asking for water, for rain, at this tree." And it rained before I got to the landing, which was 150 feet away!

Well, I told my wife about this, and she laughed. One day, she was fishing with me and my stepson. We're coming in, and I said, "We don't really need rain that badly, but I'm going to sprinkle the tree, and we'll see what happens."

And I did. I hit the paddle on the water, let the water splash against the tree, and I said, "God, please let it rain."

When we got to the landing, it started to rain. Immediately, Anne said, "Well, there was a cloud up there and it was about to bust loose anyway."

I said, "Anne, this is three out of three."

So that went on to the sixth time, and I'm telling you the truth. For six times out of six times that I've gone to this tree and asked during a drought, it has actually rained. And rained within five minutes. A big rain. A good downpour. So it makes you wonder, "What is this, a coincidence?" I believe in coincidences, but six out of six gets you to wondering what goes on with this tree.

But the Indian tribes revered this tree as a holy tree. The tree, I know, was over a hundred years old. Hurricanes have knocked it down since. The tree had been pulled over to the bank of Bayou Portage. The last time that rain was asked for, the tree was actually down and lying on the bank. And it rained. So there are a lot of theories about this, but I seem to think that, maybe, there's a pipeline from that tree area all the way to the good Lord!

Joe Fedele

TICKFAW, TANGIPAHOA PARISH

Recorded by Harry Becnel, August 25, 1983, from Joe Fedele, Italian, who lives right outside of Tickfaw, where the Mother of Grace Chapel is located.

186. A Miracle at the Mother of Grace Chapel

The chapel was just used on a yearly basis until one year, Mrs. Mary Macaluso put a wreath of roses on the statue. Like fifteen years ago. Maybe not that long. . . . She put a wreath. They called it the May Crowning of the

Mother of Grace. I think it's the fifteenth day of May. So she got the wreath from Hammond Church and brought it over here . . . Mary Macaluso. In her mind, she watched this wreath. They thought it would never die. The roses would stay perfect. . . . I would say they stayed from sixty to ninety days, until the word got out that this wreath was on the statue here. And then people would come from all over to visit this chapel and see this wreath. Then . . . our parish priest, he started a rosary once a week, Monday nights. About ninety days after. . . . And they would watch them until people would hear this, and they begin to steal a bud of roses. Then Father found out there were a couple of buds missing, so he asked Mrs. Mary Macaluso to frame it, date it, then put it away. Because he didn't think it would stay there. People would come by here from different areas, different states, and they would take items from the chapel.

Clifford Blake, Sr.

NATCHITOCHES, NATCHITOCHES PARISH

This and other tales by Blake appear on the 1980 LP recording, Cornbread for Your Husband, and Biscuits for Your Man: Mr. Clifford Blake, Sr., Calls the Cotton Press, *produced by the Louisiana Folklife Center. The original recording was made June 3, 1979, by Nicholas R. Spitzer at Blake's home in Natchitoches. Clifford Blake, an African American, is now deceased.*

187. Mr. Blue and the Dog Ghost

There was a fellow called Mr. Blue, from Shamrock. We had to pass by a grave. I said, "Mr. Blue," I said, "looka here, I got to go home."

He said, "Oh, no, man." He said, "You working now. We done did our job, so we going to park the truck and you going to help me haul some hay."

See, we was supposed to get back about ten o'clock that night. We passed by a grave on the side of the road. Had a little old mule called Jim. That little old mule snorted. I said, "Looka here. My daddy always told me when a mule snorts, there's ghosts around." He said, "Man, ain't no such thing as ghosts."

About that time, when he said that, this white dog jumped on that mule. And you talk about running! Me and him jumped out the wagon. Every time we looked behind us, we could hear something blowin, *Shhoo!*

We run about three miles, and them mules right behind us. Instead of stopping and getting back in the wagon, we ain't had time. We stayed just ahead of them mules, not to catch the wagon. But we run. It was a natural ghost.

PART IV

Beyond the Everyday World

Myths,
Animal Tales, and Magic Tales

Julia Dupuis Huval

CECILIA, ST. MARTIN PARISH

Julia Dupuis Huval, a Cajun who narrates tales in French Creole, is known by her neighbors as a great comedian. She was born and raised in Nina, a small community near Henderson, and now lives in neighboring Cecilia. Her grandfather and her mother, both from Arnaudville, were great storytellers. Huval explained that her mother told stories to her grandchildren in French. One of the favorite stories was one that her mother had learned at a picture show. After seeing a film about Uncle Remus (Walt Disney's Song of the South [1946]), she returned home and told the story of the young boy crying at the end of the film for Uncle Remus not to leave. Although Huval would have loved to continue the tradition and tell stories to her grandchildren, few of them spoke French, and it was very hard for her to translate them into English. Her repertoire includes jokes, Bouki and Lapin tales, and a wonderful märchen, "Quatorze." The following two stories were collected on February 16, 1993 by Annette Huval.

188. La chaudiérée de couche-couche (The Pot Full of Couche-Couche)

Bouki té gain un clos de coton qu'il était apé couper. Il a engagé Lapin pour vini aider li piocher le coton.

Et Bouki dit à Lapin, li dit, "Mo fait une chaudiérée de couche-couche. Pour quand nos va lâcher à midi nos sera gain du couche-couche. So bien sûr [Lapin] carrément, li commencé calculer comment li sé vini manger le couche-couche.

So li était après piocher un peu li dit, "Écoute toi, écoute toi, Bouki,

Bouki had a cotton field that he was chopping. He hired Lapin to come help pick cotton.

And Bouki says to Lapin, he says, "I'm making a pot full of couche-couche. When we take a break, we will have some couche-couche." So, of course, Lapin, right off, he started to figure how he could come and eat the couche-couche.

So, when he's been picking a little while, he says, "Listen, listen, Bouki,

This crawfish boil at Louis and Susan Mire's house provides a setting for swapping stories among friends and family. Photo: Maida Owens.

écoute toi. Il y a quelqu'un qu'après pélé moi pour un baptême."

"O," li dit, "Lapin."

Li dit, "Mo dis toi. Mo prometté mo sé couri tient un baptême."

"Ben," li dit, "Va mais reviens tout de suite."

Ça fait li va à la cuisine et li mangé un peu de couche-couche. Et li retourné dans le clos.

Bouki dit, "Comment yé pélé le petit là?"

Li dit, "Commencement."

Yé pioché un peu, yé pioché un peu. Lapin était largué. Li té gain chaud.

Li dit, "Écoute toi, écoute toi. Mais tu crois ça, quelqu'un d'autre apé pélé moi pour mo va tient un baptême."

listen. There's somebody calling me to a baptism."

"Oh," he says, "Lapin."

He says, "I tell you. I promised to go to a baptism."

"Good," he says, "Go, but come back right away."

So he goes to the kitchen, and he ate a little couche-couche. And he came back to the field.

Bouki says, "What did you name the little one?"

He says, "Beginning."

They picked a little, they picked a little. Lapin was tired. He was hot.

He said, "Listen, listen. Do you think that someone else is calling me to take part in a baptism?"

"Va, Lapin, mais sois sûr to reviens tout de suite."

"Okay, Bouki, m'a revenir."

Li arrive là-bas. Li mangé un peu de couche-couche.

Quand li retourné là-bas, Bouki dit, "Comment yé pélé cil-là?"

"Mais," li dit. "La Moitié."

Li dit, "La Moitié."

Yé pioché un autre moment, c'est té fait chaud. Lapin dit, "Il y a quelqu'un qu'apé pélé moi."

Li dit, "C'est pas pour un baptême."

"Mais," li dit, "Ça doit être. To connais mo tiens tous les petits en baptême moi."

Li dit, "Va mais reviens tout de suite."

So *retourné là-bas et li mangé tout le couche-couche.*

Quand li revini Bouki dit, "Comment yé pélé cil-là?"

"Mais," li dit, "yé appelé li Gratter Fond."

Quand yé vini pour lâcher, yé té apé marcher et Lapin té marché un petit peu derrière. Bouki té devant li. Bouki dit, "N'a pour aller manger couche-couche."

Quand yé arrivé dans la cuisine, Lapin fait comme si li était après laver ses mains dehors.

Bouki regarde dans la chaudière et il n'avait pu de couche-couche. So Bouki met ça tout ensemble que Lapin té tout mangé le couche-couche. Et le dernier petit c'était "Gratter Fond." So li té tout mangé li.

"Go, Lapin, but be sure to come back right away."

"Okay, Bouki, I'm coming back."

He gets there. He eats a little couche-couche.

When he returns, Bouki says, "What did they name this one?"

"Oh," he says. "Half."

He says, "Half."

They picked a while longer. It's very hot. Lapin says, "There's someone calling me."

He says, "It's not for a baptism."

"Oh," he says, "but it must be. You know that I go for the baptisms of all the babies."

He says, "Go, but come back right away."

So he went back and he ate all the couche-couche.

When he came back, Bouki says, "What did they name this one?"

"Oh," he says, "Scrape-the-Bottom."

When it was time to rest, they were walking, and Lapin was walking a little behind. Bouki saw in front of him. Bouki says, "Now let's go eat couche-couche."

When they got to the kitchen, Lapin acts as if he's washing his hands outside.

Bouki looks in the pot, and there wasn't any more couche-couche. So Bouki put it all together and figured out that Lapin had eaten all the couche-couche. And the last baby was "Scrape-the-Bottom." So he ate it all.

189. Quartorze (Fourteen)

*Sa maman avait été remariée.
Son beau-père voulait plus il reste.
Il n'avait pas assez de manger pour
lui. So il fallait il part. C'était le
temps il part. Et sa maman lui a dit
fallait il part faire sa vie. Li était
assez vieux pour faire sa vie. Et elle
l'a donné un* cap, *et elle l'a donné
du sirop, et puis une aiguille, et une
peau de mouton, et du fil. Elle dit,
"Les affaires t'auras de besoin dans
ta vie."*

*O, il a marché, il a marché, il a
marché. Il était lasse. So il s'est assis
dessus le bord d'un fossé ou quelque
chose. Et il a mis son* cap *par terre.
Là il a ouvert son* can *de sirop.
Avant il met son* cap *par terre, il a
ouvert son* can *de sirop et li était apé
licher son sirop. Et le bec de son* cap *a
été dans le sirop. So il a ôté son* cap
*et l'a mis par terre. Et les mouches a
été dessus le* cap. *So il a tapé, puis il
a tué quatorze mouches. So quand
il est venu pour mettre son* cap, *il a
pris un petit bâton, et il a passé ça
dans la boue. Puis il a marqué "Tué
Quatorze." Mais il a pas dit qui c'est
il avait tué. So n'importe éyoù il
arrivait, ça voulait connaître ce qu'il
avait tué. Il disait, "Tué quatorze."
C'est tout il répondait. Il a jamais dit
qu'il avait tué quatorze mouches.*

*Là, il a parti puis il a été rejoindre
un bourreau dans le bois. Il avait
marché, il avait marché jusqu'à il
avait arrivé à la maison du bourreau.*

His mama had remarried. His stepfather didn't want him to stay home; he didn't have enough for him to eat. So he had to go. It was time for him to go, and his mother told him that he had to go out and make a living. He was old enough to make his living. And she gave him a cap, and she gave him some cane syrup, and also a needle, and a sheepskin, and some thread. She says, "You will need these things to make a living."

Oh, he walked, he walked, he walked. He was tired. So he sat down on the bank of a creek or something. And he set his cap on the ground. Then he opened his can of syrup. And the brim of his cap got in the syrup. So he pulled out his cap and put it on the ground. And the flies got on the cap. So he hit it, and he killed fourteen flies. So when time came to put on his cap, he took a little stick, and he ran it through the mud. And he wrote, "Killed Fourteen" [on his cap]. But he didn't say *what* he had killed. So, no matter where he went, they wanted to know what he killed. He would say, "Killed Fourteen." That's all that he answered. He never said that he had killed fourteen flies.

Then he set out again, and he met an executioner in the woods. He'd walked, he'd walked until he'd come to the executioner's house—and the

Et la vieille femme qui soignait la place. Quand il a frappé à la porte, et lui, il a demandé s'il pouvait rentrer.

Elle dit, "Cher, tu peux pas venir ici. Le bourreau est mauvais."

Il dit, "J'ai pas peur."

"Mais," elle dit, "Rentre. Je vas te donner à manger."

So *il a rentré et elle l'a donné à manger. Un moment après ça le bourreau arrivait.*

Il dit, "Qui c'est t'après faire ici?" Mais il a vu "Tué Quatorze," so il connaissait pas ce qui c'était.

Il dit, "Je veux travailler. Tu veux me donner de l'ouvrage pour mon manger?"

"Mais," il dit, "All right. *Reste. Va coucher en haut."*

Avant il part pour coucher, c'est là où il a dit, il dit, "Demain, on va aller chercher du bois dans le bois."

Quand il a descendu, il a été au magasin chercher un cable.

L'homme a dit, "Je suis parti chercher un arbre dans le bois."

Arrivé avec le cable, l'homme dit, "C'est qui tu veux faire avec ça?"

"Mais," il dit, "J'ai pas pour amener juste un [arbre]." Il dit, "Je vas amarrer un puis je vas tous les amarrer, puis on va haler—"

"O," il dit, "Non, laisse ça. Je vas aller le chercher moi tout seul."

Il dit à le petit garçon, "Demain," il dit, "On va aller chercher un baril d'eau."

woman who looked after the place. Then he knocked at the door, and he asked if he could enter.

She says, "*Cher,* you can't come here. The executioner is evil."

He says, "I'm not afraid."

"Okay," she says, "come in. I'm going to give you something to eat."

So he came in, and she gave him something to eat. A moment later the executioner arrived. He says, "What are you doing here?" But he saw "Killed Fourteen"—so he didn't know what it was.

He says, "I want to work. Do you want to give me work for my food?"

"Okay," he says, "All right. Stay. Go sleep upstairs."

Before he goes to bed, he said, "Tomorrow, we're going to get wood in the forest."

When he came downstairs, [the boy] went to the barn looking for a rope.

The man said, "I'm off to find a tree in the woods."

[When the boy] returned with the rope, the man said, "What are you going to do with that?"

"Oh," he says, "I'm not going to get just one [tree]." He says, "I'm going to tie up one, and I'm going to tie them all together, and we're going to haul—"

"Oh," he says, "No, drop it. I'm going out to get it all alone."

He says to the little boy, "Tomorrow," he says, "we're going to get a barrel of water."

So *le lendemain matin, lève. Il a été chercher une pelle.*

Il dit, "Qui c'est que tu veux faire avec ça?"

"Mais," il dit, "Tu crois pas j'ai pour aller chercher un baril d'eau tous les jours." Il dit, "Je vas fouiller tout le puits."

"O," il dit, "Laisse ça." Il dit, "Moi je vas amener."

Il dit à la vieille femme, il dit, "Met tout le lait tu peux dans des bols." Puis il dit, "Demain on va connaître quel qui peut boire [plus] de lait ou plus de caillé.

Le petit garçon dit, "C'est là où je vas user ma peau de mouton." So il a été en haut, et il a coudu la peau de mouton avec son aiguille. Puis il l'a mis là. [Le conteur signe jusqu'au cou.]

Le lendemain matin, ils ont levé. La vieille femme avait des bols de lait et de caillé dessus la table. Il prenait un bol, l'autre prenait un. Il prenait un, l'autre prenait un.

L'homme a dit, "Mais tant qu'à ça. Mais ça c'est un petit qui peut boire du lait. Un jeune petit garçon."

"So," il dit, "Là asteur allons voir quel qu'a bu plus."

Le petit garçon dit, "Comment on va connaître?"

"Mais," il dit, "on va fendre le ventre."

Le petit garçon dit, "Tu peux fendre le mien premier."

So the sun comes up the next day. He went to find a shovel.

He says, "What are you going to do with that?"

"Oh," he says, "do you think I'm going to get a barrel of water every day?" He says, "I'm going to dig the whole well."

"Oh," he says, "drop it." He says, "I'll go get [the barrel]."

He speaks to the little boy. He speaks to the old woman, he says, "Put all the milk that you can in the bowls." Then he says, "Tomorrow we will know who can drink the most milk and eat the most cottage cheese."

The little boy says [to himself], "This is how I'm going to use my sheepskin." So he went upstairs, and he sewed up the sheepskin with his needle. Then he put it there [the teller gestures right under her neck].

The next morning they got up. The old woman had the bowls of milk and cottage cheese on the table. [The man] drank a bowlful, [the boy] drank a bowlful. One ate a bowlful, the other ate a bowlful.

The man said, "But enough of that. There's a boy who can really drink some milk. A young little boy."

"So," he says, "Now we're going to see who drank the most."

The little boy says, "How are we going to find out?"

"Well," he says, "we're going to slit open our stomachs."

The little boy says, "You can slit mine open first."

Quand il a fondu le petit garçon, ça pas tué le petit garçon.

So il dit, "Laisse moi fendre le tien asteur."

So quand il l'a fendu. Il a tué le bourreau. So c'était lui le maître de la maison après ça.

Then he slashed the little boy; it didn't kill the little boy.

So he says, "Let me slash your stomach now."

So then he slashed him. He killed the executioner. So he was the master of the house after that.

Max Greig

ST. MARTINVILLE, ST. MARTIN PARISH

Recorded on August 20, 1990, by C. Renée Harvison from Max Greig, eighty, a Cajun. He said that when he was growing up in St. Martinville in the earlier part of the century, he often heard Bouki and Lapin stories from the Creoles.

190. Bouki and Lapin in the Garden

Mr. Lapin had been, the little rabbit, he was a soft little cookie. He would go into Mr. Bouki's every night and eat up all his vegetables. Mr. Bouki decided he was going to make a little tarbaby. He put the little tarbaby in the garden, and the little rabbit, Lapin, came there at night.

He said, "Little man, what the heck are you doing here at night?"

Naturally, the little tarbaby couldn't talk. So the little rabbit said, "I'm going to slap the hell out of you with my right hand paw."

Slapped him and then his hand stayed caught. Left hand—*bam*—stayed caught. Each leg, kicked. They were all stuck. Belly. Hit him with his belly. That stayed stuck. The next morning, Mr. Bouki got up and went to his garden. Said, "Ah! You little rascal, I finally got you."

He said, "Mr. Bouki, please. Throw me in the fire, throw me in the water, but don't throw me in that briar patch across the fence. That's going to cut up all my skin." What you think that Mr. Bouki did? He throwed the little rabbit right in that briar patch. Put him at home.

The little rabbit run off and said, "You see? I'm smarter than you are!" So that's the story of Bouki and Lapin.

Nicholas L. Stouff, Jr.

JEANERETTE, ST. MARY PARISH

The following two stories were recorded from Nicholas L. Stouff, Jr., a Native American of the Chitimacha culture, at the St. Francisville Heritage Celebration, September 22,

Nick Stouff, a Chitimacha Indian, tells stories in the Storytelling
Pavilion at the Fete du Blé in Marksville during 1990 Open House.
Photo: Dayna Lee.

*1990. Stouff is a past tribal chairman of the Chitimacha nation in Charenton. A
nephew of a former chief of the Chitimacha, Stouff is well-versed in Native American
traditions, including storytelling, silver work, and carving.*

191. A Chitimacha Flood Story

We have a flood story that says when this flood came, that Noah was
building this ark for, we built a big clay pot. And we're riding out the flood
in the clay pot. Here comes two rattlesnakes who say, "We want to ride out
the flood in the pot." Say, "We're about to drown out here."

And Chitimacha and rattlesnake argued back and forth like two little
children all day long, "No" and "Yes" and "No" and "Yes."

It gets around to about dark, rattlesnakes say, "Look, we've gotta get
in that pot. We're about to drown here." Say, "We'll make a peace pact with
you. We promise if you let us ride out the flood, we'll never bite Chitimacha
again."

So rattlesnake became the totem of the Chitimacha people.

When the Indian boy went through his rituals to become a man, he
tatooed a rattlesnake on his chest to show that he was Chitimacha.

192. How Bayou Teche Was Formed

Teche is an Indian word for "snake." It seems that way back there, this big snake crawled out of the Gulf. His tail was at Atchafalaya Bay here in Morgan City. His head was up above Arnaudville over there. And he was just tearing up everything that come along. Man, he was doing some damage. So all the nations in the Gulf Coast area got together and they killed this snake. Now, when this snake died, his wiggling death like that dug out what is the Bayou Teche today.

Sarah Albritton

RUSTON, LINCOLN PARISH

Recorded September 16, 1993, by Pat Mire and Maida Owens for the video documentary, Swapping Stories. *Sarah, an African American, took a break from working at her restaurant, Sarah's Kitchen, to tell stories.*

193. She Has the Key

God made man. We were equal with man at one time, but after Eve convinced Adam to eat the fruit, God placed the man over the woman.

So, this woman, she married this man, and he ruled her with a iron hand. He didn't do anything—she had to do all the work—and she could not say a word, she couldn't complain, because God had given them men all the power.

So, she got a little unruly. She started talking back to him. And he decided he better go back and talk with the Lord again, so he'd get just a little more power.

So he went back and told the Lord his wife had started grumbling and talking back to him—he needed just a little more power to keep them under control.

So, the Lord says, "Okay, your wish is granted."

So, he went back home. He was harder on the woman than he'd ever been, because this power. And the lady got to thinking one day, she said, "Why can't I go to God?"

So, she decided, well, I'm just going to go through God and ask him to help me too and give *me* some of that power. So, she got up, and she walked the stairway to heaven, and she says, "Lord: See, my husband—he work me to death, he's mean, he's hateful, and I can't complain, I can't say anything, because you gave him all that power." She said, "Would you just give me a *little* power, so I can control him some?"

The Lord thought about it for a while, and he said, "Here." He passed her a key.

So, she looked at the key, went home. She thought about the key and thought, "Now, what good is a key? That's not power."

And the Lord says to her in a quiet voice, "Just lock the door."

So, she locked the door, and that's how the—[laughs] the woman gained control over the man: with the key locking the door. [Laughs.]

Joseph "Chelito" Campo

DELACROIX ISLAND, ST. BERNARD PARISH

The following two Isleño tales were collected by Samuel G. Armistead from Joseph "Chelito" Campo on January 4, 1981.

194. La tortuga y el conejo (The Turtle and the Rabbit)

Samuel G. Armistead: *¿Usted nos podría contar eso del conejo y la cauén?*

Chelito Campo: *Oh, la cauén. Hicieron [una porfía] la cauén y el conejo. El conejo lo dijo a la cauén, dice:—Es imposible. Tú no me puedes ganar. Dice: ¿Cómo me vas a ganar, dice, con [que] te coges tanto tiempo?*

Y ella dice:—Dame nueve días, para yo pensar lo que vamos a hacer y yo te voy a ganar.

—Está bien.—

En nueve días, se juntó con todítas las otras cauenes, ¿sabe? y les dijo:—Escucha, yo voy a ir a la punta, porque él me conoce, allá donde él tiene que parar, dice, y tú, que te pareces a mí, ponte aquí. Dice: Y el conejo va a venir, y dice, y va

Samuel G. Armistead: Could you tell us that one about the rabbit and the terrapin?

Chelito Campo: Oh, the terrapin. They had [an argument,] the terrapin and the rabbit. The rabbit said to the terrapin, he says: "It's impossible. You can't win," he says. "How're you going to beat me," he says, "when it takes you so long?"

And he says: "Give me nine days so I can think out what we're going to do and I'll beat you."

"Okay."

During those nine days, he got together with every one of the other turtles and he said to them: "Listen, I'm going to go to the finish line, because he knows me, over there where he's got to stop," he says, "and you, who look just like me, you stand

a pasar a la cauén y, para cuando
llegue a donde para, ahí está la
cauén.—¿Sabe?

here." He says: "And the rabbit's
going to come along," and he says,
"and he's going to pass the terrapin,
but when he gets to the finish line,
the terrapin is [already] there." You
know?

Y así fue andando, llegando
a donde tenía que ir y allí estaba
la cauén y dice:—Pero, ¿Cómo te
hiciste?

Dice:—Yo no sé. Dice: Yo hay
tiempo que estoy esperando por ti aquí.
[Laughs.]

So he kept going, approaching to
where he had to go and there was the
terrapin and he says: "How did you
go about doing it?"

He says: "I don't know." He says:
"I've been waiting quite a while for
you here." [Laughs.]

195. La Muerte compadre (The Partnership with Death)

Dice: Ese era uno que le dijo
la Muerte, le dijo a él:—Escucha
(porque le cristianó un niño.)
¿Sabe? Y le dijo:—Quiero ser tu
compadre.

—Ay, está bueno eso.—

Dice que: Ahí, vino, dice:—Yo
quiero hacerte millonario, dice, porque
tú eres un gran amigo mío, dice, y yo
quisiera, ya yo estoy muerto, dice, pero
quisiera que usted fuera millonario,
dice.

—Está bien. Dice:—Escucha,
ya lo voy avisar a usted: Usted no
use medecina de ninguna clase.
Usted, cuando vaya a ver al enfermo,
dile que se acueste en su cama. Y
si usted me ve, por los pies, diga:
"No hay nada para hacer para él."
Pues si yo estoy por la cabecera,
le dice: "Yo cuento en él. El se
levanta ahora mismo, si yo quiero."
¿Ve?

It goes like this:—Once there
was this fellow to whom Death said:
"Listen"—He had baptized a child
for them, you know.—And Death said
to him: "I want to be your partner."

"Oh, that's okay."

Death came along and said: "I
want to make you a millionaire," he
says, "because you're a great friend of
mine," he says, "I'm already dead,"
he says, "but I'd like you to be a
millionaire," he says.

"That's okay." He says: "Listen, I'm
going to let you know: You're not to
use medicine of any kind. When you
go to see a sick person, tell him to lie
down on his bed. And if you see me at
the foot of the bed, you say: 'There's
nothing to be done for him.' If I'm
at the head of the bed, you tell him:
'I'm counting on him. He's going to
get up this very minute, if I want him
to.' See?"

*Dice que llegaba y le ponía
la mano a ése:—Amigo,
levántate, dice. Ya tú no
tienes nada. Tú no te vas a
morir.—*

*E iba a ver los otros y el otro, y le
decía al otro:—Tú no tienes chance
hoy. No te lo quiero esconder, porque
todos nos tenemos que ir, dise. Hoy
te toca a ti and mañana me toca
a mí. ¿Ve?* [laughs] *Y así como
pasó.*

*¡Ooy! Lo hizo millonario, ya lo
creo. A ver, los millonarios esos, que
tenían tanto dinero, ellos querían
pagar para vivir. ¿Sabe? Sí. Y ahí lo
hizo millonario.*

*Samuel G. Armistead:—¿Pero qué
pasó al final?*

*Chelito Campo: Sí. Bueno.
Cuando él* [laughs] *murió: ¿Ve?
Estaba malo, dice que vio al compadre
por los pies. Dice:—¡Eh! ¡Para
aquí! Compadre no le hacía caso.
Dice:—¡Para aquí! Dice:—¡Ahí, ahí,
me vas a llevar, hombre! Me estás
mirando.—* [laughs.] *Quería que se
viniera para la cabecera: ¿Sabe?* See?
[laughs.]

[The man] would come, he would
put his hand on whoever it was:
"Friend, get up," he says. "There's
nothing wrong with you any more.
You're not going to die."

And he'd go to see someone else
and he'd say to the other one: "Today
you don't have a chance. I don't want
to keep it from you, because all of
us have to go," he says. "Today it's
your turn *and* tomorrow it's mine."
See? [Laughs.] And that's the way it
happened.

Oh! [Death] made him a millionaire. You bet he did. Of course, all
those millionaires, who had so much
money, they wanted to pay so they
could live. You know? Sure. And
there he made him a millionaire.

Samuel G. Armistead: But what
finally happened?

Chelito Campo: Yeah. Well, when
he [laughs] died: See? He was sick.
The story goes that he saw his partner
at the foot of the bed. He says: "Heh!
Up here!" The partner didn't pay
any attention. He says: "Up here!"
He says: "Down there, down there,
you're going to carry me off, man!
You're looking at me." [Laughs.] He
wanted him to come up to the head
of the bed. You know? See? [laughs.]

Bertney Langley

ELTON, JEFFERSON DAVIS PARISH

*The following three stories were collected September 18, 1993, by Pat Mire and Maida
Owens for the video documentary, Swapping Stories. Bertney Langley, a Koasati
Indian and the nephew of Bel Abbey, shared these stories with his family in Elton.*

196. How the Koasati Got Their Name

Tonight I'll tell you all a story of how we got the name *Koasati. Koasati* means "lost tribe." A while back, when [we] were living around the Alabama area, our tribe decided to move. But it was decided that the whole tribe could not move together at once. So the council decided that part of the tribe would go ahead of us, and the second group would follow, after tying up loose ends. So the first group took off and left some signs for the other group to follow.

And maybe a week or so afterwards, the second group followed. And they followed the signs, I guess, halfway up to the Mississippi River. But they lost it right after that. And, to this day, we don't know what happened to the first group, but we assume they got swept up—maybe in a trail of tears movement—and got moved to Oklahoma. But we don't know where they at today—to this day. But our second group, when they went to the Mississippi River, they ran into some explorers who asked them who they were. But naturally, since they didn't understand the language, they said *Koasa* which means, *"we are lost."* So, up until that time, we don't know what name we went by, but the explorers wrote the name *Koasati* in their journals, so from that point on, we've been known as the *Koasati,* which means "lost people."

197. How the Bat Got Its Wings

I'm going to tell you how the bat got its wings. A long time ago, the bat was a little creature who didn't have any wings, but the Creator said, "One day out of the year, you will have a game—the animals will have a game."

So it was decided that they would choose up into two teams: one were the animals who didn't have wings, and one was the birds, who had wings. So there was a little creature out there who didn't—who didn't have any wings, so he wanted to play on the animals' side. But he went and asked the animals if he could play on their team, but he was too small. So they laughed at him and made fun of him and said, "You cannot play on our team."

So, he went to the birds' side and asked if he would play on their team. But, since he didn't have any wings, the birds said, "Well, we don't know how you can play with us, since you don't have any wings, and the rules are: you have to have wings to play on our side."

As they were talking, one of the birds said, "Well, let's see how we can help him. So, as they looked around, they saw . . . a top of a drum that was left by one of the Indians, so they took the skin off the drum and made wings for the birds and put wings on him and showed him how to fly.

But, since he was just a beginner, he didn't know how to fly. So they took him on top of the treetops and dropped him, and he did like that [waving hands]. He couldn't fly straight—he was going all over the place. "So," he said, "that's that—that's the best I can do."

They said, "Well, the game is getting too close. We can't teach you how to fly straight." So they went back and put him in. So as far as the game was played—let's say like in the fourth quarter, the animals were tied with the birds. So, at that time, they decided to put the bat in there.

And the bat went and got the ball, and he was going like—like this all over [waving hands]. And there was no way they could touch him. So, he scored the winning touchdown—we could say—for the birds. So, when the game was over, the animals said, "Who was that superstar that you all had that came and we couldn't touch him? There was no way we could stop him from scoring the winning goal."

When they came to find out it was the bat, they didn't know what to do, because they had made fun of him, and he had gone out of his way to go and play for the birds. But the moral of this story is that you can't make fun of anybody, no matter what size they are or how big they are or what they can do. You have to respect whoever they are for what they are and make sure that you give them the chance to participate. And the moral, like I said, is to respect people, and that is how we are told the bat story—how the bat got its wings.

198. Learning from the Bear

I want to tell you a story about how the Indian learned from the bear.

A long time ago the Indians had to learn from the animals on how to survive. Well, it came that there were two men out there hunting for food, and they saw a bear—so they shot it with an arrow. But you know how the bear won't die quickly with, you know, like a little arrow stuck in him. So, basically what they did was try to chase it down, and they . . . chased by the bear all over the place, but the bear wouldn't die, you know. So finally, the Indian said, "Let's watch from behind the tree and see what it does."

So, as they were watching, they saw the bear pull the arrow out, you know, with his teeth. And they said, "I wonder if he's going to die now." Well, they watched and watched, and finally, the bear was . . . kind of looking at that wound, and finally, the bear started going and looking for something. And, eventually, they saw the bear go to a pine tree. They saw this pine tree, and they said, "Well, maybe he's going to climb up there or something." But, while they were watching, he went and scratched the bark, you know, like this [makes a scratching motion with his hand]. And he did that and then the Indians wondered what he was doing. But they could see something with the sap coming out of the tree bark. So, as they were watching, they saw the bear take that and put that on his wound like this. And, basically, he was stopping the bleeding.

So, after a while, they watched it and finally he did that and it quit bleeding on him. And the bear left, and the Indian said, "Let's not go and kill the bear because we have learned a lesson from this bear." He said, "Now, when we see somebody wounded, maybe we can do the same thing: take some of that salve, cover it with that, and it'll stop the bleeding, and this might help us survive." So, basically that's how the Indian learned from the bear on how to survive. So, that's one of the stories we heard from my uncle a long time ago.

Dolores Henderson

MORGAN CITY, ST. MARY PARISH

The following two stories were recorded on September 1, 1990, by C. Renée Harvison from Dolores Henderson, African American. Although Henderson tells other stories she has heard from her storytelling friends, the story included here was told to her as a young child by her great-great uncle Johnny, who kept the family children entertained.

199. Old Woman and Her Pig

This is one my uncle used to tell us. There was an old woman, who went to the market and bought a pig. She was on the way back home, and the pig wouldn't jump over the stile. So she looked around to see if she could get help. She saw a dog. She said, "Dog, dog, bite pig. Pig will not jump over the stile, and I cannot get home tonight."

The dog said, "I won't."

So she looked around some more, and she saw a stick. She said, "Stick, stick, beat dog. Dog won't bite pig. Pig won't jump over the stile, and I cannot get home tonight."

The stick said, "I won't."

So she went a little piece, and she saw some fire. She said, "Fire, fire, burn stick. Stick won't beat dog. Dog won't bite pig. Pig won't jump over the stile, and I cannot get home tonight."

So the fire said, "I won't."

Then she met some water. She told the water, "Water, water, put out fire. Fire won't burn stick. Stick won't beat dog. Dog won't bite pig. Pig won't jump over the stile, and I cannot get home tonight."

The water said, "I won't."

So she met an ox. She said, "Ox, ox, drink the water. Water won't put out the fire. Fire won't burn stick. Stick won't beat dog. Dog won't bite pig. Pig won't jump over the stile, and I cannot get home tonight."

The ox said, "I won't."

She met a butcher. She said, "Butcher, butcher, kill ox. Ox won't drink the water. Water won't put out the fire. Fire won't burn stick. Stick won't beat dog. Dog won't bite pig. Pig won't jump over the stile, and I cannot get home tonight."

The butcher said, "I won't."

So, she was getting really discouraged and went a little piece further. She saw a rope. She said, "Rope, rope, tie the butcher. Butcher won't kill ox. Ox won't drink the water. Water won't put out the fire. Fire won't burn stick. Stick won't beat dog. Dog won't bite pig. Pig won't jump over the stile, and I cannot get home tonight."

The rope said, "I won't."

So a little piece further, she saw a mouse. She said, "Rat, rat, gnaw the rope. Rope won't tie the butcher. Butcher won't kill ox. Ox won't drink the water. Water won't put out the fire. Fire won't burn stick. Stick won't beat dog. Dog won't bite pig. Pig won't jump over the stile, and I cannot get home tonight."

The rat said, "I won't."

Really discouraged, she sees a cat. She said, "Cat, cat, eat the rat. Rat won't gnaw the rope. Rope won't tie the butcher. Butcher won't kill ox. Ox won't drink the water. Water won't put out the fire. Fire won't burn stick. Stick won't beat dog. Dog won't bite pig. Pig won't jump over the stile, and I cannot get home tonight."

The cat said, "I will, if you will give me a cool drink of milk." So the old lady did, and the cat began to eat the rat, the rat began to gnaw the rope, the rope began to tie the butcher, the butcher began to kill the ox, the ox began to drink the water, the water began to put out the fire, the fire began to burn the stick, the stick began to beat the dog, the dog began to bite the pig, and the pig jumped over the stile, and the old woman got home.

200. Brer Rabbit and Tarbaby

Brer Bear was getting tired of Brer Rabbit being too smart and too sassy. And Brer Rabbit was always getting away from him. So Brer Bear thought one day, he said, "I know what I'll do. I'll just make a little tarbaby and set him out here. Maybe that'll catch him if he gets stuck to it. Then I'll be able to catch that smart Brer Rabbit."

So Brer Rabbit was coming down the road, lickety split [sings], "*Do do do do, do do do do.*" That tarbaby is sitting over there, and Brer Rabbit says, "Morning."

Brer Tarbaby, he don't answer.

Brer Rabbit said, "Morning, I says."

Tarbaby, he don't answer.

So Brer Rabbit said, "If you don't say 'Good morning,' I'm going to haul off and hit you with my right foot.

Brer Tarbaby, he don't say nothing. So Brer Rabbit, he pulls that foot back and he gave it a whack! He gets stuck. Brer Rabbit, he don't give up yet.

Brer Rabbit says, "I told you, if you don't say 'Good morning,' I'm going to hit you with my left foot."

Brer Tarbaby, he don't say nothing. Brer Rabbit pulls that foot back, and *whack*!

He says, "You mighty impudent. I told you if you don't say 'Good morning,' I'm going to hit you with my right behind foot this time."

Brer Tarbaby, he don't say nothing. So Brer Rabbit takes that right behind foot, and whack! That gets stuck too!

He still not paying attention because all he wants is for Brer Tarbaby to say "Good Morning." So Brer Rabbit said, "If you don't say 'Good morning,' I'm going to haul off and hit you with my left behind foot." *Whack*!

Brer Rabbit, he's all stuck up. All four foots are stuck up in that tarbaby. Then he said, "I give you one more time to say 'Good morning. If you don't say 'Good morning, I'm going to butt you with my head."

Tarbaby, he don't say nothing.

So Brer Rabbit hits him with his head, he's all stuck up, and Brer Bear comes out of the woods. He says, "Ah ha! I got you now."

Brer Rabbit, he's trying to figure out what he's going to do. How is he going to get away?

So Brer Bear is thinking, "What am I going to do with him now? He's all stuck up."

Brer Bear, he's thinking about what to do, and while he's thinking, Brer Rabbit's already out-thunk him. Brer Rabbit says, "Do anything you want! You can do anything! You can throw me in the water. You can throw me off the cliff. But please don't throw me in the briar patch!"

Brer Bear's thinking, "He sure don't want to get thrown in that briar patch. Maybe that's what I should do."

So Brer Bear takes him, holds on careful not to hold onto that tar. He holds onto that rabbit, and he slings him in the briar patch!

Brer Rabbit, he's over there hollering and tusseling and moving. Brer Bear, he's mighty tickled because he knows he's got that old rabbit now. Before Brer Bear could raise his head up good, *shooom*! Brer Rabbit's going down the road lickety split, "Ha, ha, ha, ha! I told you, Brer Bear, you shouldn't pay attention to what I said because us rabbits was born in the briar patch."

Tang Thi Thanh Van

LAFAYETTE, LAFAYETTE PARISH

The following five folktales were recorded at the 1990 Louisiana Folklife Festival, November 3, 1990, from Tang Thi Thanh Van, a Vietnamese American woman. Van is originally from Saigon, but has been in Louisiana since the mid-1970s, where she is a teacher. She learned these folktales as a young child from her grandmother.

201. The Legend of the Mosquito

Long, long time ago, there was a couple. A young man and a young woman. They love each other very, very much. The man said, "I will never live without you." And the wife also say that. But the wife, deep inside herself, she's very coquette. She likes nice things, jewelry, big houses, you know, servants and all that. But the man, he just wants [a] simple life. But they live happily.

But all of a sudden one day, the wife died. The husband was so, so unhappy, and he didn't want to separate from his wife's body. So he put the body in a coffin. And he put the coffin in a small canoe. . . . He said, "I'm going to find someone with a magic to resuscitate my wife, because I cannot live without my wife."

He rowed, rowed his boat along, sailing through jungles and everything. One day, he stopped by a mountain. He saw a very old man. The old man asked him, "Why are you so sad?"

He said, "Because I lost my wife, and I want to find somebody who can make her live again so that we can live happily all the time."

So the old man said, "Young man, you don't know what you're asking for."

But the young man said, "Well, whatever happen, I will be happy if my wife live again."

So the old man said, "Well, I will grant you your wish." He said, "Open the coffin, and give me your finger."

So the young man opened the coffin and gave the finger. And the old man cut his finger and let three drops of blood to his wife's mouth so his wife live again. They thanked the old man, and they were so happy. So they started sailing home. On the way, he stopped at a small town to get some provisions. He told his wife, "Just stay here and rest. I will get out and get some food."

In the meantime, there's a beautiful boat. . . . In that boat was a man. Very rich man. He looked. He saw this beautiful woman. Then he invited her over to his boat to have conversation. And then he sent her some wine, some food. She enjoyed it so much.

When the husband came back with all the food, he looked all around. There was no wife. He saw her in the next boat, and he went over to ask her to come back so that they could go. The woman said, "Well, I'm sorry. I enjoy it here. I like to be with this man. I don't want to go home with you anymore."

The husband begged and begged and begged. She said, "No, I decided to stay with this man."

The husband was so sad, but what else he could do? He said, "All right, fine. If you want, I let you go. But before you go, I don't want any part of me with you. So give me back my three drops of blood."

She said, "Oh, fine. I will do that." She wanted to do that so she could be free. So she cut her finger, three drops of blood fell out, and she died. And that way, after she died, her spirit [turned into a mosquito].

But because she gave back the blood, and she wanted to live again to be a beautiful person again, so now she became a mosquito. That's why she buzzes around people, trying to suck three drops of blood so that she can be a woman again. That's why we have the mosquito, buzzing around you, trying to get the blood, so that she [can] live again.

202. How the Tiger Got His Stripes

Why does the Tiger have stripes? Why you think the tiger have stripes? This [story] is about men and animals.

In our country, when we farm we don't have the tiller. We have to use Buffalo and put the plow behind Buffalo. The men have to guide it.

The farmer was plowing his field. The Tiger came by, and the Tiger wanted to eat the Buffalo. But the Tiger did not know how to do it. So he came by, he talked to the farmer. He said, "Farmer, the Buffalo is strong, is bigger than you. How come the Buffalo obey you?"

The farmer said, "Because I have a clever mind. I'm weaker, but I have a clever mind. That's why Buffalo obeys me."

The Tiger said, "What is a clever mind?"

He said, "I have it."

The Tiger said, "Where do you keep your clever mind?"

He said, "I keep my clever mind at home."

The Tiger said, "I want to see it."

The farmer said, "Well, if I go home, then you're going to eat my Buffalo. I cannot go home."

The Tiger said, "No, I'm not going to eat your Buffalo. Just go home, get your clever mind, and show it to me."

The farmer said, "Well, I have [a] solution. How about if I tie you [to a] tree. That way I make sure that you don't eat my Buffalo."

The Tiger said, "Okay."

So the man took a rope and wrapped the Tiger around the tree. He went home, and he came back with a torch. He set fire to the Tiger. The Tiger was burning! He said, "Oh, help, help, help please!"

But the fire burned the rope around the tree [and] freed the Tiger. But where the rope burned, it burned the Tiger. That's why now the Tiger has those stripes.

203. Why the Crow Is Black

I want to tell you one more story of the animals. This is very short. The story of the peacock and the crow.

Long time ago, the peacock and the crow, they were alike. They had very dull feathers. Gray, dull feathers. Nothing beautiful. While the other birds have beautiful feathers. One day, both of them said, "Why don't we have beautiful feathers like the pheasant, like the phoenix? It's sad how we have just very dull, gray color."

The crow said, "What about if we get some paint and we paint our feathers. We would look very pretty."

They went out and got red, blue, green, and black, and yellow [paint]. The peacock said [to] the crow, "Why don't you do me first?"

The crow said, "All right."

They sat down, and the crow start painting the peacock beautifully. Teal color, blue color, green color, yellow, purple, all the colors.

After he finished and brought a mirror for the peacock to look himself in the mirror. He said, "Oh, I'm so beautiful now. Beautiful, beautiful." He keep running around to show the other animals how beautiful he was.

The crow said, "Now it's my turn! You promise me that after I do it to you, you would do it to me."

The peacock said, "No, I'm busy. I want to go dancing and show off to the others."

But the crow said, "No, please come and do it to me."

The peacock said, "Okay. I'll do it." There's paint there. He just picked up a pot of black paint and threw it at the crow.

"Now, you, I finish." All the black paint got to the crow. That's why the crow is so black and why all the other animals stay away from him.

204. Why the Ocean Is Salty

This is another [how] story . . . how the water in the ocean is so salty. It's another why [story]. We have a lot of that kind of story. There's a man, he has two sons. [Before] he died, he tell the elder son to divide equally his wealth.

But after the father died, the eldest son [became] greedy. He took all the money, the wealth. The younger one didn't have anything to eat or anything. He had a very small hut. He had to go work for people.

Usually, during the New Year, it is a tradition to present an offering to our ancestors. The younger son did not have money to prepare food for his offering. So he went to his brother. He asked his brother to give him some money.

So the brother gave him a leg of a pig. So he took that home, and on the way, he saw a old man. The old man said, "I want to help you. If you walk toward this direction, you'll find some fairies. They are playing chess there, and they like to eat. But also they have something that help you a lot. But if they offer you anything, don't take anything. Just ask for a jar. Just ask for the jar."

So [he] went there, and those fairies smelled the food. They say, "What about give us that pig leg, and we give you some gold?"

The man said, "No, I don't want any gold, I want a jar. Your jar. The big jar over there."

Finally, the fairies said, "Okay, I give you that jar."

He give the food to the fairies. He took the jar home. But the old man said, "That jar, with that jar you can wish anything. Any of your wish will be granted, but don't overdo. Just ask enough for yourself. Don't ask too much. When you have enough, just say 'stop' and it stops."

So he took the jar home. He said, "I would like to have a house." He has a house. He said, "I would like some food." Whatever he wished he got it. The young man, he's not greedy. He just asks for what he needs.

The older brother wonder why his younger brother became rich all of a sudden. They came by and they ask him. The younger brother [was] very honest. He just told his brother the whole story. Told him that he met the fairy, the fairy gave him the jar.

The brother said, "Why don't you give me the jar, and I give you what I have?"

But the young man knew that the brother is very greedy. He said, "No, I want to keep the jar."

[That night] the brother and his wife sent somebody over, and [stole] the jar. When they got the jar, they ran away on a boat with the jar. But they did not learn the secret. How to tell the jar to give them thing and how to stop the jar.

During that time, the people in the country need salt. Salt was short, sold for a high price. They said, "Why don't we get some salt and sell it? That way, we can make a lot of money."

So they said, "Jar, please give us some salt." Salt start coming out, coming out, coming out. Pretty soon, the boat filled with salt. But they did not know how to stop it because the younger brother never told [them] what to do. So the salt keep coming out the jar, coming out the jar. Finally the boat sank, and the jar is still in the ocean producing salt. Nobody can stop the jar from making salt.

205. Why the Frog Croaks

We believe whenever the frog start making noise, that we are going to have rain. We believe that when the frog start [to] croak, that the rain will come. The story was that . . . one year, it was so dry. Trees die, animals die, and the frog, the rooster, and the horse decide to go to heaven. We believe there is some god up [there] that regulates everything. So those three animals decide to go up there and ask why didn't we have rain down here. It killed people, animals, and trees.

So they set out. The horse would carry the others to set out to go up there. They went up there, and they saw the god up there. They said, "Please, please. It is so dry down there. We need some rain because people are dying. Animals dying, trees dying."

So the god said, "We didn't know that there was no rain down there. In order for us to know that when you need the rain (when you go back down to earth), when it's so dry, then you have to call us."

They went back. After they got back, [there] was rain. Now, whenever it gets dry, the frog makes a lot of noise. The people up there hear the noise, hear the frog calling. So they make rain, for the rain to come down.

Clifford Blake, Sr.

NATCHITOCHES, NATCHITOCHES PARISH

Mr. Clifford Blake, Sr., an African American, made Natchitoches Parish his home all of his life. Blake quit school in 1927 to help his recently widowed mother take care of the family. "God give me a gift to make it," he explained, and on this faith began working at the Natchitoches Warehouse and Compress "toting dinners" for the workers. While performing this job Blake would sing his personal line, "Cornbread for your husband, and biscuits for your man." Soon he was singing other lines, but not while toting dinners; Blake had been given the responsibility of calling the cotton press: using the rhythms of his voice to coordinate the motions of the men who worked the giant metal machine that pressed the cotton into bales. For years, his deep, resonant voice rang out over the clashing noise of the machinery, with songs calling the press up and down, rhythmically encouraging the workers to move with the machinery.

In 1967, an accident at the press crushed Blake's leg, and he was forced to end his job. But he didn't forget his art, and years later he shared it with Donald W. Hatley, Nicholas R. Spitzer, and Paul Keyser. These men recorded Blake once again singing the call-response patterns he had at one time used daily to help keep the workers in rhythm and relieve them of the monotony of a wearying chore. They succeeded in capturing the sounds of what will soon be a lost art; there are only a few cotton compresses left, and these are rapidly disappearing.

They also recorded Blake's skill in another area of verbal art, storytelling. Several of the stories he told them are part of African American folktale tradition, and include animal tales and "John and Old Marster" tales. Elsewhere in this collection Blake contributes a belief legend ("Mr. Blue and the Dog Ghost").

These and other tales by Blake appear on the 1980 recording, Cornbread for Your Husband, and Biscuits for Your Man: Mr. Clifford Blake, Sr. Calls the Cotton Press. *A companion booklet by the same title provides additional information (Gregory and Hatley 1980). On April 4, 1979, Spitzer and Donald W. Hatley recorded tale #207, Mule and Ox. On June 3, 1979, Nicholas R. Spitzer recorded #206, 208, and 209 at Blake's home in Natchitoches. Clifford Blake died in 1992.*

206. Snake in a Wagon Rut

Snake in a wagon rut, and here come Brer Rabbit. He said, "Will you help me?"

The rabbit said, "If I help you, you going to bite me."

He said, "No, I'm not going to bite you."

So they got about two miles down the road, he kept a begging Brer Rabbit. Brer Rabbit said, "Now, if I take this rock off you, you promise me you wouldn't bite me?"

He said, "I swear I won't."

Taken the rock off and got down a couple of yards, snake said, "Brer Rabbit?"

He said, "What?"

He said, "My duty to bite you, and I'm going to bite you."

He said, "Didn't you tell me you wasn't going to bite me?" He said, "When a man in trouble, he'll say anything." He said, "I was in trouble, but I'm out now. And I'm going to bite you."

Brer Rabbit said, "Well, Brer Snake, I know that's your job to bite me. But I tell you what I want you to do. I want you to get back in that rut and stretch clean out just like when I found you. Then we going to make our deal, Brer Snake."

Brer Snake said, "Okay, Brer Rabbit. But when I get out, I'm going to bite you."

Old snake stretched out in the rut. Brer Rabbit put two rocks on him instead of one. He said, "Now, Brer Snake, when you was in free world, you wanted to bite me. But now you'll die." And he left them rocks on him.

207. Mule and Ox

Old Mule and Ox. They worked old Mule and Ox pretty heavy. The boss didn't have much food for them. So old Ox told old Mule one Sunday morning, he said, "Looka here, Mule!" Said, "What day we take rest?"

He said, "On Sabbath Day."

He said, "I'm going to take plenty of them." Old Ox broke the fence and went on down in the cane break.

Old Master worked old Mule kinda hard that hot day. Old Mule looked back at the Ox. Said, "Say, Master. I tell you something, you wouldn't tell it?"

Said, "No, Mule."

He said, "I can tell you where old Ox at. Down in the cane break."

Old Ox was rolling in his fat. Old Master got on old Mule, got his dogs, and they finally got old Ox. So they bringing him to the lot. Old Ox looked at old Mule, he said, "Old Mule?"

Mule said, "Um-hmm."

He said, "Your tongue is causing me to get killed. But my hide'll be tallied to your back long as the day you live." So they whip a mule with a cow hide.

208. Saul and Skeleton

Old Saul went down in a field. And he seen a skeleton hanging in a tree. He went back to the house. "Oh, Master! I seen a head hanging up in a tree!"

He said, "You lying!"

He said, "God knows I did!"

They went down there, and ain't see'd nobody. So for three mornings, they went down ever morning. Master didn't see him. So the last time, Master said, "Listen here, son. I'm going to carry you down there. And if that skeleton ain't in that tree, I'm going to hang you."

"You can hang me, boss. You can hang me, because he's there."

Got down there, wasn't nothing. But he was up there. So when old master put the rope around Saul's neck, and tighten up, this head come down. He said, "Saul?"

Saul looked around.

He said, "My tongue got me with this. Your tongue going to hang you." So that way, tongue'll hang you.

209. Brer Rabbit and the Babies

Brer Rabbit and the fox, coon, and the squirrel going to make a farm. They going to hoe and all of them going to put their dinner in the cistern. So Brer Rabbit was smart. Everyday, about nine-thirty, he'd say, "Hey!"

Old Coon say, "What's the matter, Brer Rabbit?"

"I don't know what's the matter. Somebody calling me. I got to go." Went on over there, and he'd eaten some.

He come back, "What's the matter, Brer Rabbit?"

"That woman wanted me to christen that baby. I had to christen her baby."

"All right."

About thirty minutes, "Hey!"

"What's the matter, Brer Rabbit?"

"I ain't going. I ain't going. I'm tired of christening babies."

"Go on, Brer Rabbit."

He went on, and he eat all of it up! Come back, he said, "What you name the baby?"

"All gone."

So, come on back. Went in for dinner. Didn't have no biscuits and butter. Old Coon say, "Who done been down here in this cistern and got our food?"

Brer Rabbit, "I don't know. I don't know. I don't know." Said, "I tell you what to do. You can find out who did it. I'm going to make the fire, and I'm going to stand behind you all. I'm going to show you who taking it, because whoever eat the butter going to melt." See, he going to stand behind the coon and squirrel. It happen, the possum put him ahead. All at once, they see the butter running down their leg! So Brer Rabbit, he the one eat the food. Brer Rabbit was a smart guy. He eat all the food up.

Barry Jean Ancelet

SCOTT, LAFAYETTE PARISH

Collected January 16, 1994, by Carl Lindahl from Barry Jean Ancelet at his home with his daughter Clelie and the celebrated Cajun musician Lionel LeLeux present as listeners.

As an adult, folklorist Barry Ancelet, has collected hundreds of folktales from Cajun and Creole tellers. As a child, he heard one very special magic tale from his grandmother's second husband, Edouard Dugas. As Barry recalls, M. Dugas "told all kinds of tales, but this is the only one that I remember." In his search for folktales, Barry often asked tellers if they could recall a tale like this one, about a boy and his magic dogs. He had no luck until 1993, when one of his students, Jennifer Ardoin, recorded a Creole version, quite similar to Barry's, which is now published in Cajun and Creole Folktales (Ancelet 1994, no. 19). But this is the first time that Barry's own family story has found a wider audience.

210. Gaillum, Singo, et Moliseau (Gaillum, Singo, and Moliseau)

C'était un .. jeune garçon. Il restait avec sa mère. Il avait trois chiens: s'appellaient Gaillum, Singo, et Moliseau. Et il allait dedans le bois chasser. C'étaient des chiens de chasse. Et—il allait chasser avec ses chiens, et puis quand il trouvait quelque chose il était après essayer de travailler ses chiens, il chantait après ses chiens. Il chantait:

Gaillum—illum—illum,
Gaillum—illum—illum,
Singo, Moliseau

Et c'est comme ça il appelait ses chiens. Et ses chiens étaient beaucoup dressés—et puis c'était beaucoup—ils aimaient leur maître, tu connais. Ils étaient beaucoup dévoués pour leur maître.

Ça fait, un jour, le jeune garçon ... il a tombé en amour avec une femme, une veuve—une femme qui avait déjà été mariée, mais son mari était mort. Et sa mère aimait pas la femme. Elle trouvait que quelque chose était drôle avec la femme, qu'allait pas bien. Ça fait, elle l'avait déconseillé, mais, il était en amour avec la femme, et puis, ça fait, à force de courtiser la femme, il a tombé en amour avec elle et il voulait la marier.

Et la femme était bien vaillante avec lui, tu connais. Mais elle a dit, elle disait qu'elle avait peur des chiens. Elle se fiait pas des chiens. Ça fait, il a dit, "Well," il dit, "j'aime mes chiens."

There was a . . . young man. He lived with his mother. He had three dogs: they were called Gaillum, Singo, and Moliseau. And he'd go into the woods to hunt: these were hunting dogs. And he would go hunting with his dogs, and when he found some work for his dogs to do, he sang for his dogs. He sang:

Gaillum—illum—illum,
Gaillum—illum—illum,
Singo, Moliseau.

And that was how he called his dogs. And his dogs were very well trained—and very—they loved their master, you know. They were very loyal to their master.

So one day the young boy . . . fell in love with a woman, a widow: a woman who had already been married, but her husband was dead. And his mother didn't like the woman. She thought there was something strange about the woman, that something was wrong. She didn't like her at all. So, she tried to discourage him, but he was in love with the woman, and so, in courting this woman, he fell in love with her and he wanted to marry her.

And the woman was very nice to him, you know. But she said, she said that she was afraid of the dogs. She didn't trust the dogs. So he said, "Well," he said, "I love my dogs."

Elle dit, "Well, on pourra pas faire affaire ensemble, parce que, moi, j'ai trop peur des chiens, on peut pas se marier, si tu gardes tes chiens."

Ça fait, il a dit, "Well," il faudrait il jongle à ça. Il a dit ça à sa mère, et il dit, "Elle a accepté de me marier, mais elle a peur des chiens—il faudrait je fais quelque chose avec les chiens."

Sa mère a essayé de lui dire, "Fais attention à ça tu fais. C'est pas bien, ça."

Mais il a jonglé, il a dit, "mais c'est manière bête, tu connais, manquer la chance de marier une femme pour des chiens. Des chiens c'est pas du monde," tu connais. Mais il gardait ça en arrière de sa tête. Ça fait, il à dit a sa mère, il dit, "Je vas essayer de les donner." Il a dit ça à sa pretendue."

Elle dit, "Non." Elle dit, "ça va pas faire. Tu peux pas les donner." Il faudrait que tu les tues," elle dit. "J'ai trop peur des chiens si tu les donnes."

Ça fait il a fini par décider qu'il aurait fait quelque chose avec les chiens. Ça fait, il dit, il dit à sa mère, "Je vas les tuer. Mais je vas les saigner. Et je vas garder le sang dans trois différents baquets, un pour chaque chien." Et il dit, "Si jamais je suis en tracas"—parce que elle disait qu'elle avait peur, tu connais—il dit, "Si jamais je suis en tracas, tu vas m'entendre chanter pour mes chiens, et quand je vas chanter pour

She says, "Well, we won't be able to get together, because, I'm too afraid of dogs; we can't get married if you keep the dogs."

So he said, "Well, I have to think about this." He told this to his mother, and he said, "She consented to marry me, but she is afraid of the dogs—I have to do something with the dogs."

His mother tried to tell him, "Be careful what you do. This is not good."

But he thought, he said, "But this is pretty stupid, you know: to lose the chance to marry a woman because of some dogs. Dogs aren't people," you know. But in the back of his head he remembered what his mother had said. So he said to his mother, "I'm going to try to give them away." He told that to his fiancée.

She said, "No." She says, "That won't do. You can't give them away. You have to kill them, " she says. "I'm too afraid of the dogs and if you give them away they'll come back."

He finally decided that he'd do something with his dogs. So he says, he says to his mother, "I'm going to kill them. But I'm going to drain their blood. And I'm going to keep the blood in three different buckets, one for each dog." And he says, "If ever I'm in trouble, you'll hear me singing for my dogs, and when I sing for my dogs," he says, "when you hear me, it's a sign that I'm in trouble." He says, "Take the buckets of blood and

mes chiens," il a dit, *"que tu vas*
m'entendre dire—c'est un signe que
je suis en tracas." Il dit, *"Prends*
les baquets de sang, et puis vide les
dessus les corps des chiens, et ça va
revenir en vie."

Ça fait, il a parti, il a marié la
femme, et puis, comme de fait ça a
été bien pour un élan, et puis là,
ça allait plus, et puis elle voulait
prendre le dessus de lui, tu connais,
elle voulait essayer de—et puis il a
fini par comprendre que c'est elle
qui avait tué son autre mari, pour
l'argent et pour—tu connais—pour
sa terre et pour son pouvoir. Ça fait,
et c'est ça qu'elle voulait faire avec
lui aussi. Elle l'avait, elle l'avait
pris et elle l'avait emprisonné. Elle
était au moment de le tuer, elle l'avait
d'amarré, je crois. Et elle voulait le
tuer.

Ça fait, il, il a commencé a
chanter—
Gaillum—illum—illum,
Gaillum—illum—illum,
Singo, Moliseau
—et chante et chante jusqu'à sa mère
a entendu ça. Et quand elle a entendu
ça, elle s'a rappelé que il fallait elle va
en bas et puis elle jette les baquets de
sang sur les chiens. Ça fait elle a été
en bas, elle a attrapé les baquets de
sang, et elle a garoché ça sur les corps
des chiens, puis ils ont revenu en vie.

Et puis il chantait toujours:
Gaillum—illum—illum,
Gaillum—illum—illum,
Singo, Moliseau

pour them on the bodies of the dogs,
and they will come back to life."

So he left, he married the woman,
and then, as a matter of fact, things
went well for a while, but then they
got bad. And then she wanted to get
the best of him.

So finally he understood that she
was the one who had killed her other
husband, for money and for—you
know—his land and his power. So,
that's what she wanted to do to him,
too. She had him, she made him her
prisoner. She was on the verge of
killing him. And she had him tied
up, I think. And she was going to kill
him.

So he, he started singing—
Gaillum—illum—illum,
Gaillum—illum—illum,
Singo, Moliseau.
—and sings and sings until his
mother heard it. And when she heard
that, she remembered that she had
to go and throw the buckets of blood
on the dogs. She got the buckets of
blood and poured them on the dogs'
bodies, and they came back to life.

And he was singing over and
over—
Gaillum—illum—illum,
Gaillum—illum—illum,
Singo, Moliseau.

Et puis les chiens ont entendu ça, ils ont parti à la course, droit dans sa direction, comme ils avaient tout le temps fait. Ils ont été là-bas, et puis la femme, elle avait le bougre, il était amarré, la femme avait un couteau à sa gorge, et elle était au moment de lui couper la gorge.

Et quand les chiens ont arrivé, ils ont sauté dessus elle, et puis ils l'ont tout déchirée par morceaux. Et ils ont commencé à mordre dessus les cordes, et puis ils l'ont démarré, et c'est eux qui lui ont sauvé la vie.

Et il s'a rentourné à sa mère, et puis il fallait dire à sa mère que c'est elle qu'avait eu raison, parce que la femme était pas bonne—et il a fini avec.

That's it.

And when the dogs heard that, they took off running straight in his direction just like they always had before. When they went there and the woman, she had the guy. He was tied up, and the woman had a knife at his throat, and she was on the verge of cutting his throat.

And when the dogs arrived, they jumped on her, and tore her all to pieces. And they started biting on the ropes and they untied him, and they were the ones that saved his life.

And he went back to his mother, and then he had to say that she'd been right all along, because the woman wasn't good. He had finished with her.

That's it.

Notes on the Tales

Carl Lindahl

The following notes are comparative, showing how the individual tales of this collection resemble and differ from the most commonly collected American tales, especially those from Louisiana and elsewhere in the South. Occasionally, the notes range farther afield, to West Africa, East Asia, Canada, the Caribbean, Europe, and the Spanish-speaking New World, to demonstrate the parent traditions that fed the rich mix of contemporary Louisiana folk narrative. In certain cases—such as Harold Talbert's tales—in which storytellers translate idiosyncratic personal experiences into oral art, brief notations, or none, appear. More often, however, several references will accompany a note, because the tales are both highly localized and internationally known. For example, Mary Etta Scarborough Moody's tale of "The Red-Headed Witch of Bogalusa Creek" (#179) concerns a striking and unique apparition, as well as personal experiences of trips to visit the spirit. Yet, for all its idiosyncracies, this tale contains no less than fifteen international motifs from the ghostlore of Europe and the United States. Similarly, Peter Gitz's account—both unique and personal—of the ghost known as "The Silk Lady" (#178) relies on at least ten international motifs.

Tales or narrative details possessing parallels in international folktale tradition are listed according to their numbers in Antti Aarne's and Stith Thompson's *The Types of the Folktale* (1961) and Thompson's *Motif-Index of Folk-Literature* (1955–58). Tale type numbers are listed after the prefix AT and followed by the international title in italics: for example, Wilson "Ben Guiné" Mitchell's "*O, Fiva!*" (#34) is classified AT 1705, *Talking Horse and Dog*. Motif numbers are prefaced by a letter and end with a period, followed by the standard international title in roman type. For example, Hugh McGee's "Looks Can Kill" (#128) contains motif X137. Humor of ugliness; hunter's ugliness is fatal to animals.

Books and articles containing analogues to these tales or commentary useful interpreting these stories are listed in the bibliography following the notes. Indexes of the tale types and motifs represented in this collection also appear after the bibliography.

When the notes refer to tales found in this book, the number assigned the tale appears in parentheses, preceded by the # sign: for example, Lonnie Gray's tale, "A Heaven Joke," is designated #30. The # sign is used to mark only those tales found in *Swapping Stories*; analogues from other collections are represented by the abbreviation *no.*: for example, Ancelet 1994, no. 2. I have employed this distinction to aid readers who wish to use the notes to study connections among the various tales appearing in *Swapping Stories*.

Detailed information on the cultural backgrounds of Louisiana storytellers can be found in the separate bibliography to Maida Owens's essay on the folk groups of Louisiana, which appears at the beginning of the book. I thank Barry Jean Ancelet, Samuel G. Armistead, Annette Huval, and Geoffrey Kimball for contributing to these notes, and Frank de Caro, Linda Dégh, and W. K. McNeil for their suggestions and corrections.

1–14. Harold Talbert's tales walk the thin line between the personal experience story and the tall tale. These reminiscences richly and lovingly illustrate the small-town backdrop for so many of the subsequent stories in this collection. Having sampled the 1930s as presented in Talbert's words, one can more easily imagine the world depicted by tall tale tellers Lonnie Gray, Bill Cox, and Jimmie Davis. A master at depicting the daily concerns of small town Louisiana, Talbert is also expert at pushing his accounts to the regions where fact and fantasy overlap. In the midst of delivering a vivid account of the role of the movie theater in his boyhood life, Talbert inserts the story of a boy so impressed by the lifelike quality of the cinematic experience that he shot the movie screen. A tale that begins in a sleepy town ends in frenzied flights from a man in a wild gorilla suit; a baptism nearly becomes a drowning. Because Harold Talbert's oral art makes his own life a tall tale, he draws on far fewer internationally distributed tale types than any of the other British-American narrators. Only two of his tales possess clear analogues in international oral tradition.

9. Responding to the Sermon. Jokes and personal anecdotes about the faux pas of parishioners suddenly stirred from sleep are common, both in this collection and in nationwide lore. Baughman lists ten American versions, most of which are from the South, as well as six Old World versions attesting to the popularity of the tale in Britain. Some of these tales are true, but many are fabricated: this is one instance in which art and life imitate each other closely. AT 1833, *Application of the Sermon*; X435. The boy applies the sermon. See Talbert's next tale as well as Harry Methvin's "God Works in Mysterious Ways" (#119).

10. He Prayed a Good Prayer. AT 1833; X435.

14. Talking Trash. Here Harold Talbert, all of whose reminiscences border upon the tall tale, finally commits himself fully to the form. Sharing the stage with other accomplished liars, he engages in a session of possum lore. In the repartee of these members of Possum's Unlimited, possums evolve into extraordinary animals: they fly, they hypnotize, they perform astonishing feats as registered studs.

Throughout Louisiana, one of the most common occasions for sharing oral artistry is the lying session. Male groups congregate at the country store, hunting lodge, fishing hole, local bar, or the "liars' bench" near the courthouse and goad each other to make increasingly incredible claims for whatever person or animal they fix their imaginations upon. These sessions give rise to what some people call "tall tales," and others "windies," "lies," or "talking trash." Ancelet (1980a) has a remarkable study of a French-speaking group of Louisiana tall tale tellers. The finest study of the British-American tradition is Kay Cothran's "Talking Trash" (1979). X1258. Lies about geese; X1249.5*. Lies about o'possum.

15–31. Lonnie Gray's repertoire is a classic collection of hunters' tall tales. Known worldwide among male occupational communities (such as soldiers, sailors, cowboys, lumberjacks), tall tales were particularly common throughout the sparsely inhabited American frontier, and they have maintained their popularity among rural males throughout the country. Brown (1987, 14) asserts that women seldom tell tall tales; Cothran (1979) supports her but finds that women often participate as active audience members by goading or discouraging the men. Mary Gray's repartee with her husband, captured in tales #19 and #22, shows something of the typical female role in the tall tale telling process. Gray's tales are very similar to those collected in the Ozarks by Randolph (1951, 1965), McNeil (1989) and Young and Young (1989). Indeed, he situates "A Man-Eating Varmint" (#17) and "The Mean Mountaineer" (#18) in the Ozarks.

15. A Bear-Riding Cowboy. Bears have figured as important tall tale characters as long as European Americans have lived in the United States. From T. B. Thorpe's tale "The Big Bear of Arkansas" to the most recently published collections, the bear dominates the hunting lore of the Upland South and even makes inroads in the lowlands of Louisiana. On the lore of the bear in the Ozarks, see Randolph (1951, 103–5); a more recent and general study appears in Gillespie and Mechling (1987, 133–62). The motif of the tough man riding the beast has been popular since the early nineteenth century, when Davy Crockett would appear "a-ridin' a catamount with a b'ar under each arm" (Randolph 1951, 158). X1221(d). Man rides a bear. Variant in Young and Young (1989, 49–51).

16. A Smart Bear. X1221(b). Lie: intelligent bear. Although the tale of the hog-fattening bear is quite well known (Gillespie and Mechling 1987, 147), it has not been assigned a specific motif. For related tales from the Ozarks, see Randolph (1951, 103–5).

17. A Man-Eating Varmint. This is another tale popular in the Ozarks; I collected an unpublished variant from Ernie Deane of Fayetteville, Arkansas, in 1989.

18. The Mean Mountaineer. McNeil (1989, 77, 168) records a similar story from the Ozarks and lists many published variants, principally from the Ozarks and Appalachians. E1. Person comes to life.

19. *A Rattlesnake Tale,* by Mary Gray, answers her husband's tall tales with a legend that she claims to be true. Stories of snakes that crawl on sleepers are common in the South, though seldom reported in folktale collections. Randolph (1952, 14–16, 185) prints an Ozarks variant and quotes a mountain doctor as attesting, "I know for a fact that snakes do get in people's beds sometimes." Dye (1973) presents a sampler of Louisiana snake lore, and Wilson (1987) provides a broad-based discussion of American attitudes toward snakes.

20. *It Was So Cold.* Here is another tale more common in the Ozarks and points north than in Louisiana. X1606.2.4.1*. Geese or ducks are frozen into lake: something scares them the next morning and they fly off with the whole lake. See Randolph (1951, 202) and Dorson (1946, 258).

21. *How the Farmer Saved His Pigs.* D1652.3.1. Cow with inexhaustible milk.

22. *They Buried Her Too Soon,* by Mary Gray, is another legend told in response to her husband's tall tales. The fear of being buried alive (motif S123) gave rise to many legends in nineteenth-century America and many still circulate, although modern embalming practices make the return from the grave less probable than it once was. Two tales similar to this one are reported by Baker in Indiana (1982, nos. 17, 18). The plot is also well known among the English, Irish, and French Canadians. AT 990, *The Seemingly Dead Revives*; see also R212.1.1. Man buried alive escapes from tomb when thief tries to rob it.

23. *Even after Death Did Them Part.* Though I could find no exact parallels for this tale, there are several similar stories classified under AT 1409, *The Obedient Husband*. See also Motif X597*. Jokes about new arrivals in heaven. The theme of surprises in the afterlife is very popular in American humor: McNeil (1989, 129–32) and Baker (1986, nos. 299, 300) print several such tales from the Ozarks and the Midwest.

24. *It Was So Hot.* Related to X1633.3.1*. Lizards carry chips to sit down on. Again, the Ozarks collection of Vance Randolph (1951, 183–84) offers a close parallel.

26. *The Big Fish of Corney Creek.* AT1960B, *The Great Fish.* A distant cousin of X1301.5*(e). Fish leaps, causes tidal wave. Ancelet (1994, no. 64) presents a related Cajun tale. Giant fish with great talents are a major theme in Louisiana tall tale telling; see the next tale, as well as those told by Sarah Kent (#129) and A. J. Smith (#130).

27. *Another Big Fish.* X1301.5*.(ha). Scales of big fish are used for shingles, provide new roof. Randolph (1951, 207) offers a version from Arkansas.

28. *The Devil Made Her Say It.* This well-told tale falls under the general heading X434. The parson put out of countenance. It possesses distant analogues in X425. The parson who said there is no devil, and AT 1745*, *The Parson Sees the Devil.*

29. *How to Get a Mule's Attention.* K134.6. Selling or trading a balky horse. Burrison (1991, 76) presents a similar story from the Appalachian foothills of northwest Georgia.

30. *A Heaven Joke.* X597*. Jokes about new arrivals in heaven. See the note on Lonnie's tale #23.

32–36. *Wilson "Ben Guiné" Mitchell* is recognized as one of Louisiana's great narrators. Barry Jean Ancelet (1980b; 1994, xxx, lxvii–lxix) and Carl Lindahl (Ancelet 1994, xiii) briefly discuss aspects of his life and art. These notes are adapted from Ancelet (1980b, 1994).

32. *Froumi et* Grasshopper. AT 280A, *The Ant and the Lazy Cricket.* Extremely well known from the seventeenth-century literary treatment of La Fontaine (1926, no. 1), this tale is not well reported in oral tradition. Nevertheless, Klipple (1991) lists two African versions, and Stanley Robe (1973) lists Hispanic-American versions. Ben Guiné adds a nice touch of local color by featuring the grasshopper as an accordion player; the accordion remains extremely popular among musicians in southern Louisiana.

33. *Le petit bonhomme en* Coal Tar. AT 175, *The Tarbaby and the Rabbit.* K581.2. Briar patch punishment for rabbit. This is one of the best-known tales in African-American tradition, made popular to white audiences by Joel Chandler Harris (1880, no. 2). In Louisiana, AT 175 is reported from three groups: English-speaking African Americans, like Delores Henderson, whose version appears in this book (#200); French-speaking black Creoles, including Enola Matthews (tale #49) in this book (see also Fortier 1887; reprinted in Saucier 1962, no. 33a); and Cajuns, including Max Grieg (tale #190; see also Saucier 1962, nos. 31, 33; Claudel 1978; and Ancelet 1994, no. 2). Even among such numerous and talented company, Ben Guiné's version stands out: he is the only narrator who ends his tale with the capture of Lapin (or Brer Rabbit). As Ben says, "Well then it was high time to catch Lapin, you understand! . . . You can't play with Lapin!"

34. *O, Fiva!* AT 1705, *Talking Horse and Dog,* a tale well distributed among both African-American and European-American storytellers. Ben Guiné's version is particularly closely connected with the John and Old Master cycle of jokes about the clever slave and the cruel master. Among the finest published variants is Hurston's African-American tale from Florida (1935, 182–83); Young and Young (1989, no. 70) provide a European-American example.

35. *Vieux Nèg et Vieux Blanc té gain une course.* Motif. A1671.1. Why the negro works. Many African-American narratives—most of them jokes, but nearly all of them serious on at least one level—offer an accounting for the social and economic differences between blacks and whites. Dorson (1967, 172–76) presents some similar African-American stories and numerous references.

36. *Métayer Joe.* This tale of thievery punished possesses a close parallel in the British-American tradition of the Ozarks (Randolph 1951, 95–96, 209). AT 1564**, *The Clever Granary Watcher.* J21.23. "Rise earlier."

37–48. *Bel Abbey's* tales represent the lore of the Koasati (sometimes called Coushatta) people, who began migrating from what is now Alabama to Louisiana territory in 1763, as the French colonists withdrew from Alabama and the English came to occupy it. The Koasati preferred French neighbors to English neighbors; as a consequence, on their current reservation near Elton, bordering Cajun settlements, many Koasati speak French and bear French surnames. Howard N. Martin (1966; 1977) presents myths and historical narratives collected from the related Coushatta peoples of East Texas. Notes are provided by Geoffrey Kimball (GK) and Carl Lindahl (CL).

On his father's side, Bel Abbey belonged to the family from which Koasati chiefs were elected; his mother's side was notable for its traditional doctors and ritual specialists. He and his wife of nearly forty-five years, Nora Williams (1920–1984), had three daughters (the sex of child more highly valued by the Koasati) and many grandchildren and great-grandchildren. He worried about his descendants' commitment to their Koasati heritage and language, and he occasionally gathered them together to speak to them about the importance of their culture.

Bel Abbey was in the first generation to be Christian from childhood, but he absorbed much of traditional Koasati culture from his mother, his maternal uncles, and grandparents, who were only superficially Christianized. He received little Western education, primarily a few years at the Congregational Church school; he only learned to write English while in the army during World War II. Nonetheless, he learned a great deal from his relatives, especially in regard to traditional hunting, fishing, and gathering activities; and he bent his natural curiosity and keen sense of observation to learning about the natural world. Three features that deeply colored his personality were a solid pragmatism, a respect for truth, and a skepticism concerning things that cannot be tested by the senses. Thus, though he enjoyed traditional tales, he was highly suspicious about their veracity. When telling any kind of traditional narrative, he always gave a warning introduction to the effect that the tale to follow was something that he heard, the truth of which he could not attest (GK).

37. *Learning from the Bear* is one of the medicine origin tales and the only one that Bel was willing to tell, because to him it seemed the most likely to have occurred. Other medicine origin tales incorporate fantastic elements, which Bel, pragmatic as he was, didn't like to credit as being factual (GK). B512. Medicine shown by animal. This motif is common in Native American traditions throughout the continent. Thompson (1929, no. 74) lists many versions from Northern and

Northwest Coast tribes but none from the South. Bel's nephew, Bertney Langley, tells his version of the same tale elsewhere in this book (#198) (CL).

38. The Turtle and the Rabbit Run a Race. The story refers to the box turtle, *sattapoló*, which is marked with lozenges on the shell; thus the story of their origin (GK). This aetiological legend contains many motifs common in both European and Native American traditions. A2412.5.1. Origin of spots on turtle's back; *A2356.2.9. Why tortoise has humpy back; B322.1. Hero feeds own flesh to helpful animal. Many readers will recognize this tale as a close cousin of the famous tale of the hare and the tortoise (AT 275A), but its plot is separately classified as AT 1074, *Race Won by Deception: Relative Helpers*, in which the contestants are sometimes a rabbit and turtle, but often other animals or even humans. Like AT 200D*, *Why Cat Is Indoors and Dog Outside in the Cold*, and motif A1671.1.1. Why the negro works (see tale #35 in this collection), Bel Abbey's tale describes an ancient race in which the outcome determines the relationship between the contestants for all time. Variants of AT 1074 are widely known among both African Americans and Native Americans. Baer (1981, 44–45) finds African-American versions to be derived principally from Africa (for an example, see Abrahams 1983, 75–78), but the Native American tradition is also rich. Thompson reports variants from sixteen different cultures (1929, 258–59, 359). Published collections suggest that AT 1074 possesses a long history and broad distribution among Native American peoples: see, for example, Lanman's nineteenth-century version (1856, 1:443; reprint in Botkin 1949, 505), in which a turtle races a deer; and a Zapotec version from Oaxaca, in which a toad tricks a rabbit (Boas 1912, 214–15) (CL). For a Spanish-language Isleño version of AT 1074 from St. Bernard Parish, and comments on the Spanish-language tradition of this tale, see tale #194, below, and accompanying note (CL).

39. Bel's Encounter with a Wise Owl. Bel's respect for the wisdom of the owl (B122.0.3.) is shared by many cultures, Native American, Asian, and European (CL).

40. Bel's Encounter with the Rabbit and Cow. J1741. Animal thought to be object (CL).

42. How the Buzzard Got a Pierced Nose. This is a variant of the widespread Native American tale complex, J2425. The bungling host. Franz Boas (1916) studies the North American distribution of these tales and finds many variants among Southern tribes. See also K1955. Sham doctor. The motif of posing as a doctor to kill enemies is reported widely (Thompson 1929, 352). Q451. Mutilation as punishment; S172. Mutilation: nose cut off or crushed (CL). Although some interpreters of Bungling Host tales claim that their main purpose is to illustrate the importance of hospitality, Bel does not seem to tell his tale for this reason, because in this version mutual hospitality is assumed. Rather, the focus is on the hubris *(ilakasamotilká)* of Rabbit, who tries to imitate Bear's way of providing food, even though he is unable to do so.

Another focus is the idea of the trickster tricked: here Rabbit, who usually gets the better of others, is bested by Vulture. The last word of the tale is *tafhiyám*, traditionally used as a sort of blessing to protect the teller; those who tell their tales without uttering *tafhiyám* may get a crooked back or a humpback (GK).

43. Rabbit Rolls into a Ball. J1961. Animal thought to be object (CL).

44. The Dear and the Wildcat. B2. Animal totem; J2413. Foolish imitation by animal (CL).

45–46. The First Meeting of the Indians and the Europeans. A1427. Acquisition of spiritous liquor. A Texas Coushatta tale on the first meeting of the Indians and the Europeans is found in Martin (1966, 46–47); the Texas version also concerns the introduction of alcohol but differs substantially from Bel's account (CL). Bel's story features an Orphan, a stock character in Koasati narrative. Kimball (1989, 49–50) discusses the sources of this fascination with the Orphan. By being free of kinship ties, an orphan is free to do things that others are not allowed to do, such as drinking an unknown substance. At the moment in the story when the Orphan reports that the liquor is good for inducing sleep, the Koasati audience laughs heartily. Near the end of the narrative, Bel mentions that the Spanish spoke to the Koasati "and dressed them in things such as clothing." This detail seems to be a well preserved memory of the first contact between these groups, for clothing was indeed among the first gifts given by the Spanish to the Koasati (Kimball 1987, 166–67) (GK).

47–48. A Man Loses His Breechcloth to a Bull. Although this narrative bears stylistic similarities to Bel's aetiological tales, it contains no speaking animal characters and is thus classified as a semihistorical narrative. About halfway through the tale Bel describes the pre-Western dress of the Koasati; this detail is necessary for younger listeners who may tend to forget that the Koasati did not always dress as they do now. The episode apparently occurred on the prairies of southwest Louisiana, and the "bent tree" into which the warrior escaped is probably a blackjack oak, a species still common in the region's woods and fields today. As the Koasati returned to the southwest prairies in large numbers in the 1840s and 1850s, it is likely that the incident happened between 1860 and 1880 (GK).

Enola Matthews. There is a rich mix of European and Creole motifs and styles in the repertoire of Mme. Matthews. Although she credits her Irish grandfather as the source of these tales, most of them are enormously popular in the South, and they could as easily have come from either African-American or French-American sources: for example, the plot of "*Bouki, Lapin et Rat de Bois*" (#49) is widespread among both southern blacks and French-speaking Louisianans, both black and white; and the specific characters in this version—Bouki and Lapin—derive from Louisiana Creole and not Irish tradition. On the other hand, the two magic tales that she tells— *Grandes Oreilles* and *Les trois jobs*—differ considerably from most other Louisiana

and Southern versions; while the basic plot of *Les trois* jobs (AT 313) is popular in
Cajun, African- American, and European-American märchen traditions, such details
as the ladder of bones are better known in the Old World. Mme. Matthews's tales are
characteristic, primarily, of Louisiana Creole culture and, secondarily, of Europe.
Her performances, like her tales, reflect the meeting of two cultures. She tells her
stories using both the Cajun dialect brought to Louisiana in 1765 by immigrants from
Acadia and the French Caribbean Creole language spoken by the descendants of
the slaves who worked the sugar cane plantations in nineteenth-century Louisiana.
(The following notes on Mme. Matthews's tales were written by Annette Huval and
Carl Lindahl).

   49. Bouki, Lapin, et Rat de Bois. AT 175, *The Tarbaby and the Rabbit,* extremely
popular in Louisiana: see tales #33, #190, #200, and their corresponding notes.
Already rendered famous by the nineteenth-century version appearing in Joel Chandler Harris's *Uncle Remus* (1880), the tarbaby tale attained even greater popularity
through the animated version presented in Walt Disney's *Song of the South* (1946), a
film that deeply affected Mme. Matthews. The widespread motif of the briar patch
punishment (K581.2) is found at the end of this tale. In this variant, as well as in many
other Louisiana versions (Ancelet 1994, no. 2; Saucier 1962, no. 31), the trickster
steals water from a well that he has not helped dig. There is no mention of the water
well in Uncle Remus, but Klipple lists ten variants from Africa that include water of
some sort (1991, 213–33). In this variant of AT175, there are three animals: Bouki,
Lapin, and Rat de Bois (or Possum). Bouki and Rat de Bois use tar to fashion a *catin*
(a doll in the image of a lady) to catch Lapin. Klipple lists ten versions in which the
tar baby is made to resemble a lady. Another interesting aspect of Mme. Matthews'
version is the way in which she tends to switch from Cajun to Creole French when
Lapin begins to speak in anger; the angry Lapin uses such Creole phrases as *ma
foutre, mon gain* and *t'apé vini.*

   50. Grandes Oreilles. This fascinating tale finds its closest published relatives
in AT 301, *The Three Stolen Princesses.* Part 5 of that complex tale concerns a hero,
trapped in the underworld, who promises to feed a giant bird if the creature will fly
him back to the upper world (motif F101.3). When the hero runs out of food, he
cuts off pieces of his own flesh to feed the bird (B322.1). A similar episode, told by
Cajun Lazard Daigle, was collected by Ancelet (1994, no. 26). But there are many
British-American versions as well, including tales collected by Leonard Roberts in
both Kentucky (1955, no. 1) and West Virginia (1974, no.104). The most striking
aspect of this tale is the magical power residing in the long ears of the hero. No other
American version of AT 301 shares this trait, and Thompson's *Motif-Index* can offer
only vague analogues from other traditions: Person unusual as to his ears (F511.2),

Remarkable ears (F542), Long ears (F541), and Transformation: tooth to ax head (D457.8); these motifs are most common in eastern and southern Asia.

51. *Les trois* jobs is a truncated version of AT 313, *The Girl as Helper in the Hero's Flight*, in which a monstrous father sets tasks for his daughter's suitor. This is one of the few European-derived magic tales that is enormously popular in African-American culture: the versions collected by Dorson (1967, 268–71) and Hurston (1935, 51–58) emphasize the evil of the girl's father, who is identified as the devil. European-American versions sometimes feature the father as a devil (see Randolph 1955, 3–5; Leonard Roberts 1969, no. 13), but often identify him as a king, especially as King Marrock, a name derived from Irish tradition (see Chase 1943, no. 15; Perdue 1987, nos. 6a, 6b, 6c). In most American versions, as told by both blacks and whites, the most common tasks set by the villain father are all ordinary farm jobs, but magnified to an enormous scale: cleaning huge stables, chopping down an entire forest, sorting hundreds of pounds of seeds, gathering feathers from flying birds, and draining a well with a leaky bucket. Only the last of these—the leaky bucket task (H1023.2.1)—appears in Mme. Matthews's version. The other two labors are filled with imagery more characteristic of French and other European fairy tales: climbing a glass mountain (D753.4), mounting a ladder of bones (F848.3), and securing three eggs from the top of a glass tower (H1114.1)—motifs found in French, French-Canadian, and French-Caribbean tales (Delarue 1957, 234; Thomas 1993, 263). The girl's sacrifice of her body and magical revival with a missing finger (E33), relatively rare in English-speaking American tradition, is found fairly often in French-American versions, including a French Newfoundland version collected by Thomas (1993, 247–63, 340–53) and a Cajun tale collected by Saucier (1962, no. 19). Other Louisiana versions include Saucier (1962, no. 3) and Reneaux (1993, 54–65).

52. *Les trois couillons.* This tale combines three major types in the following order: AT 1450, *Clever Elsie*; AT 1384, *The Husband Hunts Three Persons as Stupid as His Wife*; and AT 1696, *"What Should I Have Said (Done)?"* The central tale—the search for the three fools—though rarely reported in France, is slightly more common in French Canada (Thomas 1993, 153) and well attested in Ireland. The closest parallels to this section have been found among African Americans in the South (Dorson 1967, nos. 204–5; Burrison 1991, 151–53). Embedded in the quest for the fools are two additional tale types: AT 1245, *Sunlight Carried in a Bag into the Windowless House*; and AT 1286, *Jumping into the Breeches*. Both are found in Dorson's tale no. 204, and AT 1245 is found in Burrison. AT 1384 is relatively popular among European-American Southerners (Randolph 1955, 49–51; Leonard Roberts 1955, no. 58). The third *couillon* (or fool) is *Jean Sot*, or Foolish John, a popular Cajun and Creole stock character who follows instructions too literally or without adapting to

changing situations. Jean Sot is well known in France (Massignon 1968, no. 20) and French Canada (Thomas 1993). AT 1696 is often combined with other numskull tales. Ancelet (1994, nos. 32,35), Claudel (1944; 1948; 1978), Reneaux (1993, 106–15), and Saucier (1962: no. 22) have published Louisiana Jean Sot tales.

53. *Jean Sot, la vache, les chiens, et sa petite soeur.* Here is another Jean Sot tale. Present in this variant of AT 1696 is motif J2462.1. The Dog Parsley in the soup, often found elsewhere in Louisiana (Ancelet 1994, no. 35) as well as in French Canada (Thomas 1993, 242–47). Annette Huval has collected a similar version in French Creole from Julia Huval of Cecilia, who contributed two tales to this book (#188–89).

54. *La fille du Roi.* AT 1737, *The Parson in the Sack to Heaven,* is often found as part of the tale of the *Master Thief* (AT 1525), reported widely throughout Britain and the United States (Burrison 1991, 203–8; Lindahl 1988; Lindahl 1994) and in Louisiana by Ancelet (1994, no. 22), Saucier (1962, nos. 14, 15), and Claudel (1978). But this episode is also told as an independent tale by Cajuns (see Reneaux 1993, 120–23) and by African Americans throughout the South (e.g., Hurston 1935, 45–49).

55. *Séparer le maïs dans le cimitière.* AT 1791, *The Sexton Carries the Parson,* popular in European, European-American, and African-American tradition. But this particular version—in which the thieves are dividing plants of one sort or another (corn, nuts, sweet potatoes)—is a distinctively American form (McNeil 1989, 199–200). African-American versions include Dorson (1967, no. 38) and Hurston (1935, 94–95); Burrison (1991) prints three versions from the South.

56–62. *Alfred Anderson's* tales have never been previously published, but there is an available discussion of his family tradition, accompanied by two of his tales as retold by his daughter Debra Anderson Forney (Lindahl 1982).

56. *The Girls and the Alligator.* Best known in the United States and Europe as *The Wolf and the Kids* (AT 123) after the Grimms' version (1960, no. 5), this tale has been reshaped to fit the environment of southern Louisiana. Although the tale has been associated primarily with European-American traditions, it has also been collected in South Africa (Dorson 1975, 400) and from African-Caribbean peoples (Thompson 1961, 50).

57. *The Toodling Horn.* The basic plot is popular throughout the country, among both African Americans (Dorson 1967, 249–50) and European Americans (Leonard Roberts 1955, 21). Folklorists have tended to classify this tale as AT 303, *The Two Brothers* (Ranke 1934). Yet William Bascom (1992, 155–200) finds this a very common African tale and types it AT 315A. Barry Ancelet (1994, no. 19) published a Louisiana Creole version and reports its presence among Cajuns as well. In this collection, Ancelet narrates a Cajun related story—*Gaillum, Singo, et Moliseau*

(#210)—which he heard as a boy. Closely related to G275.2. Witch overcome by helpful dogs of hero.

58. *My Mama Killed Me, My Papa Ate Me*. AT 720, *My Mother Slew Me, My Father Ate Me; The Juniper Tree*. Although this tale is best known through the Grimms' German version, "The Juniper Tree" (1960, no. 47), the English-speaking tradition behind this tale is singularly strong. Scottish tradition contains many tales in which a song identical or similar to Alfred Anderson's is sung by the dead boy in bird form (Dorson 1975, 37–40). Both British-American and African-American storytellers are fond of this tale, which is especially popular in the South. Sometimes it is told as a belief legend (Randolph 1952, 53–54; Browne 1976, 151–54, 246–47; Leonard Roberts 1955, no. 27). Reneaux (1993, 159–64) presents a version from French Louisiana.

Child murder and cannibalism are so graphically depicted in this tale type that many editors of children's books excised the Grimm version from storybooks. Alfred Anderson's version is even bloodier than the Grimms', climaxing with a series of scenes in which not only the child but also the mother is cannibalized. Nevertheless, Anderson tells his tale with such aplomb the children in the audience burst into laughter at the story's end. The use of the words of *commère* and *compère*—literally meaning "co-mother" and "co-father;" and here probably refering to the godmother and godfather of the children—indicates that this tale was known among French speakers. Indeed, the opening of this tale is very similar to the opening of a version told by French-speaking whites (Saucier 1962, 54–55). E613.0.1. Reincarnation of murdered child as bird; G61. Relative's flesh eaten unwittingly.

59. *The Lazy Sisters and the Smart Sister*. AT 480, *The Kind and Unkind Girls*. This is Alfred Anderson's most overtly moralizing story, featuring an obedient child who is well rewarded. Internationally, this tale often appears in combination with *Cinderella* (AT 510A), the most popular of all magic tales (Dundes 1988a). Warren E. Roberts (1958) found it common in the New World; Reaver (1987, no. 12) prints a variant collected in Florida but derived from Louisiana oral tradition.

60. *Old Coon*. AT 1941, *Dr. Know-All*. Dorson (1967, 226–29) provides lengthy documentation of the popularity of this tale in African-American English-speaking tradition. The tale is much rarer among English-speaking whites, but it has been reported in the Ozarks as told about blacks (Randolph 1955, 133–35). Without the pun on the word "coon," the tale does not work. Among blacks in the Caribbean, the tale is told about a man named Crab who luckily identifies what is under the box when he says "Crab is caught." In a French-speaking Louisiana version collected by Saucier from white narrators, the trickster's name is Cricket (1962, 76–82). Alfred's daughter Debra tells a version of this story (Lindahl 1982, 196).

61. *Skullbone*. K1162. Talking skull refuses to talk. A version by Alfred's daughter Debra is printed and discussed by Lindahl (1982). This tale is almost certainly of

African origin. Although Randolph (1957, 3–5) collected several white versions in which a turtle appears, Halpert (Randolph 1957, 179–80) and Bascom (1977; 1992, 17–39) point out that the tale is much better known among African Americans, who tell it to underline the moral, "don't share your secrets with whites" (Lindahl 1982). See also Clifford Blake's "Saul and Skeleton" (#208), another variant of K1162.

62. *Brer Bear Meets Man.* AT 157, *Learning To Fear Man.* This animal tale is known worldwide, but in the United States it is nearly exclusively part of the African-American repertoire. Quite often in American tradition, the conflict between human beings and the animal world is taken as a metaphor for race relations. The human being, heavily armed and in control of the animal world, represents the white man, Brer Rabbit is the smart black who steers clear of the whites, and Brer Bear is the black who must learn the hard way to avoid whites. Dorson (1958) studies this tale at some length.

63–80. *Tales from the Everyday World: Family Life, Memories, and Pranks.* Most of the stories in this section are presented as personal experience tales, accounts of normal occurrences rendered memorable by humorous twists. Nevertheless, many of these spill over into the realm of the tall tale; this is a natural development, as tall tales tend to unfold in the everyday world and only gradually introduce the implausible and finally the incredible. A few other of these tales are jokes set in the typical rural landscape of times past as experienced by African Americans, British Americans, Cajuns, and Hungarian Americans. One tale (#68) represents the urban and suburban vacation pastimes of the present day.

There is a second sense in which some of these stories represent the everyday world. Five of them were collected in the types of environments where tales are most often told today: a barbershop (#67), a women's get-together (#68), a restaurant (#69–70), and a backyard barbecue party (#80).

63. *Following His Father's Example.* George Lezu's practical joke on his plow-horse bears a close resemblance to the tall tale "Red pepper for the slow ass" (X11; examples in Burrison 1991, 70, and Randolph 1965, 115).

64. *High Road to China* also emphasizes the hardships of Lezu's horse Pityu. Lezu's treatment of his horse in these two tales is reminiscent of the way in which tall tale tellers sometimes make one animal a scapegoat for the troubles of an entire community; see, for example, Zora Neal Hurston's fictional treatment of this theme in *Their Eyes Were Watching God* (1937, 81–117; also Hartsfield 1987, 119; Young and Young 1989, no. 44).

66. *He Got the Pig and the Girl* combines a very realistic account of a *fais do do* (the traditional Saturday-night Cajun courtship dance), with the tall tale theme of love magic gone bad. D1901. Witch induces love; B621.6. Pig as suitor; cf. K527.1. Poisoned food or drink fed to animal instead of man. The theme of the man who

woos a young woman but ends up pursued by an affectionate animal had enormous popularity in frontier days—for example, in the Davy Crockett almanacs, which featured the tale of the wooer dressed in a bearskin coat who disgusts his belle but wins the affections of a bear instead (Lofaro 1987 [1840], 13–14).

67. *I'm Going To Leave You*, Chère. Barber Harry Lee Leger shared this tale with his customers while cutting hair. The barbershop is one of the most popular sites for everyday storytelling; Barry Ancelet presents three Cajun tales (1994, xxxiii and tale nos. 42, 43) told by his father Elmo, another artful barber who uses tales to spice his daily work. This tale about the troubles of married couples is typical of those told in the typically all-male domain of the barbershop. Related to T298. Reconciliation of separated couple.

68. Down the Wrong Hill. Although nearly all the everyday tales presented here recreate a Louisiana landscape of years long past, this urban retelling of a recent event emphasizes current experience and imagination. Shared among twelve women friends during their regular get-together, this tale represents the informal tale telling characteristic of certain all-female and other informal groups, in which no "master narrator" appears, but rather all present contribute to the shaping of the story. For discussions of all-female story-sharing styles, see Baldwin 1985; Dégh 1995, 62–69; Kalčik 1975; Mitchell 1985.

69. Leaving Mississippi. Louisianans, like other groups, often tell tales at the expense of their neighbors. There is, for example, a rich tradition of jokes in which Louisianans best boastful men from neighboring Texas (Ancelet 1994, no. 65; Lindahl 1991). Here African American Robert Albritton capitalizes on the poor civil rights record of Mississippi, which was the focus of national attention during the 1950s and 1960s after the murders of Emmet Till (1955), Medgar Evers (1963), and three civil rights workers (1964).

70. You Think I'm Working, But I Ain't. This is part of the popular "John and Old Master" series of African-American narratives (see tales #60 and #61, above, and the section on jokes in the introduction). Clifford Blake tells a version of this tale in his recording *Cornbread for Your Husband* (1980); Hurston retells another from Florida (1935, 99–100)

71–73. Those Drivers Were No Dummies, Pulling Tires, and *Highway Robbery.* Practical jokes are, in a sense, dramatized tall tales. As a practical joke is recalled and retold, it becomes a tale itself. Recounting practical jokes has been a major form of rural entertainment through the centuries. The most respected figures of the frontier—Abraham Lincoln, for example—were fond of playing pranks and retelling them. Some figures, such as Maine's Art Church (Dorson 1964, 67–69), are remembered primarily as practical jokers, and their exploits become legendary in their communities. Rodney Cook and his boyhood friends clearly won a similar reputation in Arcadia. Rodney's first tale contains motif K2321.2. Dummy set up as a corpse to frighten people.

74. *Dentist or Proctologist?* Some of the most storied Halloween pranks involve the outhouse: the trickster turns over the outhouse, occasionally when it is occupied; or moves the outhouse, causing some poor victim to fall into the exposed latrine; or brings the outhouse into town. Some outhouses have ended up on the roofs of houses or civic buildings; Rodney Cook's trick supplies an interesting variation on this theme; Siporin (1994) supplies a broad sampling of Halloween outhouse pranks.

75. *On Top of Old Smoky.* This masterful tale is apparently part true, but quite clearly also flavored with tall tale traits; compare F989.17. Marvelously swift horse; X1242(ca). Mule is blown out of sight by explosion.

77. *That's One Tourist Who'll Never Come Back.* J1805.1. Similar sounding words mistaken for each other. Recent collections from across the country affirm that the gas station has become a major site for jokes about linguistic and cultural misunderstandings. Many such jokes focus on filling station restrooms, which seem to have replaced the outhouse as the most embarrassing place to be. Related tales appear in Dégh (1995, 333), Leary (1991, 107, 240), and Young and Young (1989, no. 58).

78. *That Darn Cat.* One of the most popular themes of contemporary legend is the dead cat that appears in an unlikely place, usually a package stolen from a car by an unlucky thief; see Brunvand 1981, 103–12; Brunvand 1986, 31–34.

79. *Big Red.* One of A. J. Smith's finest tales, this plot is well known among southern narrators; see Burrison 1991, 286; Legman 1992, 2:596–97.

80. *Swapping Stories.* Dave Petitjean's and A. J. Smith's repartee is not merely an instance of story swapping but a case of collaborative storymaking, because each man serves as straight man, audience, and helper for the other, as together they create a chain of tales based first and foremost on the stereotypical rocky relationships of married couples. Both men contribute a number of jokes and lines on cooking (J1813. Cooking processes misunderstood; W111.3. Lazy wife) and female domination of the household (T252. Overbearing wife). Following Dave Petitjean's tale of the man who hides under his bed to escape his wife, A. J. Smith changes the topic by contributing his own bed story, about a man who is afraid not of his wife, but of the dark; this begins a string of jokes about doctors (J1430. Repartee concerning doctors and patients).

Jokes based on blackened foods are popular among Cajuns. Since Cajun chef Paul Prudhomme first prepared blackened redfish in 1980, blackened foods have been associated with Cajun traditional cookery (Gutierrez 1992, 135–36)—even though the dish is not traditional and is unpopular with many Cajuns. Although Cajuns tend to like spicy food, many Cajuns believe that blackening destroys rather than enhances the taste of fish. See, for example, the story told by Cajun Marc Savoy about the first time he ate blackened catfish, at a restaurant in California. He took the fish back to his hotel room and washed off the spices so that he could enjoy the taste of the meat (Blank and Gosling 1990).

In his last joke, A. J. Smith refers to a woman who had to "take" [i.e., have] a serious operation. Here he is using typical Cajun folk speech, because French speakers would use the term *prendre* [to take] *une operation*—and often translate the expression directly when speaking English.

81–109. The Longs and Their Cousins. This sampler of political jokes and anecdotes features all manner of candidates and functionaries, but the most numerous and intense narratives are devoted to the famous Long family, led by Governor Huey Pierce Long (1893–1935), his younger brother Earl, and Huey's son Russell. The tales here give a folk view of the legendary family—a view reinforced by many of the anecdotes that Huey tells on himself in his autobiography, *Every Man a King* (1960). Another printed collection of Huey tales often told orally is Blain's *Favorite Huey Long Stories* (1937). Readers interested in other perspectives may wish to examine the biographies of Huey by H. D. Graham (1970) and T. H. Williams (1981). A. J. Liebling's *Earl of Louisiana* (1965) is a well-crafted portrait of Huey's younger brother. Stan Opotawsky (1960) attempts to chronicle the entire dynasty.

Many of the Long tales as well as the tales told by former Governor Jimmie Davis dramatize the storytelling talents of Louisiana politicians. In American political traditions, figures as diverse as Davy Crockett (Botkin 1944, 27–29) and Abraham Lincoln (Sandburg 1926, 295–313) have enhanced their popularity by storytelling. Nineteenth-century candidates used their jokes and tall tales to present themselves as everyday people—men of homespun values and simple tastes, who were nevertheless far more clever than their sophisticated opponents. In Louisiana such storytelling politicians continue to flourish in the twentieth century. Like Crockett and Lincoln, Huey Long and Jimmie Davis show great talent as tall tale tellers and sometimes use laughter as trenchantly effective weapons against their opponents.

81. Earl's Grave. Condemning one's political enemies to hell is an art that goes back at least as far as Dante; see motifs J1250. Clever verbal retorts; P422.1. Lawyers punished in hell.

Earl K. Long Memorial Park is now managed by the City of Winnfield and Earl is buried there.

82. Funeral Approval. J1805. Misunderstanding of words.

84. He Was Definitely Out. A common theme in jokes and anecdotes is the use of intimidation to change an angry charge into obsequious agreement; for an excellent Cajun tale on this theme, see Félix Richard's *La jument verte* (Ancelet 1994, no. 38). J613. Wise fear of the weak for the strong; J814.4. Flattering the villain to avoid being beaten or killed.

85. How to Save on Heating Costs. J1280. Repartee with judge; J1803. Learned words misunderstood by uneducated; X800. Humor based on drunkenness.

86. Who's on Trial? J1150. Cleverness connected with the giving of evidence; J1160. Clever pleading; X310. Jokes on lawyers.

87. 20/20 Vision. J1280. Repartee with judge.

88. His Client Was Saved. J1170. Clever judicial decisions.

89. Hugh Goes Courting, closely related to T320.3.1. Widow . . . put[s] would-be ravisher to flight—in which a widow uses her husband's weapon to run off a man who attempts to force sex on her.

90. For Better or Worse. J1086. Ignoring the unpleasant; T256. Quarrelsome Wife.

91. He Knew How to Get Votes. Here Huey shows a Lincolnesque talent for transforming his own legal failings into approval and laughter. This tale is reminiscent of one often told by and about Abraham Lincoln, whose jokes caused laughter in a courtroom and provoked the judge to fine him for contempt of court. When the judge heard Lincoln's joke from a third party, he broke out laughing himself, straightened his face, and said, "The clerk may remit Mr. Lincoln's fine" (Sandburg 1926, 2:300–301).

92. They Couldn't Fool a Polecat. This story employs the age-old theme of a man so foul that his nastiness exceeds that of the nastiest animal. Hurston provides a typical example from African Americans in Florida in which a goat faints when exposed to the odor of a man (1935, 86–87). F687. Person's remarkable odor; X599.2*. Jokes on politicians.

93. Coon Chasers and Possum Watchers. This is a good example of a politician's use of a tall tale to enhance his popularity and make his message memorable. Huey once more tells a popular tall tale. F611.2.3. Strong hero's long nursing.

94. Bull Talk. Jimmie Davis, known as the "Singing Governor" of Louisiana, is perhaps equally well known for the song "You Are My Sunshine." Davis's verbal talents, as well as his powers to persuade and amuse, are also apparent in his jokes and tall tales, which reveal an uncommon sense of humor regarding the political world. "Bull Talk," Davis's joke on himself, is sometimes told about preachers, to ridicule those who would be "holier than thou." Sarah Albritton, an African American from Ruston, tells a preacher version (#120). Also reported by Burrison (1991, 268–69); AT 1920, *Contest in Lying.*

95. Walking on Water. X960. Lie: skills of remarkable person; D1841.4.3. Walking upon water without wetting the soles or garments; D2125.1. Magic power to walk on water.

98. Wedding Special at the Barbershop. K1825.3. Disguise as barber.

99. She Was a Loyal Sam Jones Follower. There is no better testimony than this tale—and those of Sarah Kent (#107–8, below)—to the importance of politics in the daily lives of Louisianans of past generations.

100. You Never Know When Your Ass Is Going to Be in a Box Like Mine. J1190. Cleverness in law court.

101. Chaffee's Bull. A distant cousin of AT 1675, *The Ox (Ass) as Mayor.*

102. And He Knows His State Capitals Too. J1730. Absurd ignorance.

103. The Politician Gets His. AT 1704, *Anecdotes about Absurdly Stingy Persons.*

104. Huey Long and the Importance of Sticking Together. Folk heroes are often also great folktale tellers. Huey Long, like Abraham Lincoln, knew how to manipulate traditional motifs and tales to his own advantage. Joseph Aaron attests to Huey Long's power as a narrator, for Aaron remembers this detail from Huey's speech more than sixty years after hearing it.

105. Huey Long and the Pink Silk Pajama Episode. This tale, which Huey himself loved to tell (and published in his autobiography) is recounted in Blain (1937, 96–101). But Crawford Vincent's version of the tale treats Huey as a far greater hero than Huey himself does. In Huey's version, he is hung over and embarrassed when the German dignitary comes to visit, and he later apologizes to the German, claiming that illness (rather than a hangover) caused him to be wearing his pajamas. This is a far cry from Vincent's depiction of a defiant Huey who insults the ambassador.

106. Huey Let Him Sing. Like "He Knew How to Get Votes" (#91), this is an excellent example of Huey's use of his social and oral artistry to enhance his popularity.

107. Aunt Dora's Death and Aunt Tot's Vote. A Chicago proverb goes, "Vote early and often." A long-standing political accusation against Chicago's Democratic machine is that dead Chicagoans elected John F. Kennedy, for the ballots "cast" for Kennedy by dead people created Kennedy's margin of victory in Illinois and gave him his national electoral majority. The family of Aunt Dora and Aunt Tot seem to have learned both the proverb and the strategy of calling upon dead voters well before 1960.

110–23. Religious Humor. Though extraordinarily popular in oral tradition, jokes on religious topics are not well represented in the type and motif indexes. Loyal Jones (1993) presents a strong sampling of Appalachian jokes on this subject. Recent collections with sections on religious humor survey Indiana (Baker 1986, 156–77), the Ozarks (McNeil 1989, 115–32), Georgia (Burrison 1991, 76–83), and African Americans from Virginia (Dance 1978, 43–76). A particularly rich collection of Louisiana Cajun Catholic jokes on clerics has been published by Ancelet (1985);

Marcia Wallace (1975) has a collection of Southern Baptist jokes, most featuring ministers.

110. The Cajun and the Minister. J1738; X455*. Minister finds listeners are unaware of elementary knowledge of religion. This and tale #112 represent a strand of religious humor popular in the United States since colonial times. Throughout the nineteenth and early twentieth centuries, jokes set in the Appalachians and other relatively inaccessible places would feature an itinerant preacher appalled by the ignorance of the "natives." In a typical story, the preacher finally asks a native, "Don't you know that Christ died for your sins?" The native replies, "Why, no. We don't get the newspaper way out here." Mody Boatright discusses such jokes at length in *Folk Laughter on the American Frontier* (1949).

112. Trying to Get to Heaven. J1738; X455*; see note to tale #110.

113. The Man Who Stole Lumber. Évélia Boudreaux is one of the finest narrators of French-language märchen, legends, and fables. She is discussed and her French tales are presented and translated by Ancelet (1994, lviii–lx and tale nos. 13, 14, 18, 23, 27, 37, 56, 59, 101). This artful tale, narrated in English, is popular among Cajuns and has some close parallels, but no precise analogue, among the Aarne-Thompson tale types. AT 1800–1809, *Jokes about the Confessional.* V20. Confession of sins. Other jokes about confession are #121 and #122.

114. Bless Me, Father. Baker presents an analogue from Indiana (1986, no. 291).

115. Curing Corpses. J1738. Ignorance of religious matters.

116. Don't Cuss in Church. X410. A similar tale appears in Ozark tradition (see McNeil 1989, no. 162) and another is performed in Les Blank's film *In Heaven There Is No Beer?* (1984).

117. The Persimmoned Parson. Jokes about substituted communion wine and wafers are common; this one is related to AT 1836, *The Drunken Parson*; J1261.2. Disrespect for the sacrament; see also X445.1. Parson takes a drink of liquor during the sermon.

118. Brother Jimmy Walks on Water. D2125.1. Magical power to walk on water.

119. God Works in Mysterious Ways. AT 1833, *Application of the Sermon*; one of the most popular themes in Louisiana storytelling tradition. See Harold Talbert's "Responding to the Sermon" (#9), "He Prayed a Good Prayer" (#10), and their corresponding notes, above.

120. The Reverend Gets the Possum. AT 1920, *Contest in Lying.* X459. Jokes on parsons. This is a popular jest in the American South, particularly among African Americans: see Burrison 1991, 268. A European-American version (#94) also appears in this book.

121. Too Strong a Penance. AT 1800–09, *Jokes about the Confessional.* V20. Confession of sins.

122. Not Dressed to Confess. AT 1800–09, *Jokes about the Confessional.* V20. Confession of sins.

123. A Priest with a Small Parish. D1240. Magic Waters and Medicines; X459. Jokes on parsons.

124–37. Fishing and Hunting Tales are mainly of the tall variety. Although European tall tale heroes such as János Hary of Hungary and the Baron von Münchausen of Germany often involve themselves in great social feats—such as overturning kingdoms and defeating armies—the American tall tale teller most often pits himself against nature. The theme of nature's abundance dominates in this collection, as elsewhere in the United States.

124. The Possum Gets Jerry. X1249.5*. Lies about opossum. For more possum lore, see tale #14, above.

126. That Squirrel Could Really Fish. AT 1960C, *The Great Catch of Fish* (X1150.1.); X1302*(d). Extraordinary bait used to catch large fish. This tale offers an excellent application of the idea of unlimited good. Even mistakes produce abundance in the tall tale world.

127. Mosquitoes Save a Life. The mosquito is one animal that almost never gets a kind word from tall tale tellers. By tradition these pernicious insects sharpen their bills with whetstones, kidnap babies, and carry off oxen. In Ancelet's collection of Cajun tales, mosquitoes weigh two hundred pounds and fly off with houses (1994, no. 84). Among the hundreds of bad mosquitoes found in the *Motif-Index* (X1286), there are few good. This story offers a neat inversion of the typical mosquito lore. When mosquitoes and snakes are worked into the same story, there is usually a more negative evaluation of the mosquito. Related to X1286.5(a). Deadly bite of mosquito: Mosquitoes are so deadly that people bitten by mosquitoes have rattlesnakes bite them to counteract the mosquito venom. The best summary of mosquito tales is by Halpert (1990).

128. Looks Can Kill. A parallel version is found in Burrison (1991). Several motifs can be identified in this tale: X1124. Hunter catches or kills game by ingenious or unorthodox method; X137. Humor of ugliness. Hunter's ugliness fatal to animals.

129. A Tale about a Catfish. AT 1960B, *The Great Fish* (X1301). Ancelet (1994, 64) has a Cajun version; see also Lonnie Gray's tales #26 and #27 in this collection, as well as the following story.

130. Does He Drive, Too? AT 1960B, *The Great Fish* (X1301). Fond de Culotte—which literally means "seat of the pants" in Cajun—is a *tit-nom,* or nickname, applied to a foolish person.

131. A Well-Dressed Deer. A common tall tale theme concerns the stupid hunter who mistakes a domestic animal or a human for wild game. Numerous tales, for example, feature a novice hunter who shoots a woman when she tells him, "I'm game." See Baker 1986, no. 238; classified as E57.2 by Clements in his *Types of the Polack Joke* (1969).

132. Fish or Talk. J1250. Clever verbal retorts.

133. The Dog That Walked on Water. Dave Petitjean's masterful joke has a close analogue in Revon Reed's classic, *Le chien qui marchait sur l'eau* (Ancelet 1994, no. 31). Both men are Cajuns, but Petitjean's tale, recorded two decades after Reed's French-language performance, is told in English. Petitjean, who grew up speaking French, preserves a few French words as well as many aspects of the English dialect spoken by older Cajuns, who often created colorful idioms; for example, the term "full bleed" was used to describe purebred, or "full blood" dogs. D2125.1. Magic power to walk on water; J1600. Practical retorts; X1215.13*. Remarkable dog.

134. The Alligator Peach Tree. This basic plot is one of the most common in American tall tale literature, but the animal whose skull becomes the host for a tree is almost always a deer when the tale is told elsewhere. The Louisiana bayous and the tall tale tellers' love of working their surroundings into their stories produce this variation. This story is found in the famous eighteenth-century collection of tales by the Baron von Münchausen, but it has been reported in the United States far more often than in any other country. Among the most recent published variants is one from Florida (Reaver 1987, 81). AT1889C, *Fruit Tree Grows from Head of Deer Shot with Fruit Pits* (X1130.2).

135. All His Ducks in a Row. AT 1890E, *Gun Barrel Bent.* X1122.3. Lie: ingenious person bends gun barrel to make spectacular shot. Baughman reports this tale exclusively from the New World, but it too is related to a tale in the eighteenth-century collection of Baron von Münchausen. The tale is popular with French Americans; Ancelet (1994, no. 73) has a version from Lazard Daigle (no relation to Pierre Daigle, narrator of the present story.)

136. A Frog Gigging Story. X1342. Lies about frogs; X1201. The great animal; X1130. Lie: unusual experience of hunter.

137. Tit Jean, the Greatest Liar of Them All. This is one of the most popular of American tales about great liars. Among the many places recording the tale are Florida (Reaver 1987, 21), Illinois (Dorson 1964, 357) and Maine (Dorson 1964, 67). AT 1920B, *"I Have Not Time To Lie"* (X905.4); AT 1895, *Man Wading in Water Catches Many Fish in His Boots* (X1112); X1154. Lie: Unusual catch by fisherman. The figure of Tit Jean appears in all manner of Louisiana French tales, but especially in märchen and tall tales, where he occupies a position similar to that of Jack in British-American lore. For some Louisiana French märchen in which he appears, see Saucier (1962, 56–65). Ray Robinson tells this tale in his book, *Tales of the Louisiana Bayous* (1984).

138. The Terrorism of Bonnie and Clyde. Folklore projects two opposed images of Bonnie and Clyde. In central Texas, where Bonnie Parker (b. 1911) and Clyde Barrow (b. 1909) spent their youth, a wealth of stories, still circulating, depicts them as romantic Robin Hoods. One man brought up with those legends, Bob Benton, went on to coauthor the screenplay of the famous film *Bonnie and Clyde* (dir. Arthur Penn, 1967), starring Warren Beatty and Faye Dunaway, who did much to spread the romantic image of the couple throughout the nation (Towne 1972; Wake and Hayden 1972). A second folk tradition, far more negative, casts Clyde as "The Texas Rattlesnake" and Bonnie as "Suicide Sal" (Nash 1973, 43), a couple of cold-blooded killers. This is the portrait of Bonnie and Clyde that emerges from the Louisiana tales of Clarence Faulk and Julienne Cole. Faulk states accurately that Bonnie and Clyde shot down poor, innocent people; "far from Robin Hood types," the couple "preyed on their fellow poor and killed them ruthlessly, thoughtlessly. They were hated by their own kind" (Nash 1973, 40). An equally legendary bank robber, John Dillenger, is reported to have called Bonnie and Clyde "a couple of punks. They're giving bank-robbing a bad name" (Nash 1973, 40). Thirteen murders are attributed to Bonnie and Clyde and their gang; nine of the victims were law officers (Nash 1973, 39–40).

139. Bonnie and Clyde Almost Rob the Ruston State Bank. Clarence Faulk remembers Bonnie Parker as smoking a cigar. Indeed Bonnie promoted the image of herself as a cigar smoker, and she once posed for a photo with a cigar in her mouth. Later, however, she told one of her hostages, "Tell the public I don't smoke cigars. It's the bunk" (Nash 1973, 43).

140. The Day Bonnie and Clyde Were Killed: May 23, 1934. As Clarence Faulk reports, "over a hundred" shells (one report states 187) hit Bonnie and Clyde, who died with their "pistols in their hands." But, apparently, the couple had no opportunity to use their guns, because the police ambush was successful and the two "died instantly. Clyde had been driving in his socks and Bonnie had a sandwich in her mouth" (Nash 1973, 45).

143. Winn Parish Night Riders. Attached to this story of robbery are a number of motifs. The woman who entices visitors to board with her and then kills them exists in both social reality and in folk legend and is probably best known in the case of Belle Gunness, the Lady Bluebeard of La Porte, Indiana (Langlois 1985). The motif of people so sinister that they impale babies on knives or bayonets is also widespread (S100. Revolting murders or mutilations). The phenomenon of the night riders, or vigilance committees, is dealt with in tales by French-speaking Creoles Inez Catalon and Westley Dennis (Ancelet 1994, nos. 104–6).

144. The Legend of Lying Horse Rock. N591. Curse on treasure.

145. The Traveling Salesman. D1654.3.1. Indelible mark; cf. H215.4. Ineradicable handprint proves innocence; E613.6. Reincarnation as dove.

146. Eugene Bunch, the Robin Hood of Southeast Louisiana. Robin Hood motifs abound in this tale. The tale of "robbing the robber"—stealing from the man who stole the poor woman's money and returning the money to the original owner—appears in one of the earliest surviving Robin Hood tales, "The Geste of Robin Hood" (Child 1882–98, no. 117), written in England in the fifteenth century. Also shared with the Robin Hood story is the belief of murder by treachery. These motifs also appear in American legends about Jesse James, Sam Bass, Pretty Boy Floyd, and Billy the Kid, to name a few. See Randolph's tale about Jesse James (1958, 91–92, 157) collected in the Ozarks in 1950. Rosenberg (1982, 171–74) and Steckmesser (1966) provide brief surveys of related tales.

147. Ben Lilly, Strongman of Morehouse Parish. The local strong man is one of the major figures of folk legendry; see the discussion on historical legends in the introduction. Stories of local strongmen also abound in Louisiana's Cajun tradition, often attached to such legendary constables as Joe Hanks and Martin Weber, who took on the formidable job of keeping order at dance halls in the first half of this century, when fist- and knife-fights abounded. Ancelet (1994, nos. 111–12) presents tales about the Cajun strongman Martin Weber.

Benjamin Vernon Lilly (1856–1936) has become a local legend in several locales. He first visited Louisiana at age twelve, after running away from his parents' home in Mississippi and walking to Morehouse Parish to live with his uncle Vernon. In J. Frank Dobie's account of *The Ben Lilly Legend,* Lilly was not only a legendary strongman in Louisiana (Dobie 1950, 29–49), but later also a legendary hunter and tracker in Texas, Mexico, and the Rocky Mountains (101–69). Dobie's account of Ben Lilly's Louisiana years was based largely on oral traditions in Morehouse Parish, including stories from four residents of Bastrop, the home of James B. Rider, narrator of the present tale. For a reporter's firsthand account of a Lilly bear hunt in East Texas in 1906, see Abernethy (1968, 123–36).

F610. Remarkably strong man; C631. Tabu: breaking the sabbath (cf. Dobie 1950, 39); F628.1.1.4. Strong man kills bear (cf. Dobie 1950, 75–76); F652. Marvelous sense of smell; F685. Marvelous withstander of cold. Ben has much in common with the marvelous companions of märchen fame; see, for example, the band of heroes in Cajun Elby Deshotels's tale, *Jean L'Ours et la fille du Roi* (Ancelet 1994, no. 20).

148. The Legend of the Brooch. This is one of innumerable Lafitte legends currently in oral circulation in Louisiana; see also stories #163 and #169. Other published tales include several in Saxon et al. (1945, 258–65, 275) and a more recent buried treasure tale in Langley et al. (1995, 13).

Jean Lafitte (also spelled Laffite; 1780?–1826) was born in France, but he made his name on the Gulf Coast, where he engaged in smuggling and, by 1810, commanded a pirate band based on Grand Terre Island off the Lousiana shore. In 1813, Louisiana Governor William Claiborne offered a $500 reward for Lafitte's capture; Lafitte responded with a $1,500 reward for Claiborne. But when the United States fought England in the War of 1812, Lafitte allied his band with the Americans, supported General Andrew Jackson at the Battle of New Orleans, and earned a presidential pardon for his loyalty. However, he soon returned to piracy. As his Grand Terre headquarters had been destroyed by the American government, he relocated to Galveston Island (now part of Texas), from which he was driven in 1821 to resume his wanderings. The date and place of his death are uncertain. Gonzalez (1981) has written a good biography of Lafitte.

149. Shine and the Titanic. African-American toasts, discussed briefly in the introduction to this book, are most often performed in all-male, adult settings. Arthur Pfister changed his normal version of "Shine and the Titanic" to make it more suitable for a live festival audience. The text printed here is the version that Pfister himself wrote down for that live performance. F696. Marvelous swimmer.

Though focused on a major historical event, this rhymed narrative stretches the notion of historical legend almost past its limits. After the sinking of the Titanic in 1912, legends sprang up concerning the celebrated African-American boxing champion Jack Johnson: the story went that Johnson had not been allowed to board the segregated ocean liner and thus his life was spared. The relationship of Johnson to Shine, the hero of this toast, is unclear, but most toast singers now regard Shine as an imaginary and not a historical figure. Roger Abrahams (1970, 120–29) documents verses related to this toast as early as 1918 and presents evidence that related rhymes centered around other African-American heroes were in circulation before the sinking of the Titanic. Saxon et al. (1945, 373–74) present parts of a similar toast collected in New Orleans in the 1930s.

151. Old Levi Loved His Goats. Some historical legends focus not on heroes but on local characters who become the target of their neighbors' more or less innocent anecdotes and practical jokes. Anecdotes of Captain Horace Smith collected in Maine by Richard Dorson (1964, 65–67) bear some resemblance to the Old Levi tale. Lyle Saxon's *Gumbo Ya Ya* (1945) presents tales about local characters in the African- American neighborhoods of New Orleans.

152. The Cournair. *Cournair* is a French term for "cuckold," used to deride a man whose wife cheats on him. Q411.0.1.1. Adulterer Killed. Ray Robinson, the present teller, presents a written version in his book, *Tales of the Louisiana Bayous* (1984).

153–56, 194–95. The Isleños of St. Bernard Parish. The following notes are supplied by Samuel G. Armistead, who also transcribed and translated all the book's Isleño texts (153–56, 194–95).

The Isleños live in six small communities in lower St. Bernard Parish, about thirty-five miles southeast of New Orleans: Delacroix ("The Island"), Woods Lake, Reggio, Yscloskey, Shell Beach, and Hopedale. They are descendants of colonists from the Canary Islands, who arrived in Louisiana in 1778, as part of a colonization initiative supported by the Spanish governor, Bernardo Gálvez. Traditionally, they have been trappers, fishermen, duck hunters, shrimp trawlers, oystermen, crabbers, and alligator hunters. The Isleños are intensely and justifiably proud of their Hispanic heritage. Having lived in relative isolation from the dominant French- and English-speaking communities of Louisiana for more than two hundred years and, at the same time, having never completely broken their ties with the Canary Islands and with other Spanish-speaking areas, the Isleños have kept, down to the present day, the distinctive Louisiana-Spanish dialect that developed in their Delta communities. Isleño Spanish has retained many of its original Canarian characteristics, in both lexicon and phonology, but it has also borrowed a substantial vocabulary from American Spanish, from Cajun French, and from English, as well as from Portuguese, by way of the numerous Portuguese loanwords in Canarian Spanish. Isleño folklore is similarly eclectic, combining ancestral Canarian items with others borrowed from other Hispanic areas: Andalusia, Castile, Asturias, Catalonia, Spanish Caribbean islands, Mexico, and the American Southwest. There are also certain limited influences from the Cajun French song repertoire and, more recently, even from country and western music. A distinctively local and specifically Isleño creation are the satirical narrative poems, known as *décimas*, which allude to events in local history and to the perils and travails of local activities. The *décimas* also poke fun at the weaknesses and foibles of local individuals, but others may re-create centuries-old themes, having their origins in the medieval ballads (*romances*) of Spanish tradition. Together with these poetic narratives, the Isleños also have a well-developed repertoire of traditional folktales.

The *décima* was originally characterized by a ten-verse stanza, embodying a complex consonantal rhyme scheme (typically: *abba-ac-cddc*) and having octosyllabic verses, but in St. Bernard Parish, while the term *décima* has survived, the songs themselves now usually consist of anisosyllabic (predominantly octosyllabic) quatrains, with assonant rhyme in every second verse, reflecting the influence of Spanish ballad meter and of the *corrido* of Mexico, Central America, and the U.S. Southwest.

Irvan Perez, who lives in Poydras (St. Bernard Parish), is a great singer of traditional *décimas* and is the foremost authority on Isleño language and folklore. His unflagging enthusiasm and devotion to his ancestral heritage have contributed incalculably to the current revival of local and international interest in Isleño popular culture. His superb knowledge of the Isleño dialect includes total control of an exhaustive lexicon covering every animal, bird, reptile, fish, insect, plant, and tree native to the local marshlands (*la plería*), as well as every detail of the traditional material culture of the Isleño community. In 1991, Irvan Perez was awarded a National Heritage Fellowship, from the National Endowment for the Arts, in recognition of his artistry and his dedication to maintaining the traditional culture of the Isleño people. The four *décimas* included here were sung by Irvan Perez in 1989 and can be heard on the cassette recording, *Spanish Décimas from St. Bernard Parish,* produced by the Louisiana Folklife Center, at Northwestern State University, in Natchitoches.

153. La vuelta del marido. This song reflects one of the favorite themes of Pan-European balladry: the husband returns from war, unrecognized, and before revealing his true identity, tests the fidelity of his unsuspecting wife. *The Husband's Return* (in -é- assonance) is a very old text-type in the Hispanic tradition. Its earliest known analogue figures in a medieval French manuscript dating from the 1400s and the earliest Spanish text was printed in 1605. The ballad is still sung essentially wherever Spanish is spoken today, from Spain, the Canary Islands, and throughout Spanish America, to the most distant reaches of the Hispanic world, such as the Philippines and the Judeo-Spanish communities of Morocco, the Balkans, and the Near East. The Isleño versions show particular affinity to texts collected in the American Southwest. For the song's origin and distribution in Hispanic lands, as well as for other Isleño variants, see Armistead (1978, 45–46; 1983, 42–43; 1992, 64–65). Compare these motifs: N741. Unexpected meeting of husband and wife; N741.4. Husband and wife reunited after long separation and tedious quest; K1813. Disguised husband visits his wife. Concerning the Isleños and their folk literature, see MacCurdy (1975) and Armistead (1992); for their history, Din (1988); for their language, MacCurdy (1950) and Lipski (1990).

154. La vida de un jaibero. For two other Isleño texts, see Armistead (1992, 30–31).

155. La pesca del camarón. For another Isleño version, sung by Chelito Campo, see Armistead (1992, 34–35). AT 1960C, *The Great Catch of Fish,* and 1960H, *The Great Ship,* as well as the motifs: X1150.1. The great catch of fish; X1061. Lie: great boat or ship of remarkable man; X1061.1. Remarkable size of great ship; for more parallels: Armistead (1992, 25, n. 15).

156. Setecientos setentaisiete. Inspired by a new Isleño cultural awareness and deep pride in their distinctive Hispanic origins, the song is, without doubt, the only *décima* that uses data taken from written history, in offering a succinct historical overview of the Isleño community's beginnings, travails, and subsequent development. For another rendition by Irvan Perez, see Armistead (1992, 37–38).

159–65. Buried Treasure stories, though extremely common throughout the U.S., are underrepresented in the best recent collections (e.g., Burrison 1991). Treasure legends straddle the boundary between the everyday and the supernatural. Some narratives, such as "The Widow's Buried Gold" (#157), unfold in the real world, while others, such as "A Moaning Ghost and Buried Treasure" (#165), are filled with otherworldly occurrences. Even when ghosts fail to appear (as in "Buried Treasure Money Used to Build a Catholic Church" [#158]), there is often perceived to be something eerie or cursed about treasure. The idea that one cannot get something for nothing seems to lie behind the elusiveness of buried money—and behind the curses that attend it when it is finally discovered. Saxon et al. (1945, 258–71) summarize many legends collected in the Depression Era and present a table of thirty-three treasure legends and treasure hunts from the state; Jameson (1993, 63–89) presents five Louisiana treasure tales; and Langley et al. (1995) print eleven more from Louisiana Cajuns, African Americans, and German Americans. Harry Middleton Hyatt's large collection of African-American hoodoo and conjuration lore (1970–78) contains references to Louisiana magical beliefs and practices related to searching for buried treasure (see, for example, de Caro 1974, 33). For an Isleño legend from St. Bernard Parish, see Armistead (1992, 151, n.3; 153, no. 11.2).

157. The Widow's Buried Gold. N511.1. Treasure buried by men; S32. Cruel stepfather.

158. Buried Treasure Money Used to Build a Catholic Church. Although there is nothing overtly supernatural about this story, the narrator implies that there is something more than coincidental about the way in which the two churches built with the buried money burned to the ground at seven-year intervals. N591. Curse on treasure; Z71.5. Formulistic number: seven.

159. Family Misfortunes. N513.4. Treasure hidden in river; N534. Treasure discovered by accident.

160. Found Silver. Another story about the outlaw West; see "Winn Parish Night Riders" (#144, above). N512. Treasure in underground cavern; S100. Revolting murders or mutilations.

161. Buried Money near Highway 171. Related to N557. Treasure disappears after being uncovered.

162. A Barrel of Money. N511.1.8.

163. Buried Treasure of Jean Lafitte. N513.5. Treasure buried in sunken ship. Two other Lafitte tales appear in this book (#148, #169).

The numerous legends of Lafitte's buried treasures are doubted by historians, who point out that he was short of funds when he left the Gulf coast. Nevertheless, thousands of people have searched for his loot. For a brief biography of Lafitte and references to other published Lafitte treasure tales, see the note to tale #148, above.

164. The Haint Took It. This mysterious memorate is filled with supernatural references. The narrator understands some of them but still is unsure of the exact nature of the ritual used by the treasure hunter. N553.1. Tabu: Incontinence while treasure is being raised; N553.2. Unlucky encounter causes treasure-seekers to talk and thus lose treasure; N554. Ceremonies and prayers used at unearthing of treasure; N557. Treasure disappears after being uncovered. The motif of sacrificing slaves to guard treasure has no number, but it is related to N554.1. Sacrifices at unearthing of treasure; and E291. Ghost protects hidden treasure.

165. A Moaning Ghost and Buried Treasure. C401.3. N571.2*(a). Bird as ghostly treasure guard. E402.1.1.2. Ghost Moans.

166. Failure to Heed a Warning. The *avertissements* that Velma Duet describes have their parallels in British American tradition. Known as "tokens" in the South and "forerunners" in the Northeast, such supernatural phenomena usually predict an unchangeable future (see Dorson 1964, 63–64).

167. Veiled Eyes. The caul, or veil, is a portion of the membrane covering the fetus that emerges with the infant at birth, sometimes giving the appearance that the infant is wearing a hat or veil. The idea that those born with cauls possess special powers is widespread in European and American folk belief. C401.3. Tabu: speaking while searching for treasure; T588. Motifs associated with the placenta; T589.4. Birth with veil brings luck. See Cassetta et al. (1981, nos. 25060–25112); Hand (1961–64, nos. 244–45); H. Roberts (1927, no. 12).

168. The Rooster Knows. The belief that the cock's crow means company is reported throughout the rural United States; see Hand (1961–64, 3938–66).

169. The Ghosts of Jean Lafitte's Pirates. E265.2. Meeting ghost causes madness; N570. Guardian of treasure; N576. Ghosts prevent men from raising treasure. Other Lafitte tales are #148 and #163, above.

170. A Brush with the Loup Garou. Often spelled or pronounced *rou garou* in Cajun Louisiana, the *loup garou* is the French term for "werewolf," a human being transformed into a wolf. Unlike the typical Hollywood victim, who becomes a wolf when bitten by another werewolf, a French American can become a wolf simply by committing a sin. As John Verret explains, when "you do something wrong, . . . then . . . God turns his back on you. Then the devil takes over." In French Canadian *loup garou* stories, missing mass on Sunday is sometimes enough to turn a man into a monster (Dorson 1975, 465). Although most British Americans are familiar with werewolves principally through horror films, the Cajun *loup garou* has long been a subject of folk belief and oral storytelling (see Ancelet et al. 1991, 215; Sarrazin et al. 1968). Dorson records similar *loup garou* stories from French Americans in Michigan (1952, 71–78). Motifs: D113.1.1. Werewolf; D142.0.1. Transformation: woman to cat; D712.4. Disenchantment by drawing blood; Z72.1. Year and a day; C423.1. Tabu:

revealing the marvelous; E721.1. Soul wanders from body in sleep. See also tales #174 and #176, below.

171. A Brief Encounter with a Ghost. E422.4.4(ea). Female revenant in form of nun.

172. Feu Follet ("Fool's Fire," or *ignus fatuous*) is the Cajun term for the glowing apparition known to most Americans as the will-o'-the-wisp. Usually interpreted in folk belief as a ghost or a spirit, the will-o'-the-wisp is explained by geologists as a miasma, or glowing swamp gas. Note that John Verret sees the *feu follet* not merely as a spirit, but as Hell's angel. Another Cajun belief holds the *feu follet* to be the wandering soul of an unbaptized baby (Ancelet et al. 1991, 215; Bourque 1968; Ditchy and Reinecke 1966, 49–50). Dorson reports similar beliefs from French Americans in Michigan (1952, 86). F491. Will-o'-the-Wisp; F491.1. Will-o'-the-Wisp leads people astray; A302. Angel of Hell.

173. Two Mysteries of Bayou Go to Hell. D915. Magic river; D1976.1. Transportation during magic sleep. Anderson (1958) recounts tales of a similar haunted Louisiana bayou from newspaper accounts published in 1847; but, while Anderson's bayou is imaginary, Bayou Go to Hell is the name of an actual bayou located in Terrebonne Parish.

174. An Oyster-Culling Loup Garou. Unlike the fearsome *loup garou* described by John Verret, the creature who visits the oyster cullers in this tale is helpful and friendly, if a bit greedy; the workmen are not afraid of this beast; see motif N810. Supernatural helpers. Perhaps the oldest surviving French werewolf tale, the twelfth-century poem *Bisclavret,* features a similarly friendly werewolf (Marie de France 1986, 68–72). Much like the werewolf described by John Verret (#170), the oyster-culling *loup garou* is disenchanted by a blow from a pole (D712.3. Disenchantment by striking); but while Verret's werewolves bleed, this being seems to be more shadow than substance. D113.1.1. Werewolf.

175. The Shadow Companion. Like the previous legend, this haunting tale features a supernatural companion who is more friend than foe, a creature that shares the protagonist's time and his fate—and perhaps his soul as well. Such creatures are sometimes known as "familiars" (in some English traditions) or as "animal companion spirits" (in some Native American traditions). Unlike the spirit described here, the familiars of American folklore are most often considered evil and associated with witchcraft. F403.2.2.1. Familiar spirit in animal form; F403.2.2.3. Familiar spirit equivalent to man's soul; E765.2. Life bound up with that of animal; person to live as long as animal does; D712.3. Disenchantment by striking.

176. Loup Garou *as Shadow Companion.* Glen Pitre's storytelling skills are clearly part of his family heritage; but, like every great narrator, Glen makes this tale uniquely his own. Themes and episodes from the two previous tales, told by Glen's father, are reshaped in this version, which Glen learned from his uncle. Here, once more, the supernatural being is a lifelong companion. D113.1.1. Werewolf; N810. Supernatural helpers; F403.2.2.3. Familiar sprit equivalent to man's soul; E765.2. Life bound up with that of animal; person to live as long as animal does; D712.4. Disenchantment by drawing blood.

177. *Lifesaving Sirens.* B81. Mermaid. Here is another tale displaying the helpful side of supernatural beings. In European and American legends mermaids and sirens tend to drown or abduct sailors; the life-threatening sirens of Book 12 of the *Odyssey* are typical. In coastal Brittany, however, there is a tradition that sirens are lifesavers (B53.1. Drowning man rescued by siren). Brittany was the French homeland for some of the Acadians who migrated to Louisiana; perhaps that group influenced the mermaid tradition represented in this tale.

Dorson (1967, 250–54) documents a substantial tradition of mermaid tales from African Americans in the South; like the mermaids featured in this tale, those of black legendry often nurture mortal men, but, like mermaids elsewhere, they also tend to abduct their men and live with them undersea before taking them safely back to land.

178. *The Silk Lady.* This account incorporates many of the typical motifs of European-American ghostlore. Like ghosts throughout the country, she is a glowing apparition (E421.3. Luminous ghosts) of a woman dressed in white (E422.4.4[a]. Female revenant in white clothing) who appears only at night, floating in the air (F411.2), moaning (E402.1.1.2), screaming (E402.1.1.3), frightening sensitive animals (B733. Animals spirit-sighted), making horses rear (E421.1.2(a). Ghost scares horse), and attacking people (E261. Wandering ghost makes attack). But this creature has some more distinctive, haunting qualities, represented in her "silky eyes" (cf. E421.3.3. Ghost with glowing face) and long silky fingernails (E422.1.8. Revenant with peculiar nails). Finally, she is a family ghost, a female that seems to prefer haunting males, especially Peter Gitz and his male ancestors, whom she has visited since the 1850s. The Silk Lady bears some resemblance to the famous ghost of "Mona Lisa" said to stalk City Park in New Orleans; see Chambers (1983), Senn (1983), and Orso (1993).

179. *The Red-Headed Witch of Bogalusa Creek.* Across the country, ghosts stalk lovers' lanes, and adolescents who travel with their dates to visit lonely places tell each other hair-raising stories about the spirits of frustrated lovers or sex maniacs. Many people, like Mary Etta Scarborough Moody, visit these sites to see for themselves if the ghosts and monsters are really there. During such ritual visitations, the storytellers act out the plot of the legend, and when (and if) they return to the company of their friends, they tell the story of their experiences. Their accounts become part of the legend process. Like so many "lovers' lane" legends across the

country, Moody's account is in two parts: half is the story she heard as a child, and the other half is an account of her own experience with the Red-Headed Witch. G213. Witch with extraordinary eyes; G219.4. Witch with very long hair; G224.4. Person sells soul to devil in exchange for witch powers; G242. Witch flies through air; G262. Murderous witch; T93.3. Disappointed lover a suicide; E334.4. Ghost haunts suicide spot; E266.1. Ghost of suicide drags people into stream; Q503. Wandering after death as punishment; M210. Bargain with devil; D1841.4.3. Walking upon water without wetting the soles or garments; F411.2. Spirit walks on water; G221.3. Witch has extraordinary strength; D2172.1. Magic repetition: person must keep on doing or saying thing until released. If you catch her, she'll take your place.

180. The Hammering Ghost of Minden. E402.1.8(g). Ghost uses hammer, saw, plane in woodworking shop. Wind in curtains mistaken for ghost; E338.1. Nonmalevolent ghost haunts house or castle.

181. Bloody Mary. Among the most common aspects of children's unofficial education is learning schoolhouse ghost stories and rituals. Grade-school ghosts appear most often in the bathroom, when the lights are suddenly switched off. Children scare each other and test their own courage by turning out the lights while staring in the mirror. The figure one sees in the mirror just as the room grows dark is supposed to be the ghost, often named "Bloody Mary" or "Mary Whales" (see Langlois 1981). One relatively recent twist of plot present in this story is the alien factor. In much contemporary lore, extraterrestrials are taking on the roles once reserved for ghosts.

182. The Headless Man of Black Bayou. E272. Road-ghosts; E413.1. Execution victim cannot rest in grave; E422.1.1. Headless revenant.

183. Evie Sees the Headless Man. E422.1.1. Headless revenant.

184. Who's Gon'na Sleep with Me? This simple but artful scare story usually ends with a practical joke. When the spirit has drawn close to the victim, the tale teller yells out "gotcha" and grabs the listener, producing screams and frightened laughter. Although legends tend to be belief narratives, this story might be classified a humorous antilegend, a tale that exploits certain beliefs and fears but then deflates them by turning a frightening narrative into a joke. This is a variant of one of the most popular American folktales, AT 366, *The Man from the Gallows.* In most versions the action begins when a man steals a special object or a body part from a corpse. The corpse pursues the thief into his house, and the tale teller ends by screaming and grabbing one of the listeners. Among the best-known American versions is "The Golden Arm," celebrated by Mark Twain in his essay, "How to Tell a Story." Grider (1980) discusses American variants of AT 366. Motif Z13.1. Tale-teller frightens listener: yells "Boo" at exciting point.

185. A Holy Tree. D950. Magic Tree; F811. Extraordinary Tree; D1542.1. Magic object produces rain; D2143. Rain produced by magic.

186. A Miracle at the Mother of Grace Chapel. Too often folklorists associate legendry solely with the eerie or evil side of the supernatural. Yet such hopeful Christian legends as the following are also part of the corpus. This group narration preserves the authentic flavor of the way in which legends are most often shared and spread: through group participation in which two or more tellers create a "negotiated text." D2167.3. Flowers magically kept from withering; V268. Miracles performed under protection of Virgin Mary; V268.5. Image of Virgin Mary works miracles.

187. Mr. Blue and the Dog Ghost. Belief in and fear of dog ghosts has long been part of African-American folk belief. Stories similar to this are reported elsewhere in Louisiana (Martin 1968), in Texas (Brewer 1976, 89–93) and in the Caribbean. A relatively rare British-American dog ghost story come from West Virginia (Musick 1977, 21). E521.2. Ghost of dog; B733. Animals spirit-sighted; closely related to E421.1.2. Ghost visible to horses alone.

188. La chaudiérée de couche-couche. AT 15, *The Theft of Honey (Butter) by Playing Godfather.* Julia Huval's well-told tale belongs to a rich African-American, Creole, and European-American tradition. Reported in the famous Grimm collection (1960, no. 2), in Africa (Klipple 1991), and in France (Massignon 1968, no. 54), AT 15 is also well known in French-speaking Canada (Dorson 1975, 445–48) and Missouri (Carrière 1937, nos. 6, 7). African-American variants include two collected by Dorson (1967, nos. 1, 2) and one Louisiana tale by Clifford Blake (#209, below). AT 15 has been popular among Louisiana Cajuns and Creoles (Ancelet 1994, no. 1; Reneaux 1992, 26–30). This variant is particularly interesting for its local flavor. In most international versions, rabbit steals either honey or butter, but here he steals couche-couche, a local Cajun and Creole food. As Madame Huval explains, her family had no butter. She does not remember eating butter as a child.

189. Quartorze. A variant of AT 1640, *The Brave Tailor.* Often the young boy kills seven flies in one blow, but in this variant, he kills fourteen and then writes *Tué Quatorze* on his cap. Motifs associated with this variant are K1741.3. Bringing the whole well; and K1741.1. Felling the whole forest. Legaré (1980, 127–35) prints a variant from French-speaking Mauritius in which the young boy is called Monsieur Quatorze and is forced to leave because his family is so poor. "Fourteen" is also the name of the hero in some British-American tales (Perdue 1987, no. 2). Other variants are found in France (Massignon 1968) and French Canada (Lemieux 1973, 221–52), where the young tailor writes on his cap, "I killed a thousand at one blow!" Motif K1951.1. Boastful fly-killer: seven at a blow.

190. Bouki and Lapin in the Garden. The tale of the tarbaby and the briar patch, made world famous by Joel Chandler Harris's Brer Rabbit stories and by Walt Disney's

1946 cartoon rendition, has been collected from French-speaking Americans since the nineteenth century; see Fortier (1895, 108). Similar tales have been collected in French-speaking Missouri (Carrière 1937). AT 175; K741. Capture by tar baby; K581.2, Briar-patch punishment for rabbit. Three other Louisiana variants of this story—#33, #49, #200—appear in this book.

191. *A Chitimacha Flood Story*. A1010. Deluge. Stories of a flood that covered the earth in the distant past, destroying much of humanity, are found throughout the world (Dundes 1988b; Pessoa 1948). A1029.3. Escape from deluge in pot or jar, a motif that is often recorded in South America; B2. Animal totems. This Chitimacha tale of the friendship between humans and snakes stands in stark contrast with Clifford Blake's "Snake in a Wagon Rut" (#206) and other African-American and European-American tales that explain the origin of antagonism between snakes and people. Orso and Plaisance (1974) print a variant of this tale and provide some cultural background on the Chitimacha.

192. *How Bayou Teche Was Formed*. A930.1.1. Snake as Creator of Rivers and Lakes.

193. *She Has the Key*. African-American oral traditions contain a significant proportion of tales that more or less humorously explain the origins of current social relationships. Wilson "Ben Guiné" Mitchell's tale of the race between black and white men (#35 in this collection) supplies just one example (see also Dorson 1967, 171–86). Yet there are many other tales devoted specifically to the relationships between men and women (e.g., Hurston 1935, 80–81; Abrahams 1985, no. 3). This one bears a close resemblance to an African-American tale retold by Zora Neale Hurston in *Mules and Men* (1935, 33–38); in Hurston's Florida variant, the lucky woman has three keys of power over her husband: the keys to the kitchen, the nursery, and the bedroom. A1557. Why woman is master of her husband.

194. *La tortuga y el conejo*. This and the following tale represent the Spanish-language folktale tradition of the Isleños of St. Bernard Parish, whose culture and *décima* traditions are briefly described in Samuel G. Armistead's notes to tales #153–56; the following notes are also by Armistead.

In addition to their locally created tradition of narrative poetry, the *Isleños* also cultivated an extensive repertoire of traditional folktales, anecdotes, and legends. Joseph "Chelito" Campo, of Delacroix Island (*La Isla*), is one of the great old-time *décima* singers and, like Irvan Perez, has an extensive repertoire of other folklore forms as well: lyric songs (*coplas*), children's rhymes, riddles (*adivinas*), proverbs (*dichetes*), and personal narratives. Chelito is also an expert raconteur, who has preserved the old folktale tradition down to the present day. He is a great folk artist, who loves to perform and who reacts with zest to enthusiastic interest in his art. Varying his intonation and changing voices, Chelito punctuates his narratives with exclamations, asides, commentary, and laughter, constantly dramatizing his stories and allowing us to imagine how a rich tradition of Hispanic folktales must once have flourished among the Isleños, gathered of an evening at a trapper's *campa* somewhere out on the *plería* or on some shrimp boat, hove to for the night, far out on the Gulf. The folktales edited and translated here were collected by Samuel G. Armistead, at Delacroix Island, on January 4, 1981.

The plot of *La tortuga y el conejo,* known worldwide, is told by Castilian speakers in Spain, Spanish speakers throughout the New World, Portuguese speakers in Brazil and the Cape Verde Islands, and Catalan speakers in Catalonia. For another Isleño version, also told by Joseph (Chelito) Campo, see Armistead (1992, 143–144), where further parallels and Pan-Hispanic variants are listed. AT 1074, *Race Won by Deception: Relative Helpers* (motif K11.1). For a Koasati Native American version of AT 1074, see Bel Abbey's tale #38 in this volume; the note to #38 comments on African-American and Native American versions of the tale.

195. La Muerte compadre. This is a widely diffused story, known throughout Europe and in European settlements in the New World, as well as in Arabic, Armenian, Hebrew, and Turkish versions from the Middle East. Many texts have been reported from Spanish-, Portuguese-, and Catalan-speaking areas, both on the Iberian Peninsula and overseas. This tale, also collected by MacCurdy (1952, no. 2) in a more extensive form, represents AT 332, *Godfather Death.* The present text was edited and translated by Armistead (1992, 139–41, where further references are provided).

197. How the Bat Got Its Wings. Because bats blur the boundaries between mammals and birds, they are the subject of many tales that attempt to explain their mixed characteristics. In Africa and among native North American cultures, the confusing status of the bat is often explained in terms of a game or war between the animals and the birds. Usually the bat is seen as a cheater or a fence-sitter who sides with the birds when they are ahead and with the mammals when the tide turns; the two sides then call a truce and the bat is punished for switching sides by being forced to sleep upside down during the day and come out only at night. This Koasati tale is far friendlier to the bat, who becomes a surprise hero in the contest between birds and beasts. Like so many related stories, this tale also explains the strange characteristics of bats—in this case, its zigzag flight pattern A2377. Origin of animal characteristics: wings. B449.3. Helpful bat. Cf. AT 222A, *Bat in War of Birds and Quadrupeds* (B261.1); A2442. Method and position of bird's flight. Another version of this tale appears in Langley et al. (1995, 47–53) with two other stories narrated by Bertney Langley.

198. Learning from the Bear. Bertney Langley learned this tale from the great Koasati narrator Bel Abbey. Bel's version also appears in this collection; see tale #37 and its corresponding note.

199. Old Woman and Her Pig. AT 2030; Z41. This variant follows almost word-for-word the text that appears in Joseph Jacobs's classic, *English Fairy Tales* (New York, 1902), one of the best-selling fairy tale collections in United States history. Dolores Henderson's only significant departure from this text is a kindness she shows the butcher. The tale generally runs, "rope hang butcher," rather than "rope tie butcher." For an elaborated Ozarks variant see Young and Young 1989, no. 68.

200. Brer Rabbit and the Tarbaby. See tales #33, #49, #190, and their corresponding notes.

201. The Legend of the Mosquito. A2034. Origin of mosquitoes. Tales turning on this theme have been widely collected in China, Japan, and India. K2213.5. Faithless resuscitated wife. This particular tale is closely related to AT 612, *The Three Snake-Leaves.* E113. Resuscitation by blood, a motif common in India as well as in the Western world; cf. A2034.3. Mosquitoes from ashes of bad woman. Eberhard (1937) identifies several Chinese variants. The negative view of the mosquito expressed in this story is common in folklore worldwide; see, for example, the notes to "Mosquitoes Save a Life," tale #127 above.

202. How the Tiger Got His Stripes. A2413.4. Origin of stripes of tiger. Enmity story. A2494.10.1. Enmity between tiger and man. A motif common in south and southeast Asia.

203. Why the Crow Is Black. A2219.1. Animal has color spilled on him: cause of his color. A2411.2.1.6. Origin of color of crow; A2411.2.6.7. Origin of color of peacock; A2522.5. Why crow is disliked. Abundant stories from India and other parts of South and East Asia are devoted to the origin of the peacock's feathers. Stories about the crow, however, like the crow itself, are much more common worldwide. In most traditions, the crow is turned black as a punishment for evil intent or actions. In this Vietnamese tale, however, the crow is good-natured and generous, guilty of nothing more than gullibility.

204. Why the Ocean is Salty. AT 565, *The Magic Mill.* Variants of this tale are found in medieval and modern Europe as well as in East Asia. Ancelet (1994, no. 23) records a variant in Cajun French. A1115.2. Why the sea is salt: magic salt mill. This Vietnamese legend possesses close relatives in international traditions, particularly in Iceland and China. The most common western variants feature a sea-captain who steals a magic salt mill and orders it to grind without knowing that only the true owner can stop the mill. D1039.2. Magic salt; D1171.7.1. Magic jar; D1651. Magic object obeys master alone. J514. One should not be too greedy; W151.0.1. Cauldron of greed.

205. Why the Frog Croaks. A1131.0.1. Regulation of rains. Thompson documents this motif for China and India. A2426.4.1.2. Why frog croaks in wet weather (documented in Korea); B98. Mythical frog.

206. *Snake in a Wagon Rut.* Clifford Blake, the narrator of tales #206–9, grew up in conditions not far removed from slavery; hence, it is not surprising that his tales are filled with a strong sense of struggle. Such narratives as "Saul and Skeleton" (#208) date back to slavery days and depict a world of antagonism between white masters and their black slaves. But he continues to tell them because they proved crucial to his life's experience. As he points out in an autobiographical anecdote, "God Give Me a Gift" (Blake 1980), he left home to find new work because he didn't want to be a slave. His creativity with music and the spoken word helped him find jobs that lifted him out of servitude. Thus, though records of extraordinarily trying times, his tales carry liberating messages that illustrate the talents that helped free their teller.

AT 155, *The Ungrateful Animal Returned to Captivity.* This tale has strong roots in both African and European tradition. Aarne and Thompson (1961) list nearly fifty African variants. African-American examples are found as early as Joel Chandler Harris's *Nights of Uncle Remus* (no. 46). The European tradition of this tale goes back to Aesopian fable (Halm 1852), and versions are very popular among Spanish speakers in the New World. Outside the American South, this tale usually involves a man and a snake; it is most often told to reinforce the idea that humans and certain animals will never get along, that certain traditional animosities cannot be overcome. Dorson (1967, 106) presents an African-American version in which the snake bites and kills the good Samaritan. Ancelet (1994, no. 11) prints a Louisiana Creole version from Mary Fentroy of Cade. J1172.3. Ungrateful animal returned to captivity; W154.2.1. Rescued animal threatens rescuer.

207. *Mule and Ox.* This tale, like the one that precedes it and the ones that follow it, projects a world of extremely limited resources in which suffering is inevitable. It possesses an analogue in A1459.1.5. Origin of horsewhips.

208. *Saul and Skeleton.* K1162. Talking skull refuses to talk. See Alfred Anderson's "Skullbone" (#61 in this collection) and its corresponding note.

209. *Brer Rabbit and the Babies.* AT 15, *The Theft of Honey (Butter) by Playing Godfather.* This is one of the most popularly reported animal tales in the African-American repertoire. In almost all cases, Brer Rabbit is working together with a group of other animals; by pretending to hear distant voices summoning him to attend a baptism, he manages to evade the work assigned him. Tale tellers have two basic strategies of dealing with Brer Rabbit's transgressions. If Brer Rabbit is working for a white overseer (as in Dorson 1967, no. 2), he becomes the hero in a struggle against injustice. If, on the other hand, Brer Rabbit is part of a community pledged to share labor, he becomes the lazy villain. Clifford Blake's version falls into this second category; it is similar to the tale told by J. D. Suggs (Dorson 1967, no. 1). For

another version and further notes, see Julia Huval's "*La chaudiérée de couche-couche,*" tale #188 in this book.

 210. Gaillum, Singo, et Moliseau. AT 303, *The Twins, or Blood Brothers.* This is an excellent example of a cante-fable, a story that mixes prose with singing and chanting. Barry Jean Ancelet, the teller of this tale, presents a similar version in his *Cajun and Creole Folktales* (1994, no. 19). Cante-fables are generally more popular in African-American traditions (both Creole- and English-speaking) than among European Americans, but AT 303 has been popular with French Canadians (cf. Thomas 1993, 201–5) and British-American storytellers. Alfred Anderson's story, "The Toodling Horn"—tale #57 in this book—features four dogs that rescue their master from a life-threatening situation. William Bascom (1992, 155–200) would classify Ancelet's tale as a special variant of AT 315A, *Dogs Rescue Master from Tree Refuge.* Ancelet, who learned French—and this tale—from his grandparents, also contributes an English-language tale to this collection, #122, above.

Folktale Bibliography

The following bibliography lists sources in which readers can find information on Louisiana storytellers, their stories, and related stories and storytelling traditions from elsewhere in the United States and throughout the world. All books and articles cited in this book from Carl Lindahl's introductory essay forward receive full citations below. Readers interested in reading more about Louisiana's traditional cultures and nonnarrative folk traditions are referred to Maida Owens's introductory essay "Louisiana's Traditional Cultures: An Overview" and its accompanying "Louisiana Folklife Bibliography".

Aarne, Antti, and Stith Thompson. 1961. *The Types of the Folktale*. 3rd ed. *Folklore Fellows Communications*, no. 184. Helsinki: Suomalainen Tiedeakatemia.

Abernathy, Francis E. 1966. *Tales from the Big Thicket*. Austin: University of Texas Press.

Abrahams, Roger D. 1970. *Deep Down in the Jungle: Negro Narrative Folklore from the Streets of Philadelphia*. 2nd ed. Chicago: Aldine.

———, ed. 1983. *African Folktales: Traditional Stories of the Black World*. New York: Pantheon.

———, ed. 1985. *Afro-American Folktales: Stories from Black Tradition in the New World*. New York: Pantheon.

Ancelet, Barry Jean. 1977. " '*Je suis surement pas un conteur de contes, mais . . .* ': Oral Literature of French Louisiana." M.A. thesis, Indiana University.

———. 1980a. "Talking Pascal in Mamou: A Study in Folkloric Competence." *Journal of the Folklore Institute* 17:1–24.

———. 1980b. "Creole Tales from Louisiana." *Revue de Louisiane/Louisiana Review* 9:61–68.

———. 1984. " 'La Truie dans la berouette': Étude comparée de la tradition orale en Louisiane francophone." Ph.D. dissertation, Université d'Aix en Provence.

———. 1985. "*Ote voir ta sacrée soutane*: Anti-Clerical Humor in Louisiana French Oral Tradition." *Louisiana Folklore Miscellany* 6, no. 1:26–33.

———. 1989. "The Cajun Who Went to Harvard: Identity in the Oral Tradition of South Louisiana." *Journal of Popular Culture* 23 (1): 101–14.

———. 1994. *Cajun and Creole Folktales: The French Oral Tradition of South Louisiana.* New York: Garland.

Ancelet, Barry Jean, Jay Edwards, and Glen Pitre. 1991. *Cajun Country.* Jackson: University Press of Mississippi.

Anderson, John Q. 1958. "Some Mythical Places in Louisiana." *Louisiana Folklore Miscellany* 1, no. 3:1–10.

———. 1960. "Folkways in Writing about Northeast Louisiana before 1865." *Louisiana Folklore Miscellany* 1, no. 4:18–32.

Armistead, Samuel G. 1978. "Romances tradicionales entre los hispanohablantes del estado de Luisiana." *Nueva Revista de Filología Hispánica* 27:39–56.

———. 1983. "Más romances de Luisiana." *Nueva Revista de Filología Hispánica* 32:41–54.

———. 1992. *The Spanish Tradition in Louisiana, I: Isleño Folkliterature* (with musical annotations by Israel J. Katz). Newark, Del.: Juan de la Cuesta.

Aswell, James R., et al. 1985. *God Bless the Devil! Liars' Bench Tales.* Knoxville: University of Tennessee Press.

Baer, Florence C. 1981. *Sources and Analogues of the Uncle Remus Tales. Folklore Fellows Communications,* no. 228. Helsinki: Suomalainen Tiedeakatemia.

Baker, Ronald L. 1982. *Hoosier Folk Legends.* Bloomington: Indiana University Press.

———. 1986. *Jokelore: Humorous Folktales from Indiana.* Bloomington: Indiana University Press.

Baldwin, Karen. 1985. "'Woof!' A Word on Women's Roles in Family Storytelling." In Jordan and Kalčik 1985, 149–62.

Ball, John. 1959. "Style in the Folktale." *Folklore* 67:170–72.

Bascom, William. 1977. "African Folktales in America 1: The Talking Skull Refuses to Talk." *Research in African Literatures* 8:266–91.

———. 1992. *African Folktales in the New World.* Bloomington: Indiana University Press.

Baughman, Ernest W. 1966. *Type and Motif-Index of the Folktales of England and North America.* Indiana University Folklore Series, no. 20. The Hague: Mouton.

Bennett, Louise. 1979. *Anansy and Miss Lou.* Kingston, Jamaica: Sangster's Book Store.

Biebuyck-Goetz, Brunhilde. 1977. "And This is the Dying Truth: Mechanisms of Lying." *Journal of the Folklore Institute* 14:73–95.

Blain, Hugh Mercer. 1937. *Favorite Huey Long Stories*. Baton Rouge: O. Claitor.

Blake, Clifford. 1980. *Cornbread for Your Husband and Biscuits for Your Man: Mr. Clifford Blake, Sr., Calls the Cotton Press*. LP record. Recorded by Nicholas R. Spitzer, Paul Keyser, and Donald W. Hatley.

Blank, Les. 1984. *In Heaven There is No Beer?* ½" Video Presentation. Berkeley, Calif.: Flower Films.

Blank, Les, and Maureen Gosling. 1990. *Yum, Yum, Yum: A Taste of the Cajun and Creole Cooking of Louisiana*. ½" Video Presentation. Berkeley, Calif.: Flower Films.

Boas, Franz. 1912. "Notes on Mexican Folk-Lore." *Journal of American Folklore* 25:204–66.

———. 1916. *Tsimshian Mythology*. Report of the Bureau of American Ethnology, no. 31. Washington, D.C.: Bureau of American Ethnology.

Boatright, Mody C. 1949. *Folk Laughter on the American Frontier*. New York: Macmillan.

Botkin, Benjamin A., ed. 1944. *A Treasury of American Folklore*. New York: Crown.

———. 1949. *A Treasury of Southern Folklore*. New York: Crown.

Bourque, Daniel. 1968. "*Cauchemar* and *Feu Follet*." *Louisiana Folklore Miscellany* 2, no. 4:69–84.

Brandon, Elizabeth. 1964. "'Traiteurs' or Folk Doctors in Southwest Louisiana." In Dorson 1964, 261–66.

Brewer, J. Mason. 1976. *Dog Ghosts/The Word on the Brazos*. Austin: University of Texas Press.

Brown, Carolyn S. 1987. *The Tall Tale in American Folklore and Literature*. Knoxville: University of Tennessee Press.

Browne, Ray B. 1976. *"A Night with the Hants" and Other Alabama Folk Experiences*. Bowling Green, Ohio: Bowling Green University Popular Press.

Brunvand, Jan Harold. 1981. *The Vanishing Hitchhiker: American Urban Legends and Their Meanings*. New York: Norton.

———. 1984. *The Choking Doberman and Other "New" Urban Legends*. New York: Norton.

———. 1986. *The Mexican Pet: More "New" Urban Legends and Some Old Favorites*. New York: Norton.

Burrison, John A. 1991. *Storytellers: Folktales and Legends from the South*. Paperback edition. Athens: University of Georgia Press.

Carlson, Flo. 1970. "A Collection of Cajun Superstitions and Supernatural Tales." *Louisiana Folklore Miscellany* 3, no. 1:28–37.

Carrière, Joseph Médard. 1937. *Tales from the French Folklore of Missouri.* Evanston and Chicago: Northwestern University Press.

Cassetta, Anna, Wayland D. Hand, and Sondra B. Thiederman, eds. 1981. *Popular Beliefs and Superstitions: A Compendium of American Folklore, from the Ohio Collection of Newbell Niles Puckett.* 3 vols. Boston: G. K. Hall.

Chambers, E. O. 1983. "The Mona Lisa Legend of City Park, New Orleans." *Louisiana Folklore Miscellany* 5, no. 3:31–39.

Chase, Richard. 1943. *The Jack Tales.* Boston: Houghton Mifflin.

Child, Francis James. 1882–1898. *The English and Scottish Popular Ballads.* 5 vols. Boston: Houghton Mifflin.

Christian, Renée Harvison. 1993. "The Louisiana Storytelling Project: An Appreciation." *Louisiana Folklore Miscellany* 8:49–54.

Claudel, Calvin. 1944. "Louisiana Tales of Jean Sot and Bouqui and Lapin." *Southern Folklore Quarterly* 8:287–99.

———. 1948. "Foolish John Tales from the French Folklore of Louisiana." *Southern Folklore Quarterly* 12:157–59.

———. 1978. *Fools and Rascals: Louisiana Folktales.* Baton Rouge: Legacy Publishing.

Clements, William M. 1979. *The Types of the Polack Joke. Folklore Forum,* Bibliographical and Special Series, no. 3.

Clements, William M., and W. E. Lightfoot. 1972. "The Legend of Stepp Cemetery." *Indiana Folklore* 5:91–141.

Cothran, Kay. 1979. "Talking Trash in the Okefenokee Swamp Rim." In *Readings in American Folklore,* ed. Jan H. Brunvand. New York: Norton. Pp. 215–35.

Crowley, Daniel J. 1966. *I Could Talk Old-Story Good: Creativity in Bahamian Folklore.* Berkeley: University of California Press.

Dance, Daryl Cumber. 1978. *Shuckin' and Jivin': Folklore from Contemporary Black Americans.* Bloomington: Indiana University Press.

de Caro, Francis A. 1974. "Hyatt's Hoodoo Odyssey—A Review Article." *Revue de Louisiane* 3, no. 1 (Summer 1974): 29–38.

Dégh, Linda. 1971. "The Belief Legend in Modern Society." In Hand 1971, 55–68.

———. 1972. "Folk Narrative." In *Folklore and Folklife: An Introduction,* ed. Richard M. Dorson. Chicago: University of Chicago Press.

———. 1976. "Symbiosis of Joke and Legend: A Case of Conversational Folklore." In *Folklore Today: A Festschrift for Richard M. Dorson,* ed. Linda Dégh et al. Bloomington: Research Center for Language and Semiotic Studies. Pp. 101–22.

———. 1981. *Indiana Folklore: A Reader.* Bloomington: Indiana University Press.

———. 1983. "Does the Word 'Dog' Bite? Ostensive Action: A Means of Legend Telling." *Journal of Folklore Research* 20:5–34.

———. 1989. *Folktales and Society: Story-Telling in a Hungarian Peasant Community.* 2nd ed. Bloomington: Indiana University Press.

———. 1995. *Narratives in Society: A Performer-Centered Study of Narration. Folklore Fellows Communications,* no. 255. Helsinki: Suomalainen Tiedeakatemia.

Din, Gilbert C. 1988. *The Canary Islanders of Louisiana.* Baton Rouge: Louisiana State University Press.

Ditchy, Jay K., ed. "Louisiana French Life and Folklore: From the Anonymous Breaux Manuscript." Trans. George Reinecke. *Louisiana Folklore Miscellany* 2, no. 3.

Dobie, J. Frank. 1950. *The Ben Lilly Legend.* Boston: Little, Brown.

Dorson, Richard M. 1946. *Jonathan Draws the Longbow.* Cambridge, Mass.: Harvard University Press.

———. 1952. *Bloodstoppers and Bearwalkers: Folk Traditions of the Upper Peninsula.* Cambridge, Mass.: Harvard University Press.

———. 1958. *Negro Tales from Pine Bluff, Arkansas, and Calvin, Michigan.* Bloomington: Indiana University Press.

———. 1964. *Buying the Wind: Regional Folklore in the United States.* Chicago: University of Chicago Press.

———. 1967. *American Negro Folktales.* Greenwich, Conn.: Fawcett.

———. 1975. *Folktales Told around the World.* Chicago: University of Chicago Press.

Dundes, Alan. 1971. "On the Psychology of Legend." In Hand 1971, 21–36.

———. 1988a. *Cinderella: A Casebook.* Madison: University of Wisconsin Press.

———. 1988b. *The Flood Myth.* Berkeley: University of California Press.

Dye, Robert. 1973. "Snake-Lore in Louisiana." *Louisiana Folklore Miscellany* 3, no. 3:17–24.

Eberhard, Wolfram. 1937. *Typen Chinischer Volksmärchen. Folklore Fellows Communications,* no. 120. Helsinki: Suomalainen Tiedeakatemia.

Edwards, Jay, and Maida Bergeron. 1991. "Folk Medicine." In Ancelet, Edwards and Pitre 1991, 95–100.

Fauset, Arthur H. 1927. "Negro Folktales from the South." *Journal of American Folklore* 40:213–303.

Ferris, William. 1979. *Blues from the Delta.* Garden City, N.Y.: Doubleday.

Fortier, Alcée. 1887. "Bits of Louisiana Folk-Lore." *Transactions and Proceedings of the Modern Language Association* 3:101–68.

———. 1895. *Louisiana Folktales in French Dialect and English Translation.* Memoirs of the American Folklore Society, no. 2. Boston: Houghton Mifflin.

Fry, Gladys-Marie. 1975. *Night Riders in Black Folk History.* Knoxville: University of Tennessee Press.

Gaudet, Marcia. 1992. "Bouki, the Hyena, in Louisiana and African Tales." *Journal of American Folklore* 105:66–72.

Gillespie, Angus K., and Jay Mechling. 1987. *American Wildlife in Symbol and Story.* Knoxville: University of Tennessee Press.

Glimm, James York. 1983. *Flatlanders and Ridgerunners: Folktales from the Mountains of Northern Pennsylvania.* Pittsburgh: University of Pittsburgh Press.

Gonzalez, Catherine. 1981. *Lafitte: The Terror of the Gulf.* Austin, TX: Eakin.

Gould, Philip. 1980. Les Acadiens d'Asteur: *Today's Cajuns.* Lafayette: Acadiana.

Graham, Hugh Davis. 1970. *Huey Long.* Englewood Cliffs, N.J.: Prentice Hall.

Gregory, H. F., and Donald W. Hatley, eds. 1980. "Cornbread for Your Husband and Biscuits for Your Man: Mr. Clifford Blake, Sr., Calls the Cotton Press." *Louisiana Folklife* 5, no. 1.

Grider, Sylvia. "From the Tale to the Telling: AT 366." In *Folklore on Two Continents: Essays in Honor of Linda Dégh.* Ed. Nikolai Burlakoff and Carl Lindahl. Bloomington, Ind.: Trickster. Pp. 49–56.

Grimm, Jakob, and Wilhelm Grimm. 1960. *The Grimms' German Folk Tales.* Trans. Francis P. Magoun, Jr., and Alexander H. Krappe. Carbondale: Southern Illinois University Press.

Gutierrez, C. Paige. 1992. *Cajun Foodways.* Jackson: University Press of Mississippi.

Halm, Karl von. 1852. *Aisopeion Mython Synagoge.* Leipzig.

Halpert, Herbert. 1991. "Mosquitoes on the Runway." *Western Folklore* 50: 145–61.

Hand, Wayland D., ed. 1961–64. *Popular Beliefs and Superstitions from North Carolina.* Vols. 6 and 7 of the Frank C. Brown Collection of North Carolina Folklore. Gen. ed., Newman Ivey White. Chapel Hill: University of North Carolina Press.

———, ed. 1971. *American Folk Legend: A Symposium.* Berkeley: University of California Press.

Harris, Joel Chandler. 1880. *Uncle Remus and His Friends.* Boston: Houghton Mifflin.

———. 1883. *Nights With Uncle Remus: Myths and Legends of the Old Plantation.* Boston: Houghton Mifflin.

Hartsfield, Mariella Glenn. 1987. *Tall Betsy and Dunce Baby: South Georgia Folktales.* Athens: University of Georgia Press.

Hennigson, Gustav. 1965. "The Art of Perpendicular Lying: Concerning a Commercial Collecting of Norwegian Sailors' Tall Tales." *Journal of the Folklore Institute* 2:180–219.

Hurston, Zora Neale. 1935; rpt., 1978. *Mules and Men.* Bloomington: Indiana University Press.

———. 1937; rpt., 1978. *Their Eyes Were Watching God.* Urbana: University of Illinois Press.

Hyatt, Harry Middleton. 1970–78. *Hoodoo, Conjuration, Witchcraft, Rootwork,* 5 vols. St. Louis: Western Publishing.

Jacobs, Joseph. 1902. *English Fairy Tales.* New York: A. L. Burt.

Jameson, W. C. 1992. *Buried Treasures of the South.* Little Rock: August House.

Jamison, C. V. 1905. "A Louisiana Legend Concerning Will o' the Wisp." *Journal of American Folklore* 18:250–51.

Jones, Loyal. 1993. *The Preacher Book.* Little Rock: August House.

Jordan, Rosan, and Susan Kalčik, eds. 1985. *Women's Folklore, Women's Culture.* Philadelphia: University of Pennsylvania Press.

Kalčik, Susan. 1975. " 'Like Anne's Gynecologist or the Time I Was Almost Raped': Personal Narratives in Women's Rap Groups." *Journal of American Folklore* 88:3–11.

Kimball, Geoffrey. 1987. "A Grammatical Sketch of Apalachee." *International Journal of American Linguistics* 53:136–74.

———. 1989. "Peregrine Falcon and Great Horned Owl: Ego and Shadow in a Koasati Tale." *Southwest Journal of Linguistics* 9:45–74.

———. 1991. *Koasati Grammar.* Lincoln: University of Nebraska Press.

Klipple, May A. 1991. *African Folk-Tales with Foreign Analogues.* New York: Garland.

La Fontaine, Jean de. 1923. *Les fables.* Paris: Garnier.

Langley, Linda, Susan LeJeune, and Claude Oubre. 1995. *Les Raconteurs: Treasure Lore and More.* Folklife Series, vol. 1. Eunice: Louisiana State University at Eunice.

Langlois, Janet. 1981. "Mary Whales, I Believe in You." In Dégh 1981, 196–224.

————. 1985. *Belle Gunness: The Lady Bluebeard*. Bloomington: Indiana University Press.

Lanman, Charles. 1856. *Adventures in the Wilds of the United States and British American Provinces*. Philadelphia: J. W. Moore.

Leary, James P. 1991. *Midwestern Folk Humor*. Little Rock: August House.

Legaré, Clément. 1980. *La bête à sept têtes et autres contes de la Mauricie*. Montréal: La Quinze.

Legman, Gershon. 1982. *No Laughing Matter: An Analysis of Sexual Humor*. 2 vols. Bloomington: Indiana University Press.

Lemieux, Germaine. 1973. *Les vieux m'ont conté: contes franco: ontariens*, vol. 1. Montréal: Éditions Bellermin.

Levine, Lawrence W. 1978. *Black Culture and Black Consciousness*. New York: Oxford University Press.

Liebling, Abbott Joseph. 1970. *The Earl of Louisiana*. Baton Rouge: Louisiana State University Press.

Lindahl, Carl. 1982. "Skallbone, The Old Coon, and the Persistence of Specialized Fantasy." *Western Folklore* 41:192–204.

————. 1984. "Feindschaft zwischen Tieren und Mensch (AaTh 159B, 285D)." In *Enzyklopädie des Märchens*. Berlin: Walter de Gruyter.

————. 1985. "Gevater Stehen (AaTh 15)." In *Enzyklopädie des Märchens*. Berlin: Walter de Gruyter.

————. 1986. "Psychic Ambiguity at the Legend Core." *Journal of Folklore Research* 23:1–20.

————. 1988. "Who Is Jack? A Study in Isolation." *Fabula* 29:373–82.

————. 1991. "*Grand Texas*: Accordion Music and Lifestyle on the Cajun *Frontière*." *French American Review* 62, no. 2:26–36.

————. 1994. "Jacks: The Name, the Tales, the American Traditions." In *Jack in Two Worlds*. Ed. William B. McCarthy. Chapel Hill: University of North Carolina Press. Pp. xiii-xxxiv.

Lipski, John M. 1990. *The Language of the "Isleños": Vestigial Spanish in Louisiana*. Baton Rouge: Louisiana State University Press.

Lofaro, Michael A., ed. 1987. *The Tall Tales of Davy Crockett: The Second Nashville Series of Crockett Almanacs, 1839–1841*. Knoxville: University of Tennessee Press.

Long, Huey Pierce. 1961. *Every Man a King: The Autobiography of Huey P. Long*. New York: Quadrangle.

MacCurdy, Raymond R. 1950. *The Spanish Dialect in St. Bernard Parish, Louisiana*. Albuquerque: University of New Mexico Press.

———. 1975. "Los isleños de la Luisiana: Supervivencia de la lengua y el folklore canarios." *Anuario de Estudios Atlánticos* 21:471–591.

Mangione, Jerre Gerlando. 1972. *The Dream and the Deal: The Federal Writers' Project, 1935–1943.* New York: Avon.

Marie de France. 1986. *The Lays of Marie de France.* Ed. Glyn Burgess and Keith Busby. New York: Penguin.

Martin, Howard N. 1966. "Tales of the Alabama-Coushatta Indians." In Abernethy 1966, 33–57.

———. 1977. *Myths and Folktales of the Alabama-Coushatta of Texas.* Dallas: Southern Methodist University Press.

Martin, Malcolm J. 1968. "A Ghost Dog." *Louisiana Folklore Miscellany* 2, no. 4:103–4.

Massignon, Geneviève. 1968. *Folktales of France.* Chicago: University of Chicago Press.

McNeil, W. K. 1985. *Ghost Stories from the American South.* Little Rock: August House.

———. 1989. *Ozark Mountain Humor.* Little Rock: August House.

Mitchell, Carol. 1985. "Some Differences in Male and Female Joke-Telling." In Jordan and Kalčik 1985, 163–86.

Montell, W. Lynwood. 1986. *Killings: Folk Justice in the Upper South.* Lexington: University Press of Kentucky.

Musick, Ruth Ann. 1965. *The Tell-Tale Lilac Bush and Other West Virginia Ghost Tales.* Lexington: University Press of Kentucky.

———. 1977. *Coffin Hollow and Other Ghost Tales.* Lexington: University Press of Kentucky.

Nash, Jay Robert. 1973. *Bloodletters and Badmen: A Narrative Encyclopedia of American Criminals from the Pilgrims to the Present.* New York: M. Evans.

Opotawsky, Stan. 1960. *The Longs of Louisiana.* New York: Dutton.

Orso, Ethelyn G. 1993. "New Light on an Old Story: The Mona Lisa Legend as Ancient Folklore." *Louisiana Folklore Miscellany* 8:17–24.

Orso, Ethelyn, and E. Charles Plaissance. 1975. "Chitimacha Folklore." *Louisiana Folklore Miscellany* 3, no. 4:35–41.

Oster, Harry M. 1968. "Negro Humor: John and Old Marster." *Journal of the Folklore Institute* 5:42–57.

Owens, Maida. 1993. "The Louisiana Storytelling Program." *Practicing Anthropology* 14, no. 2:31–34.

Paredes, Américo. 1966. "The Décima on the Texas-Mexican Border: Folksong as an Adjunct to Legend." *Journal of the Folklore Institute* 3:154–67.

Perdue, Charles. 1987. *Outwitting the Devil: Jack Tales from Wise County, Virginia.* Santa Fe: Ancient City.

Perez, Irvan. 1988. *"Spanish Décimas from St. Bernard Parish."* Liner notes by S. G. Armistead. Cassette recording. Natchitoches: Louisiana Folklife Center.

Pessoa, Maria Alice Moura. 1948. "A Bibliographic Study of the Deluge Myth in the Americas." M.A. thesis, Columbia University.

Preston, Dennis. 1982. "Ritin' Fowklower Daun 'Rong." *Journal of American Folklore* 95:305–26.

Randolph, Vance. 1951. *We Always Lie to Strangers: Tall Tales from the Ozarks.* New York: Columbia University Press.

———. 1952. *Who Blowed Up the Church House? and Other Ozark Tales.* With notes by Herbert Halpert. New York: Columbia University Press.

———. 1955. *The Devil's Pretty Daughter and Other Ozark Folk Tales.* With notes by Herbert Halpert. New York: Columbia University Press.

———. 1957. *The Talking Turtle and Other Ozark Folktales.* With notes by Herbert Halpert. New York: Columbia University Press.

———. 1958. *Sticks in the Knapsack and Other Ozark Folktales.* With notes by Ernest Baughman. New York: Columbia University Press.

———. 1965. *Hot Springs and Hell, and Other Folk Jests and Anecdotes from the Ozarks.* Hatboro, Penn.: Folklore Associates.

Ranke, Kurt. 1934. *Die Zwei Brüder: Eine Studie zur vergleichenden Märchenforschung. Folklore Fellows Communications,* no. 114. Helsinki: Suomalainen Tiedeakatemia.

Reaver, J. Russell. 1987. *Florida Folktales.* Gainesville: University of Florida Press.

Reneaux, J. J. 1993. *Cajun Folktales.* Little Rock: August House.

Robe, Stanley. 1973. *Index of Mexican Folktales: Including Narrative Texts from Mexico, Central America, and the Hispanic United States.* Berkeley: University of California Press.

Roberts, Hilda. 1927. "Louisiana Superstitions." *Journal of American Folklore* 40:144- 208.

Roberts, John W. 1989. *From Trickster to Badman: The Black Folk Hero in Slavery and Freedom.* Philadelphia: University of Pennsylvania Press.

Roberts, Leonard. 1955. *South from Hell-fer-Sartin.* Lexington: University Press of Kentucky.

———. 1969. *Old Greasybeard: Tales from the Cumberland Gap.* Hatboro, Penn.: Folklore Associates.

———. 1974. *Sang Branch Settlers*. Austin: University of Texas Press.

Roberts, Warren E. 1958. *The Kind and Unkind Girls: Aa-Th 480 and Related Tales*. Supplemental series of *Fabula*. Series B, vol. 1. Berlin: Walter de Gruyter.

Robinson, Ray. 1984. *Tales of the Louisiana Bayous*. Gray: Cypress.

Rosenberg, Bruce A. 1982. *The Code of the West*. Bloomington: Indiana University Press.

Sandburg, Carl. 1926. *Abraham Lincoln: The Prairie Years*. 2 vols. New York: Harcourt.

Sarrazin, Jean, Laura Kraus, and Donald Krintzman. 1968. "'Werewolves' on Bayou Lafourche." *Louisiana Folklore Miscellany* 2, no. 4:34–44.

Saucier, Corinne. 1962. *Folktales from French Louisiana*. New York: Exposition.

Saxon, Lyle, Edward Dreyer, and Robert Tallant. 1945. *Gumbo Ya Ya: A Collection of Louisiana Folktales*. Baton Rouge: Louisiana Library Commission.

Senn, Mary C. 1983. "Mona Lisa, Is That You?" *Louisiana Folklore Miscellany* 5, no. 3:27–30.

Siporin, Steve. 1994. "Halloween Pranks: 'Just a Little Inconvenience.'" In *Halloween and Other Festivals of Death and Life*, ed. Jack Santino. Knoxville: University of Tennessee Press. Pp. 45–61.

Stack, Carol B. 1974. *All Our Kin: Strategies for Survival in a Black Community*. New York: Harper and Row.

Stahl, Sandra. 1977. "The Personal Experience Narrative as Folklore." *Journal of the Folklore Institute* 14:9–30.

Steckmesser, Kent Ladd. 1966. "Robin Hood and the American Outlaw." *Journal of American Folklore* 79:350–59.

Summers, Montague. 1966. *The Werewolf*. New York: University Books.

Thomas, Gerald. 1993. *The Two Traditions: The Art of Storytelling amongst French Newfoundlanders*. St. John's, Newfoundland: Breakwater.

Thompson, Stith. 1929. *Tales of the North American Indians*. Bloomington: Indiana University Press.

———. 1946. *The Folktale*. New York: Dryden.

———. 1955–58. *Motif-Index of Folk-Literature: A Classification of Narrative Elements in Folktales, Ballads, Myths, Fables, Mediaeval Romances, Exempla, Fabliaux, Jest-Books, and Local Legends*. 2nd ed. 6 vols. Bloomington: Indiana University Press.

Titon, Jeff Todd. 1977. *Early Downhome Blues*. Urbana: University of Illinois Press.

Towne, Robert. 1972. "A Trip with Bonnie and Clyde." In Wake and Hayden 1972, 174–77.

Vlach, John. 1971. "One Black Eye and Other Horrors: A Case for the Humorous Anti- Legend." *Indiana Folklore* 4, no. 2:95–140.

Wake, Sandra, and Nicola Hayden, eds. 1972. *Bonnie and Clyde*. London: Lorrimer.

Wallace, Marcia. "Jokes Southern Baptists Tell." *Louisiana Folklore Miscellany* 3, no. 4:70–84.

Welsch, Roger. 1972. *Shingling the Fog and Other Plains Lies*. Chicago: Swallow.

Williams, T. Harry. 1981. *Huey Long*. New York: Vintage.

Wilson, David S. 1987. "The Rattlesnake." In *American Wildlife in Symbol and Story*, ed. Angus K. Gillespie and Jay Mechling. Knoxville: University of Tennessee Press. Pp. 41–72.

Young, Richard, and Judith Dockrey Young. 1989. *Ozark Tall Tales*. Little Rock: August House.

Index of Tale Types

In this index, tales from *Swapping Stories* are identified according to their respective numbers in Aarne's and Thompson's *The Types of the Folktale* (1961).

Index of Motifs

In this index, tales from *Swapping Stories* are identified according to their respective numbers in Stith Thompson's *Motif-Index of Folk-Literature* (1955–58). Motifs which end with asterisks "*" or lower-case letters in parentheses "(a)" refer to the supplemental numbers and titles that appear in Ernest W. Baughman's *Type and Motif-Index of the Folktales of England and North America* (1966). Thus, the following is a Thompson motif: X1301. Lie: the great fish; but this is a supplemental motif introduced by Baughman: X1301.5*(e). Fish leaps, causes tidal wave.

Motif number and international title	Number and title of tale as it appears in *Swapping Stories*
A302. Angel of Hell.	172. *Feu Follet*
A930.1.1. Snake as creator of rivers and lakes.	192. How Bayou Teche Was Formed
A1010. Deluge.	191. A Chitimacha Flood Story
A1029.3. Escape from deluge in pot or jar.	191. A Chitimacha Flood Story
A1115.2. Why the sea is salt: magic salt mill.	204. Why the Ocean Is Salty
A1131.0.1. Regulation of rains.	205. Why the Frog Croaks
A1427. Acquisition of spiritous liquors.	45,46. The First Meeting of the Indians and the Europeans
A1459.1.5. Origin of horsewhips.	207. Mule and Ox
A1557. Why woman is master of her husband.	193. She Has the Key
A1671.1 Why the negro works.	35. *Vieux Nèg et Vieux Blanc té gain une course*
A2034. Origin of mosquitoes.	201. The Legend of the Mosquito
A2034.3. Mosquitoes from ashes of bad woman.	201. The Legend of the Mosquito
A2219.1. Animal has color spilled on him: cause of his color.	201. Why the Crow Is Black
A2356.2.9. Why tortoise has humpy back.	38. The Turtle and the Rabbit Run a Race

K1955. Sham physician.

K2213.5. The faithless resuscitated wife.

K2321.2. Dummy set up as a corpse to frighten people.

M210. Bargain with devil.

N511.1. Treasure buried by men.

N511.1.8. Treasure buried in chest, cask, kettle, or cannon barrel.

N512. Treasure in underground cavern.

N513.4. Treasure hidden in river.

N513.5. Treasure buried in sunken ship.

N528. Treasure found in hollow of tree.

N534. Treasure discovered by accident.

N553.1. Tabu: Incontinence while treasure is being raised.

N553.2. Unlucky encounter causes treasure-seekers to talk and thus lose treasure.

N554. Ceremonies and prayers used at unearthing of treasure.

N554.1. Sacrifices at unearthing of treasure.

N557. Treasure disappears after being uncovered.

N570. Guardian of treasure.

N571.2*(a). Bird as ghostly treasure guard.

N576. Ghosts prevent men from raising treasure.

42. How the Buzzard Got a Pierced Nose

201. The Legend of the Mosquito

71. Those Drivers Were No Dummies

179. The Red-Headed Witch of Bogalusa Creek

157. The Widow's Buried Gold
159. Family Misfortunes

160. Found Silver

159. Family Misfortunes
163. The Buried Treasure of Jean Lafitte

160. Found Silver

159. Family Misfortunes

164. The Haint Took It

164. The Haint Took It

164. The Haint Took It

164. The Haint Took It

160. Found Silver
161. Buried Money near Highway 171
164. The Haint Took It
169. The Ghosts of Jean Lafitte's Pirates

165. A Moaning Ghost and Buried Treasure

169. The Ghosts of Jean Lafitte's Pirates

T589.4. Birth with veil brings luck.

V20. Confession of sins.

167. Veiled Eyes
113. The Man Who Stole Lumber
121. Too Strong a Penance
122. Not Dressed to Confess

V268. Miracles performed under
protection of Virgin Mary.

185. A Holy Tree
186. A Miracle at the Mother of
Grace Chapel

V268.5. Image of Virgin Mary works
miracles.

185. A Holy Tree
186. A Miracle at the Mother of
Grace Chapel

W111.3. The lazy wife.

80. Swapping Stories

W151.0.1. Cauldron of greed.

204. Why the Ocean Is Salty

W154.2.1. Rescued animal threatens
rescuer.

206. Snake in a Wagon Rut

X11. Red pepper for the slow ass;
man tries it on himself.

63. Following His Father's Example

X137. Humor of ugliness. Hunter's
ugliness fatal to animals.

128. Looks Can Kill

X310. Jokes on lawyers.

86. Who's on Trail?

X410. Jokes on parsons.

123. A Priest with a Small Parish

X425. Parson who said there is no
devil.

28. Devil Made Her Say It

X434. Parson put out of countenance.

28. Devil Made Her Say It

X435. The boy applies the sermon.

9. Responding to the Sermon
10. He Prayed a Good Prayer
119. God Works in Mysterious
Ways.

X445.1. Parson takes a drink of liquor
during the sermon.

117. The Persimmoned Parson

X455*. Minister finds listeners
are unaware of elementary
knowledge of religion.

110. The Cajun and the Minister
112. Trying to Get to Heaven

X459. Jokes on parsons.

117. The Persimmoned Parson
123. A Priest with a Small Parish

X597*. Jokes about new arrivals in
heaven.

23. Even After Death Did Them
Part
30. A Heaven Joke

X599.2*. Jokes on politicians.

92. They Couldn't Fool a Polecat
94. Bull Talk

X1286.5(a). Deadly bite of mosquito: Mosquitoes are so deadly that people bitten by mosquitoes have rattlesnakes bite them to counteract the mosquito venom. — 127. Mosquitoes Save a Life

X1301. Lie: the great fish. — 26. The Big Fish of Corney Creek
129. A Tale about a Catfish
130. Does He Drive, Too?

X1301.5* (e). Fish leaps, causes tidal wave. — 26. The Big Fish of Corney Creek

X1301.5* (ha). Scales of big fish are used for shingles. — 27. Another Big Fish Story

X1302* (d). Extraordinary bait used to catch large fish. — 126. That Squirrel Could Really Fish

X1342. Lies about frogs. — 136. A Frog Gigging Story

X1606.2.4.1*. Geese or ducks are frozen into lake: . . . they fly off with the whole lake. — 26. It Was So Cold

X1633.3.1*. Lizards carry chips to sit down on. — 24. It Was So Hot

Z13.1. Taleteller frightens listener, yells "Boo" at exciting point. — 184. Who's Gon'na Sleep with Me?

Z41. The old woman and her pig. — 199. Old Woman and Her Pig

Z71.5. Formulistic number: seven. — 158. Buried Treasure Money Used to Build a Catholic Church

Z72.1. Year and a day. — 170. A Brush with the *Loup Garou*

Index of Titles

Index of Storytellers

Teller's Name and Story Number(s)